GRAPHIS DIAGRAM 1

THE GRAPHIC VISUALIZATION OF QUANTITATIVE
INFORMATION, PROCEDURES, AND DATA

DIE GRAPHISCHE VISUALISIERUNG VON QUANTITATIVER
INFORMATION, ABLÄUFEN UND KOMPLEXEN SACHVERHALTEN

LA VISUALISATION GRAPHIQUE D'INFORMATIONS
QUANTITATIVES, DE PROCESSUS SÉQUENTIELS ET DE DONNÉES
COMPLEXES

EDITED BY/HERAUSGEGEBEN VON/RÉALISÉ PAR
B. MARTIN PEDERSEN

PUBLISHER AND CREATIVE DIRECTOR: B. MARTIN PEDERSEN
ASSISTANT EDITORS: HEINKE JENSSEN, BRITA POLZER
DESIGNERS: MARINO BIANCHERA, MARTIN BYLAND
PHOTOGRAPHER: WALTER ZUBER

GRAPHIS PRESS CORP, ZURICH (SWITZERLAND)

GRAPHIS PUBLICATIONS

GRAPHIS, International bi-monthly journal of graphic art and photography

GRAPHIS DESIGN ANNUAL, The international annual on design and illustration

GRAPHIS PHOTO, The international annual of photography

GRAPHIS POSTER, The international annual of poster art

GRAPHIS PACKAGING VOL. 5, An international survey of packaging design

GRAPHIS DIAGRAMS VOL. 2, The graphic visualization of abstract, technical and statistical facts and functions

GRAPHIS COVERS, An anthology of all GRAPHIS covers from 1944-86 with artists' short biographies
    and indexes of all GRAPHIS issues

GRAPHIS ANNUAL REPORTS, An international compilation of the best designed annual reports

FILM + TV GRAPHICS 2, An international survey of the art of film animation

GRAPHIS-PUBLIKATIONEN

GRAPHIS, Die internationale Zweimonatszeitschrift für Graphik und Photographie

GRAPHIS DESIGN ANNUAL, Das internationale Jahrbuch über Design und Illustration

GRAPHIS PHOTO, Das internationale Jahrbuch der Photographie

GRAPHIS POSTER, Das internationale Jahrbuch der Plakatkunst

GRAPHIS PACKUNGEN BAND 5, Internationaler Überblick der Packungsgestaltung

GRAPHIS DIAGRAMS BAND 2, Die graphische Darstellung abstrakter, technischer und statistischer Daten und Fakten

GRAPHIS COVERS, Eine Sammlung aller GRAPHIS-Umschläge von 1944-86 mit Informationen über die Künstler
    und Inhaltsübersichten aller Ausgaben der Zeitschrift GRAPHIS

GRAPHIS ANNUAL REPORTS, Ein internationaler Überblick der Gestaltung von Jahresberichten

FILM + TV GRAPHICS 2, Ein internationaler Überblick über die Kunst des Animationsfilms

PUBLICATIONS GRAPHIS

GRAPHIS, La revue bimestrielle internationale d'arts graphiques et de la photographie

GRAPHIS DESIGN ANNUAL, Le répertoire international de la communication visuelle

GRAPHIS PHOTO, Le répertoire international de la photographie

GRAPHIS POSTER, Le répertoire international de l'art de l'affiche

GRAPHIS EMBALLAGES VOL. 5, Répertoire international des formes de l'emballage

GRAPHIS DIAGRAMS VOL. 2, La représentation graphique de faits et donnés abstraits, techniques et statistiques

GRAPHIS COVERS, Recueil de toutes les couvertures de GRAPHIS de 1944-86 avec des notices biographiques
    des artistes et le sommaire de tous les numéros du magazine GRAPHIS.

GRAPHIS ANNUAL REPORTS, Panorama international du design de rapports annuels d'entreprises

FILM + TV GRAPHICS 2, Un panorama international de l'art du film d'animation

PUBLICATION No. 190 (ISBN 3-85709-423-0)

© Copyright under Universal Copyright Convention

Copyright 1988 by Graphis Press Corp., 107 Dufourstrasse, 8008 Zurich, Switzerland

No part of this book may be reproduced in any form without written permission of the publisher

Printed in Japan by Toppan

Typeset in Switzerland by Setzerei Heller, Zurich

Typefaces: Garamond ITC Light Condensed, Futura Extra Bold

HISTORICAL DIAGRAMS

Diagrams from various sectors in the visualization of facts, functions, and sequences

HISTORISCHE DIAGRAMME

Darstellungen aus verschiedenen Bereichen der Visualisierung von Fakten, Funktionen, Abläufen

DIAGRAMMES HISTORIQUES

Représentations tirées de divers secteurs de la visualisation de faits, fonctions et opérations

COMPARATIVE, STATISTICAL DIAGRAMS

VERGLEICHENDE, STATISTISCHE DIAGRAMME

DIAGRAMMES STATISTIQUES COMPARATIFS

FLOW AND ORGANIZATIONAL DIAGRAMS

ABLAUF- UND GLIEDERUNGSDIAGRAMME

ORGANIGRAMMES ET DIAGRAMMES DE STRUCTURE

TECHNICAL FUNCTIONAL DIAGRAMS AND REPRESENTATIONS

TECHNISCHE FUNKTIONSDIAGRAMME UND DARSTELLUNGEN

DIAGRAMMES FONCTIONNELS ET REPRÉSENTATIONS TECHNIQUES

CARTOGRAPHICAL DIAGRAMS

KARTOGRAPHISCHE DIAGRAMME

CARTOGRAMMES

ARCHITECTURAL PLANS AND REPRESENTATIONS

ARCHITEKTONISCHE PLÄNE UND DARSTELLUNGEN

PLANS ET REPRÉSENTATIONS ARCHITECTURAUX

SCIENTIFIC AND SEMI-SCIENTIFIC DIAGRAMS

WISSENSCHAFTLICHE UND POPULÄR-WISSENSCHAFTLICHE DIAGRAMME

DIAGRAMMES SCIENTIFIQUES ET DE VULGARISATION

ABBREVIATIONS

ARGENTINA	ARG
AUSTRIA	AUT
BELGIUM	BEL
CANADA	CAN
DENMARK	DEN
FRANCE	FRA
GERMANY (WEST)	GER
GREAT BRITAIN	GBR
IRAQ	IRQ
ITALY	ITA
JAPAN	JPN
NETHERLANDS	NLD
SPAIN	SPA
SWEDEN	SWE
SWITZERLAND	SWI
USA	USA

ABKÜRZUNGEN

ARGENTINIEN	ARG
BELGIEN	BEL
DÄNEMARK	DEN
DEUTSCHLAND (BRD)	GER
FRANKREICH	FRA
GROSSBRITANNIEN	GBR
IRAK	IRQ
ITALIEN	ITA
JAPAN	JPN
KANADA	CAN
NIEDERLANDE	NLD
ÖSTERREICH	AUT
SCHWEDEN	SWE
SCHWEIZ	SWI
SPANIEN	SPA
USA	USA

ABRÉVIATIONS

ALLEMAGNE OCCIDENTALE	GER
ARGENTINE	ARG
AUTRICHE	AUT
BELGIQUE	BEL
CANADA	CAN
DANEMARK	DEN
ESPAGNE	SPA
ETATS-UNIS	USA
FRANCE	FRA
GRANDE-BRETAGNE	GBR
IRAK	IRQ
ITALIE	ITA
JAPON	JPN
PAYS-BAS	NLD
SUÈDE	SWE
SUISSE	SWI

REMARKS

■ We extend our heartfelt thanks to contributors throughout the world who have made it possible for us to publish a wide and international spectrum of the best work in this field. Our thanks also to Harriet Höppner and Christoph Göldlin of the Design School, Zürich, for their valuable support.

■ Entry instructions may be requested at:
Graphis Press Corp., Dufourstrasse 107,
8008 Zurich, Switzerland

ANMERKUNGEN

■ Unser herzlicher Dank gilt den Einsendern aus aller Welt, die es uns durch ihre Beiträge möglich gemacht haben, ein breites, internationales Spektrum der besten Arbeiten zu veröffentlichen. Gleichzeitig danken wir Frau Harriet Höppner und Herrn Christoph Göldlin von der Schule für Gestaltung, Zürich, für ihre Unterstützung.

■ Teilnahmebedingungen:
Graphis Verlag AG, Dufourstrasse 107,
8008 Zurich, Schweiz

AVERTISSEMENT

■ Toute notre reconnaissance va aux artistes du monde entier dont les envois nous ont permis de constituer un vaste panorama international des meilleurs travaux. Nous aimerions remercier en même temps Mme Harriet Höppner et M. Christoph Göldlin de la Schule für Gestaltung à Zurich pour leur collaboration.

■ Demande de participation:
Editions Graphis SA, Dufourstrasse 107,
8008 Zurich, Suisse

Diagrams offer unique opportunities for communication. They are arresting, they are capable of delivering complex messages quickly, they transcend language barriers, and they are memorable. Their impact can far exceed the total value of their graphic excitement and the information they embody. They are a marvelous synthesis of art and science.

The best and the brightest of chart makers have the gift of both intelligence and drama. Like a great painting or an eloquent scientific presentation, a truly great diagram will stimulate the viewer and leave a longstanding impression.

It is not easy to forget the horror of Napoleon's retreat in the winter of 1812 after viewing Minard's amazing depiction of his Russian campaign on page 40.

What makes that simple map so eloquent, so memorable and, I dare say, so poetic? For one thing, the true route of the troops is clearly presented. For another the army shrivels before our eyes as it crosses the Berezina River and struggles on as a mere thread to reunite with a rear guard unit. But, I submit, the illustrator rivets our attention and wins his place in graphic history by adding the day-to-day drop in temperatures; in so doing, he grips the viewer as effectively as a film by Kurasawa or Eisenstein. All this was done in black ink on paper 127 years ago and remains "the diagram to beat".

The field of graphics has come a long way since 1861. Diagrams have become a primary means of communication. They are no longer perceived as supplements to texts or as mere decorations. They meet the needs of an age which has witnessed an exponential growth of statistical information that has to be translated into a form that is simple to comprehend, meaningful and, one hopes, memorable.

At the same time, the designer's resources have become staggering.

We are living in a world where such mundane items as credit cards and news magazines are not only produced in full color with metallic tints but they are also likely to contain holograms, scratch-and-sniff patches and musical messages.

Some of us may never again touch pencil or pen. We work with screens that are able to display statistics in previously impossible dimensions. We are able to include multiple levels of information in ways that are both easy to follow and easy to remember. But therein lies a danger: we can design presentations that could themselves become more memorable than the information we are trying to transmit.

A chart is, by definition, a sober serious communication effort. The very presence of a chart or diagram implies a sincere desire to inform. It embodies an unspoken contract. It promises to make something easier to understand. In the fact of this implied sincerity, obfuscation in a chart is a betrayal of trust. It is equivalent to posting unclear traffic signs on a highway.

The chartist/artist also has a moral obligation to keep his client honest and protect that client's credibility by avoiding diagrams that mislead – those that use geometric proportions to represent arithmetic changes, truncated charts that distort proportional relationships, charts that mix scales without adequate explanatory notation, and charts that feature trivial material at the expense of the important.

Some thinkers have defined man as the quintessential tool maker or game player. One could also define the human being as gatherer, preserver and sharer of information. Consider the charts and diagrams spread over the caves of southern France drawn some 20 000 years ago. These illustrations, their facts and figures, are so incredibly lucid that present-day scholars can speculate about the beliefs, rituals and triumphs of our forebears. Scientists have interpreted the bone engraving from La Marche pictured on page 14 to be a lunar notation system related to the foaling time of wild mares. It utilizes simple symbols that link the animal to certain dates. The fact that 20th century scientists can deduce such a message, indeed any sort of message, from a Cro-Magnon scribe is testimony to the ability of a pictograph to transcend all cultural and language barriers.

The bone carving from La Marche is remarkably similar in its juxtaposition of elements to one of the most technically sophisticated communication efforts ever produced. On page 14 there is a space-age diagram which also depicts time notations and human beings. It compresses our knowledge of the makeup of the universe into a cartoonlike message to be read by intelligent aliens in outer space. It is engraved on a gilded aluminum plate mounted on the side of Pioneer 10, the first spacecraft designed to travel beyond our solar system. The message starts by identifying the home planet of the vehicle and its trajectory. Above, a structure that consists of a pattern of lines which indicate time intervals of pulsars as observed from our planet. The quantities are given in binary code, the simplest mathematical "language". The designers of the diagram then embark on a more challenging task: to depict the living beings who launched the spacecraft.

The hoped-for sequence of understanding here is an immediate recognition of simple pulsar signals followed by an understanding of the human images, whereas the scholars who studied the stone age carvings were able to make sense of the time notations because they recognized the depictions of the animals.

The 19th century cartographer, the Cro-Magnon bone carver and the space-age communications specialist are alike in that they have created works that were conceived primarily with a true intent to inform. There is no self-conscious attempt to impress anyone with clever decorations. They don't look as if they were constructed with design competitions in mind. Yet they are, all three, most impressive and indeed worthy of the highest design awards.

The nicest thing about this volume is that it is much more a source of inspiration than of specific ideas to be copied. The most outstanding of these examples of graphic communications are so appropriately related to their source material that they don't lend themselves to transplantation. This book's greatest value is as a stimulus ... and as a yardstick.

The next time I find myself trying to add one more layer of "necessary" information into a single diagram, I will be forced to measure my efforts against the eminently spare engraving on the side of the Pioneer spacecraft.

When I am next tempted to reinvent the calendar, I hope I will remember the timeless simplicity of the Cro-Magnon scribe's lunar notations.

And when, at year's end, I resort to charts, graphs and diagrams to explain the financial outcome of the endeavors of thousands of people, I will wish that I could endow those graphic presentations with some small fraction of the human drama the French cartographer managed to put into his simple recording of a few facts.

LESLIE A. SEGAL is president of Corporate Annual Reports Inc., New York. He has been responsible for the design and production of over 600 annual reports for some of America's leading corporations. Many of the pioneering disclosure charts and graphics designed for these clients were reproduced widely in the financial press and have since become standard format in American corporate annual reports.

Diagramme bieten einzigartige Möglichkeiten der Kommunikation. Sie fallen auf, können in kurzer Zeit komplexe Botschaften übermitteln, überwinden Sprachbarrieren und bleiben im Gedächtnis haften. Ihre Wirkung kann weit über den gestalterischen und inhaltlichen Wert hinausgehen. Sie sind eine wunderbare Synthese von Kunst und Wissenschaft.

Die besten Gestalter von Diagrammen zeichnen sich durch Intelligenz und eine dramatische Begabung aus. Ein wirklich gutes Diagramm wird den Betrachter wie ein spannendes Gemälde oder eine gelungene wissenschaftliche Präsentation anregen und einen tiefen Eindruck bei ihm hinterlassen.

Es ist nicht leicht, die entsetzlichen Verluste bei Napoleons Rückzug im Winter 1812 zu vergessen, nachdem man Minards hervorragende Darstellung des Russlandfeldzugs auf Seite 40 gesehen hat.

Was macht eine einfache Karte so ausdrucksstark, so eindrucksvoll und – wie ich sagen möchte – so poetisch? Einerseits wird die Route der Truppen klar definiert. Vor unseren Augen schrumpft die Armee beim Überqueren des Beresina-Flusses zusammen und kämpft sich dann, zu einer dünnen Linie geworden, weiter voran, um sich mit einer Nachhut zusammenzuschliessen. Der Illustrator verdankt unsere Aufmerksamkeit und seinen Platz in der Geschichte aber dem Hinzufügen einer Darstellung des täglichen Rückgangs der Temperaturen; dadurch wird seine Graphik so packend wie ein Film von Kurasawa oder Eisenstein. All dies wurde vor 127 Jahren in schwarzer Tinte zu Papier gebracht, ein Diagramm, das bis heute unschlagbar ist.

Seit 1861 hat sich auf dem Gebiet der Graphik viel getan. Diagramme wurden ein bedeutendes Medium der Kommunikation. Sie gelten nicht mehr als Textergänzungen oder gar Ausstaffierungen; vielmehr werden sie einem Zeitalter gerecht, in dem die Umsetzung statistischer Information in einfache, leicht verständliche, aussagekräftige und – hoffentlich – eindrucksvolle Darstellungen, eine immense Bedeutung erlangt hat.

Gleichzeitig sind die Möglichkeiten des Graphikers schier endlos

geworden. Wir leben in einer Welt, in der so mondäne Dinge wie Kreditkarten und Zeitschriften nicht nur vierfarbig mit zusätzlichen Metallfarben gedruckt werden, sondern unter Umständen auch Hologramme, Reib-und-Riech-Streifen oder gar musikalische Grüsse enthalten.

Einige von uns greifen vielleicht nie mehr zu Bleistift oder Feder. Wir arbeiten an Bildschirmen und können Statistiken in bisher ungeahnten Dimensionen präsentieren. Wir können mit verschiedenen Ebenen arbeiten und zwar so, dass sie leicht verständlich und leicht zu behalten sind. Aber hierin liegt eine Gefahr: wir können Präsentationen machen, die als solche eindrucksvoller sein können als die Information, die es zu vermitteln gilt.

Ein Diagramm ist, im Sinne des Wortes, ein nüchterner, ernsthafter Versuch der Kommunikation. Schon die Tatsache seiner Existenz wird gleichgesetzt mit dem Wunsch, zu informieren. Damit schliesst man stillschweigend einen Vertrag. Es wird versprochen, zum leichteren Verständnis einer Sache beizutragen. Angesichts der hier unterstellten Aufrichtigkeit ist eine bewusste Irreführung durch ein Diagramm ein Vertrauensmissbrauch. Es kommt einer unklaren Signalisierung auf Autobahnen gleich.

Der Gestalter/Künstler hat seinem Kunden gegenüber die moralische Verpflichtung zur Aufrichtigkeit. Um dessen Glaubwürdigkeit zu erhalten, muss er irreführende Darstellungen vermeiden, wie z.B. geometrische Proportionen bei rechnerischen Veränderungen, reduzierte Diagramme mit verzerrten Proportionen, Diagramme mit verschiedenen Massstäben ohne entsprechende Erklärung oder Überbetonung von Unwichtigem auf Kosten von Wichtigem.

Nach der Definition einiger Denker ist der Mensch im Grunde seines Wesens ein Werkzeughersteller oder ein Spieler. Man könnte ihn auch als Sammler, Verwahrer und Teilhaber von Informationen bezeichnen. Man denke an die Darstellungen und Diagramme in den Höhlen Südfrankreichs, die vor ca. 20 000 Jahren entstanden. Diese Illustrationen, ihre Inhalte und Figuren sind so unglaublich anschaulich, dass die Studenten heute Spekulationen über den Glauben, die Rituale und Erlebnisse unserer Vorfahren anstellen können.

Wissenschaftler haben die Knochengravierungen von La Marche, Seite 14, als ein Mondzeitsystem definiert, das sich auf die Trächtigkeitsdauer wilder Stuten bezieht. Einfache Symbole sind hier eingesetzt, die das Tier mit bestimmten Tagen des Jahres in Verbindung bringen. Die Tatsache, dass Wissenschaftler des 20. Jahrhunderts eine solche Botschaft verstehen, d.h. jede Art von Botschaften in Cro-Magnon-Gravierungen, zeugt von der Fähigkeit des Piktogramms, alle Kultur- und Sprachbarrieren zu überwinden.

Die Knochengravierung von La Marche ist in der Anordnung der Elemente einem der technisch anspruchsvollsten Kommunikationsmedien bemerkenswert ähnlich. Das als Botschaft an mögliche hochentwickelte Lebewesen im All kreierte Diagramm unseres Raumfahrtzeitalters (S. 14) zeigt Zeitwerte und Menschen. In komprimierter Form stellt es unser Wissen von der Beschaffenheit des Universums dar. Auf eine vergoldete Aluminiumplatte graviert, wurde es auf einer Seite von Pioneer 10 angebracht, der ersten Raumsonde, die für einen Flug ausserhalb unseres Sonnensystems bestimmt war. Die Botschaft beginnt mit der Identifizierung des Heimatplaneten in Verbindung mit der Flugbahn der Raumsonde. Darüber befindet sich eine sternförmige Anordnung von Linien, die sich auf die Zeitabstände der radioelektrischen Emissionen der Pulsare beziehen, wie sie von der Erde aus beobachtet werden. Die Quantitäten sind im Binärcode angegeben, der einfachsten mathematischen «Sprache». Schliesslich ging es für die Gestalter noch um die delikate Aufgabe, die Lebewesen darzustellen, die diese Raumsonde ins All schickten. Man hofft, dass die ausserirdischen Wesen die Botschaft in folgender Reihenfolge dechiffrieren: Sofortiges Erkennen der einfachen Signale der Pulsare, Begreifen der Bilder von Mann und Frau – anders als bei den mit den Höhlenmalereien beschäftigten Studenten, die auf der Basis der von ihnen erkannten Tiere auf die Zeit rückschliessen konnten.

Den Kartographen des 19. Jahrhunderts, den Cro-Magnon-Knochengravierer und den Kommunikationsspezialisten des Raumfahrtzeitalters verbindet die gemeinsame ehrliche Absicht, zu informieren. Da gibt es keinen selbstgefälligen Versuch, irgendjemanden durch geschickte Dekoration zu beeindrucken. Die Diagramme sehen nicht aus, als seien sie für Design-Wettbewerbe geschaffen, und doch sind sie alle drei äusserst eindrucksvoll und der höchsten Auszeichnung würdig.

Das Bemerkenswerteste an diesem Buch ist die Tatsache, dass es vielmehr eine Quelle der Inspiration ist als eine Vorlage für Nachahmungen. Die besten dieser Beispiele graphischer Kommunikation sind so eng mit der Aufgabe verbunden, dass sie nicht übertragen werden können. Der grösste Wert dieses Bandes liegt in der Anregung – und dem Setzen eines Massstabes für Qualität.

Wenn ich wieder vor der Aufgabe stehe, noch weitere «notwendige» Informationen in ein einziges Diagramm einzubringen, werde ich meine Kräfte an der bestechenden Einfachheit der Tafel auf der Pioneer-Raumsonde messen müssen.

Beim nächsten Versuch, den Kalender neu zu erfinden, hoffe ich, mich an die zeitlose Einfachheit der Cro-Magnon-Gravierung des Mondkalenders zu erinnern.

Und wenn ich mich am Jahresende mit Diagrammen aller Art befassen muss, um das finanzielle Ergebnis der Bemühungen von Tausenden von Leuten darzustellen, hoffe ich, ein kleines bisschen von dem menschlichen Drama einbringen zu können, das jener französische Kartograph so hervorragend durch die einfache Aufführung einiger weniger Fakten darstellte.

LESLIE A. SEGAL ist Direktor der Corporate Annual Reports, Inc. in New York. Er war verantwortlich für die graphische Gestaltung der über 600 Jahresberichte, die seine Firma für führende amerikanische Gesellschaften produziert hat. Manche für diese Berichte entworfenen Diagramme und Graphiken wurden von Finanz-Fachorganen als richtungsweisende Beispiele abgedruckt, und sie sind seither zur Norm in geschäftlicher Berichterstattung geworden.

Les diagrammes offrent des possibilités de communication exceptionnelles. Ils captent le regard, sont capables de transmettre rapidement des messages complexes, se jouent des barrières linguistiques, ont un pouvoir de rappel élevé. Leur impact peut dépasser la valeur totale de la stimulation graphique qu'ils procurent et de l'information qu'ils incarnent. Ils représentent une merveilleuse synthèse entre l'art et la science.

Les meilleurs créateurs de graphiques se caractérisent par un double talent: une intelligence sans faille et le don de la mise en scène dramatique. Tout comme un tableau de maître ou une présentation scientifique éloquente, un diagramme réalisé selon les règles de l'art stimulera le lecteur et lui laissera une impression durable.

Il n'est pas facile d'oublier les horreurs de la retraite de Russie de l'armée napoléonienne au vu du graphique de Mignard (p. 40).

Qu'est-ce qui rend donc cette simple carte si pathétique, si mémorable et, risquons le mot, si poétique? Une raison tient à la représentation exacte de la route suivie par les troupes françaises. Et puis, on voit l'armée s'effriter sous nos yeux au fur et à mesure de la traversée de la Berezina et de l'avance en colonne mince tentant de garder le contact avec l'arrière-garde. Il y a plus encore: l'illustrateur force notre attention et conquiert une place dans l'histoire de l'art graphique en ajoutant la chute continue des températures; ce faisant, il tient le lecteur en haleine aussi sûrement que le ferait un film de Kurasawa ou d'Eisenstein. Tout cela a été réalisé à l'encre noire sur papier il y a 127 ans et reste «le diagramme-record à battre.»

Le domaine des graphiques a bien changé depuis 1861. Les diagrammes ont accédé au rang d'outils de communication essentiels. On ne les considère plus comme de simples suppléments au texte, voire comme des éléments du décor. Ils satisfont aux besoins d'une époque qui a connu une croissance exponentielle du volume d'informations statistiques à traduire sous une forme simple à assimiler, riche de signification et aussi mémorable que possible.

En même temps, les ressources à la disposition des designers se sont multipliées à un rythme effarant. Nous vivons dans un monde où des articles banals tels que les cartes de crédit et les magazines d'information ne sont pas seulement produits en polychromie avec des tons métalliques, mais sont susceptibles de renfermer des hologrammes, des zones préparfumées découvertes par grattage et des messages musicaux.

Certains d'entre nous risquent de ne plus toucher à un crayon ou à une plume. Nous travaillons sur des écrans capables de nous afficher des statistiques dans des dimensions qu'il aurait été impossible d'imaginer précédemment. Nous sommes en mesure d'inclure de multiples niveaux d'information d'une manière à la fois facile à suivre et facile à se remémorer. Pourtant il y a là un danger: nous sommes en mesure de concevoir des présentations qui risquent d'être plus mémorables en soi que l'information que nous cherchons à transmettre. Et ça, en tout état de cause, c'est contraire à l'éthique.

Un graphique est par définition un effort de communication sobre et sérieux. La présence même d'un graphique ou diagramme implique un désir sincère d'informer. Une représentation graphique incorpore un contrat tacite. Elle promet de donner toute la clarté désirable à un phénomène ou à un processus. En égard à cette sincérité implicite, l'obscurité d'un graphique équivaut à une trahison. C'est comme si l'on plaçait sur une autoroute des panneaux de signalisation équivoques.

Le graphiste a aussi l'obligation morale de faire respecter l'intégrité de l'information à son client et de protéger la crédibilité de ce dernier en évitant tout diagramme prêtant à confusion – par exemple ceux qui traduisent en proportions géométriques les variations arithmétiques, les graphiques tronqués qui déforment les relations proportionnelles, les graphiques mélangeant les échelles sans fournir d'explication satisfaisante ou ceux qui montent en épingle des informations triviales au détriment de l'essentiel.

Certains penseurs ont voulu définir l'homme comme le faiseur d'outils ou l'esprit ludique par excellence. On pourrait aussi définir l'homme comme l'être qui recueille, préserve et partage l'information. Regardez les graphiques et tableaux qui ornent les parois des grottes préhistoriques du midi de la France et ont quelque 20 000 années d'âge.

Ces illustrations, les faits et les personnages qu'on y trouve sont incroyablement lucides, à tel point que les chercheurs peuvent aujourd'hui en déduire toutes sortes de conclusions quant aux croyances, rituels et triomphes de nos ancêtres. Des savants ont interprété la gravure sur os provenant de La Marche, en France (page 14) comme un système de notations mettant en relation les lunaisons et la période de gestation des juments sauvages. Des symboles simples à interpréter y relient la silhouette de l'animal à certains jours de l'année. Le fait que des savants du XXe siècle sont en mesure de déduire un tel message rédigé par un scribe de Cro-Magnon, voire tout simplement de le reconnaître pour tel, est un beau témoignage des vertus d'un pictogramme qui se joue de toutes les barrières culturelles et linguistiques.

L'os gravé de La Marche ressemble étonnamment, pour ce qui est de la juxtaposition de ses éléments, à l'un des efforts de communication technique les plus sophistiqués que l'humanité ait produits. On trouvera à la page 14 un diagramme de l'ère spatiale où figurent des notations temporelles et des êtres humains. Il comprime notre connaissance de la structure de l'univers en un message de B.D. que des extraterrestres doués d'intelligence pourront déchiffrer. Ce message est gravé sur une plaque d'aluminium doré scellée au flanc de Pioneer 10, la première sonde spatiale conçue pour quitter le système solaire. Le message identifie tout d'abord la planète d'origine de la sonde et indique sa trajectoire. Au-dessus, on voit une structure en étoile, qui se réfère aux intervalles de temps des émissions radioélectriques des pulsars observés depuis la Terre. Les quantités sont indiquées dans le code binaire, le «language» mathématique le plus simple. Puis les designers du graphique ont entrepris une tâche plus délicate en représentant les êtres vivants qui ont envoyé la sonde dans l'espace. On espère que le déchiffrement par des intelligences extraterrestres se fera dans l'ordre suivant: reconnaissance immédiate des simples signaux de pulsars, compréhension des images de l'homme et de la femme – alors que les savants qui ont étudié les gravures rupestres ont pu identifier la notation temporelle utilisée parce qu'ils avaient préalablement reconnu les animaux représentés.

Le cartographe du XIXe siècle, le graveur sur os de Cro-Magnon et le spécialiste des communications de l'ère spatiale ont ceci en commun qu'ils ont réalisé des œuvres conçues en premier lieu pour véhiculer de l'information. On n'y trouve pas de tentative prétentieuse pour impressionner qui que ce soit par des effets ornementaux. Ces graphiques ne donnent pas l'impression d'avoir été conçus en vue de participer à un concours de design. Pourtant tous trois sont impressionnants et en fait dignes d'être récompensés d'un premier prix de design.

La chose la plus agréable en ce qui concerne le présent volume, c'est qu'il constitue bien davantage une source d'inspiration qu'un recueil d'idées précises à copier. Les exemples les plus marquants des chefs-d'œuvre en matière de communication graphique qui y sont réunis sont tellement adéquats à leur matériel statistique ou factuel de base qu'ils ne se prêtent pas à la transplantation. La valeur exceptionnelle du présent ouvrage découle de son pouvoir de stimulation… et d'émulation.

La prochaine fois que je serai tenté d'ajouter une couche supplémentaire d'information «nécessaire» à un diagramme, j'essaierai de m'inspirer de la sobriété de la gravure inscrite au flanc de la sonde Pioneer.

La prochaine fois que je serai tenté de réinventer le calendrier, j'espère être capable de me rappeler la simplicité intemporelle des notations lunaires du scribe de Cro-Magnon.

Et lorsqu'à la fin de l'année j'aurai recours à des graphiques, tableaux et diagrammes pour expliquer les résultats financiers de l'effort de milliers de personnes, j'espère pouvoir imbiber ces représentations graphiques d'une portion minime du drame humain que le cartographe français a réussi à glisser dans son compte rendu tout de sobriété de quelques faits touchant à l'Histoire.

LESLIE A. SEGAL est président de Corporate Annual Reports, Inc., New York. Responsable de la conception et réalisation de plus de 600 rapports annuels pour les principaux groupes industriels américains, il a vu un grand nombre des techniques nouvelles de visualisation graphique adoptées pour ces rapports passer dans l'usage de la presse financière et des publications d'entreprises.

■ 1 Space-age diagram which was mounted on the side of Pioneer 10 and meant to be read by intelligent aliens in space. This diagram was the brain-child of the American astrophysicist Carl Sagan.

■ 1 Diagramm des Raumfahrtzeitalters, das auf der Seite von Pioneer 10 montiert wurde und als Botschaft an intelligente Wesen im All gedacht war. Die Idee zu diesem Diagramm stammt von dem amerikanischen Astro-Physiker Carl Sagan.

■ 1 Diagramme de l'ère spatiale vissé au flanc de Pioneer 10 à l'intention des intelligences extraterrestres. C'est l'astronome américain Carl Sagan qui en eut l'idée.

■ 1a Fragment of an antler tool, found in La Marche, France. This is the earliest known artifact, interpreted as a lunar notation system indicating the foaling time of wild mares.

Special reference is made to these two diagrams in the preface on pages 8/9.

■ 1a Fragment eines Geweihs aus La Marche, Frankreich. Es ist das früheste bekannte Artefakt. Die Gravierung wird als ein Mondzeitsystem gedeutet, das sich auf die Trächtigkeitszeit wilder Stuten bezieht.

Im Vorwort auf S. 10/11 wird speziell auf diese beiden Diagramme eingegangen.

■ 1a Fragment d'un andouiller façonné en outil, découvert à La Marche, (France). C'est l'artefact le plus ancien comportant un système de notations lunaires en fonction de la période de gestation des juments sauvages.

On trouvera de plus amples informations sur ces diagrammes dans la préface p. 12 et 13.

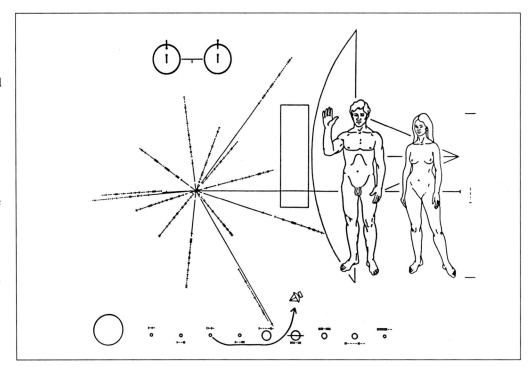

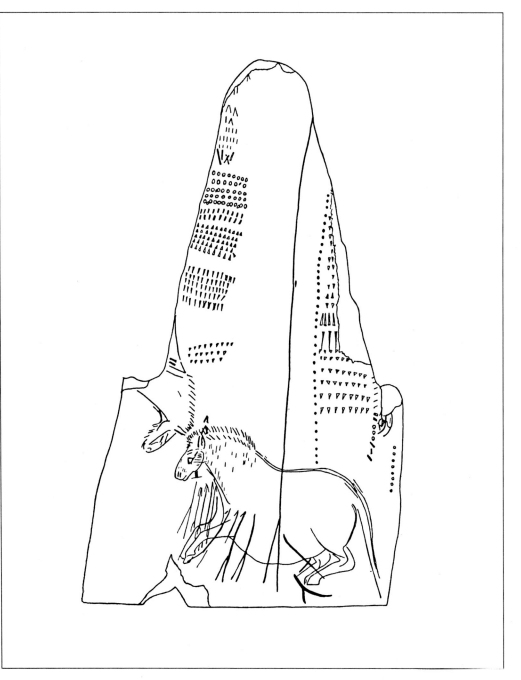

The need to explain complex facts with the aid of visual diagrams is as old as the cultural history of mankind and can be traced throughout its various stages of development and epochs up to the present day.

The oldest illustration in this book originates from ancient Egypt. It relates to the tomb paintings of the Sennejem in Western Thebes *(Fig. 2)*. Particularly interesting in this diagram is the fact that the two deceased persons are simultaneously portrayed in a variety of different activities, a condition that we find again in current flow diagrams.

Especially archaic are the Eskimo woodcuts from Greenland shown further on *(Fig. 3)*, in which by the most simple means the contours of the fiords and mountains of the rugged Greenland coast are portrayed in abstract form.

The illustrations on the following pages show how man has studied the design of his environment in order to better understand the complicated structures of nature. Through this conversion the unknown, the mystique, loses its fearful danger. The designer experiences his environment and endows it with a human stamp. At the same time he conveys his knowledge to his fellow creatures and to posterity.

The Renaissance finally set standards in science that are valid to this day. A new age brought with it a new conception of the world. The new world was as round as a ball, considering itself as part of the cosmos. Therefore the Ebsdorf World Map *(Fig. 5)*, with its narrow outer boundaries, has become a curiosity whose design is nevertheless exemplary for its time.

The Renaissance's scientific way of looking at things led to a new understanding of human life itself. It was realized that man was a part of nature, man's thoughts were all-embracing. Man himself was an object of discovery, and in this connection nature studies took precedence as scientific drawing.

In his lifetime Dürer won great acclaim for his naturalistic art. One story has him sending a selfportrait to his doctor who lived a great distance away. In this portrait Dürer painted a finger pointing to a certain place on his bare body. The drawing enabled the physician to diagnose Dürer's ailment and to give him appropriate instructions for a cure.

Dürer's scientific talent is not only evident in his famous nature studies, but also in the then new medium of the printed book ("Instructions on Measuring", Nuremberg 1525). This work, perfect too in its typography, deals with technical-architectural diagrams, and specifically with perspective, which is explained for the first time as we know it today *(Fig. 18)*.

Leonardo da Vinci was not only a great painter, but - typical for the Renaissance - also a great inventor, discoverer, architect, and engineer. He was one of the first to study the human body from the inner parts, and he set standards for all subsequent anatomical studies. *(Fig. 13)*. Apart from this he invented waterpumps, flying machines, and also machines of war. The technocrat was born. From its point in time technology, mechanics, and architecture became the greatest challenge for planners, designers, and draftsmen. An increasing number of exact plans, drafts, and functional instructions were required to fulfill the growing demands of a technological society. At first they were end-grained woodcuts, later, copper engravings and steel etchings were used as illustrations in print. There was a close cooperation necessary between the creative brains and the leading wood and copper engravers of that time in order to satisfy the high demands of a feudal epoch. Nowadays only a few of the names of these great masters of their crafts are known to us - those who, with great devotion, sensitivity and unsurpassed handicraft talent made printing possible and with it the spread of countless printed works.

The total abstract diagram of complex data and facts, the diagram in its actual present sense, is probably an invention of the end of the 18th century. We place a purely statistical curved diagram *(Fig. 28, 29)* of 1786 in juxtaposition to a weather diagram of 1971 - and see, astonishingly, that really very little has changed in the fundamentals. Classic, and particularly impressive are the two French diagrams *(Figs. 26, 27)*. The novelty in these two diagrams is the presentation of geographic and time factors in one and the same table. Added to this is the definition of qualitative and quantitative data, so that many various facts are woven into a network leading finally to a complex and yet very clear statement.

It is understandable that with a network based on facts or statistical data, there is a great temptation to expand the level of calculable reality of a subject. Indeed the diagram is being increasingly used to present facts in such a way as to be able to work out a possible pattern for future development. How quickly, however, the vision of the future becomes a castle in the air, is amusingly shown in the illustration *(Fig. 30)* by the English architect Cockerell (1848).

Finally, Le Corbusier leads us with his 'Modulor' diagram back to the principles of proportion. A comparison with Leonardo's and Dürer's studies is forced upon us. As different as they are, the illustrations shown demonstrate how rich is the scope of presentation of complex facts over the centuries. And it becomes clear how, in every epoch of mankind's cultural history, his own strong modes of expression have been realized.

Das Bedürfnis, komplexe Sachverhalte mit Hilfe visueller Darstellungen zu erklären, ist so alt wie die Kulturgeschichte der Menschheit und lässt sich durch alle Entwicklungsstufen und Epochen verfolgen.

Die älteste Abbildung in diesem Buch stammt aus dem alten Ägypten. Es handelt sich um das Grabgemälde des Sennedjem in Theben-West (Abb. 2). Interessant ist bei dieser Darstellung die Tatsache, dass sich das porträtierte verstorbene Menschenpaar in einem Kontext der Gleichzeitigkeit befindet, ein Sachverhalt, den wir auch in heutigen Ablaufdiagrammen wiederfinden.

Besonders archaisch wirkt die anschliessend gezeigte Eskimo-Holzschnitzerei aus Grönland (Abb. 3), welche mit einfachsten Mitteln die Konturen einer von Fjorden und Gebirgen zerklüfteten grönländischen Küste in abstrahierter Form wiedergeben.

Die Abbildungen auf den folgenden Seiten zeigen, wie sich der Mensch mit der Natur gestalterisch auseinandersetzte. Durch diese Umsetzung verliert das Unbekannte, Mystische seine beängstigende Gefährlichkeit. Der Gestalter erfährt seine Umwelt und gibt ihr eine menschliche Prägung. Gleichzeitig vermittelt er seinen Zeitgenossen und der Nachwelt seine Erkenntnisse.

Die Renaissance setzt schliesslich den bis heute gültigen Massstab an Wissenschaftlichkeit. Ein neuer Zeitgeist bringt auch ein neues Weltbild hervor. Die neue Welt ist rund wie ein Ball, sie versteht sich als Teil des Kosmos. So wurde die Ebsdorfer Weltkarte (Abb. 5) zu einem Kuriosum, dessen Gestaltung jedoch beispielhaft für jene Zeit ist.

Die wissenschaftliche Betrachtungsweise der Renaissance führt auch zu einem neuen Verständnis des Menschseins; man versteht sich als Teil der Natur, man denkt ganzheitlich. Der Mensch wird Gegenstand der Forschung, und in diesem Zusammenhang erhält die Naturstudie als wissenschaftliche Zeichnung eine vorrangige Bedeutung.

Schon zu Lebzeiten erringt Albrecht Dürer grossen Ruhm wegen seiner naturnahen Darstellungskunst. Von ihm wird berichtet, dass er seinem an einem entfernten Ort lebenden Leibarzt ein Selbstporträt zustellen liess, auf welchem Dürer mit dem Finger auf eine bestimmte Stelle seines entblössten Körpers weist. Aufgrund dieser Zeichnung konnte der Arzt Dürers Leiden diagnostizieren.

Dürers wissenschaftliche Begabung ist nicht nur durch seine Naturstudien belegt, sondern auch durch das damals neue Medium des gedruckten Buches (Unterweysung der Messung). Dieses auch in typographischer Hinsicht vollkommene Werk widmet sich der technisch-architektonischen Darstellung, vor allem der Perspektive, welche hier für heutige Begriffe erstmals richtig erklärt wird. (Abb. 18).

Leonardo da Vinci war nicht nur ein grosser Maler, sondern – was typisch für die Renaissance ist – auch Forscher, Erfinder, Architekt und Ingenieur. Als einer der ersten Menschen erforschte er den menschlichen Körper auch von innen und setzte so Massstäbe für alle späteren Anatomiestudien (Abb. 13). Ausserdem erfand er Wasserpumpen, Flugmaschinen – und auch Kriegsmaschinen. Der Technokrat war geboren. Von diesem Zeitpunkt an wird Technik, Mechanik und Architektur wie kaum ein anderes Gebiet zur grossen Herausforderung für Planer, Gestalter und Zeichner. Als Arbeitsgrundlage werden immer mehr genaue Pläne, Risse und Funktionsanleitungen verlangt, um den wachsenden Ansprüchen gerecht zu werden. Anfänglich sind es Stirnholzschnitte, später Kupferstiche und Stahlstiche, die für die Illustration der gedruckten Medien verwendet werden. Zwischen den Kreativen jener Zeit und den ausführenden Holz- und Kupferstechern war eine enge Zusammenarbeit notwendig, um die hohen Ansprüche einer feudalen Epoche zu befriedigen. Heute sind uns nur in Ausnahmefällen die Namen dieser grossen Meister ihres Fachs bekannt, die mit grosser Hingabe, Einfühlungsvermögen und unübertroffenem handwerklichen Geschick den Druck und damit die Verbreitung unzähliger gedruckter Erzeugnisse möglich machten.

Die gänzlich abstrakte Darstellung komplexer Daten und Fakten, das Diagramm im eigentlichen, heutigen Sinne, dürfte eine Erfindung des auslaufenden 18. Jahrhunderts sein. Klassisch und ganz besonders eindrucksvoll sind die beiden französischen Diagramme (Abb. 26, 27). Das Novum in beiden Diagrammen ist die Darstellung von geographischen und zeitlichen Faktoren in einer Tafel. Hinzu kommt die Definition sowohl qualitativer als auch quantitativer Werte. So werden hier viele verschiedene Sachverhalte in ein Netzwerk verwoben, was schliesslich zu einer komplexen und doch deutlichen Aussage führt.

Das Diagramm wird immer wieder dazu benutzt, um Sachverhalte überhöht darzustellen, nicht zuletzt in der Absicht, Modelle einer möglichen Zukunft errechnen zu können. Wie schnell jedoch die Vision einer Zukunft zur Utopie der Luftschlösser wird, zeigt auf amüsante Weise das Bild (Abb. 30) des englischen Architekten Cockerell von 1848.

Schliesslich führt uns Le Corbusier mit seinem Modulor-Diagramm (Abb. 33) zurück zur Proportionslehre. Ein Vergleich mit den Studien Leonardos und Dürers drängt sich auf. Die hier gezeigten Abbildungen zeigen, wie facettenreich sich das Gebiet der Darstellung komplexer Sachverhalte durch die Jahrhunderte gewandelt hat, und es wird deutlich, wie in jeder Epoche der menschlichen Kulturgeschichte die eigenen starken Ausdrucksmöglichkeiten wahrgenommen werden.

Le besoin d'expliciter des données complexes au moyen de représentations visuelles s'affirme dans l'histoire des civilisations dès leur origine. On en retrouve l'expression à travers tous les avatars de la pensée humaine jusqu'à nos jours.

La plus ancienne illustration reproduite dans cet ouvrage provient de l'aire égyptienne ancienne. Il s'agit de la peinture qui orne la tombe de Sennedjem à Thèbes-Ouest *(fig. 2)*. Ce qui est particulièrement intéressant dans cette scène, c'est que le couple défunt est représenté dans un contexte de simultanéité comme le ferait un organigramme de nos jours. Le bois esquimau du Groenland que nous montrons ensuite *(fig. 3)* a l'air particulièrement archaïque en retraçant sous une forme abstraite, avec les moyens les plus simples, les contours de la côte déchiquetée avec ses fjords et ses montagnes.

Les illustrations des pages suivantes font comprendre comment l'homme s'est expliqué progressivement avec son environnement sur le plan conceptuel, afin de mieux pouvoir se représenter les structures complexes de la nature. Cette transposition enlève à l'inconnu, au mystique sa charge de menaces et d'angoisses. L'artiste perçoit l'environnement sous un jour qui lui donne forme humaine. En même temps, il communique ses découvertes à ses contemporains et à la postérité.

C'est la Renaissance qui met au point l'approche scientifique encore valable aujourd'hui. A époque nouvelle, conception nouvelle du monde et de l'univers. La Terre est désormais ronde comme un ballon et s'insère dans un tissu cosmique. C'est ainsi que la mappemonde d'Ebsdorf strictement limitée quant à son ouverture sur l'extérieur *(fig. 5)* se mue en curiosité même si sa facture est représentative de l'art du temps.

L'optique scientifique de la Renaissance entraîne une révision déchirante de la vision de l'homme conçu désormais comme partie intégrante de la nature, d'un ensemble holistique. L'homme devient lui-même objet de recherches, ce qui confère à l'étude d'après nature la valeur d'un dessin scientifique essentiel à la compréhension.

De son vivant déjà, Albrecht Dürer fut célèbre pour son art de la représentation proche de la nature. On raconte qu'il fit un jour parvenir à son médecin personnel habitant un endroit éloigné un autoportrait sur lequel il désignait du doigt la partie endolorie de son anatomie. Ce dessin du corps dénudé de son patient permit au médecin de faire son diagnostic et de lui envoyer les instructions de soins nécessaires.

Les capacités scientifiques de Dürer ressortent non seulement de ses célèbres études naturelles, mais aussi de l'ouvrage qu'il publia à Nuremberg en 1525, donc de son recours à un média alors tout nouveau. La publication en question, parfaite également au plan de la typographie, est consacrée à la représentation technique et architecturale et notamment à la perspective, dont elle fournit la première explication valable qui soit parvenue jusqu'à nous *(fig. 18)*.

Léonard de Vinci n'a pas seulement été un très grand peintre, mais aussi (et c'est typique de l'homme de la Renaissance) un chercheur, inventeur, architecte et ingénieur de grand talent. Il fut l'un des premiers à explorer l'intérieur du corps humain et traça la voie à toutes les études d'anatomie à suivre *(fig. 13)*. Il inventa la pompe à eau, des machines volantes et même des machines de guerre. C'est avec lui que la technocratie voit le jour. Depuis cette époque, la technique, la mécanique et l'architecture constituent les domaines privilégiés où s'exerce la créativité des projeteurs, des concepteurs et des dessinateurs. Pour fonder un projet, on exige désormais des plans, projections verticales et modes d'emploi précis et détaillés. Le bois de fil, puis le cuivre et l'acier fournissent les matériaux des graveurs qui fournissent l'illustration aux médias de l'imprimerie. Les créatifs de l'époque entretenaient une étroite collaboration avec les artisans de la gravure afin de donner toute satisfaction aux tenants du pouvoir féodal. Ce n'est qu'exceptionnellement que nous connaissons nommément l'un ou l'autre des grands maîtres de l'estampe dont l'ardeur à la tâche, la sensibilité frémissante et le savoir-faire artisanal inégalable ont permis la mise sous presse et la diffusion d'innombrables imprimés.

L'abstraction totale dans la représentation de données et faits complexes, soit le diagramme au sens propre, celui qu'il a aujourd'hui, est probablement une conquête de la fin du XVIIIe siècle. En comparant un graphique purement statistique de 1786 *(fig. 28, 29)* et un graphique météo de 1971, nous constatons à notre étonnement que la méthode de représentation a au fond peu changé. Remarquables en soi et par leur classicisme, les deux diagrammes français *(fig. 26, 27)* présentent une nouveauté de poids: l'interprétation de faits géographiques et temporels sur un même tableau. Il s'y ajoute la définition de données aussi bien quantitatives que qualitatives, ce qui fait qu'un ensemble de paramètres fort divers sont organisés au sein d'une structure complexe, mais parfaitement intelligible.

On comprend aisément qu'une vision mettant un réseau des faits ou des données statistiques aboutisse à une modélisation parfois abusive du réel calculable. Le diagramme est en effet régulièrement utilisé pour surfaire les données réelles, ce qui permet par exemple de calculer des modèles prospectifs. Une belle démonstration du caractère utopique de telles projections dans l'avenir est fournie de manière plaisante par la vision de l'architecte anglais Cockerell en 1848 *(fig. 30)*.

En notre siècle, l'inventeur du Modulor *(fig. 33)*, Le Corbusier, nous ramène au calcul des proportions et, partant, à Léonard et à Dürer. Les illustrations présentées ici témoignent de la diversité du facettage du réel qu'opèrent les techniques de représentation graphique de données complexes depuis des siècles. Nous y trouvons également l'affirmation du pouvoir d'expression propre à chaque époque de civilisation.

◄■ 2 *(Preceding page)* Representation of a part of life after death (Grave of the Sennedjem - No. 1 - 19. Dyn., Western Thebes.) with the falconheaded sun god in the pediment bringing momentary light to the gloominess of the underworld. Below is the deceased with his wife offering prayers to the deity and at work in the fields - being a stage of purgatory. This form of the simultaneous portrayal of events can also be found in many modern diagrams. From *Ägypten* (Egypt), Silva Verlag, Zürich, with photographs by Maximilian Bruggmann.

■ 3 Wood carvings by the Eskimos of Greenland representing the topography of the coastal fiords. Courtesy of the National Museum of Denmark, Department of Ethnography, and of the Gronlands Landsmuseum.

◄■ 2 *(Vorangehende Seite)* Darstellung eines Teils des Jenseits (Grab des Sennedjem - Nr. 1 - 19. Dyn., Theben-West) mit dem falkenköpfigen Sonnengott im Giebelfeld, der vorübergehend Licht in die Finsternis der Unterwelt bringt. Darunter der Verstorbene mit seiner Gemahlin beim Anbeten von Gottheiten und bei Feldarbeiten, die eine Stufe der Läuterung sind. Diese Form der gleichzeitigen Darstellung von Handlungen ist auch in vielen modernen Diagrammen zu finden. Aus *Ägypten,* Silva-Verlag, Zürich, mit Photos von Maximilian Bruggmann.

■ 3 Hölzer der Grönland-Eskimos, aus denen die Topographie der fjordenreichen Küsten ablesbar ist. Mit freundlicher Genehmigung des National Museum of Denmark, Department of Ethnography, und des Gronland Landsmuseum.

◄■ 2 *(Page précédente)* Représentation d'une partie de l'audelà (tombe de Sennedjem no 1, XIXe dynastie, Thèbes-Ouest) avec, au tympan, le dieu solaire à tête de faucon qui porte temporairement la lumière dans l'obscurité du «pays souterrain». En bas, le défunt et son épouse adorant les divinités et engagés dans les travaux des champs, étape de sa purification. Cette forme de représentation simultanée se retrouve dans nombre de diagrammes modernes. Extrait du livre *Ägypten,* Ed. Silva, Zurich, avec photos par Maximilian Bruggmann.

■ 3 Bois des esquimaux du Groenland indiquant la topographie des côtes riches en fjords. Avec l'aimable autorisation du National Museum of Denmark, Department of Ethnology, et du Gronlands Landsmuseum.

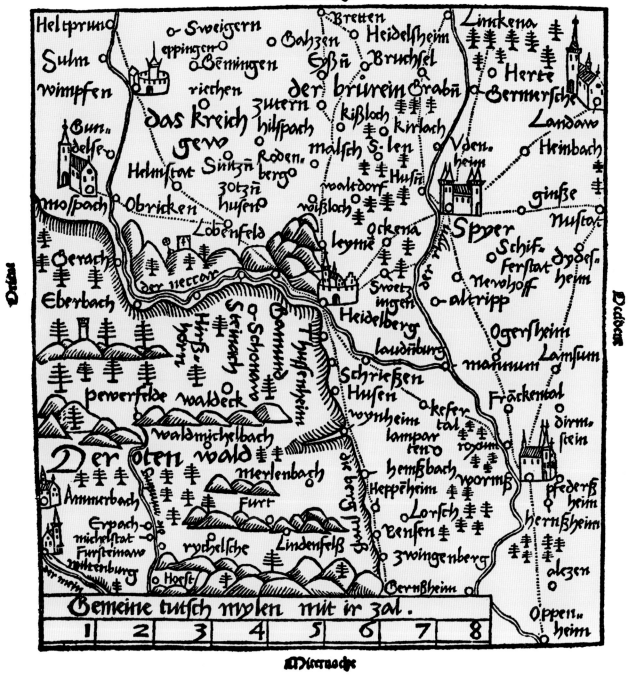

■ 4 Regional map of Heidelberg and environs. Woodcut by Sebastian Münster, 1528, for a book. From *Vom alten Bild der Welt* (From old Impressions of the World) by Werner Beck, courtesy of the *Nationale Forschungs- und Gedenkstätten der klassischen deutschen Literatur,* Weimar.

■ 4 Regionalkarte von Heidelberg und Umgebung. Buchholzschnitt von Sebastian Münster, 1528. Aus *Vom alten Bild der Welt* von Werner Becker, mit freundlicher Genehmigung der Nationalen *Forschungs- und Gedenkstätten der klassischen deutschen Literatur* in Weimar.

■ 4 Carte de la région de Heidelberg. Gravure sur hêtre par Sebastian Münster, 1528. Illustration tirée de l'ouvrage *Vom alten Bild der Welt* de Werner Becker, reproduite avec l'autorisation des *Nationale Forschungs- und Gedenkstätten der klassischen deutschen Literatur* à Weimar.

■ 5 The Ebstorf map of the world originating from 1235. It shows an impression of a world of limited vision. Based on an 1896 print from the picture archives of the Austrian National Library, Vienna.

■ 5 Die Ebstorfer Weltkarte, entstanden um 1235. Sie zeigt die Vorstellung einer nach aussen eng begrenzten Welt. Nach einem Druck von 1896 aus dem Bild-Archiv der Österreichischen Nationalbibliothek, Wien.

■ 5 La mappemonde d'Ebstorf, dessinée vers 1235. Elle fournit l'image d'un monde étriqué, sans ouverture sur l'extérieur. D'après une gravure de 1896 figurant dans les archives de la Bibliothèque nationale autrichienne à Vienne.

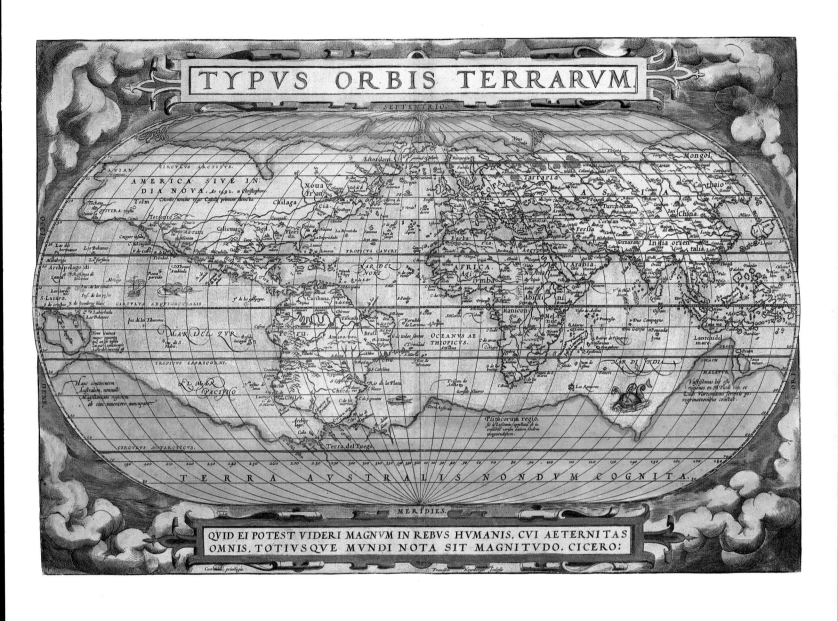

■ 6 Map of the world circa 1570/73 by Abraham Ortelius, which depicts Australia as "a land unknown to man". The quotation by Cicero liberally translated, means: "Ah, what human endeavours can be regarded as great when compared to the eternal greatness of the whole world?" From the Ryhiner collection of the Municipal and University Library, Berne.

■ 6 Erdkarte um 1570/73 von Abraham Ortelius, welche den Erdteil Australien als «von niemandem bekanntes Land» bezeichnet. Der Satz von Cicero lautet sinngemäss: «Ach, was kann in menschlichen Dingen schon Grosses gesehen werden angesichts der ewigen Grösse dieser ganzen Welt.» Aus der Ryhiner-Sammlung der Stadt- und Universitätsbibliothek Bern.

■ 6 Planisphère terrestre d'Abraham Ortelius, vers 1570/73, où l'Australie figure comme «pays connu de personne». La citation de Cicéron signifie: «Que peut-on donc voir de grand dans les entreprises humaines si l'on considère l'immensité éternelle de tout cet univers!» Document figurant à la collection Ryhiner de la Bibliothèque municipale et universitaire de Berne.

■ 7 Miniature of a medieval handwriting entitled: Christian kings and ancient philosophers observe the firmament. From the picture archive of the Austrian National Library, Vienna.

■ 8 Diagram by Sir William Herschel, German-born British astronomer, published in 1784 to explain the form of the galaxies. The earth is depicted with an S in the cluster of stars reaching from a to b. Herschel, through systematic observation of the heavens, developed the theory of stellar evolution. It was he who discovered the planet Uranus. He was knighted in 1816. From *Observations Tending to Investigate the Construction of the Heavens,* by Frederick William Herschel (Orig. name). Philosophical Transactions, London 1784.

■ 7 Miniatur einer mittelalterlichen Handschrift: Christliche Könige und Philosophen der Antike betrachten den Sternenhimmel. Bild-Archiv der Österreichischen Nationalbibliothek, Wien.

■ 8 Von William Herschel im Jahre 1784 veröffentlichtes Schema, das die Form der Milchstrasse erklären soll. Die Erde ist hier mit S in der von a bis b reichenden Sternansammlung gekennzeichnet. Herschel war der erste, der dank seiner systematischen Sternzählungen die Milchstrassen- und mit ihr die Fixsternforschung auf sicheren wissenschaftlichen Boden stellte. Aus *Observations tending to investigate the Construction of the Heavens,* von Frederick William Herschel. Philosophical Transactions, London 1784.

■ 7 Miniature illustrant un manuscrit du Moyen Age: rois chrétiens et philosophes y contemplent le ciel étoilé. Document tiré des archives iconographiques de la Bibliothèque nationale autrichienne à Vienne.

■ 8 Schéma censé expliquer la forme qu'a prise la Voie lactée, publié par l'astronome William Herschel en 1784. La Terre est identifiée par le sigle S parmi les étoiles groupées entre les points a et b. Grâce à ses comptages systématiques d'étoiles, Herschel a été le premier à établir sur de solides bases scientifiques l'étude de la Voie lactée et des étoiles fixes. Extrait de l'ouvrage original de Frederick William Herschel, *Observations tending to investigate the Construction of the Heavens,* paru dans les Philosophical Transactions, Londres 1784.

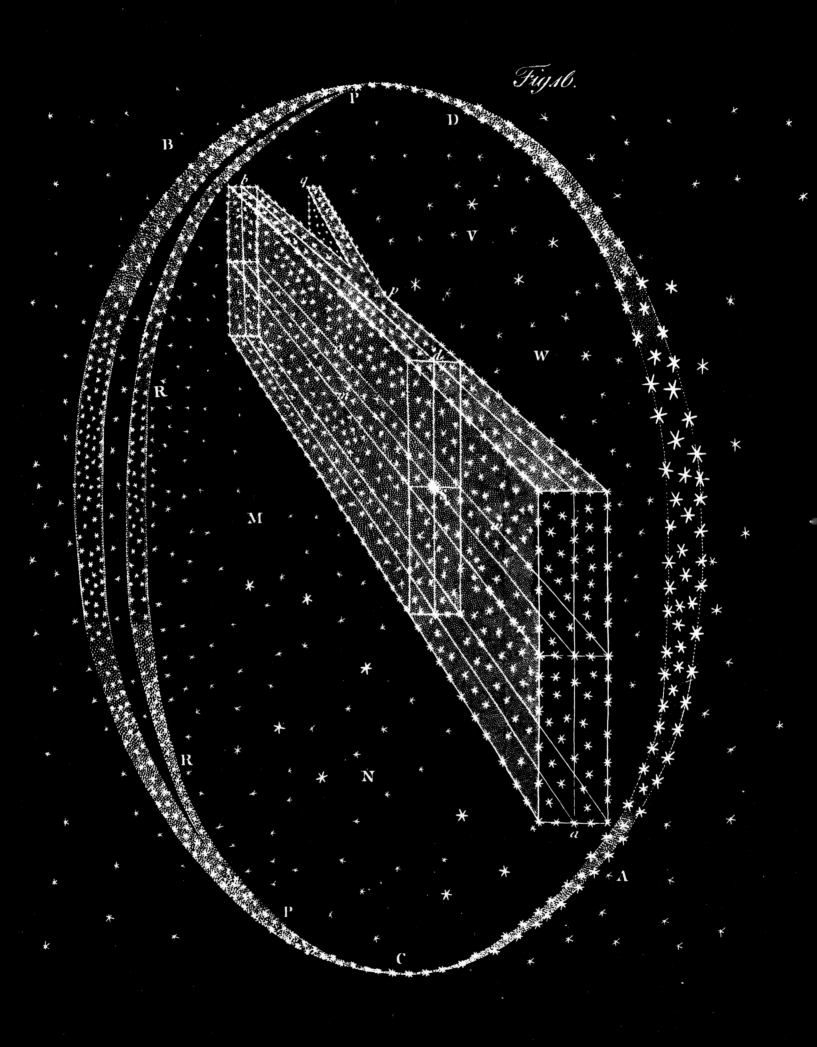

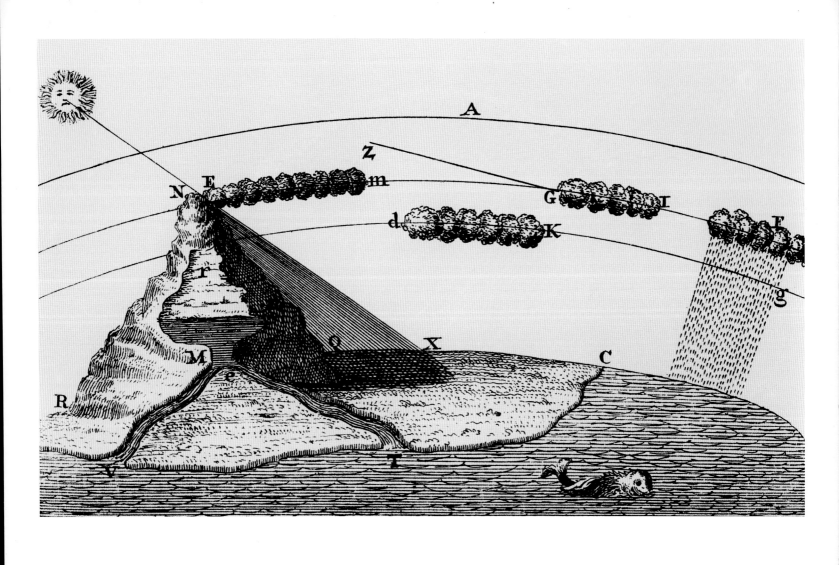

■ 9 The circulation of water according to Stephen Switzer (1729). Under the influence of the sun's heat, mist rises until, in a cooler atmospheric layer, it condenses to vapor and clouds (F, G). It turns to rain, seeps through the earth, collects in springs (r) and finally – through the emptying of the springs – it returns once more to the seas. Science Museum Library, London.

■ 9 Der Kreislauf des Wassers nach Stephen Switzer (1729). Unter dem Einfluss der Sonnenwärme steigt der Wasserdunst empor, bis er sich in einer kühleren Luftschicht zu Dampf und Wolken verdichtet (F, G), zu Regen wird, in den Boden sickert, sich in den Brunnenstuben (r) der Erde sammelt und schliesslich durch die Entleerung der Quellen wieder ins Meer gelangt. Science Museum Library, London.

■ 9 Le cycle de l'eau d'après Stephen Switzer (1729). Sous l'influence du rayonnement solaire, l'eau s'évapore dans l'atmosphère où elle se condense en vapeur et en nuages au contact de couches d'air froides (F, G). Elle se déverse ensuite en pluie, s'infiltre dans le terrain, se rassemble dans la nappe phréatique (r) qui alimente les sources, d'où elle rejoint la mer. Science Museum Library de Londres.

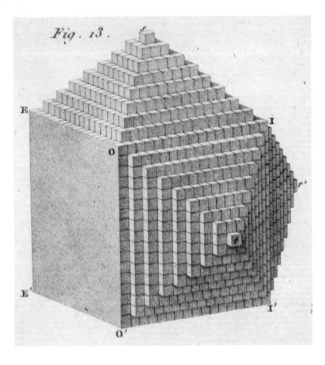

LE DODÉCAÈDRE À PLANS TRIANGULAIRES et ses Modifications. Pl. VI.

Fig. 1. 2. 3. 4. 5. 6. 7. 8. 9.
10. 11. 12. 13. 14. 15. 16. 17. 18.
19. 20. 21. 22. 23. 24. 25. 26. 27.
28. 29. 30. 31. 32. 33. 34. 35. 36.
37. 38. 39. 40. 41. 42. 43. 44. 45. 46.

Desfontaines del. et Sculp.

Fig. 13.

■ 10, 11 Diagrams from the field of crystallography. Above, variations of the hexagonal dodecahedron with twelve triangular surfaces. (*Cristallographie* by Romé de l'Isle, 1763). Below, an illustration of the structure based on Abbé Réne-Just Haüy's theory: the permanence of crystal form is due to equilibrium between the inter-molecular (and inter-atomic) forces, thus conjecturing the "space lattice" of the crystal. (*Treatise on Mineralogy*). Central Library, Zürich.

■ 10, 11 Darstellungen aus dem Bereich der Kristallographie. Oben Varianten des hexagonalen Dodekaeders mit zwölf dreieckigen Flächen. (*Cristallographie* von Romé de l'Isle, 1763). Darunter ein Strukturbild, anhand dessen Abbé René-Just Haüy das Dekreszenzgesetz erklärt, wonach sich gewisse Formen durch die von Ebene zu Ebene regelmässig abnehmende Zahl der Materiepartikelchen erklären (*Traité de Minéralogie* von Haüy, 1807). Zentralbibliothek Zürich.

■ 10, 11 Représentations cristallographiques. En haut, variantes du dodécaèdre hexagonal comportant douze faces triangulaires. (*Cristallographie* de Romé de l'Isle, 1763). En bas, une image structurale qui sert à l'abbé René-Just Haüy à expliquer la loi de décroissance du nombre des particules de matière au fur et à mesure qu'on descend l'échelle des niveaux d'organisation, d'où la variabilité des formes. (*Traité de minéralogie*, 1807). Bibl. centrale, Zurich.

■12 Tantric diagram of kundalini Yoga (system of practices for the purification of mind and body). Yogis consider and worship the Hindu supreme goddess Shakti that is lying dormant within the body as a coiled serpent (kundalini) and which must be aroused to reach liberation. Shakti is here represented by Prakriti – meaning kinetic energy in Hindu tantrism. Collection Dr. Frank R. Reiter, Berlin.

■12 Tantrisches Diagramm des Kundalini Yoga (Methode zur Vervollkomm-nung des menschlichen Körpers und der Aktivierung der psychologisch-neuro-logischen Körperzentren). Die hier verkörperte Schakti wird vom weiblichen Prin-zip Prakriti repräsentiert, das im Hindu-Tantrismus die kinetische Energie bedeutet. Sammlung Dr. Frank R. Reiter, Berlin.

■12 Diagramme tantrique du Kundalini Yoga (méthode de perfectionnement de l'organisme humain et d'activation de centres orga-niques neuropsychologi-ques). La Chakti incarnée ici est représentée par le principe féminin de la Pra-kriti qui signifie l'énergie cinétique dans le tantrisme hindou. Collection du Dr Frank R. Reiter, Berlin.

■13 Study of the female organs, by Leonardo da Vinci. Pen and ink, and wash, over black crayon, 47 x 32.8 cm. Windsor Castle, Royal Collection. (Copyright: Her Majesty the Queen)

■13 Studie der weiblichen Organe, von Leonardo da Vinci. Feder, Tinte, laviert, über schwarzer Kreide, 47 x 32,8 cm. Windsor Castle, Royal Collection. (Copyright: Her Majesty The Queen)

■13 Etude des organes féminins par Léonard de Vinci. Dessin à la plume passé au lavis sur craie noire, 47 x 32,8 cm. Collec-tion Royale de Windsor. (Copyright: Sa Majesté la Reine Elisabeth)

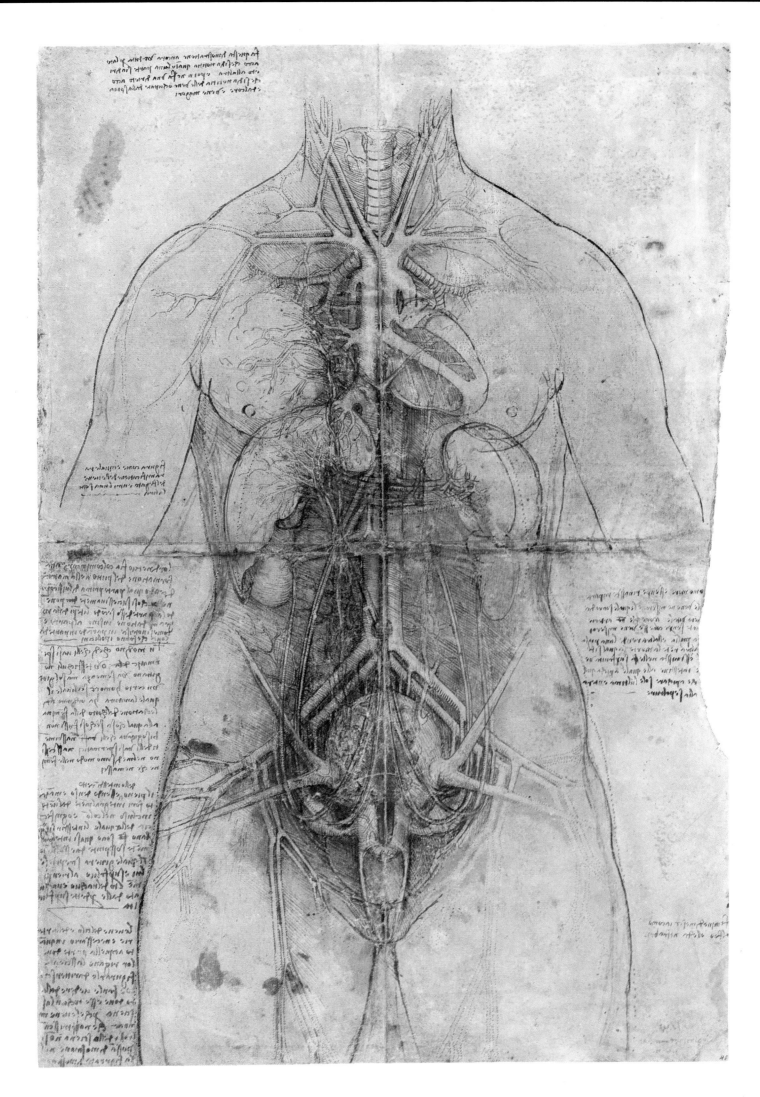

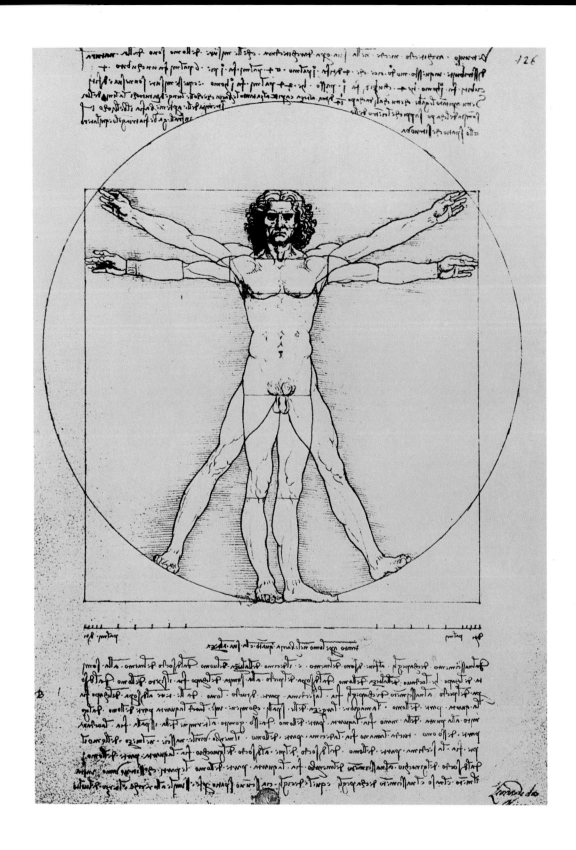

■ 14 Leonardo da Vinci's famous "Figure of Vitruvius" with which he explained the Vitruvius principal of proportions which reads as follows: "The natural center of the human body is the navel. If the man lies with outstretched arms on his back and a compass point is placed at his navel, his fingers and toes are at the circumference: the human figure can also be placed in a square, in which the height from the skull to the sole of the foot is as wide as the outstretched arms." Document held by the picture archives of the Galleria dell'Academia, Venice.

■ 14 Leonardo da Vincis berühmte «Figur zu Vitruv», mit der er die Prinzipien des Vitruvs über die Proportionen erläutert: «...Beim menschlichen Körper ist die natürliche Mitte der Nabel. Liegt ein Mann mit ausgestreckten Armen und Beinen auf dem Rücken, und wird auf seinem Nabel ein Zirkel angesetzt, so werden seine Finger und Zehen die Kreislinie berühren; ebenso kann man die menschliche Gestalt auch in ein Quadrat einpassen, da die Höhe vom Scheitel bis zur Fusssohle gleich der Breite der ausgestreckten Arme ist.» Galleria dell'Accademia, Venedig.

■ 14 La célèbre «Figure de Vitruve» où Léonard de Vinci explique les principes de Vitruve quant aux proportions: «Le centre naturel du corps humain, c'est le nombril. Lorsqu'un homme est couché sur le dos, bras et jambes écartés, la branche d'un compas posé sur son nombril esquissera un cercle passant par ses doigts et ses orteils; on peut de même inscrire la figure humaine dans un carré, puisque la hauteur de l'homme, du sommet du crâne à la plante des pieds, égale sa largeur d'un bout à l'autre des bras écartés.» Galleria dell'Accademia à Venise.

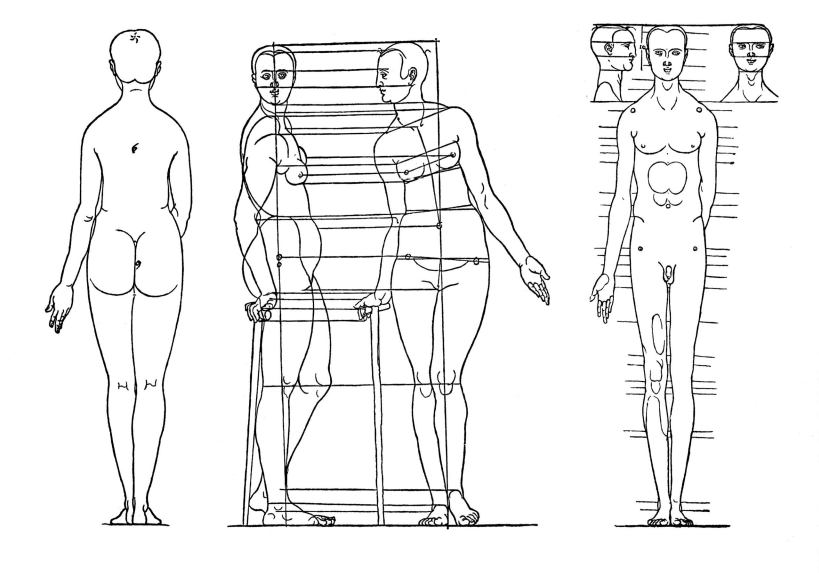

■ 15 Woodcut by Albrecht Dürer on the subject of the principals of the human body. The title of the work: "Herein is a comprehension in four books about human proportions discovered and described by Albrecht Dürer of Nuremberg for the advantage of all those who appreciate this art." Publisher: Jeronymus Formschneider 1528 for Dürer's widow.

■ 15 Holzschnitt von Albrecht Dürer zum Thema der Prinzipien menschlicher Proportionen: Der Titel des Werkes. «Hierin sind begriffen vier Bücher von menschlicher Proportion durch Albrechten Dürer zu Nuremberg erfunden und beschriben zu Nutz all denen, so zu dieser Kunst lieb tragen.» Herausgeber: Jeronymus Formschneider 1528 für die Witwe Dürers.

■ 15 Bois d'Albrecht Dürer traitant des principes des proportions humaines et illustrant l'étude intitulée «Ouvrage contenant quatre traités des proportions humaines inventées par Albrecht Dürer de Nuremberg et exposées pour l'instruction de tous ceux qui se vouent à cet art.» Ouvrage publié en 1528 par les soins de Jeronymus Formschneider à l'intention de la veuve de Dürer.

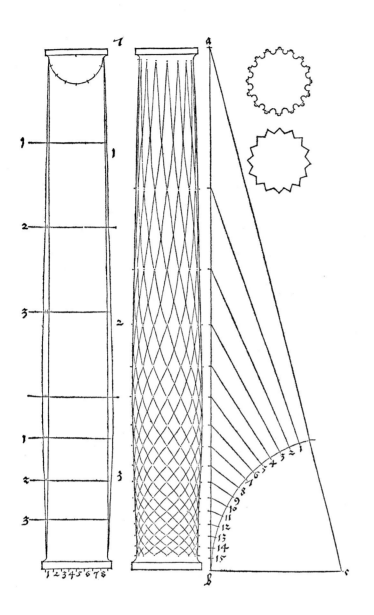

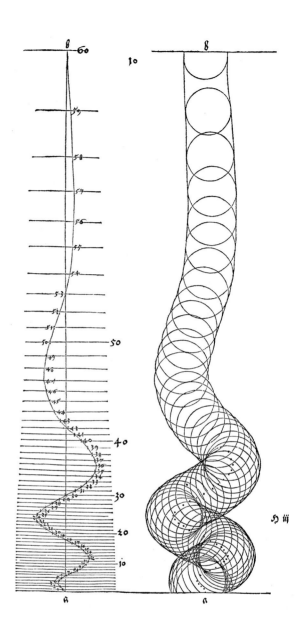

■ 16, 17 Explanations by Albrecht Dürer for the use of endless patterns, here rhombuses and circles for various constructions.

■ 18 A mechanical apparatus to produce perspective illustrations, a subject which has been studied intensely by Albrecht Dürer.

All illustrations on this double spread originate from a facsimile print based on the original *Underweysung der Messung,* (Instructions on Measuring), Nuremburg, 1525, by Albrecht Dürer, with the title "Instructions on Measuring with the Compass and Level", by Josef Stocker-Schmid, Dietikon, Zürich, and published by Alvin Jaeggli, Library of the ETH (Federal Institute of Technology) Zurich.

■ 16, 17 Erläuterungen von Albrecht Dürer für den Einsatz von Endlosmustern, hier Rauten und Kreise, für verschiedene Konstruktionen.

■ 18 Ein mechanischer Apparat zur Herstellung perspektivischer Bilder, ein Thema, mit dem sich Dürer ausführlich beschäftigt hat.

Alle Abbildungen auf dieser Doppelseite stammen aus einem Faksimiledruck nach der Urausgabe *(Underweysung der Messung,* Nürnberg 1525, von Albrecht Dürer) mit dem Titel *Unterweisung der Messung mit dem Zirkel und Richtscheit,* von Josef Stocker-Schmid in Dietikon-Zürich verlegt und von Alvin Jaeggli, Bibliothek der Eidgenössischen Technischen Hochschule, in Zürich herausgegeben.

■ 16, 17 Explications d'Albrecht Dürer pour l'utilisation de motifs décoratifs en continu, en l'occurence de losanges et de cercles, pour divers domaines d'application.

■ 18 Appareil mécanique pour la production de vues éclatées. C'est là un sujet auquel Albrecht Dürer a voué mainte réflexion et étude.

Toutes les illustrations de cette double page proviennent d'un fac-similé de l'édition originale *(Underweysung der Messung,* Nuremberg 1525, par Albrecht Dürer) aux Editions Josef Stocker-Schmid à Dietikon-Zürich sous le titre de «Instructions pour la mesure au compas et à la réglette», publié par J. Stocker-Schmid et procuré par Alvin Jaeggli, de la Bibliothèque de l'Ecole Polytechnique Fédérale de Zurich.

mit einem anderen puncten aber also piß das du die gantzen lauten gar an die tafel punctirst / dann
zeuch all puncten die auf der tafel von der lauten worden sind mit linien züsamē / so sichst du was dar-
auß wirt / also magst du ander ding auch abzeychnen. Dise meynung hab ich hernach aufgerissen.

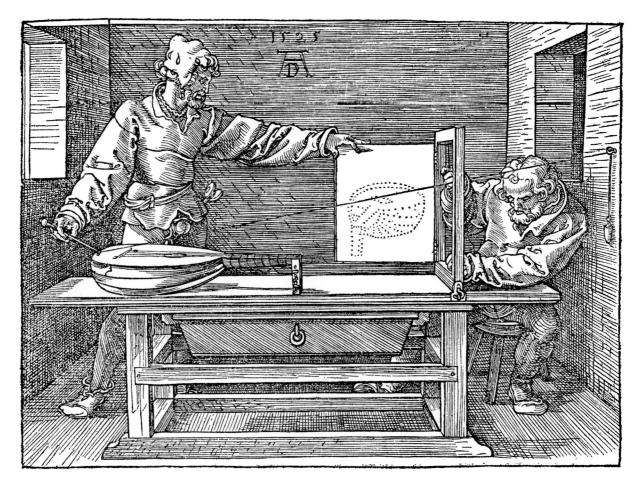

Vnd damit günstiger lieber Herr will ich meinem schreyben end geben / vnd so mir Got genad ver-
leycht die bücher so ich von menschlicher proporcion vñ anderen darzü gehörend geschryben hab mit
der zeyt in druck pringen / vnd darpey meniglich gewarnet haben / ob sich yemand vnder-
steen wurd mir diß außgangen büchlein wider nach zü drucken / das ich das
selb auch wider drucken will / vñ auß lassen geen mit meren vnd
grösserem züsatz dañ ietz beschehen ist / darnach mag
sich ein yetlicher richtē / Got dem Herren
sey lob vnd eer ewigklich.

N iij

Gedruckt zü Nüremberg.
Im. 1 5 2 5. Jar.

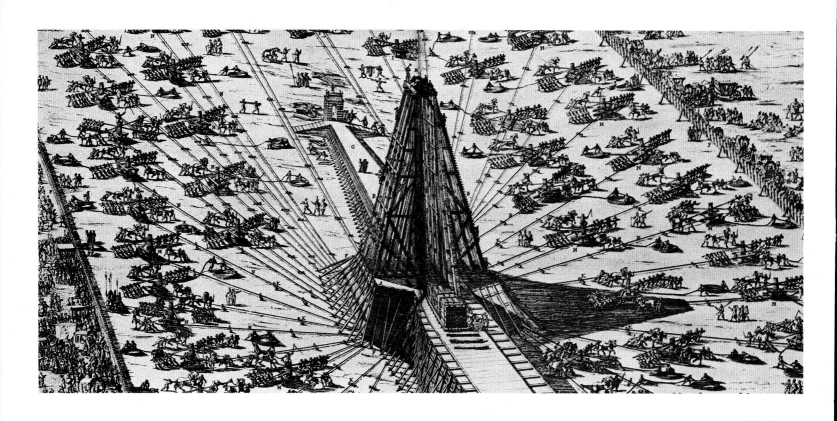

■ 19 The construction of the Obelisk of Caligula in St. Peter's Square in Rome on 10th September 1586. 800 men and 140 horses worked on winches under the supervision of architect and engineer Domenico Fontana. Bibliothèque Nationale, Paris.

■ 19 Die Aufstellung des Obelisken von Caligula auf dem St.-Peters-Platz in Rom am 10. September 1586. 800 Mann und 140 Pferde arbeiteten an Erdwinden unter der Aufsicht des Architekten und Ingenieurs Domenico Fontana. Bibliothèque Nationale, Paris.

■ 19 L'érection de l'obélisque de Caligula sur la place Saint-Pierre de Rome, le 10 septembre 1586. 800 hommes et 140 chevaux furent mobilisés pour hisser le monument à l'aide de treuils sous la direction de l'architecte et ingénieur Domenico Fontana. Bibliothèque Nationale, Paris.

■ 20 Diagram of the flight path of canonballs. The illustration shows that the range of fire is dependent on the angle of inclination of the mortar. Map by Paulus Puchner, Dresden 1577. Mathematics-Physical Salon, Dresden.

■ 20 Darstellung der Flugbahnen von Kanonenkugeln. Hier wird verdeutlicht, dass die Schussweite vom Neigungswinkel des Mörsers abhängt. Karte von Paulus Puchner, Dresden 1577. Mathematisch-Physikalischer Salon, Dresden.

■ 20 Représentation des trajectoires de boulets de canon. On voit ici que la portée d'un mortier dépend de l'angle d'inclinaison. Carte de Paulus Puchner réalisée à Dresde en 1577. Mathematisch-Physikalischer Salon, Dresde.

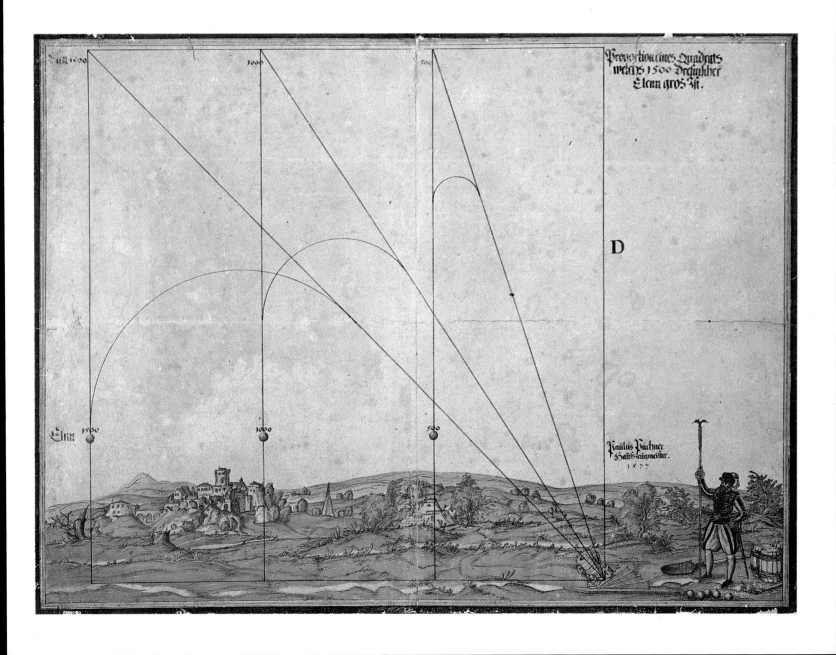

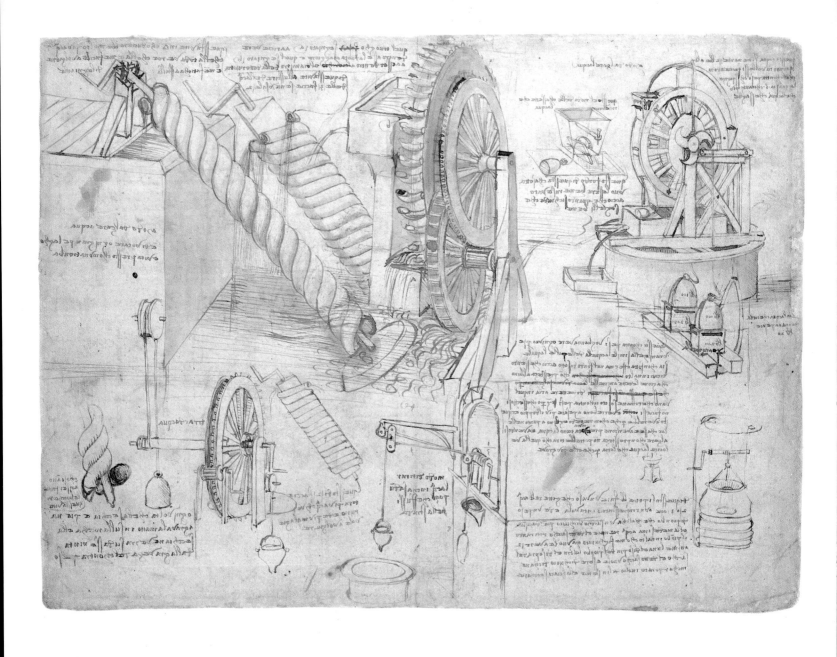

■ 21 The function of a well pump with a water lifting mechanism shown in a drawing by Leonardo da Vinci from the Codex Atlanticus (26 v.) from the Ambrosiana Library, Milan.

■ 22 Agostino Ramelli, one of Leonardo da Vinci's successors, also designed a water pump *(Le Diverse et Artificiose Macchine,* 1588). His specific interest was in the plunger (piston) pump, shown here, and he studied the possibility of a conversion from the rotating movement to a reciprocal movement. Bibliothèque Nationale, Paris.

■ 21 Die Funktion einer Brunnenpumpe mit Wasserhebewerk, Zeichnung von Leonardo da Vinci aus dem Codex Atlanticus (26 v.) aus der Mailänder Bibliothek Ambrosiana.

■ 22 Agostino Ramelli, ein Nachfolger Leonardo da Vincis, stellte ebenfalls eine Wasserpumpe dar *(Le Diverse et Artificiose Macchine,* 1588). Sein besonderes Interesse galt den hier gezeigten Kolbenpumpen, und er beschäftigte sich mit einer Umwandlung der rotierenden Bewegung in eine Hin- und Herbewegung. Bibliothèque Nationale, Paris.

■ 21 Fonction d'une pompe de puisage avec système d'élévation d'eau. Dessin de Léonard de Vinci tiré du Codex Atlanticus (26 v.) conservé à la Bibliothèque Ambrosiana de Milan.

■ 22 Agostino Ramelli, successeur de Léonard de Vinci, a également imaginé une pompe de puisage dans *Le Diverse et Artificiose Macchine,* 1588. Il vouait un intérêt particulier aux pompes alternatives présentées ici et s'occupait des possibilités de transformation du mouvement rotatif en un mouvement de va-et-vient. Bibliothèque Nationale, Paris.

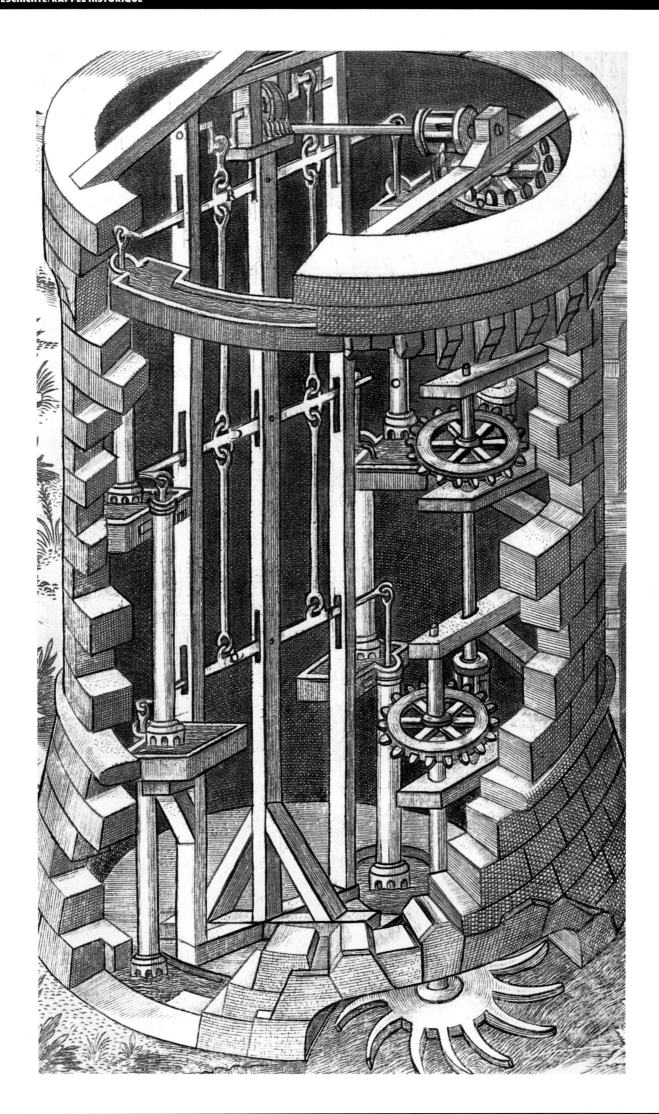

■ 23 Cross section of the first practical steam engine, developed in 1711 by Thomas Newcomen and John Cawley. Steam admitted from the boiler to the cylinder allowed the piston to be raised by a heavy counterpoise on the side of the beam and the jet of cold water entered the cylinder and condensed the steam. The piston was consequently forced down by the pressure of the atmosphere which activated the pump. Musée des Arts et Métiers, Paris.

■ 24 Single part of a crane that served to load and unload barges in the 19th century. From the collection of Charles Dollfus.

■ 25 Part of a 19th century steam engine (developed by von Heilmann in 1890).

■ 23 Schnitt durch die erste in der Praxis verwendbare Dampfmaschine, 1711 von Newcomen und Cawley entwickelt. Der Ausgleichhebel ist an einer Seite an den Pumpstangen befestigt, auf der anderen mit einem Kolben. Durch Dampf im Zylinder wurde der Hebel nach oben gedrückt. Stellte man die Dampfzufuhr ab und spritzte Wasser in den Zylinder, so drückte der Luftdruck den Kolben herunter, was die Pumpe betätigte. Musée des Arts et Métiers, Paris.

■ 24 Einzelteile eines Krans, der im 19. Jahrhundert zur Ent- und Beladung von Frachtkähnen diente. Sammlung Charles Dollfus.

■ 25 Teil einer Dampflokomotive aus dem 19. Jahrhundert (1890 von Heilmann entwickelt).

■ 23 Vue en coupe de la première machine à vapeur utilisable dans la pratique, celle qu'inventèrent Newcomen et Cawley en 1711. Le levier de compensation est fixé d'un côté aux bielles, de l'autre à un piston. La vapeur du cylindre pousse le levier vers le haut. En coupant l'alimentation en vapeur et en injectant de l'eau dans le cylindre, la pression d'air abaisse le piston, ce qui met la pompe en marche. Musée des Arts et Métiers de Paris.

■ 24 Pièces constitutives d'une grue du XIXe siècle qui servait au chargement et déchargement des péniches. Coll. Charles Dollfus.

■ 25 Partie d'une locomotive à vapeur du XIXe siècle (construite en 1890 par Heilmann).

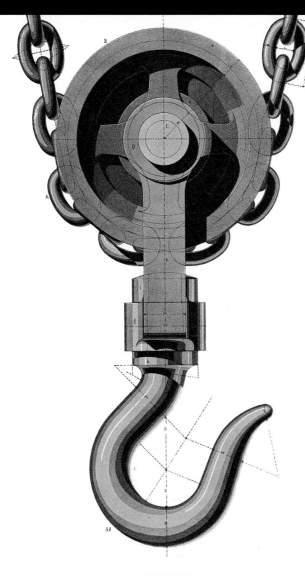

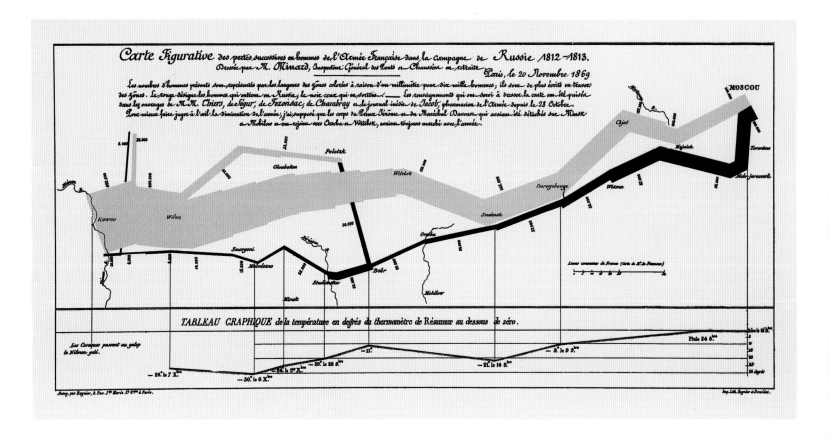

■ 26 Losses suffered by Napoleon's army in the Russian campaign 1812–1813. The brown line illustrates the losses on the march to Moscow. The path of the retreat from Moscow is depicted by the dark lower band. The temperature line (shown in Réaumur minus degrees) and corresponding dates show very clearly how the extreme cold contributed to the casualities. Charles Joseph Minard, (1869). Bibliothèque de l'Ecole Nationale des Ponts et Chaussées, Paris.

■ 26 Diagramm der fortgesetzten Verluste von Napoléons Armee beim Russlandfeldzug 1812–1813. Die braune Linie verdeutlicht die Verluste beim Marsch auf Moskau, die Schwarze die Verluste beim Rückzug. Sehr deutlich wird der Zusammenhang mit der Kälte, die im unteren Teil in Minustemperaturen (Réaumur), auch mit dem jeweiligen Datum versehen, angezeigt ist. Charles Joseph Minard. Bibliothèque de l'Ecole Nationale des Ponts et Chaussées, Paris.

■ 26 Représentation graphique des pertes continues de l'armée de Napoléon durant la campagne de Russie de 1812–1813. La ligne brune indique les pertes lors de l'avancée sur Moscou, la noire celles de la retraite. Le rapport est évident avec la chute des températures au-dessous de zéro portées au bas du graphique de Charles Joseph Minard en degrés Réaumur, avec les dates. Bibliotèque de l'Ecole Nationale des Ponts et Chaussées, Paris.

■ 27 Train schedule for Paris to Lyon in the 1880's. Arrivals and departures, as well as the length of stops, are depicted by horizontal lines. The stations are separated in proportion to their actual distance. The slope of the vertical lines reflects the speed of the trains – the more vertical the line, the faster the train. A less dense grid would have contributed to better readability. E. J. Marey. *La Méthode Graphique*, Paris 1885.

■ 27 Fahrplan für die Strecke Paris–Lyon. Ankunfts- und Abfahrtszeiten lassen sich an den horizontalen Linien ablesen, sowie auch die Aufenthaltsdauer. Der Abstand zwischen den Stationen entspricht proportional der wirklichen Distanz. Der Neigungswinkel der vertikalen Linien zeigt die Schnelligkeit der Züge (je steiler, desto schneller). Ein weniger starker Raster hätte noch zur besseren Lesbarkeit beigetragen. E. J. Marey. *La Méthode graphique*, Paris 1885.

■ 27 Horaire de chemin de fer, trajet Paris-Lyon. Lignes horizontales: heures d'arrivée et de départ, temps d'arrêt dans les gares. L'écart entre les gares correspond proportionnellement aux distances sur le terrain. L'angle d'inclinaison des lignes verticales indique la vitesse des trains (qui augmente avec la verticalité). Une trame moins forte aurait accru la lisibilité de l'ensemble. Extrait de l'ouvrage d'E. J. Marey, *La Méthode graphique*, Paris 1885.

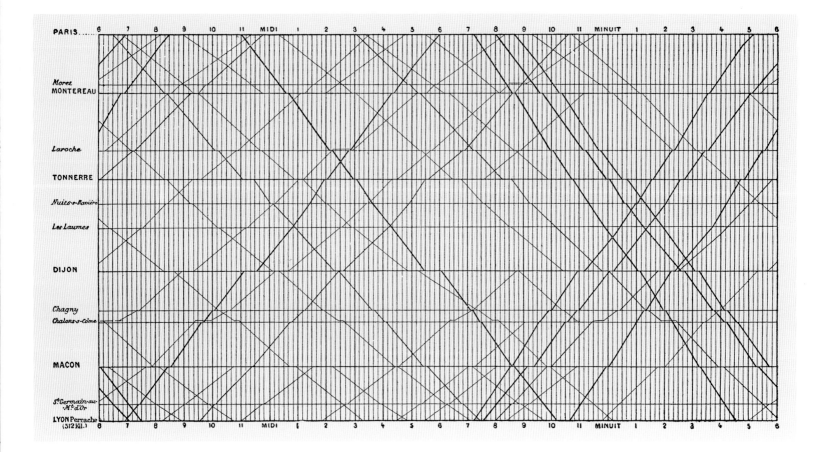

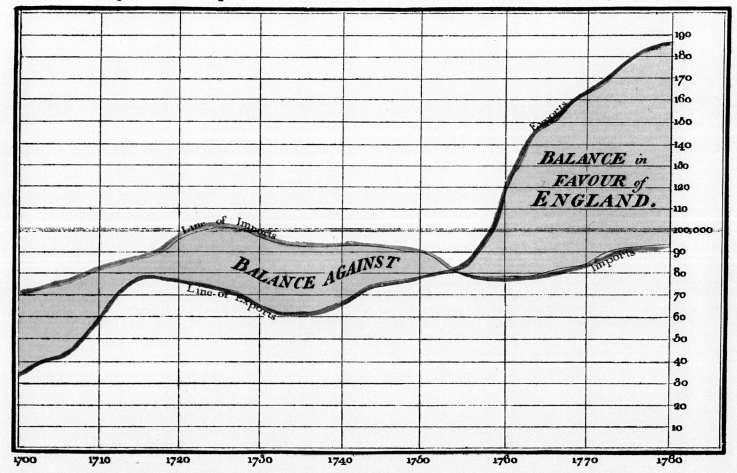

Exports and Imports to and from **DENMARK** & **NORWAY** from 1700 to 1780.

BALANCE in FAVOUR of ENGLAND.

BALANCE AGAINST

Line of Imports

Line of Exports

Exports

Imports

190
180
170
160
150
140
130
120
110
100,000
90
80
70
60
50
40
30
20
10

1700   1710   1720   1730   1740   1750   1760   1770   1780

The Bottom line is divided into Years, the Right hand line into £10,000 each.

Published as the Act directs, 1st May 1786, by Wm. Playfair   Neele sculpt 352, Strand, London.

■ 28 An etching to illustrate the development of England's exports to Norway between the years 1700 and 1780. On the right the value in £ 10 000 is given. By William Playfair, 1786.

■ 28 Eine Radierung für die Darstellung der Entwicklung der Exporte von England nach Norwegen zwischen 1700 und 1780. Auf der rechten Seite ist der Wert in £ 10 000.– angegeben. Von William Playfair, 1786.

■ 28 Eau-forte représentant l'évolution des exportations anglaises vers la Norvège de 1700 à 1780. Leur valeur figure sur la droite en dizaines de milliers de livres sterling. Gravure exécutée en 1786 par William Playfair.

■ 29 Positive and negative illustrations of a recording of the hours of sunshine over one year at different times of day. Here, to compare, is the stronger effect of a negative version of the original by J. Monkhouse and H.R. Wilkinson *(Maps and Diagrams)*.

All illustrations on this page are taken from the book *The Visual Display of Quantitative Information* by Edward R. Tufte.

■ 29 Positiv- und Negativdarstellung einer Aufzeichnung der Sonnenscheindauer übers Jahr zu verschiedenen Tageszeiten. Hier wird im Vergleich die stärkere Wirkung einer Negativvariante des Originals von J. Monkhouse und H. R. Wilkinson *(Maps and Diagrams)* hervorgehoben.

Alle Abbildungen auf dieser Seite stammen aus dem Buch *The Visual Display of Quantitative Information* von Edward R. Tufte.

■ 29 Valeurs positives et négatives d'un enregistrement annuel de l'ensoleillement à différentes heures de la journée. A titre comparatif, on fait ressortir ici l'impact accru d'une variante négative de l'original dû à J. Monkhouse et H. R. Wilkinson dans leur étude *Maps and Diagrams.*

Toutes les illustrations de cette page sont extraites de l'ouvrage *The Visual Display of Quantitative Information* d'Edward R. Tufte.

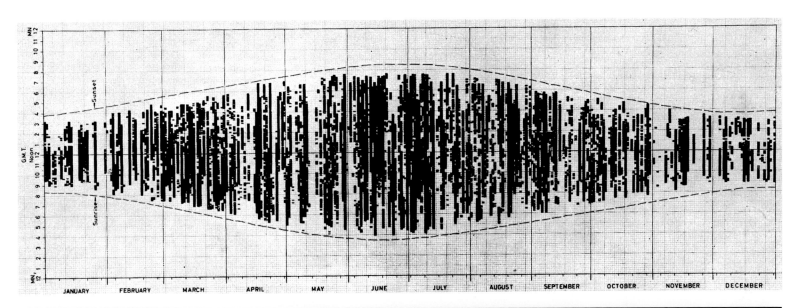

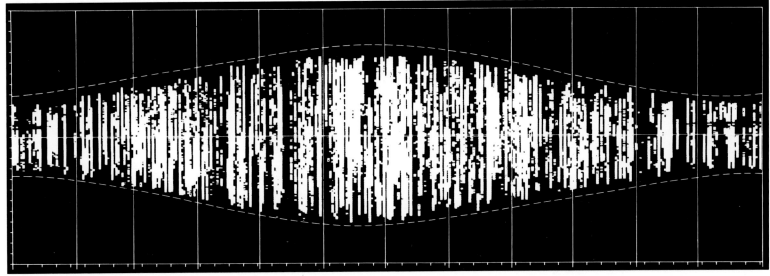

■ 30 "The Professor's Dream", 1848, by the English architect Charles Robert Cockerell: The knowledge of building history as basis for the builder's liberation from traditional styles. Watercolor, paper on canvas. Royal Academy of Arts, London.

■ 30 «The Professor's Dream», 1848, von Charles R. Cockerell: Die Kenntnisse der Baugeschichte als Grundlage für die Befreiung der Baumeister von traditionellen Stilen. Aquarell, Papier auf Leinwand. Royal Academy of Arts, London.

■ 30 «Le Rêve du professeur», 1848, aquarelle par Charles R. Cockerell: la connaissance de l'histoire de l'architecture servant à libérer les architectes du joug des styles de construction traditionnels. Royal Academy of Arts, Londres.

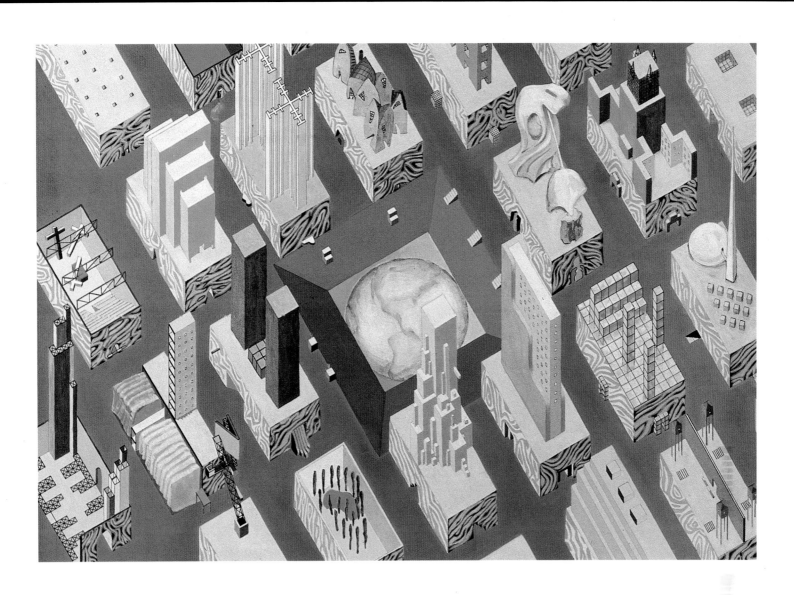

■ 31 The modern "Professor's Dream" – a Utopian vision of the "City with the Imprisoned Globe". Rem Koolhaas, The Office of Metropolitan Architecture, Rotterdam. (Available as poster at the Edition Lidiarte, Berlin.)

■ 31 Der moderne «Traum des Professors», eine utopische Vision der «Stadt mit dem gefangenen Globus». Rem Koolhaas, The Office of Metropolitan Architecture, Rotterdam. (Als Plakat bei Edition Lidiarte, Berlin, erhältlich.)

■ 31 La version moderne du «rêve du professeur», une vision utopique de la «ville au globe captif». Rem Koolhaas, The Office of Metropolitan Architecture, Rotterdam. (Existe en affiche aux Editions Lidiarte de Berlin.)

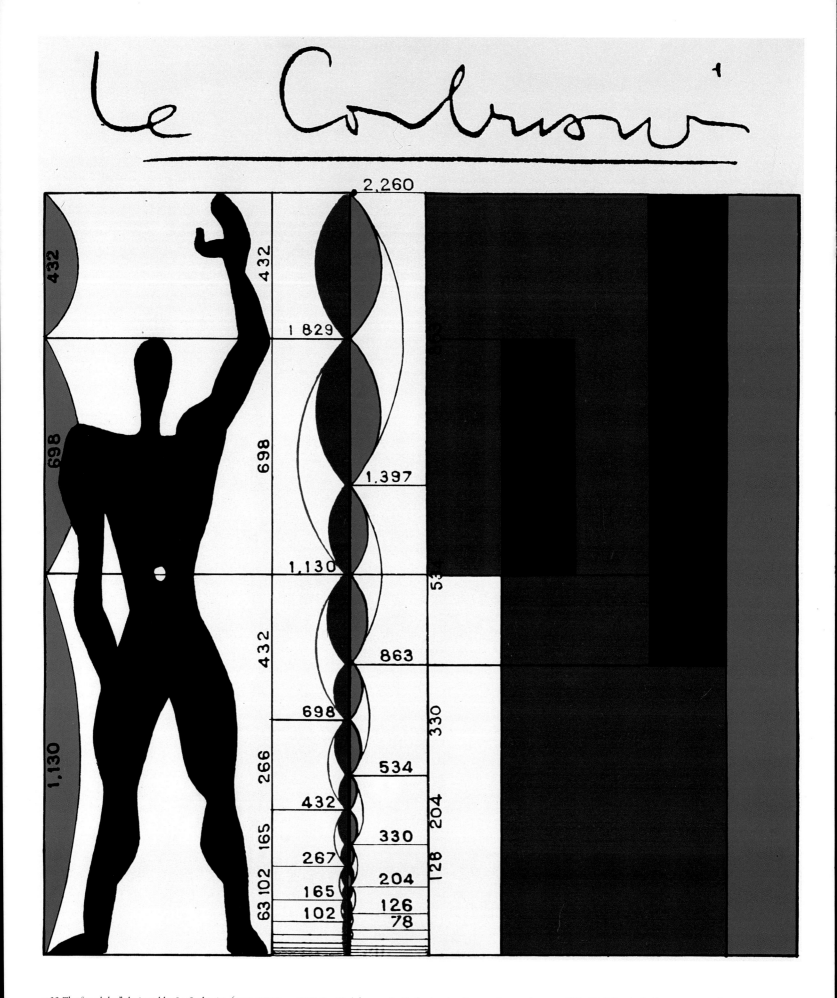

■ 32 The "modulor" designed by Le Corbusier (now patented), a mathematical system based on human proportions which he used for all his architectural plans. From *Le Corbusier, Œuvre complet 1938–1946* by Willy Boesiger; copyright Verlag für Architektur, Artemis Verlag, Zürich.

■ 32 Der Modulor von Le Corbusier, der dieses auf menschlichen Proportionen basierende Berechnungssystem für alle seine architektonischen Pläne verwendete. Aus *Le Corbusier, Œuvre complet 1938–1946* von Willy Boesiger; Copyright Verlag für Architektur, Artemis Verlag, Zürich.

■ 32 Le Modulor du Corbusier, qui a utilisé pour tous ses dessins d'architecture ce système de calcul basé sur les proportions humaines. Extrait de *Le Corbusier, Œuvre complet 1938–1946* par Willy Boesiger, copyright by Verlag für Architektur, Editions Artemis, Zurich.

STATISTIKEN UND VERGLEICHE

In the selection for this section, which is devoted to comparative statistical diagrams, legibility and aesthetics in the interpretation play an equally important role. GRAPHIS DIAGRAM is not a textbook, therefore the simplest forms of diagrams are not reproduced; these can be found in the form of line and column diagrams in specialized technical books and dissertations where they fulfill their purpose admirably. This chapter presents diagrams whose tasks are both complex or simple. The solutions are convincing because of the thoroughly thought-out concept, careful planning in the implementation; their technique, imagination, and originality.

A fundamental prerequisite in the choice of suitable form for representation is the understanding of figures. It is obvious that the designer must cooperate closely with the client's statisticians and other experts. The basic idea for the interpretation, though, is chiefly left to him, and in this the medium and the targeted public both play a decisive part. The fact that a diagram may be intended for the layman should not, however, lead the designer to limit himself to the minimum. In every case the designer must create a powerfully stated, thoroughly planned, aesthetically appealing diagram that everyone can understand immediately – after it has inspired a closer study. And anyway there is hardly a diagram appearing in annual reports, company brochures, house organs, general and trade magazines or books that is only meant for laymen. The diagram reader is almost always one of a very mixed public comprised of specialists and interested non-specialists. To solve this problem the designer's top priority is the moral duty towards the client and to the reader; to avoid misleading diagrams – as for instance a distortion of proportions, or a jumble of measurements without sufficient elucidation, or overemphasizing insignificancies at the cost of the essentials etc. If he does not comply with this duty, this form of communication is a betrayal of trust, since a graphic representation serves solely the purpose of explanation, on the basis of the general assumption – that the use of a diagram stands for the wish to inform.

Obviously it is quite legitimate to favor a diagram that takes a longer-term period into consideration, e.g. in an annual report that has to document a slack business year the successful diagram thus shows that ups and downs are only part of the firm's development, to be coped with and overcome.

If the year was successful it is understandable that the client opts for a conspicuous, carefully-conceived diagram that he can place in his report as an eye-catcher. The relatively simple column diagrams become particularly effective when the illustrative style of the report is taken up. This is what Wilmington Trust *(Figs. 43–49)* opted for in their annual report, and why Guardsman Chemicals *(Figs. 88, 89)* decided on a very painterly style in their report – also prevalent in the diagrams. An imaginative solution that turns column diagrams into eye-catchers is also the use of photography, as the annual report for the Bank of New England *(Figs. 50–53)* clearly demonstrates. In Hewlett Packard's annual report computer circuit components are used for the columns *(Fig. 81)*. A very appealing idea to show statistics is the tomato appearing in the annual report of the food concern H. J. Heinz Company *(Fig. 101)*. It becomes a glowing spot of color in an otherwise black-and-white printed report. In the annual reports for Ranstad Holding *(Fig. 106)*, the Dutch Electricity Works *(Fig. 45)*, and the National Steel Company *(Figs. 39–41)*, the firm's symbol in each case is integrated cleverly into the diagrams without it becoming a disturbing embellishment. Outstanding examples for the graphic interpretation of extremely complex data – relating to, among other things, very great time stretches – are the diagrams for the Holderbank Cement Factory *(Figs. 90–92)* and for the magazine *Wirtschaftswoche (Figs. 82, 83)*. In Bergen Brunswig Corporation's annual report *(Fig. 107)* the diagrams are formed by block-shaped elements that are symbolic, representing the firm's acquisitions (in the cover illustration shown as additional parts of a solid foundation block that symbolizes the parent company). Pictorial elements in this form of diagram are only of assistance when they are symbolic – as in the diagram of the social structure of the USA *(Fig. 102)* – and are not merely distracting accessories.

The use of abstract, non-pictorial diagrams is a surprisingly new departure. Only in the years between 1750 and 1800 did there begin to emerge statistical diagrams showing information on quantities and periods – long after the triumphant recognition in mathematics. The reason for the relatively late appearance of this form of diagram may lie in the high demands placed on the designer: statistical and mathematical understanding on the one side, plus imagination and creative flair on the other.

Bei der Auswahl für diesen Sektor, der vergleichenden, statistischen Diagrammen gewidmet ist, spielen Lesbarkeit und Ästhetik der Umsetzung eine gleichbedeutende Rolle. Da es sich bei GRAPHIS DIAGRAM nicht um ein Lehrbuch handelt, wird hier, wie auch in allen anderen Sektoren, auf die Wiedergabe der einfachsten Formen von Diagrammen verzichtet, die man in Form von Linien- und Säulendiagrammen vor allem in Fachbüchern und Dissertationen findet, wo sie auch durchaus ihren Zweck erfüllen. Dieses Kapitel behandelt Diagramme, denen sowohl komplexe als auch einfache Aufgaben zugrunde liegen. Die Lösungen überzeugen durch sorgfältige, durchdachte Umsetzung, durch Phantasie und Originalität.

Eine Voraussetzung bei der Wahl der geeigneten Form der Darstellung ist das Verständnis der Zahlen. Es ist selbstverständlich, dass der Designer eng mit den Statistikern oder anderen Experten seines Auftraggebers zusammenarbeiten muss. Die Grundidee für die Umsetzung ist aber in den meisten Fällen ihm überlassen, und hier spielen für seine Entscheidung auch das Medium und das Zielpublikum eine Rolle. Die Tatsache, dass ein Diagramm unter Umständen für Laien bestimmt ist, sollte jedoch nicht dazu führen, sich auf das Minimum zu beschränken; in jedem Fall sollte sich der Graphiker bemühen, ein aussagekräftiges, durchdachtes, ästhetisch ansprechendes Diagramm zu schaffen, das jeder bei sorgfältiger Betrachtung verstehen kann. Hinzu kommt, dass kaum ein Diagramm, das in Jahresberichten, Firmenbroschüren, Hauszeitschriften, Publikums-und Fachzeitschriften oder Büchern erscheint, nur für Laien bestimmt ist. Es handelt sich meistens um ein sehr gemischtes Publikum, das aus Fachleuten und interessierten Laien besteht.

An erster Stelle bei der Lösung seiner Aufgabe steht für jeden Graphiker die moralische Verpflichtung – gegenüber Auftraggeber und Leser –, irreführende Diagramme zu vermeiden, wie z.B. die Verzerrung von Proportionen, gemischte Massstäbe ohne ausreichende Erklärungen, Überbetonung von Unwichtigem auf Kosten von Wichtigem usw. Hält er sich nicht an diese Verpflichtung, so wird diese Form der Kommunikation zur Farce.

Selbstverständlich ist es legitim, sich z.B. bei einem Jahresbericht, der ein schwieriges Geschäftsjahr dokumentieren muss, für ein Diagramm zu entscheiden, das eine längerfristige Periode berücksichtigt, die ein konstantes Auf und Ab als eine Entwicklung erkennen lässt, die

zu verkraften und durch geeignete Massnahmen zu bewältigen ist. War das Jahr erfolgreich, ist es verständlich, wenn der Auftraggeber sich für auffallende, sorgfältig ausgearbeitete Diagramme entscheidet, die er als Blickfang in seinem Bericht einsetzt. Besonders wirkungsvoll präsentieren sich z.B. relativ einfache Säulendiagramme, in denen der illustrative Stil des Berichtes aufgenommen wird. So entschied man sich bei den Jahresberichten von Wilmington Trust *(Abb. 43-49)* und von Guardsman Chemicals *(Abb. 88, 89)* für einen sehr malerischen Stil, der auch die Diagramme prägt. Eine einfallsreiche Lösung, die einfache Säulendiagramme zum Blickfang macht, ist auch der Einsatz von Photographie, wie im Jahresbericht der Bank of New England *(Abb. 50-53)* wirkungsvoll demonstriert wird. Im Jahresbericht für Hewlett-Packard bilden Computer-Schaltelemente die Säulen *(Abb. 81)*. Eine besonders ansprechende Darstellung einer Statistik ist die Tomate im Jahresbericht für den Nahrungsmittelkonzern H. J. Heinz Company *(Abb. 101)*: sie wird zu einem leuchtenden Farbfleck in einem im übrigen schwarzweiss gedruckten Bericht. In den Jahresberichten der Ranstad Holding *(Abb. 106)*, der holländischen Elektrizitätswerke *(Abb. 45)* und der National Steel Company *(Abb. 39-41)* wird das jeweilige Firmensymbol in den Diagrammen sinnvoll eingesetzt, ohne dass es zu störendem Beiwerk wird. Hervorragende Beispiele für die diagrammatische Umsetzung sehr komplexer Daten – es galt u.a. sehr grosse Zeitspannen darzustellen – sind die Diagramme für die Cementfabrik Holderbank *(Abb. 90-92)* und für die *Wirtschaftswoche (Abb. 82, 83)*. Im Jahresbericht der Bergen Brunswig Corporation *(Abb. 107)* bekommen als Diagramme eingesetzte blockförmige Elemente zusätzlich Symbolcharakter: sie stehen für Akquisitionen der Firma, die in der Umschlagillustration als Bauelemente eines soliden Grundblocks (der Mutterfirma) dargestellt sind.

Die Verwendung abstrakter, nicht bildhafter Diagramme ist eine überraschend junge Erfindung. Erst zwischen 1750 und 1800 entstanden statistische Diagramme, die Mengen und Zeiträume angaben, lange nach triumphalen Erkenntnissen in der Mathematik. Der Grund für das relativ späte Aufkommen dieser Form des Diagramms mag in den hohen Ansprüchen liegen, die es an den Gestalter stellt: statistisches und mathematisches Verständnis auf der einen Seite sowie Phantasie und gestalterisches Können auf der anderen.

Notre sélection pour ce chapitre consacré aux diagrammes statistiques comparatifs a été dictée par les critères de la lisibilité et de l'esthétique qui entrent à parts égales dans une transposition réussie. GRAPHIS DIAGRAM n'ayant pas le caractère d'un manuel d'enseignement, nous avons renoncé, tout comme dans les autres chapitres, à reproduire les formes les plus simples de ce genre de diagrammes que l'on retrouve sous forme de graphiques à lignes ou à bandes principalement dans les ouvrages spécialisés et les thèses où ils conviennent parfaitement pour l'utilisation qui en est faite. Le présent chapitre traite de diagrammes inspirés par des tâches aussi bien complexes que simples. Les solutions emportent l'adhésion par les soins et l'intelligence apportés à la transposition, l'imagination et l'originalité qui y sont à l'œuvre.

La condition essentielle lors du choix de la forme de représentation appropriée, c'est la compréhension des données chiffrées. Le designer est tenu de collaborer avec les statisticiens ou autres spécialistes désignés par son client. Pourtant, c'est bien à lui que revient en général l'idée de base de la transposition; or, son choix est aussi dicté par le médium employé et le public visé. Le fait qu'un diagramme donné s'adresse éventuellement à un public non averti ne devrait pas entraîner un traitement minimaliste de la part du graphiste. Celui-ci doit bien au contraire chercher dans tous les cas d'espèce à réaliser un diagramme expressif, conçu avec soin, qui en appelle au sens esthétique et puisse être compris de tous sans aucune équivoque après un examen attentif – dans la mesure où il incite à un tel examen. Il s'y ajoute le fait que la plupart des diagrammes publiés dans les rapports annuels, les brochures et revues d'entreprises et les livres sont rarement destinés aux seuls amateurs. Ils s'adressent bien plus souvent à un public mixte composé de spécialistes aussi bien que de lecteurs ignorants en la matière.

Le graphiste inspiré observe comme priorité n° 1 à l'égard de son client comme de ses lecteurs l'engagement moral qui vise à éviter d'induire le public en erreur en manipulant les proportions, en changeant d'échelle sans en avertir le lecteur, en accentuant des faits insignifiants au détriment d'informations essentielles, etc. Dans la mesure où il ne respecte pas cette obligation, ce mode de communication se pervertit, car une représentation graphique ne peut servir qu'à l'élucidation de faits et données; étant donné cette fonction de principe, le lecteur est amené à supposer que l'apparition d'un diagramme coïncide avec le désir de communiquer une information utile.

Lorsqu'un rapport annuel doit faire état d'un parcours difficile au cours de l'exercice écoulé, il est évidemment légitime d'opter pour un graphique pluriannuel établissant que la marche des affaires suit un mouvement en dents de scie qu'il s'agit d'amortir et de pallier par un train de mesures approprié. Lorsque l'exercice s'est soldé par un coquet bénéfice, le client aura tout aussi naturellement tendance à privilégier des diagrammes captant le regard et préparés avec soin pour en consteller son rapport. Une efficacité particulière revient à cet égard aux graphiques à bandes relativement simples à mettre en œuvre et qui reprennent le style illustratif du rapport. C'est ainsi que les rapports de Wilmington Trust *(fig. 43-49)* et de Guardsman Chemicals *(fig. 88, 89)* ont opté pour un style très pictural, que l'on retrouve dans la partie diagrammatique. Une solution ingénieuse pour mettre en vedette de simples graphiques à bandes consiste à les illustrer de photos, comme le démontre de façon remarquable le rapport annuel de la Bank of New England *(fig. 50-53)*. Le rapport de Hewlett-Packard utilise des circuits logiques pour ordinateurs en lieu et place des bandes du graphique *(fig. 81)*. Une représentation fort séduisante de données statistiques s'incarne dans la tomate du rapport du groupe alimentaire H. J. Heinz Company *(fig. 101)*, qui fait figure de tache couleur étincelante dans un texte par ailleurs imprimé en noir et blanc. Dans les rapports de Ranstad Holding *(fig. 106)*, des Forces motrices néerlandaises *(fig. 45)* et de la National Steel Company *(fig. 39-41)*, l'emblème de l'entreprise est intégré judicieusement dans les diagrammes sans y constituer un ornement factice. De remarquables exemples de la transposition graphique de données très complexes – notamment en ce qui concerne les longues périodes représentées – se trouvent dans les diagrammes réalisés pour la Cimenterie Holderbank *(fig. 90-92)* et le magazine *Wirtschaftswoche (fig. 82, 83)*. Dans le rapport annuel de la Bergen Brunswig Corporation *(fig. 107)*, les éléments-blocs employés comme diagrammes se voient dotés d'une valeur symbolique additionnelle: ils représentent en effet les acquisitions du groupe, ce qui fait qu'on les retrouve sur la couverture comme «briques» d'une solide construction monobloc figurant la société mère. Les éléments illustratifs n'ont de sens dans ce genre de diagrammes que lorsqu'ils ont valeur de symboles – comme on le voit dans la figuration de la structure sociale des Etats-Unis *(fig. 102)* – au lieu d'être de simples ajouts superfétatoires.

Le recours à des diagrammes abstraits, non figuratifs est d'invention récente, ce qui n'est pas sans surprendre. C'est seulement entre 1750 et 1800 que l'on vit naître les diagrammes statistiques indiquant des quantités et des durées, longtemps après que les mathématiques eurent remporté leurs grands triomphes scientifiques. La raison de ce retard dans la réalisation du diagramme statistique comparatif peut tenir aux exigences élevées qu'il impose au concepteur qui doit être informé des statistiques et des mathématiques, d'une part, et disposer par ailleurs de ressources imaginatives et d'un talent créatif certain.

■ 34–38 Covers of the Japanese magazine *Daily Industrial News.* The diagrams relate to the contents of these issues. *34:* a market forecast with details of anticipated demand for semiconductors. *35:* the prospects for highly-developed technology and precision mechanics. *36:* shares of Japanese products on the international electronics market. *37:* forecast of the domestic requirements of electronic articles for private households. *38:* the proportion of employees working in high-tech industries in various US states. (JPN)

■ 34–38 Umschlagseiten der japanischen Zeitschrift *Daily Industrial News.* Die Diagramme beziehen sich auf den Inhalt der Ausgaben. *34:* Eine Marktprognose mit Angabe der zu erwartenden Nachfragesteigerung für Halbleiter. *35:* Die Aussichten für hochentwickelte Technologie und Feinmechanik. *36:* Anteile japanischer Produkte am Elektronikmarkt. *37:* Prognose der Inlandnachfrage nach elektronischen Artikeln für Privathaushalte. *38:* Der Anteil der in hochtechnisierten Industrien Beschäftigten in verschiedenen US-Staaten. (JPN)

■ 34–38 Couvertures du magazine japonais *Daily Industrial News.* Les diagrammes se rapportent au contenu des divers numéros. *34:* Evolution prévisionnelle du marché des semi-conducteurs en fonction de la demande croissante. *35:* Perspectives en matière de technologie de pointe et de mécanique de précision. *36:* Part du marché de l'électronique revenant aux produits japonais. *37:* Evolution prévisionnelle de la demande intérieure privée en matière d'appareils électroniques. *38:* Répartition de la main-d'œuvre des industries de pointe au sein des Etats-Unis. (JPN)

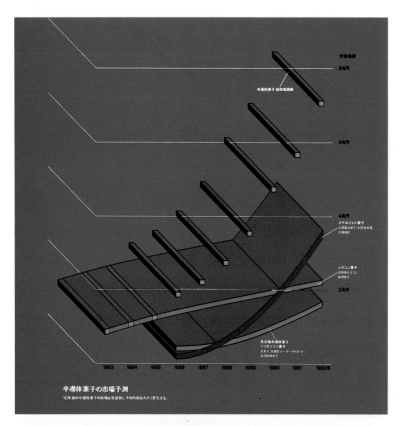

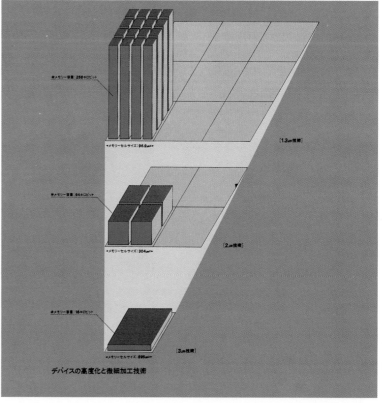

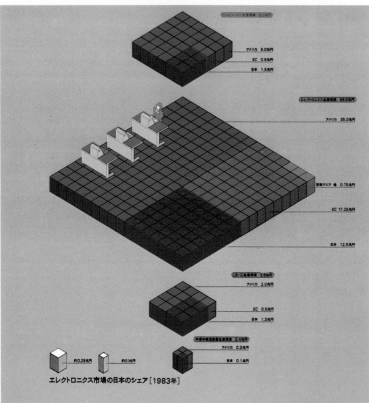

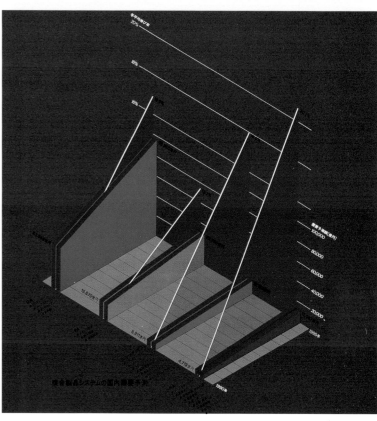

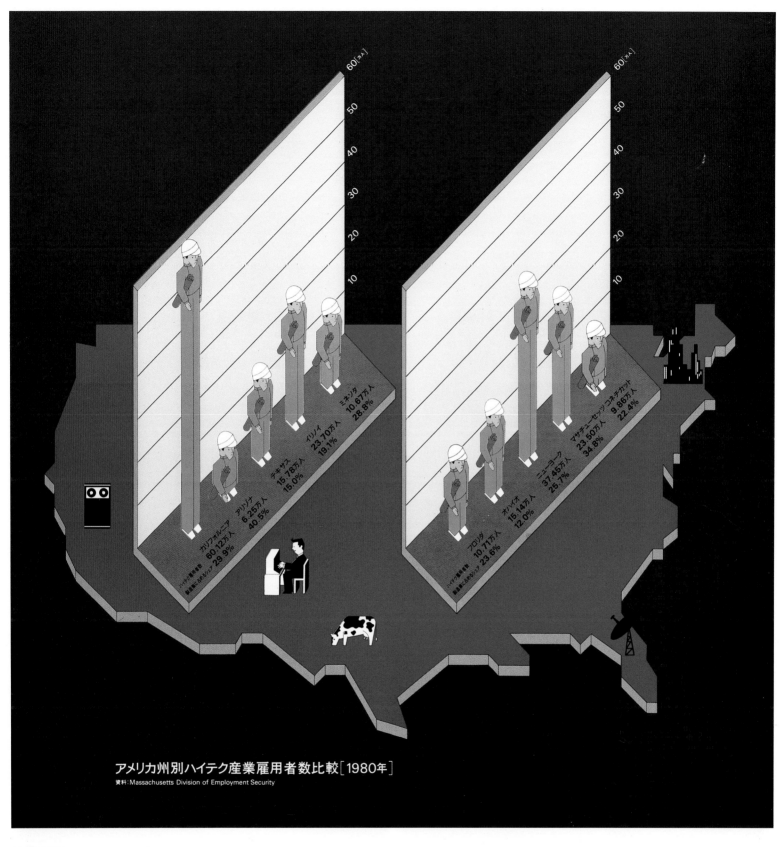

アメリカ州別ハイテク産業雇用者数比較［1980年］
資料：Massachusetts Division of Employment Security

ART DIRECTOR:
KENZO NAKAGAWA
DESIGNER:
KENZO NAKAGAWA/
SATCH MORIKAMI
AGENCY:
NIPPON DESIGN CENTER
PUBLISHER:
NIKKAN KOGYO SHINBUN-SHA
■ 34–38

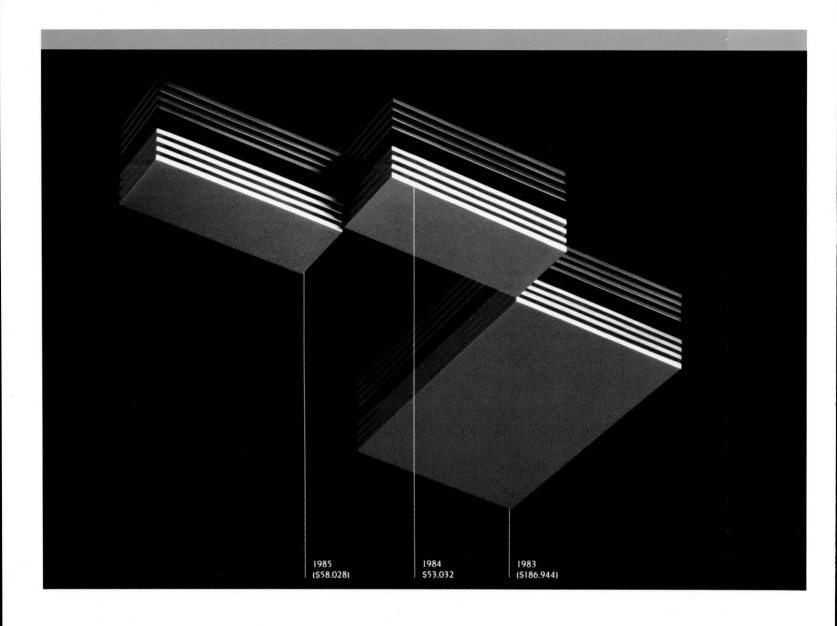

1985
($58,028)

1984
$53,032

1983
($186,944)

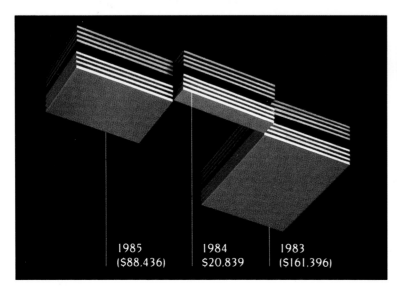

1985
($88,436)

1984
$20,839

1983
($161,396)

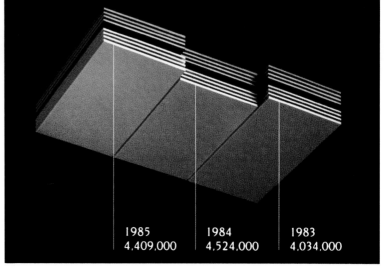

1985
4,409,000

1984
4,524,000

1983
4,034,000

DESIGNER:
ROBERT ADAM/SCOTT PIPITONE
ART DIRECTOR:
ROBERT ADAM
AGENCY:
ADAM, FILIPPO & MORAN
CLIENT:
NATIONAL STEEL CORP.
◄■ 39-41

DESIGNER:
GEORGE TSCHERNY
ART DIRECTOR:
GEORGE TSCHERNY
AGENCY:
GEORGE TSCHERNY
CLIENT:
W.R. GRACE & CO.
►■ 42

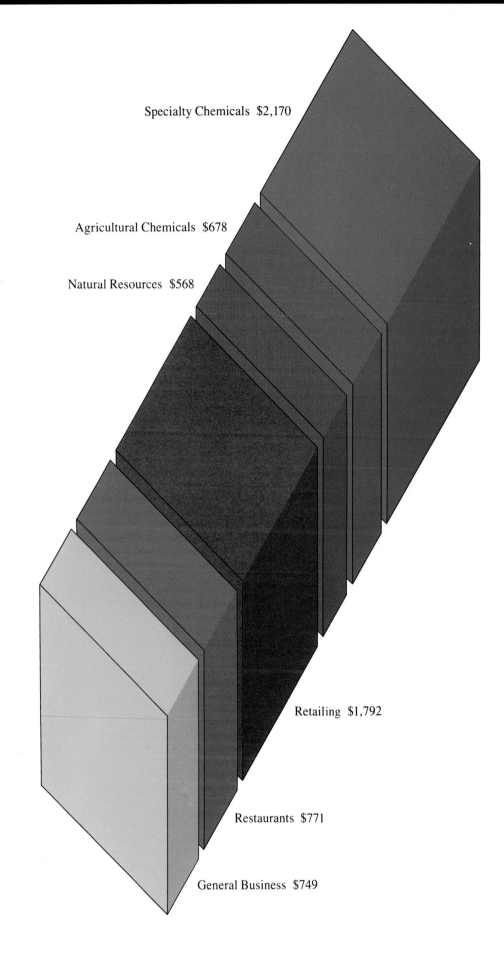

Specialty Chemicals $2,170

Agricultural Chemicals $678

Natural Resources $568

Retailing $1,792

Restaurants $771

General Business $749

■ 39-41 Three-year comparisons of the state of business, from the 1985 annual report of the National Steel Company, Pittsburgh, Pennsylvania. (USA)

■ 42 Graphic representation of the *1984* sales of W.R. Grace & Co. New York, categorized according to the various business sectors. (USA)

■ 39-41 Dreijahresvergleiche des Geschäftsgangs aus dem Jahresbericht 1985 der National Steel Company, Pittsburgh, Pennsylvania. (USA)

■ 42 Graphische Darstellung der Verkäufe von 1984 der W. R. Grace & Co. New York, aufgeteilt nach den verschiedenen Geschäftszweigen. (USA)

■ 39-41 Evolution triennale comparative du chiffre d'affaires, dans le rapport annuel pour 1985 de la National Steel Company de Pittsburgh en Pennsylvanie. (USA)

■ 42 Représentation graphique du chiffre d'affaires réalisé en 1984 par la société W.R. Grace & Co., de New York - ventilé par secteurs d'activité. (USA)

DESIGNER:
JOEL KATZ
ARTIST:
SEYMOUR MEDNICK
ART DIRECTOR:
JOEL KATZ
AGENCY:
KATZ WHEELER DESIGN
CLIENT:
WILMINGTON TRUST COMPANY
■ 43-49

■ 43-46 Representations from an annual report of the Wilmington Trust Company, Wilmington, Delaware. *43:* the liquid resources from 1981 to 1985 of the State of Delaware as well as expenditure during this period. *44:* decrease in Delaware's debts from 1981 to 1985. *45:* percentage of Delaware's rate of unemployment compared with all other US states from 1980 - 84. *46:* the high per capita income in the state of Delaware compared with the per capita income in all other US states from 1979 - 83. (USA)

■ 47-49 Five-year comparisons from the 1984 annual report of the Wilmington Trust Company. (USA)

■ 43-46 Malerische Darstellungen aus einem Jahresbericht der Wilmington Trust Company, Wilmington, Delaware. *43:* Die flüssigen Mittel von 1981 bis 1985 des Staates Delaware sowie Ausgaben in dieser Zeit. *44:* Abnahme der Verschuldung Delawares von 1981 bis 1985. *45:* Prozentualer Vergleich der Arbeitslosenrate in Delaware gegenüber allen Staaten der USA von 1980-84. *46:* Das hohe Pro-Kopf-Einkommen im Staate Delaware gegenüber dem Pro-Kopf-Einkommen aller US-Staaten von 1979-83. (USA)

■ 47-49 Fünfjahresvergleiche aus dem Jahresbericht 1984 der Wilmington Trust Company. (USA)

■ 43-46 Représentations figurant dans un rapport annuel de la Wilmington Trust Company. *43:* Liquidités 1981-1985 de l'Etat du Delaware comparées aux dépenses de la même période. *44:* Réduction de la dette publique du Delaware entre 1981 et 1985. *45:* Taux de chômage comparés du Delaware et de tous les autres Etats de l'Union au cours de la période 1980-1984. *46:* Mise en relief du revenu élevé par habitant dans l'Etat du Delaware comparé aux autres Etats de l'Union pour la période 1979-1983. (USA)

■ 47-49 Comparaisons quinquennales figurant dans le rapport annuel 1984 de la Wilmington Trust Co. (USA)

Unemployment Rates:
Delaware vs. United States
One of the most important in-
dicators of the strength of a
state's economy is its ability
to provide jobs for its resi-
dents. 1984 marked the third
consecutive year in which Delaware's unemployment rate
averaged more than a full
percentage point below the
national average. Source:
Delaware Development Office.

Personal Income Growth:
Delaware vs. United States
(adjusted for inflation)
Growth of personal income is
a key measure of economic
prosperity. In this regard, Delaware rebounded remarkably
from the 1979 recession and
was virtually unaffected by the
severe downturn of the early
1980s. Personal income grew
4.4% after inflation in 1982,
nearly twice the rate for the
total United States. The trend
continued in 1983, with an increase of 3.5% for Delaware,
compared with 2.4% for the
nation. Source: Delaware
Development Office.

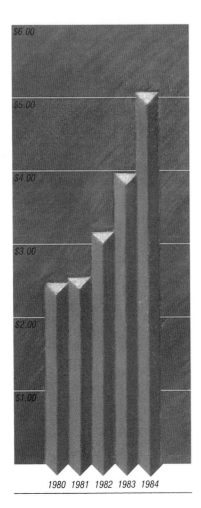

1980 1981 1982 1983 1984

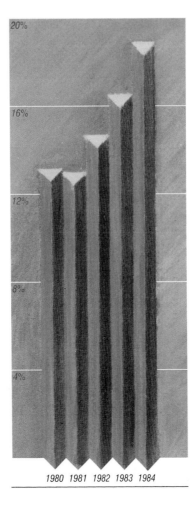

1980 1981 1982 1983 1984

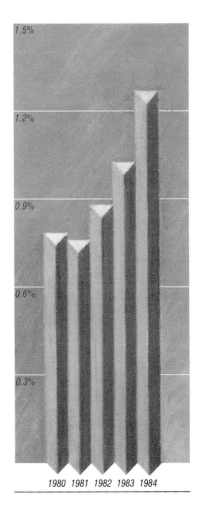

1980 1981 1982 1983 1984

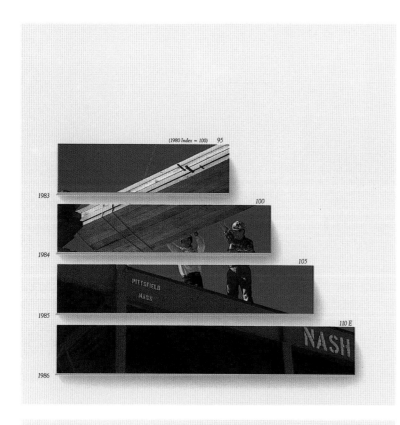

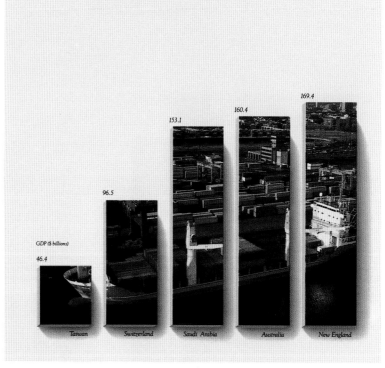

■ 50-53 Photographs cut into columns that represent the economic development of the Bank of New England Corp. and New England itself. *50:* manpower development. *51:* new buildings in New England, *52:* loans, *53:* cash deposits of the Bank of New England Corp. All pictures are taken from the 1985 annual report of the Bank of New England Corp. (USA)

■ 54 Development of the sales of products available only on prescription, from 1969-1985. Perspective illustration from the annual report of the Bergen Brunswig Corp. (USA)

■ 50-53 Aus Photographien zusammengesetzte Säulen, die die wirtschaftliche Entwicklung der Bank of New England Corp. und des Gebietes von Neuengland darstellen. *50:* Arbeitsmarktentwicklung; *51:* Neubauten in Neuengland; *52:* Darlehen; *53:* Geldeinlagen der Bank of New England Corp. Alle Bilder stammen aus dem Jahresbericht 1985 der Bank. (USA)

■ 54 Entwicklung der Verkäufe von rezeptpflichtigen Produkten in den Jahren 1969 bis 1985. Perspektivische Darstellung aus dem Jahresbericht der Bergen Brunswig Corp. (USA)

■ 50-53 Photos découpées en bandes pour illustrer l'essor économique de la Bank of New England Corp. et des six Etats de Nouvelle-Angleterre. *50:* Evolution du marché du travail régional, *51:* évolution du bâtiment (constructions nouvelles), *52:* croissance des prêts, *53:* et des dépôts de la banque. Du rapport annuel 1985 de la Bank of New England Corp. (USA)

■ 54 Evolution des ventes de médicaments sujets à prescription de 1969 à 1985. Représentation en perspective cavalière. Rapport annuel de la Bergen Brunswig Corp. (USA)

DESIGNER:
MICHAEL BENES
PHOTOGRAPHER:
RUSSELL SCHLEIPMAN
ART DIRECTOR:
MICHAEL BENES
AGENCY:
*MICHAEL BENES
COMMUNICATIONS*
CLIENT:
BANK OF NEW ENGLAND
◄■ 50–53

DESIGNER:
C. CLAUDIA JEFFERIES
ART DIRECTOR:
RON JEFFERIES
AGENCY:
THE JEFFERIES ASSOCIATION
CLIENT:
BERGEN BRUNSWIG CORP.
►■ 54

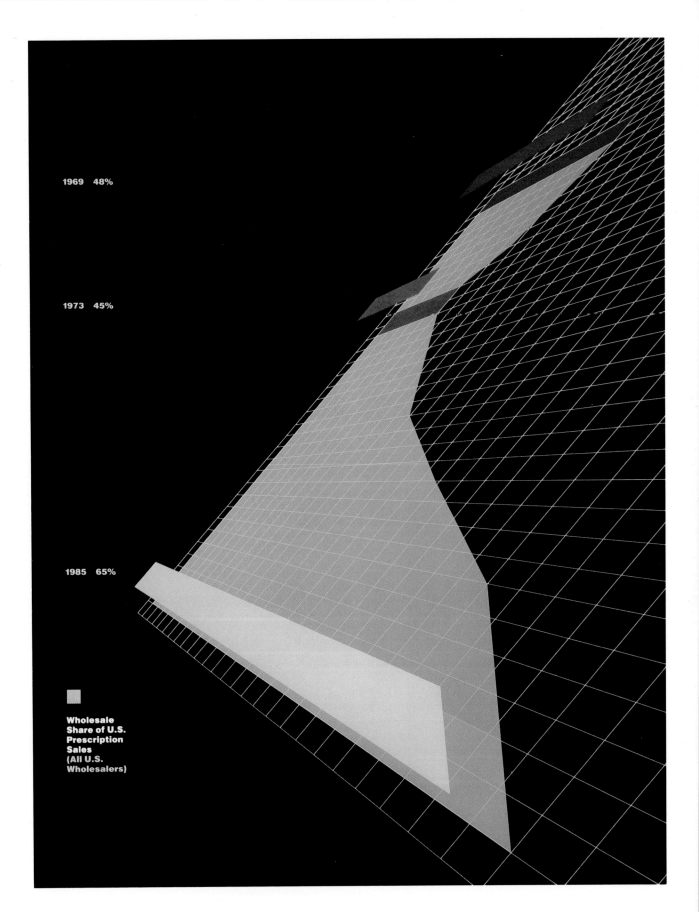

1969   48%

1973   45%

1985   65%

Wholesale
Share of U.S.
Prescription
Sales
(All U.S.
Wholesalers)

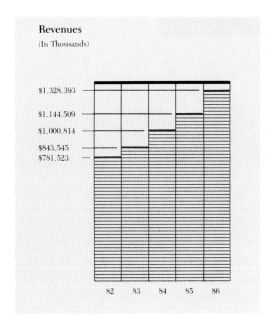

Revenues
(In Thousands)

$1,328,393
$1,144,509
$1,000,814
$843,545
$781,523

82 83 84 85 86

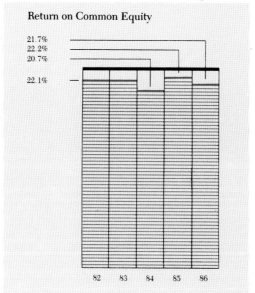

Return on Common Equity

21.7%
22.2%
20.7%

22.1%

82 83 84 85 86

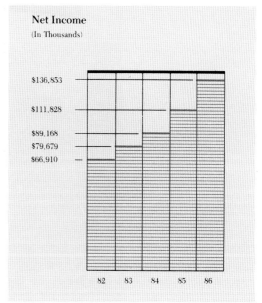

Net Income
(In Thousands)

$136,853
$111,828
$89,168
$79,679
$66,910

82 83 84 85 86

DESIGNER:
AL GLUTH
ART DIRECTOR:
AL GLUTH/JOHN WEAVER
AGENCY:
GLUTH WEAVER INC.
CLIENT:
*BROWNING-FERRIS
INDUSTRIES, INC.*
▲■ 55-57

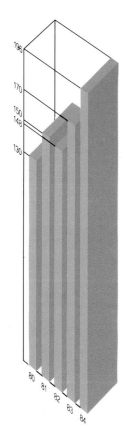

196
170
150
148
130

80 81 82 83 84

2.67
2.35
2.25
2.12
2.04

80 81 82 83 84

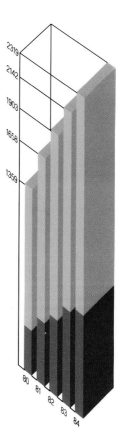

2319
2142
1903
1658
1359

80 81 82 83 84

DESIGNER:
BENNETT ROBINSON
ART DIRECTOR:
BENNETT ROBINSON
AGENCY:
CORPORATE GRAPHICS INC.
CLIENT:
*CONTEL
(CONTINENTAL TELECOM INC.)*
◄■ 58-60

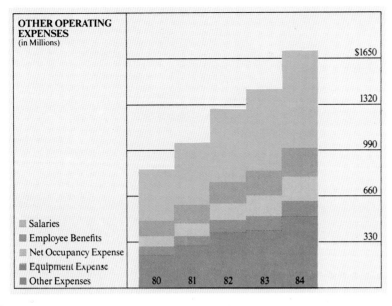

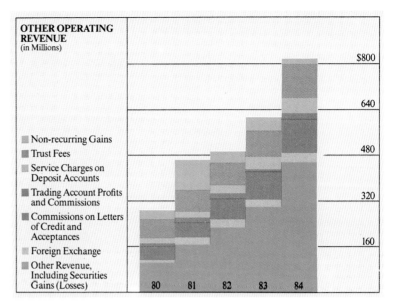

DESIGNER:
MARK ULRICH
ART DIRECTOR:
ANTHONY RUSSELL
CLIENT:
MANUFACTURERS HANOVER
▲■ 61, 62

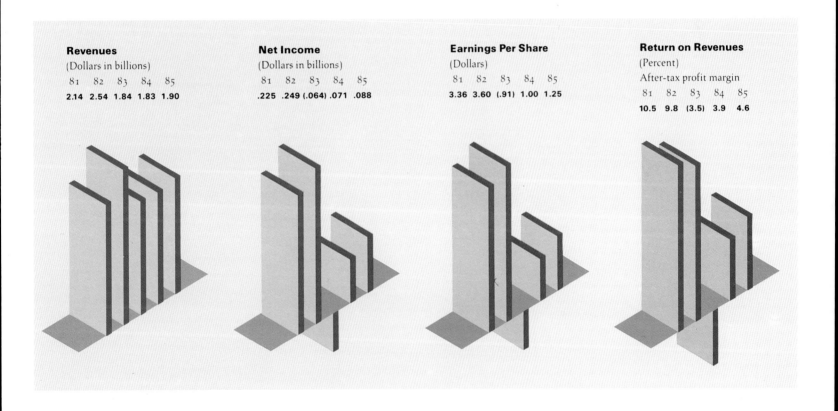

Revenues
(Dollars in billions)
81 82 83 84 85
2.14 2.54 1.84 1.83 1.90

Net Income
(Dollars in billions)
81 82 83 84 85
.225 .249 (.064) .071 .088

Earnings Per Share
(Dollars)
81 82 83 84 85
3.36 3.60 (.91) 1.00 1.25

Return on Revenues
(Percent)
After-tax profit margin
81 82 83 84 85
10.5 9.8 (3.5) 3.9 4.6

■ 55-57 From an annual report of Browning-Ferris Industries Inc., Houston, Texas; the financial development from 1982 to 1986. (USA)

■ 58-60 Bar diagrams of various financial data of the Continental Telecom Inc., Atlanta, Georgia. From their 1984 annual report. (USA)

■ 61, 62 Revenues *(61)* and expenditure chart *(62)* of the Manufacturers Hanover Corp. of New York, from 1980-1984. (USA)

■ 63 Bar diagrams from the 1985 annual report of Baker International showing details of its financial position. (USA)

■ 55-57 Aus einem Jahresbericht der Browning-Ferris Industries Inc., Houston, Texas. Die finanzielle Entwicklung von 1982 bis 1986. (USA)

■ 58-60 Graphische Darstellung verschiedener Finanzdaten der Continental Telecom Inc., Atlanta, Georgia. Aus ihrem Jahresbericht 1984. (USA)

■ 61, 62 Einnahmen- *(61)* und Ausgabenskala *(62)* der Manufacturers Hanover Corp., New York, in den Jahren 1980-84. (USA)

■ 63 Im Jahresbericht 1985 der Baker International Corp. veröffentlichte Entwicklung der Finanzen. (USA)

■ 55-57 Diagrammes tirés d'un rapport annuel de Browning-Ferris Industries Inc., Houston (Texas). On y représente l'évolution financière du groupe de 1982 à 1986. (USA)

■ 58-60 Représentation graphique de diverses données financières relatives aux résultats de la Continental Telecom Inc. d'Atlanta. Extrait du rapport annuel 1984. (USA)

■ 61, 62 Echelle des revenus *(61)* et dépenses *(62)* de la Manufacturers Hanover Corp. de New York pour les années 1980-1984. (USA)

■ 63 Progression des résultats financiers de la Baker International Corp., tirée du rapport annuel pour 1985. (USA)

■ 64 Chart with three-dimensional impact showing sales in various business sectors and the development relating to shares, published in an annual report of Monogram Industries, Inc., Santa Monica. (USA)

■ 65-68 Charts showing various data relating to customers of Merrill Lynch, taken from their brochure "Mergers and Acquisitions". The illustrative section was additionally varnished. (USA)

■ 64 Dreidimensional wirkende graphische Darstellung der Verkäufe, aufgeteilt in verschiedene Geschäftszweige, und der Aktienentwicklung. Aus einem Jahresbericht der Monogram Industries Inc. (USA)

■ 65-68 Graphische Darstellungen verschiedener Daten und Fakten aus dem Kundenkreis der Investmentfirma Merrill Lynch, veröffentlicht in der Broschüre «Fusionen und Übernahmen». Der Illustrationsteil wurde zusätzlich lackiert. (USA)

■ 64 Diagrammes donnant une impression de relief, pour la représentation du chiffre d'affaires ventilé par secteurs d'activité et de l'évolution de données financières corrélées. Rapport de Monogram Industries, Inc. (USA)

■ 65-68 Représentations graphiques de divers faits et données relatifs à la clientèle de Merrill Lynch, tirées de la brochure «Fusions et Acquisitions». Les illustrations sont pelliculées specialement. (USA)

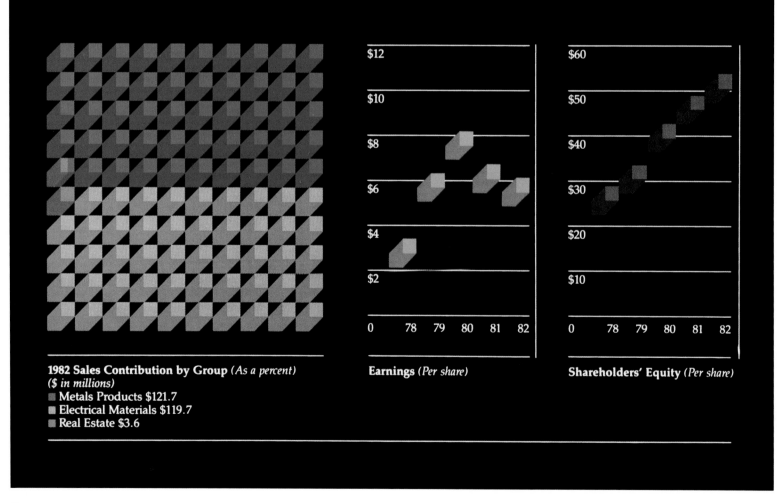

1982 Sales Contribution by Group *(As a percent)*
($ in millions)
■ **Metals Products $121.7**
■ **Electrical Materials $119.7**
■ **Real Estate $3.6**

Earnings *(Per share)*

Shareholders' Equity *(Per share)*

DESIGNER:
C. CLAUDIA JEFFERIES
ART DIRECTOR:
RON JEFFERIES
AGENCY:
THE JEFFERIES ASSOCIATION
CLIENT:
MONOGRAM INDUSTRIES, INC.
■ 64

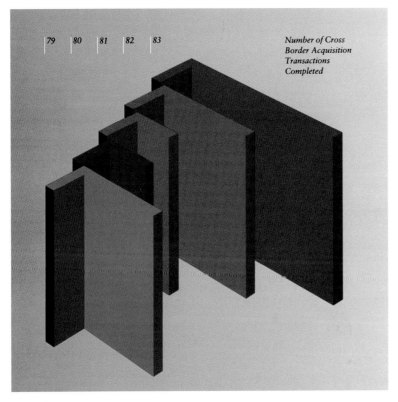

79 80 81 82 83

Number of Cross Border Acquisition Transactions Completed

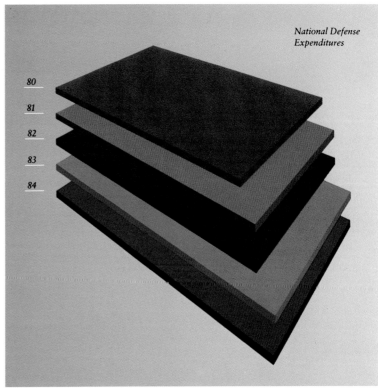

National Defense Expenditures

80
81
82
83
84

Price/Book Value Multiples Paid in the Acquisition of Commercial Banks

80 81 82 83 84

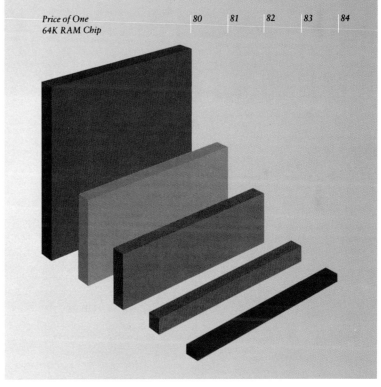

Price of One 64K RAM Chip

80 81 82 83 84

DESIGNER:
LESLIE SMOLAN/ALYSSA ADKINS
ART DIRECTOR:
LESLIE SMOLAN
AGENCY:
CARBONE SMOLAN ASSOCIATES
CLIENT:
MERRILL LYNCH
■ 65–68

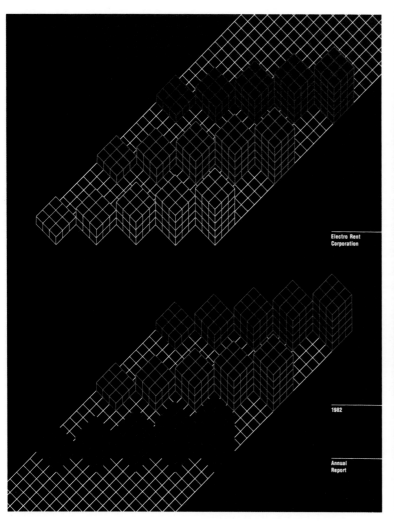

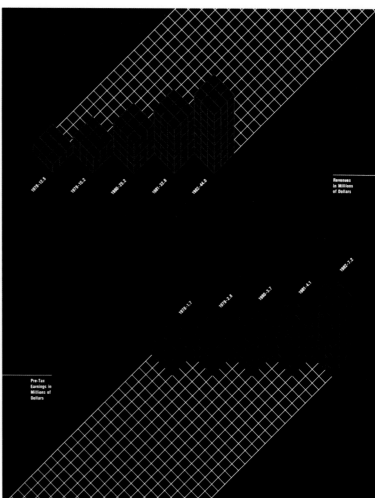

DESIGNER:
RIK BESSER
ARTIST:
PAUL BICE
ART DIRECTOR:
RIK BESSER
AGENCY:
RUNYAN & ASSOCIATES
CLIENT:
ELECTRO RENT CORPORATION
■ 69, 70

■ 69, 70 From the annual report of the Electro Rent Corp., Santa Monica. *69:* cover, *70:* parallel-perspective diagrams showing the revenues and the various appliances available in the years 1978-82. (USA)

■ 71-73 Representations of the financial development of Mony Pension Investment Facilities, in comparison with the Dow Jones Industrial Index and the Standard and Poor's 500 index. Four-color print with specially blended inks in full-tone technique and stripped-in shading. (USA)

■ 69, 70 Aus dem Jahresbericht der Electro Rent Corp., Santa Monica. *69:* Umschlag, *70:* parallel-perspektivische Darstellungen der Einnahmen und der zur Verfügung stehenden Geräte in den Jahren 1978-82. (USA)

■ 71-73 Die finanzielle Entwicklung der Mony Pension Investment Facilities, New York, im Vergleich zum Dow-Jones-Index und zum Standard and Poor's 500 Index. Vierfarbendruck mit speziell ausgemischten Farben in Volltontechnik mit zusätzlich eingestrippten Schattierungen. (USA)

■ 69, 70 Rapport annuel de l'Electro Rent Corp. *69:* Couverture, *70:* représentation en perspective cavalière des recettes enregistrées dans les années 1978-1982 et du stock d'appareils disponible durant la même période. (USA)

■ 71-73 Evolution financière de Mony Pension Investment Facilities, New York, mise en relation avec l'indice Dow Jones des valeurs industrielles et l'indice Standard and Poor's 500. Quadrichromie avec couleurs spécialement dissociées sans tramage, avec adjonction de dégradés. (USA)

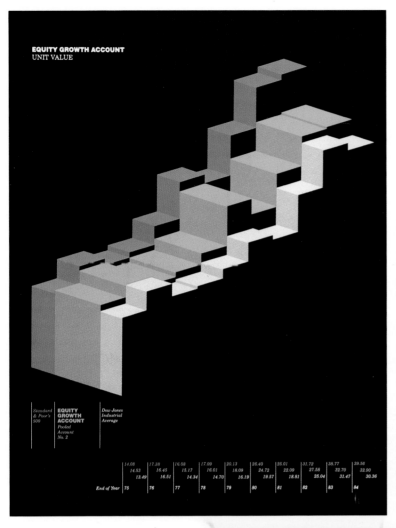

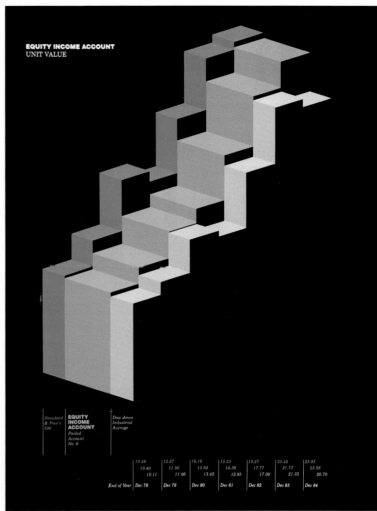

DESIGNER:
D. BRUCE ZAHOR
ART DIRECTOR:
D. BRUCE ZAHOR
AGENCY:
ZAHOR + BENDER INCORPORATED
CLIENT:
*MONY PENSION INVESTMENT
FACILITIES*
■ 71-73

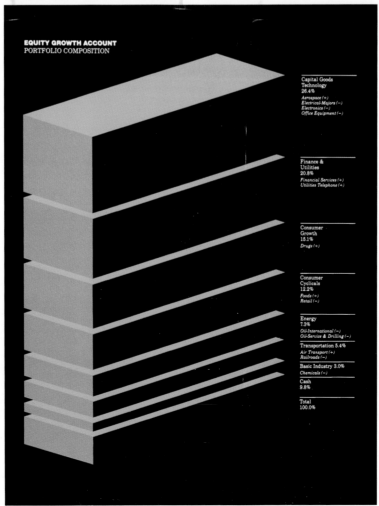

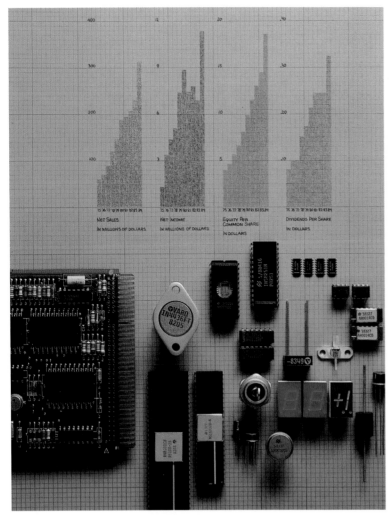

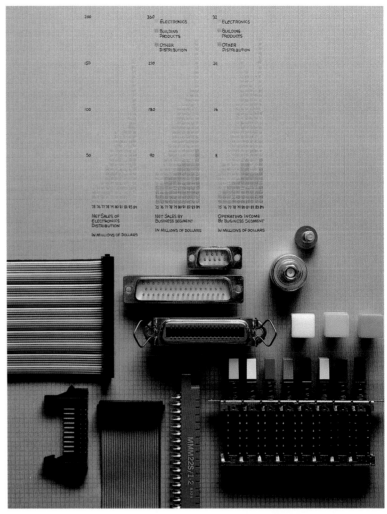

DESIGNER:
Al Briggs
ART DIRECTOR:
Al Briggs
AGENCY:
Alfred Wesley Briggs, Inc.
CLIENT:
Bell Industries, Inc.
▲■ 74, 75

DESIGNER:
Kenton Lotz
ART DIRECTOR:
Ron Jefferies
AGENCY:
The Jefferies Association
CLIENT:
Baker International Corp.
▼■ 76, 77

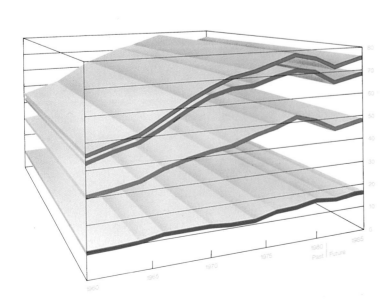

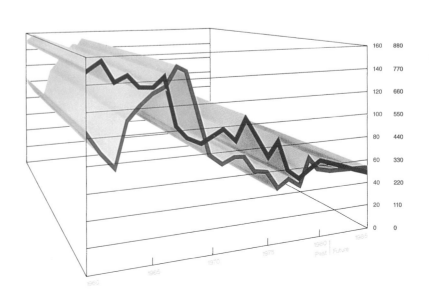

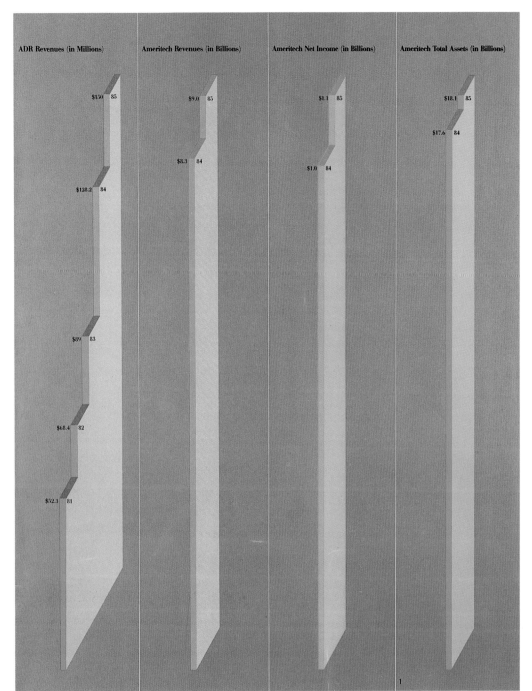

DESIGNER:
ROB FRANKLE
ART DIRECTOR:
ROGER COOK/DON SHANOSKY
AGENCY:
*COOK AND SHANOSKY
ASSOC., INC.*
CLIENT:
APPLIED DATA RESEARCH, INC.
■ 78

■ 74, 75 From an annual report of Bell Industries, Inc. Diagrams and photographed articles illustrate some of the items in the company's range of products. (USA)

■ 76, 77 From the 1982 Baker International Corp. annual report. *76:* energy consumption in the USA (from bottom to top) coal, oil, gas, various. *77:* development of the geological occurrences of oil and gas. (USA)

■ 78 Financial data of Applied Data Research, Inc. and their parent company *Ameritech.* The background was printed with an additional silver tone. (USA)

■ 74, 75 Aus einem Jahresbericht der Bell Industries, Inc.: Gezeichnete Diagramme und photographierte Artikel aus dem Produktsortiment der Firma. (USA)

■ 76, 77 Aus dem Jahresbericht 1982 der Baker International Corp. *76:* Energieverbrauch in den USA (von unten nach oben) Kohle, Öl, Gas, anderes. *77:* Entwicklung der geologischen Vorkommen von Öl und Gas. (USA)

■ 78 Finanzdaten der Applied Data Research, Inc. und ihrer Mutterfirma *Ameritech.* Der Hintergrund wurde mit einer zusätzlichen Silberfarbe bedruckt. (USA)

■ 74, 75 Rapport annuel de Bell Industries, Inc.: diagrammes dessinés et photos de divers produits figurant dans l'assortiment de l'entreprise. (USA)

■ 76, 77 Rapport annuel de la Baker International Corp. pour 1982. *76:* Consommation énergétique des Etats-Unis; de bas en haut, charbon, pétrole, gaz, autres. *77:* Evolution des réserves prouvées de gaz et de pétrole. (USA)

■ 78 Résultats financiers d'Applied Data Research, Inc. et de sa société mère *Ameritech.* Couleur argent supplémentaire pour l'arrière-plan. (USA)

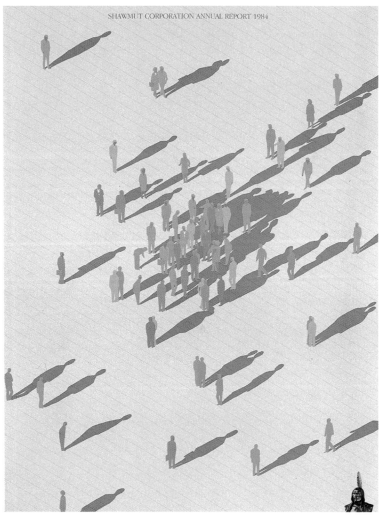

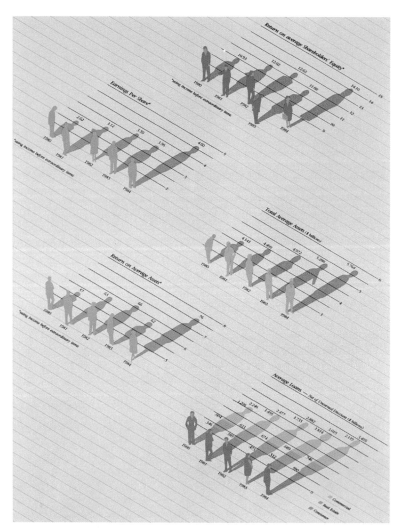

DESIGNER:
MICHAEL BENES
ARTIST:
MICHAEL BENES/DAVID HANNUM
AGENCY:
BENES COMMUNICATIONS
CLIENT:
SHAWMUT CORPORATION
■ 79, 80

■ 79, 80 From the 1984 annual report of the Shawmut
Corp., Boston. The shadow play on the cover *(79)* is also
used for the financial statistics *(80)*. (USA)

■ 81 Financial highlights of Hewlett-Packard Ltd., London,
graphically illustrated through computer components. From
the 1985 annual report. (GBR)

■ 79, 80 Aus dem Jahresbericht 1984 der Shawmut Corp.,
Boston: Das Schattenspiel auf dem Umschlag *(79)* wird
auch für die finanzielle Statistik verwendet *(80)*. (USA)

■ 81 Finanzielle Höhepunkte der Hewlett-Packard Ltd.,
London, die durch Computerschaltelemente graphisch dargestellt werden. Aus dem Jahresbericht 1985. (GBR)

■ 79, 80 Rapport annuel de la Shawmut Corp.: le jeu
d'ombres de la couverture *(79)* se retrouve dans la partie
illustrative des statistiques financières *(80)*. (USA)

■ 81 Les brillants résultats financiers de Hewlett-Packard
Ltd. sont représentés graphiquement par des circuits logiques d'ordinateur. Tiré du rapport annuel pour 1985. (GBR)

DESIGNER:
STEPHEN GIBBONS
ARTIST:
DAVID WORTH
ART DIRECTOR:
AZIZ CAMI
AGENCY:
LINE & LINE
CLIENT:
HEWLETT-PACKARD LTD.
■ 81

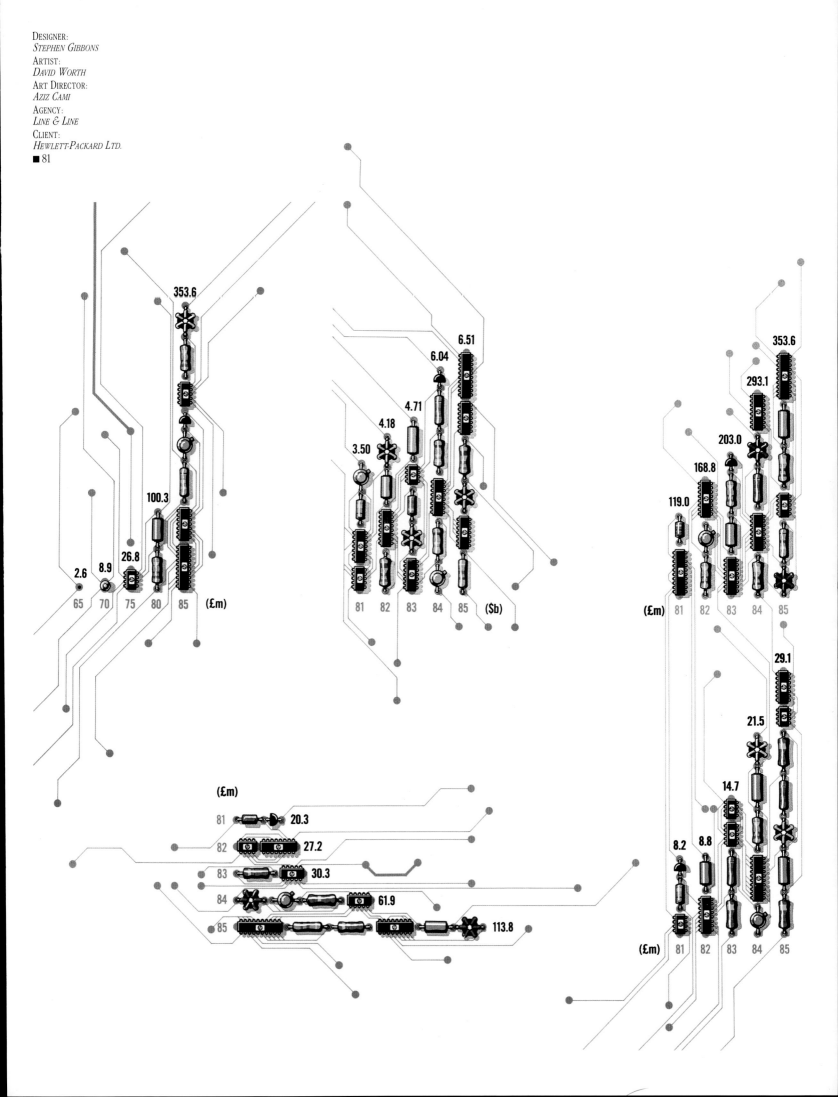

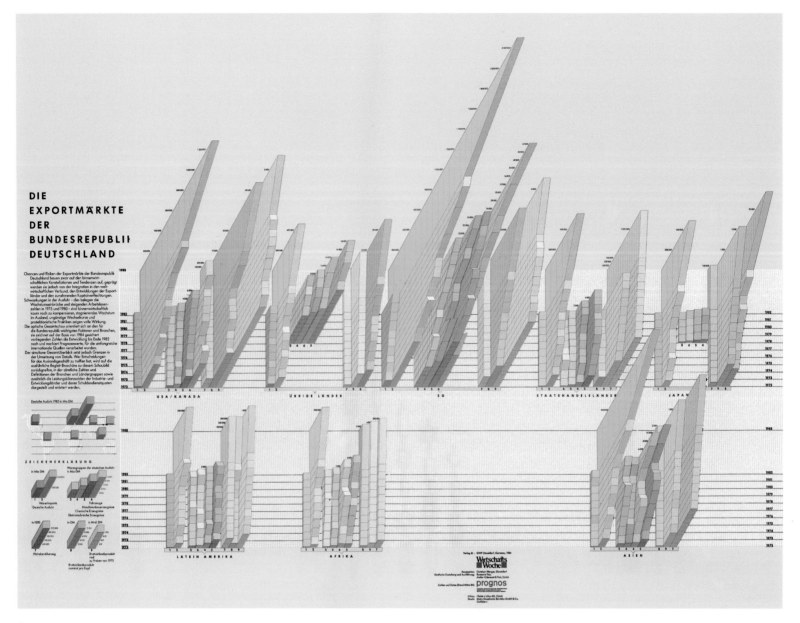

DESIGNER:
ROSMARIE TISSI
ART DIRECTOR:
ROSMARIE TISSI
AGENCY:
ODERMATT & TISSI
CLIENT:
WIRTSCHAFTSWOCHE
■ 82, 83

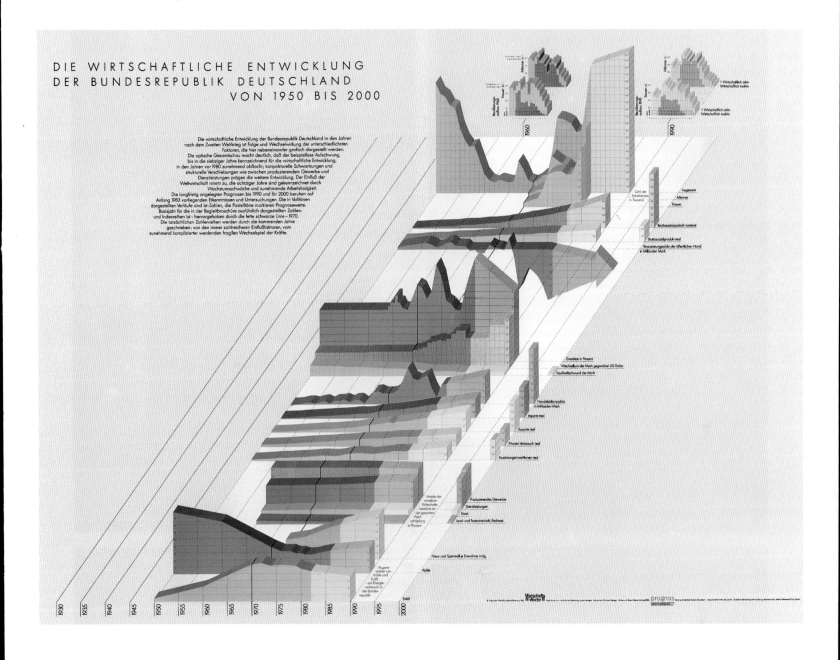

DIE WIRTSCHAFTLICHE ENTWICKLUNG
DER BUNDESREPUBLIK DEUTSCHLAND
VON 1950 BIS 2000

■ 82, 83 Illustrations with 3-D appearance to show export markets and economic development of West Germany, published in the *Wirtschaftswoche* magazine. The total overview presented in these graphs is limited in detail, therefore more specific information is provided in a supplementary brochure. (GER)

■ 82, 83 Dreidimensional wirkende Darstellungen der Exportmärkte und der wirtschaftlichen Entwicklung der Bundesrepublik Deutschland, veröffentlicht im Magazin *Wirtschaftswoche*. Diese Schaubilder werden durch eine Broschüre mit spezifischen Angaben ergänzt, die im Gesamtüberblick nicht enthalten sind. (GER)

■ 82, 83 Représentations tridimensionnelles des marchés d'exportation et de la croissance économique de la RFA, parues dans le magazine *Wirtschaftswoche*. La vue d'ensemble que procurent ces graphiques limite évidemment l'interprétation de détail, que l'on trouve en revanche dans la brochure annexe. (GER)

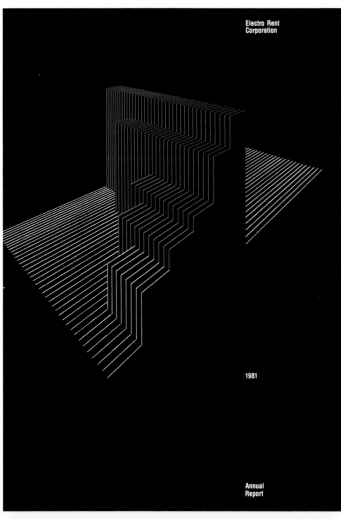

Electro Rent
Corporation

1977	1978	1979	1980	1981
.9	1.7	2.8	3.7	4.1

1981

Annual
Report

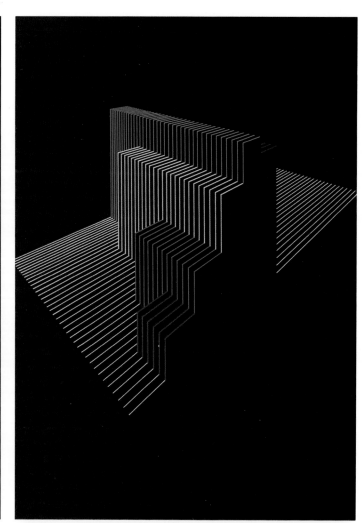

1977	1978	1979	1980	1981
14.8	20	34.4	48.8	66.1

Electro Rent
Corporation

1977	1978	1979	1980	1981
.9	1.7	2.8	3.7	4.1

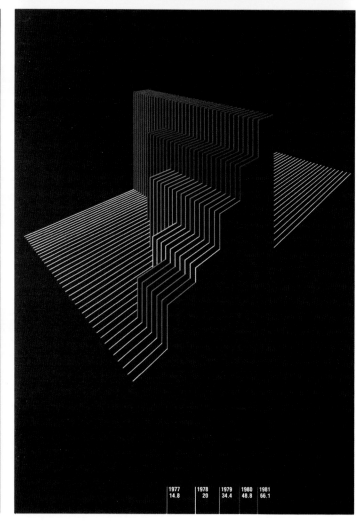

1977	1978	1979	1980	1981
14.8	20	34.4	48.8	66.1

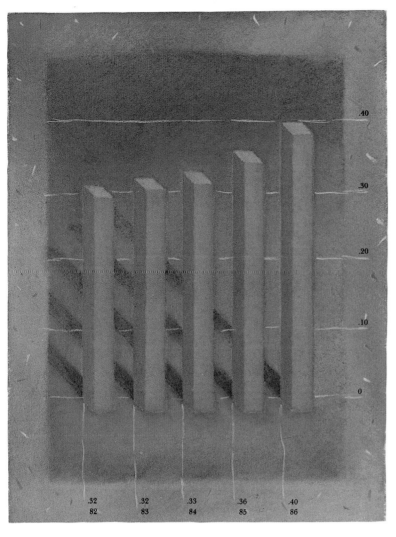

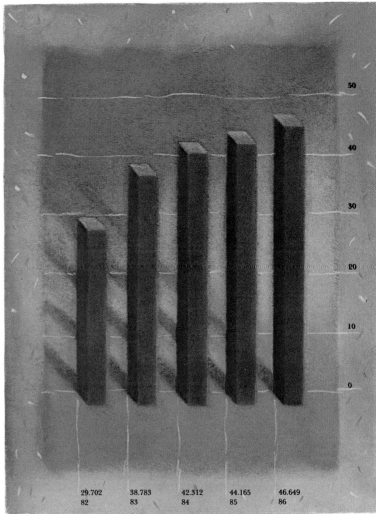

DESIGNER:
RIK BESSER
ARTIST:
PAUL BICE/KENJI MATSUMOTO
ART DIRECTOR:
RIK BESSER
AGENCY:
RUNYAN & ASSOCIATES
CLIENT:
ELECTRO RENT CORPORATION
◀■ 84-87

DESIGNER:
SUSAN BENNETT
ARTIST:
LINDA NELSON/GOULD GRAPHICS
ART DIRECTOR:
THOMSON DAWSON
AGENCY:
DAWSON + COMPANY DESIGN
CLIENT:
GUARDSMAN CHEMICALS, INC.
■ 88, 89

■ 84-87 Five year comparative studies from the 1981 annual report of the Electro Rent Corporation. Development of revenues (before and after taxes) is illustrated, and also the inventory of appliances for the leasing business. (USA)

■ 88, 89 Large bar graphs in soft pastel shades were used full page for the 1986 annual report of Guardsman Chemicals Inc. of Michigan, to emphasize the company's good performance and positive outlook. Bands of texture cropped from the pastel illustrations were used for the different introductory section headings. (USA)

■ 84-87 Fünfjahresvergleiche aus dem Jahresbericht 1981 der Electro Rent Corporation. Dargestellt ist die Entwicklung des Einkommens (vor und nach Abzug der Steuern) und der Gerätebestand für das Leasing-Geschäft. (USA)

■ 88, 89 Ganzseitige Säulendiagramme in sanften Pastelltönen wurden für den Jahresbericht 1986 der Guardsman Chemicals Inc. verwendet, um die gute Geschäftsentwicklung und die positiven Zukunftsaussichten zu unterstreichen. Ausschnitte aus diesen Pastellen wurden für schmale Balken benutzt, die die verschiedenen Kapitel einleiten. (USA)

■ 84-87 Comparaisons quinquennales illustrant le rapport annuel 1981 de l'Electro Rent Corporation. On y représente l'évolution des revenus (avant et après impôts) et du stock d'appareils mis en leasing. (USA)

■ 88, 89 Graphiques à bandes aux tons pastel sur pleine page, dans le rapport annuel 1986 de Guardsman Chemicals Inc., illustrant les affaires prospères et les excellentes perspectives du groupe. Divers détails de ces pastels ont été utilisés sous forme de bandes étroites placées en tête des différents chapitres du rapport. (USA)

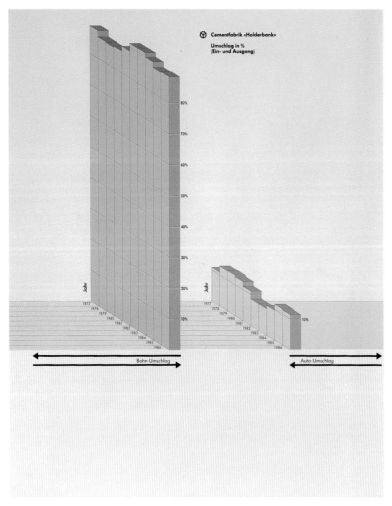

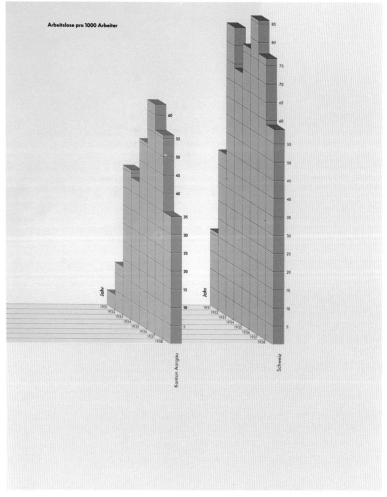

DESIGNER:
ROSMARIE TISSI
ART DIRECTOR:
ROSMARIE TISSI
AGENCY:
ODERMATT & TISSI
CLIENT:
CEMENTFABRIK "HOLDERBANK"
■ 90–92

DESIGNER:
SUSAN GARLAND
ART DIRECTOR:
RON JEFFERIES
AGENCY:
THE JEFFERIES ASSOCIATION
CLIENT:
FLUOROCARBON COMPANY
▼■ 93, 94

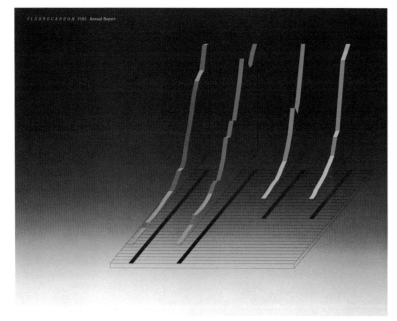

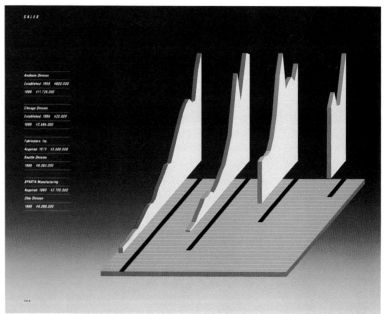

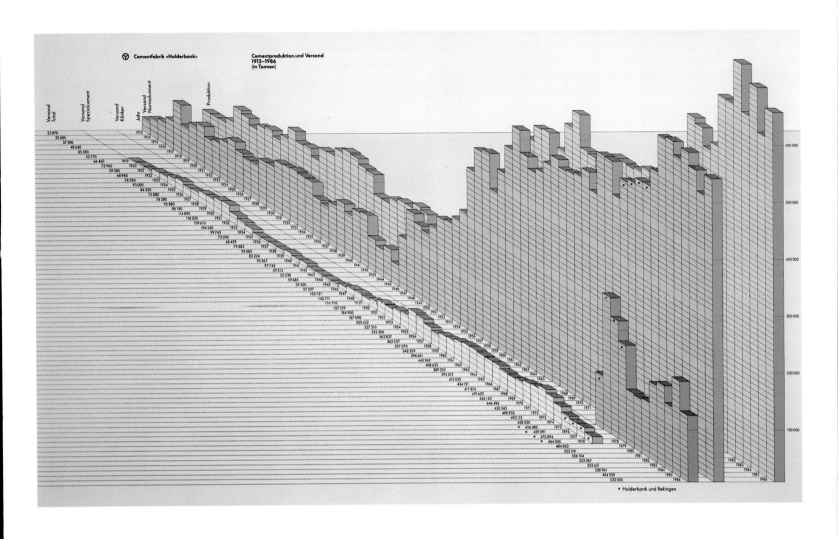

■ 90-92 Graphic charts with three-dimensional appearance for the Swiss cement company "Holderbank". *90* shows a ten year comparison of the railway and auto shipment, *91* the unemployment figures in the years 1931 to 1938 in canton Aargau in comparison with the whole of Switzerland. *92* is a double-spread graph to show cement production development and delivery (total and classified in three subregions) from 1913-1986. (SWI)

■ 93, 94 Diagrams with a three-dimensional appearance to show the business development of the Fluorocarbon Company, from the 1985 annual report. The colors serve to identify the various departments. The numerical values given on the same pages are accordingly underlined, the explanatory text on the opposite pages is printed in the same color. (USA)

■ 90-92 Graphische Darstellungen für die Schweizerische Cementfabrik «Holderbank». *90* zeigt Zehnjahresvergleiche des Bahn- und des Auto-Umschlags in %, *91* die Arbeitslosenquoten in den Jahren 1931-1938 im Kanton Aargau im Vergleich zur gesamten Schweiz. *92* ist eine doppelseitige Darstellung der Entwicklung der Zementproduktion und des Versands (total und aufgeteilt in drei Teilbereiche) von 1913-1986. (SWI)

■ 93, 94 Dreidimensional wirkende Darstellungen der Geschäftsentwicklung der Fluorocarbon Company, aus dem Jahresbericht 1985. Die Farben dienen zur Identifizierung der verschiedenen Abteilungen. Die auf der gleichen Seite angegebenen Zahlenwerte sind entsprechend unterstrichen, der erläuternde Text auf der gegenüberliegenden Seite ist in der jeweiligen Farbe gedruckt. (USA)

■ 90-92 Représentations graphiques pour la cimenterie suisse «Holderbank». *90:* Comparaisons décennales de l'acheminement par voies ferrée et par la route, en pourcent, *91:* taux de chômage du canton d'Argovie pour la période 1931-1938 comparé au reste de la Suisse. *92:* double page représentant l'évolution de la production et de l'expédition du ciment de 1913 à 1986, avec le chiffre global et trois chiffres sectoriels. (SWI)

■ 93, 94 Représentations tridimensionnelles du chiffre d'affaires de la Fluorocarbon Company dans le rapport annuel de 1985. Un code couleur sert à identifier les différents départements de cette entreprise. Les données chiffrées de la page même sont soulignées, le texte explicatif de la page opposée est imprimé dans la couleur correspondante. (USA)

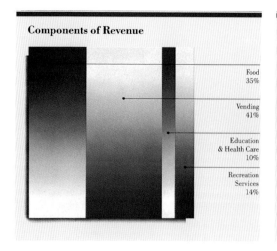

Components of Revenue

Food 35%
Vending 41%
Education & Health Care 10%
Recreation Services 14%

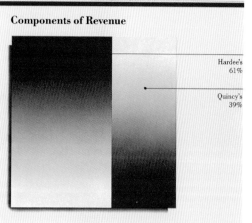

Components of Revenue

Hardee's 61%
Quincy's 39%

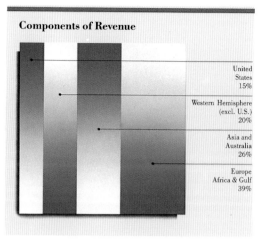

Components of Revenue

United States 15%
Western Hemisphere (excl. U.S.) 20%
Asia and Australia 26%
Europe Africa & Gulf 39%

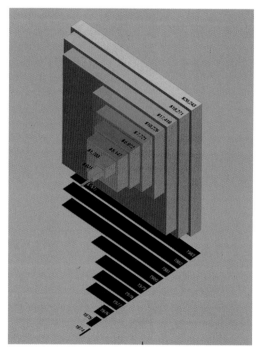

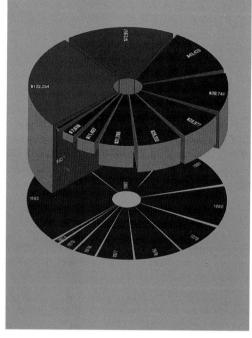

■95-97 From the 1985 annual report of Transworld Corp. The colors identify its various companies. The division of the rectangles shows the proportion of the different business sectors/areas. (USA)

■98-100 From the 1983 annual report of the Clabir Corp. *98:* ten-year comparison of the share capital; *99:* accrued assets; *100:* development of dividends. (USA)

■101 This tomato from the 1977 annual report of the foodstuffs company *Heinz* represents the cost proportion per dollar unit of the end price. (USA)

■95-97 Aus dem Jahresbericht 1985 der Transworld Corp. Die Farben dienen zur Identifizierung der Firmen dieser Gruppe. Die Aufteilung der Rechtecke verdeutlicht prozentuale Anteile der Geschäftsbereiche/Gebiete. (USA)

■98-100 Aus dem Jahresbericht 1983 der Clabir Corp. *98:* Zehnjahresvergleich des Aktienkapitals, *99:* Darstellung der Aktiva, *100:* Entwicklung der Dividenden. (USA)

■101 Diese Tomate aus dem Jahresbericht 1977 des Lebensmittelkonzerns *Heinz* zeigt die Kostenanteile pro Dollareinheit des Endpreises. (USA)

■95-97 Rapport annuel 1985 de la Transworld Corp. Le code couleur a trait aux différentes sociétés du groupe. Les rectangles figurent la part en pour-cent qui revient aux secteurs et zones géographiques d'activité. (USA)

■98-100 Rapport annuel 1983 de la Clabir Corporation. *98:* Evolution du capital social sur dix ans, *99:* interprétation des actifs, *100:* évolution des dividendes versés. (USA)

■101 Cette tomate illustrant le rapport annuel du groupe alimentaire *Heinz* décompose en secteurs circulaires les facteurs de coût rapportés au prix final, par dollar. (USA)

DESIGNER:
BLOCH GRAULICH WHELAN INC.
AGENCY:
L. P. THEBAULT COMPANY
CLIENT:
TRANSWORLD CORP.
◄■ 95-97

DESIGNER:
THOMAS D. MORIN
ART DIRECTOR:
THOMAS D. MORIN
AGENCY:
JACK HOUGH ASSOC.
CLIENT:
CLABIR CORP.
◄■ 98-100

DESIGNER:
BENNETT ROBINSON
PHOTOGRAPHER:
MICHAEL PATEMAN
ART DIRECTOR:
BENNETT ROBINSON
AGENCY:
CORPORATE GRAPHICS, INC.
CLIENT:
H.J. HEINZ COMPANY
►■ 101

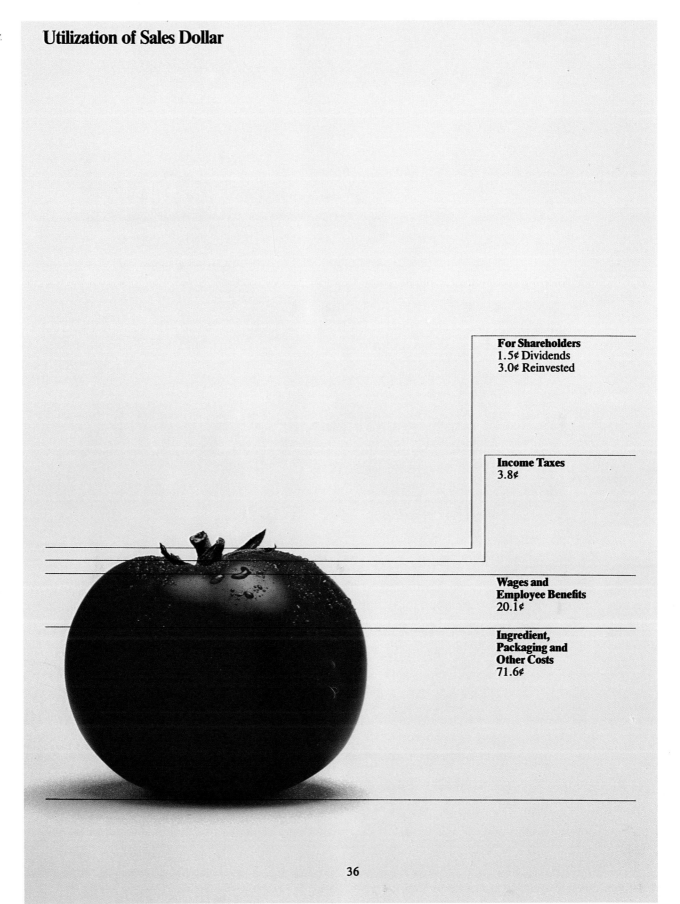

Utilization of Sales Dollar

For Shareholders
1.5¢ Dividends
3.0¢ Reinvested

Income Taxes
3.8¢

**Wages and
Employee Benefits**
20.1¢

**Ingredient,
Packaging and
Other Costs**
71.6¢

36

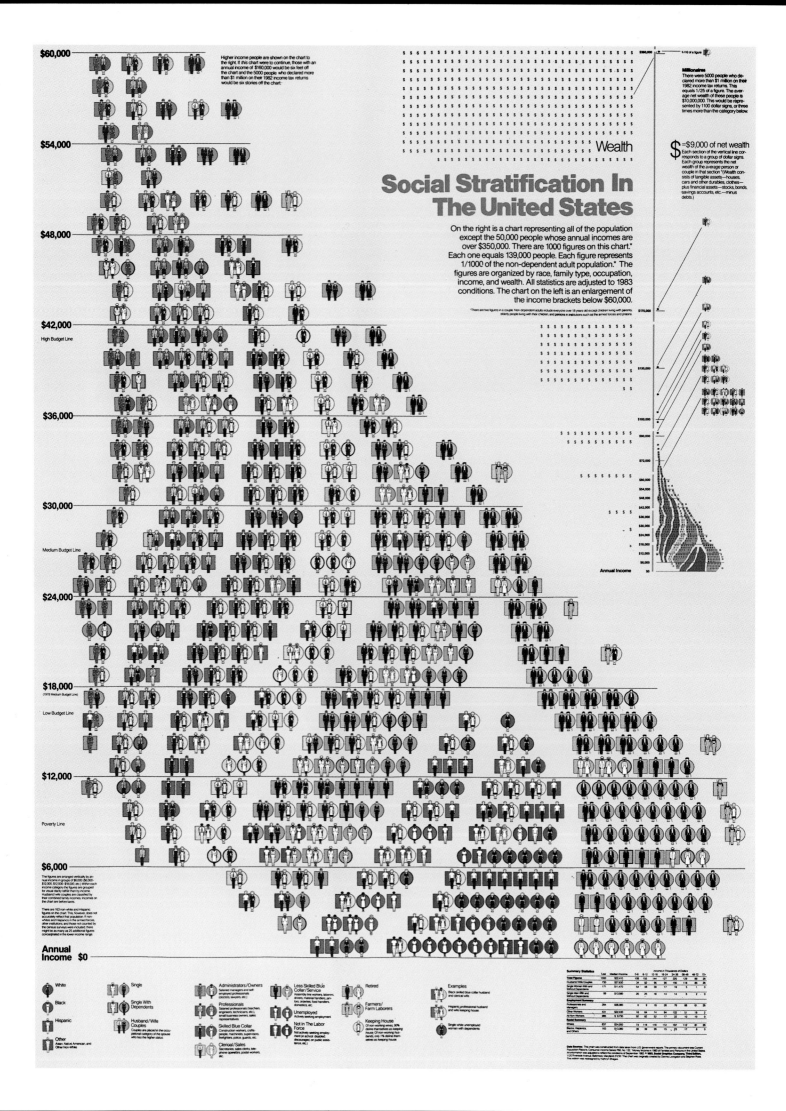

Social Stratification In The United States

On the right is a chart representing all of the population except the 50,000 people whose annual incomes are over $350,000. There are 1000 figures on this chart.* Each one equals 139,000 people. Each figure represents 1/1000 of the non-dependent adult population.* The figures are organized by race, family type, occupation, income, and wealth. All statistics are adjusted to 1983 conditions. The chart on the left is an enlargement of the income brackets below $60,000.

Wealth

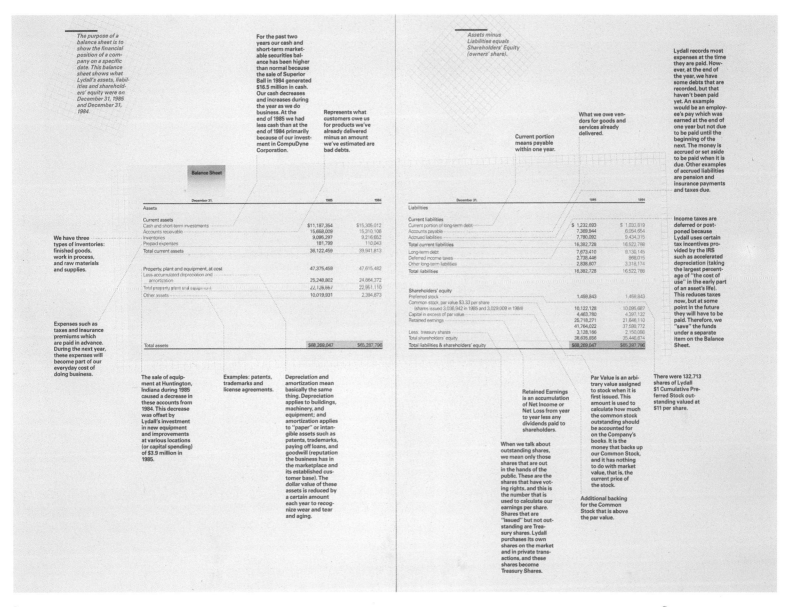

DESIGNER:
KATHRYN SHAGAS
ART DIRECTOR:
KATHRYN SHAGAS
CLIENT:
SOCIAL GRAPHICS COMPANY
◀■ 102

DESIGNER:
KURT GIBSON
ART DIRECTOR:
ROBERT APPLETON
AGENCY:
APPLETON DESIGN INC.
CLIENT:
LYDALL, INC.
■ 103

■ 102 Poster with an overview of the annual income of the population of the USA, classified according to race, marital status, sex, and occupation. (USA)

■ 103 Double spread from the 1985 annual report for the employees of Lydall Inc. The individual text blocks explain the balance sheet in easier terms. (USA)

■ 102 Plakat mit einer Übersicht des Jahreseinkommens der Bevölkerung der USA, aufgeteilt nach Rasse, Zivilstand, Geschlecht und Beschäftigung. (USA)

■ 103 Doppelseite aus dem Jahresbericht 1985 für die Angestellten der Lydall Inc. Die einzelnen Textblocks erklären die in einer Bilanz üblichen Begriffe. (USA)

■ 102 Affiche présentant le revenu annuel de la population des Etats-Unis ventilé par races, catégories d'état-civil, sexes et occupations. (USA)

■ 103 Double page du rapport annuel 1985 de la Lydall Inc. destinée au personnel. Les divers groupes de textes expliquent les termes spécialisés utilisés dans un bilan. (USA)

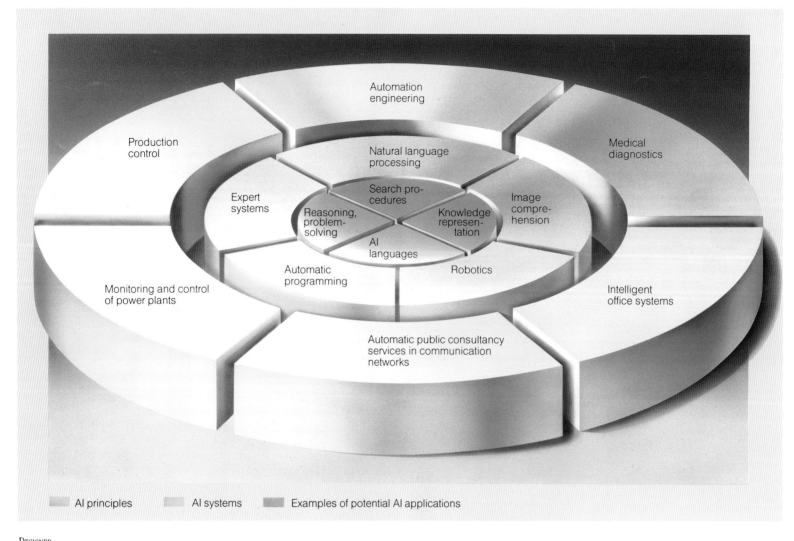

Automation engineering

Production control

Medical diagnostics

Natural language processing

Expert systems

Search procedures

Image comprehension

Reasoning, problem-solving

Knowledge representation

AI languages

Monitoring and control of power plants

Automatic programming

Robotics

Intelligent office systems

Automatic public consultancy services in communication networks

AI principles   AI systems   Examples of potential AI applications

DESIGNER:
HEINZ HENKEL
ARTIST:
WINFRIED FRASE
ART DIRECTOR:
PETER RADOWITZ
CLIENT:
SIEMENS AG
■ 104

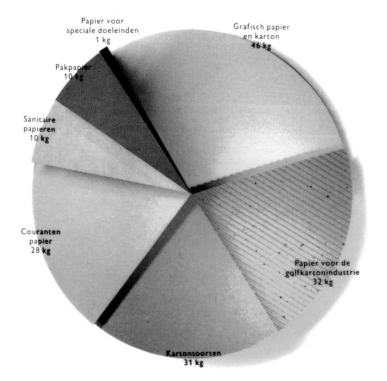

Papierverbruik per capita per soort in Nederland
(Bron CBS/VNP)
Totaal 158 kg

Papier voor speciale doeleinden
1 kg

Grafisch papier en karton
46 kg

Pakpapier
10 kg

Sanitaire papieren
10 kg

Couranten papier
28 kg

Papier voor de golfkartonindustrie
32 kg

Kartonsoorten
31 kg

DESIGNER:
ANDRÉ TOET
ARTIST:
VICENZO TRACQUILIO
ART DIRECTOR:
ANDRÉ TOET
AGENCY:
SAMENWERKENDE OUTWERPERS
CLIENT:
PROOST EN BRANDT NV
■ 105

■ 104 Pie-chart presenting the basis, systems and range of applications of AI (Artificial Intelligence). (GER)

■ 105 Graph showing the per capita consumption of various paper qualities in Holland. From an annual report for Proost en Brandt NV. (NLD)

■ 106 Diagram of the cost distribution and net gain in 1985, of the total turnover calculated percentually, from an annual report of Randstad Holding NV. The firm's symbol serves to liven up the graphics. (NLD)

■ 104 Kreisdiagramm der Grundlagen, Systeme und Anwendungsbereiche von AI (Artificial Intelligence). (GER)

■ 105 Darstellung des Pro-Kopf-Verbrauchs verschiedener Papiersorten in den Niederlanden. Aus einem Jahresbericht für Proost en Brandt NV. (NLD)

■ 106 Darstellung der Kostenverteilung und des Nettogewinns 1985, ausgerechnet in Prozenten des Gesamtumsatzes, aus einem Jahresbericht der Randstad Holding NV. Das Firmenzeichen dient zur graphischen Auflockerung. (NLD)

■ 104 Diagramme circulaire: fondements, systèmes, domaines d'application de l'intelligence artificielle AI. (GER)

■ 105 Représentation de la consommation par habitant de diverses qualités de papier aux Pays-Bas. Rapport annuel de Proost en Brandt NV. (NLD)

■ 106 Graphique de la répartition des coûts et du bénéfice net de l'exercice 1985, en pour-cent du chiffre d'affaires global, dans un rapport annuel de la Randstad Holding NV. Le sigle du groupe sert à aérer la composition. (NLD)

DESIGNER:
BEN BOS
AGENCY:
TOTAL DESIGN
CLIENT:
RANDSTAD UITZENDBUREAU
■ 106

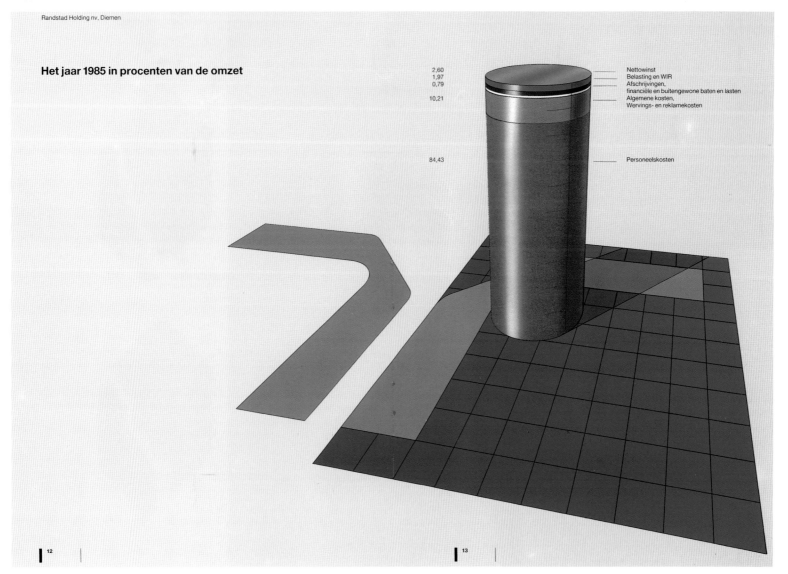

Randstad Holding nv, Diemen

Het jaar 1985 in procenten van de omzet

2,60
1,97
0,79

10,21

84,43

Nettowinst
Belasting en WIR
Afschrijvingen,
financiële en buitengewone baten en lasten
Algemene kosten,
Wervings- en reklamekosten

Personeelskosten

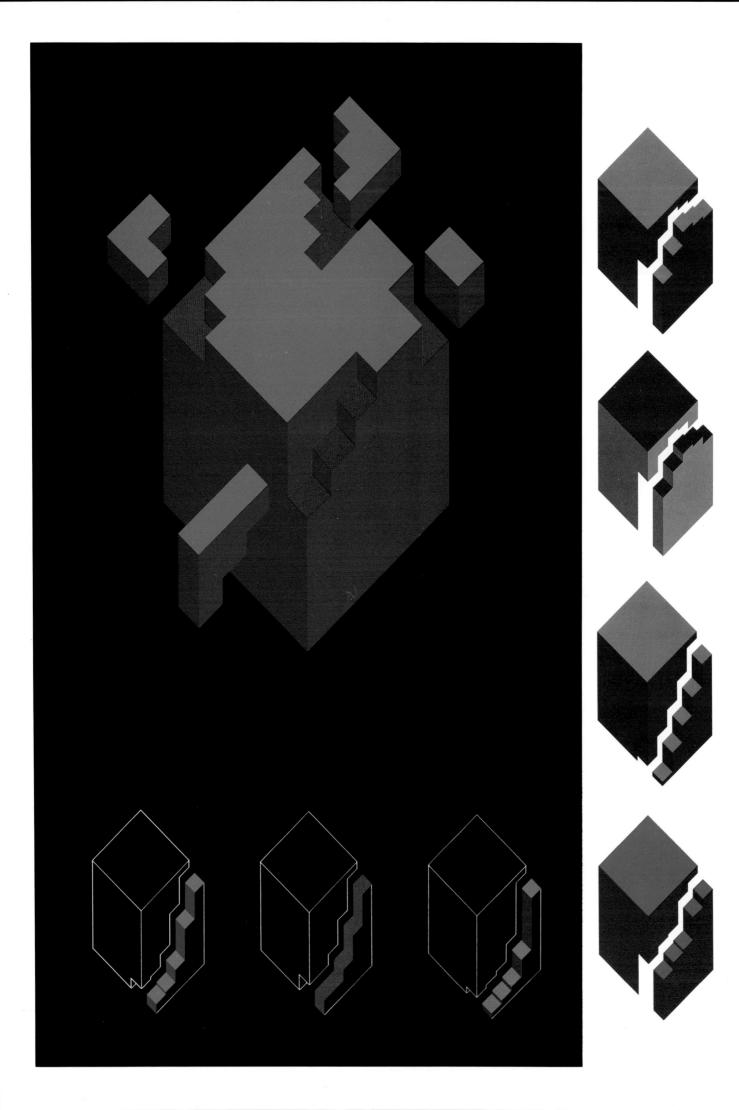

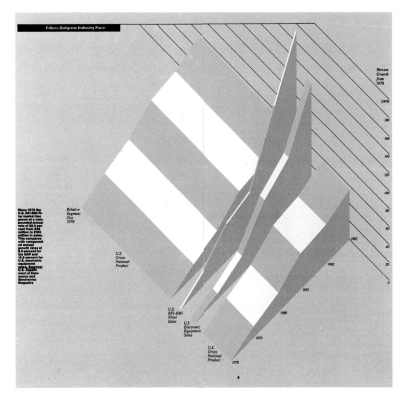

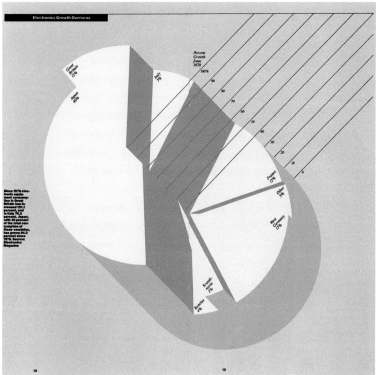

DESIGNER:
C. Claudia Jefferies
ART DIRECTOR:
Ron Jefferies
AGENCY:
The Jefferies Association
CLIENT:
Bergen Brunswig Corporation
◀■ 107

DESIGNER:
Wayne Webb
ARTIST:
Jerome Linz
ART DIRECTOR:
Wayne Webb
AGENCY:
Robertz, Webb + Co.
CLIENT:
Corcom Inc.
■ 108, 109

■ 107 Graph to show the steady growth of the company Bergen Brunswig through acquisitions and internal developments. Companies recently taken over form the components that serve to strengthen the basic element – the solid well-managed parent company. This basic element is again underpinned by a comparative five-year survey in the smaller graphs. From the annual report of 1986. (USA)

■ 108, 109 Double spreads from the 1983 annual report of Corcom Inc., producers of filters for computer and digital electronic equipment. *108* shows the growth of this industrial sector from 1978–83 in comparison to the GNP of the United States, and the sales of electronic systems. *109* gives an overview of the electronics growth in Europe and Japan. The broken pie-chart shows the total consumption percentwise of the countries; the percentual growth in comparison to 1978 can be read from the height of the points in relation to the percentage tables. (For example, Great Britain = 101.1%.) (USA)

■ 107 Graphische Darstellung des ständigen Wachstums der Firma Bergen Brunswig durch Akquisitionen und interne Entwicklungen. Kürzlich übernommene Firmen sind hier Bauteile, die ein festes Grundelement (die solide, gut eingeführte Mutterfirma) noch verstärken. Dieses Element wird in verschiedenen Fünfjahresvergleichen wieder aufgenommen. Aus dem Jahresbericht für 1986. (USA)

■ 108, 109 Doppelseiten aus dem Jahresbericht 1983 der Corcom Inc., Hersteller von Filtern für Computer und digital-elektronische Geräte. *108* zeigt das Wachstum dieses Industriezweiges von 1978–83 im Vergleich zum Bruttosozialprodukt der USA und den Verkäufen elektronischer Geräte. *109* gibt einen Überblick über das Wachstum der Elektronikindustrie in Japan und Europa. Das zerteilte Kreisdiagramm zeigt den Anteil am Gesamtverbrauch der Länder; das prozentuale Wachstum im Vergleich zu 1978 lässt sich am Stand der Spitzen im Verhältnis zur Prozenttabelle ablesen (z.B. Grossbritannien = 101.1%). (USA)

■ 107 Représentation graphique de la croissance continue de la société Bergen Brunswig due à des acquisitions et à des développements internes. Les sociétés d'acquisition récente sont figurées par des éléments de construction qui viennent renforcer les fondations solides de la société mère bien introduite. Image reprise dans les diagrammes relatifs aux comparaisons quinquennales. Rapport annuel 1986. (USA)

■ 108, 109 Doubles pages du rapport annuel 1983 de la Corcom Inc., qui fabrique des filtres pour ordinateurs et appareils électroniques numériques. *108* Croissance de cette branche de l'industrie 1978–1983 rapportée au P.N.B. des Etats-Unis et aux ventes d'appareils électroniques. *109* Vue d'ensemble de la croissance de l'industrie électronique japonaise et européenne. Le camembert éclaté montre la part des principaux pays consommateurs; la croissance en pourcent depuis la base 0 en 1978 ressort de la position des pointes par rapport au tableau des pourcentages (101,1% pour la Grande-Bretagne). (USA)

Net Income
(Dollars in thousands)

'80 $2,771 '81 $5,603 '82 $7,337 '83 $9,468 '84 $12,084

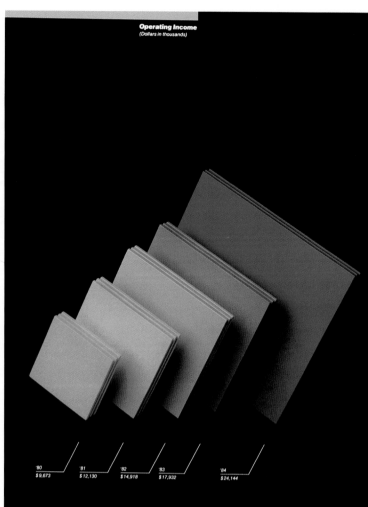

Operating Income
(Dollars in thousands)

'80 $9,673 '81 $12,130 '82 $14,918 '83 $17,932 '84 $24,144

DESIGNER:
HENRY GOERKE
ARTIST:
NICK FASCIANO
PHOTOGRAPHER:
JERRY STRAPOCHIELLO
ART DIRECTOR:
JACK HOUGH
AGENCY:
JACK HOUGH ASSOC.
CLIENT:
GENERAL DEFENSE CORP.
■ 110–112

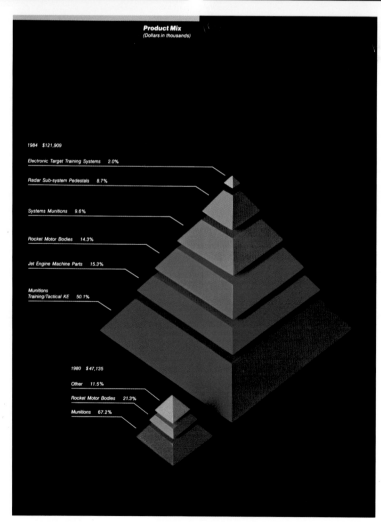

Product Mix
(Dollars in thousands)

1984 $121,909

Electronic Target Training Systems   2.0%
Radar Sub-system Pedestals   8.7%
Systems Munitions   9.6%
Rocket Motor Bodies   14.3%
Jet Engine Machine Parts   15.3%
Munitions
Training/Tactical KE   50.1%

1980 $47,135

Other   11.5%
Rocket Motor Bodies   21.3%
Munitions   67.2%

DESIGNER:
ERWIN SCHMÖLZER
ART DIRECTOR:
ERWIN SCHMÖLZER
AGENCY:
*ATELIER FÜR KUNST + DESIGN
E. SCHMÖLZER*
CLIENT:
ALLGEMEINE SPARKASSE
►■ 113–116

■ 110-112 Full page, three dimensional graphs of revenue developments and the turnover proportions of various product groups, from the 1984 annual report of the General Defense Corporation. (USA)

■ 113-116 Computer-aided graphs for the 1985 business report of the Allgemeine Sparkasse Linz. *113* shows the number of employees (in three groups), *114* the profit margin in percentage of average balance-sheet total, *115* credit proportion of four receiving groups, all in five year comparisons. *116* origin and application of funds (in millions of Austrian schillings). (AUT)

■ 110-112 Ganzseitige, dreidimensional wirkende Darstellungen von Einkommensentwicklungen und Umsatzanteilen der verschiedenen Produktgruppen, aus dem Jahresbericht 1984 der General Defense Corporation. (USA)

■ 113-116 Computer-unterstützte graphische Darstellungen für den Geschäftsbericht 1985 der Allgemeinen Sparkasse Linz. *113* zeigt den Mitarbeiterstand, aufgeteilt in drei Gruppen, *114* die Zinsspanne in Prozent der Durchschnittsbilanzsumme, *115* Kreditanteile von vier Empfängergruppen, alle im Fünfjahresvergleich. *116:* Herkunft und Verwendung der Mittel in Millionen Schilling. (AUT)

■ 110-112 Représentations pleine page produisant un effet tridimensionnel: évolution des revenus et part de chaque groupe de produits au chiffre d'affaires global. Rapport annuel 1984 de la General Defense Corporation. (USA)

■ 113-116 Représentations graphiques assistées par ordinateur, pour le rapport annuel 1985 de l'Allgemeine Sparkasse (Caisse d'épargne) de Linz. *113:* Effectifs du personnel en 3 groupes, *114:* marge d'intérêt en pour-cent du bilan moyen, *115:* part de quatre groupes de preneurs de crédit dans les crédits totaux, le tout sur cinq ans. *116:* Origine et utilisation des fonds. (AUT)

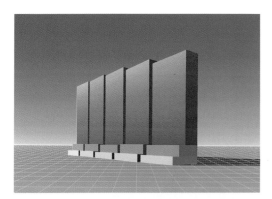
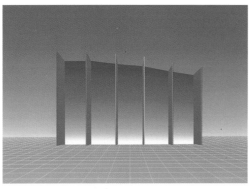
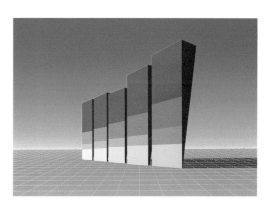
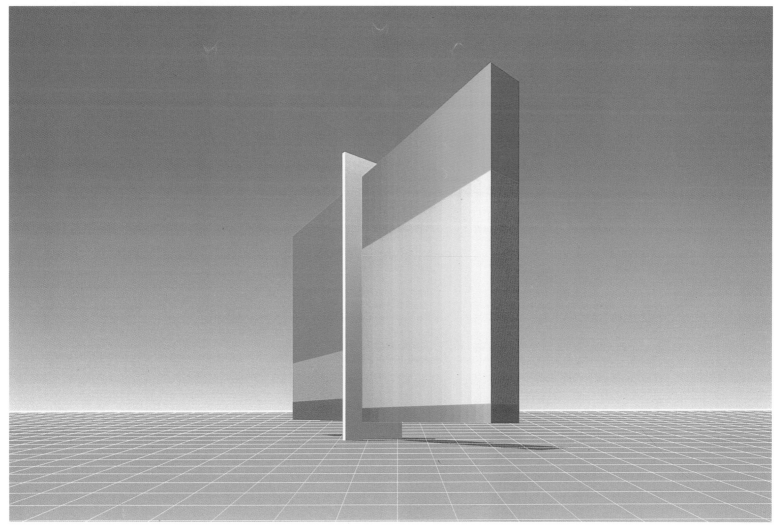

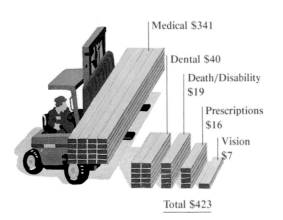

Medical $341
Dental $40
Death/Disability $19
Prescriptions $16
Vision $7
Total $423

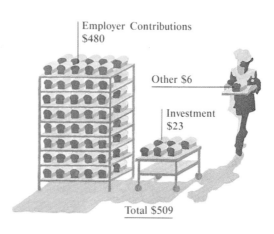

Employer Contributions $480
Other $6
Investment $23
Total $509

DESIGNER:
MARY BETH BOSTRUM-CYBUL
ARTIST:
B. J. JOHNSON
ART DIRECTOR:
JACQUELINE KOHN/
MARY BETH BOSTRUM-CYBUL
AGENCY:
HILL AND KNOWLTON, INC.
CLIENT:
CENTRAL STATES, SOUTHEAST
AND SOUTHWEST AREAS HEALTH
AND WELFARE AND PENSION
FUNDS
■ 117–119

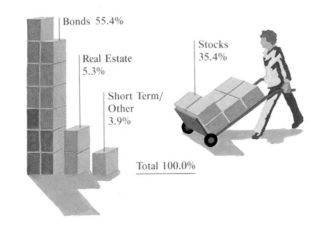

Bonds 55.4%
Real Estate 5.3%
Stocks 35.4%
Short Term/ Other 3.9%
Total 100.0%

DESIGNER:
KOJI TAKEI
ART DIRECTOR:
TOM OHMER
AGENCY:
ADVERTISING DESIGNERS, INC.
CLIENT:
FINANCIAL FEDERATION INC.
■ 120, 121

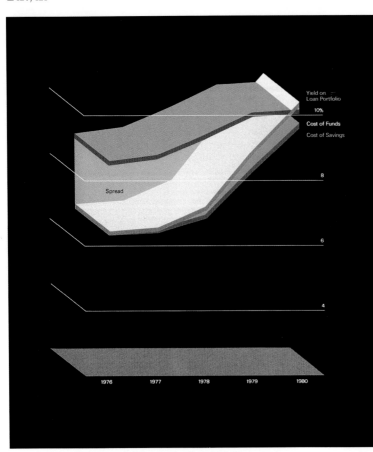

Yield on Loan Portfolio
10%
Cost of Funds
Cost of Savings
8
Spread
6
4
1976 1977 1978 1979 1980

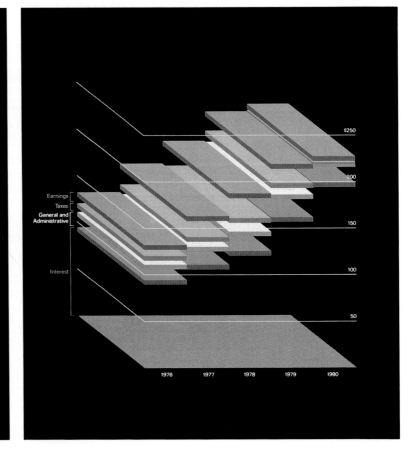

$250
200
Earnings
Taxes
General and Administrative
150
Interest
100
50
1976 1977 1978 1979 1980

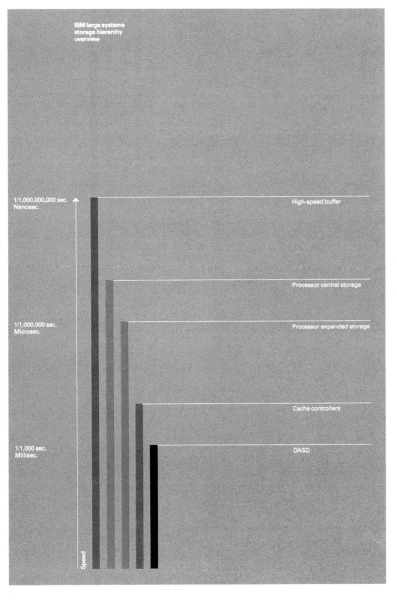

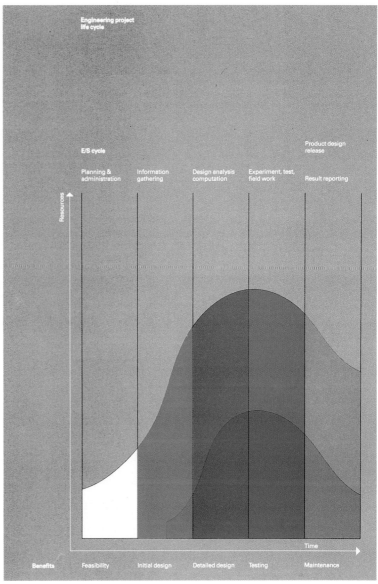

DESIGNER:
DANI PIDERMAN
ART DIRECTOR:
JOHN CRAINE
AGENCY:
TROLLER ASSOCS
CLIENT:
IBM, WHITE PLAINS
■ 122, 123

■ 117–119 Examples of the graphs designed to communicate statistical information to a largely blue-collar audiance, from the 1984 annual report of a sickness and pension fund. (USA)

■ 120, 121 Full-page diagrams from the 1980 annual report of the Financial Federation Inc. showing interest rate analysis and allocation of revenues. The colors indicate the various factors and are repeated in all the diagrams of the report. (USA)

■ 122, 123 Comparative diagrams from a prospectus about an IBM computer system, the "IBM 3090 processor", and an overview into the IBM large systems storage hierarchy. *123* shows an engineering project life cycle. (USA)

■ 117–119 Darstellungen aus dem Jahresbericht 1984 einer Kranken- und Pensionskasse. Aufgabe war es, den vorwiegend aus Arbeitern bestehenden Mitgliedern statistische Daten zu erläutern. (USA)

■ 120, 121 Ganzseitige Diagramme aus dem Jahresbericht 1980 eines Finanzinstituts. Dargestellt sind Geschäftsentwicklungen über fünf Jahre. Die Farben, die zur Kennzeichnung der verschiedenen Faktoren verwendet wurden, wiederholen sich in allen Diagrammen des Berichts. (USA)

■ 122, 123 Aus einem Prospekt über ein IBM-Computersystem. Hier ein Überblick über verschiedene Speicherkapazitäten und eine Darstellung des Ablaufs eines technischen Projekts von der Planungsstufe bis zum Unterhalt. (USA)

■ 117–119 Diagrammes du rapport annuel 1984 d'une caissemaladie et retraites. Il s'agissait d'expliquer les données statistiques aux membres, qui se recrutent surtout dans le monde ouvrier. (USA)

■ 120, 121 Graphiques pleine page dans le rapport annuel 1980 d'un institut financier, représentant l'évolution des affaires sur cinq ans. Les couleurs attribuées aux différents facteurs de croissance sont reprises dans les autres diagrammes. (USA)

■ 122, 123 Diagrammes comparatifs dans le prospectus relatif à un système informatique IBM: aperçu des différentes capacités de mémoire et ordinogramme d'un projet technique, de la planification jusqu'aux travaux d'entretien. (USA)

82		19.4
81		9.8
80		6.0
79		3.0
78		1.8

82		4.9
81		4.1
80		1.4
79		.8
78		.7

82	17.5	.7
81	12.7	1.6
80	15.4	.2
79	11.7	.2
78	8.9	.3

82		27.6
81		12.9
80		3.6
79		1.2
78		.6

82		39.2
81		24.6
80		13.4
79		12.3
78		7.1

82	5.0	1.0
81	3.5	.6
80	3.5	.1
79	3.6	.4
78	4.1	1.1

82		42.0
81		36.5
80		21.2
79		15.9
78		12.8

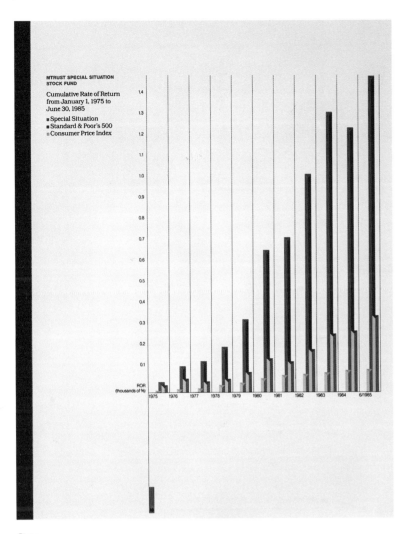

MTRUST SPECIAL SITUATION
STOCK FUND

Cumulative Rate of Return
from January 1, 1975 to
June 30, 1985

■ Special Situation
■ Standard & Poor's 500
▨ Consumer Price Index

DESIGNER:
JOHN WEAVER
ART DIRECTOR:
JOHN WEAVER/AL GLUTH
AGENCY:
GLUTH WEAVER INC.
CLIENT:
DIGICON INC.
◀■ 124

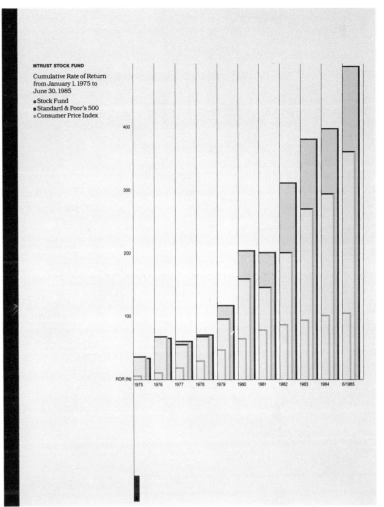

MTRUST STOCK FUND

Cumulative Rate of Return
from January 1, 1975 to
June 30, 1985

■ Stock Fund
■ Standard & Poor's 500
▨ Consumer Price Index

DESIGNER:
ROBIN AYRES
ART DIRECTOR:
ROBIN AYRES
AGENCY:
RBMM & A
CLIENT:
MTRUST
■ 125, 126

■ 124 Compilation of various five-year comparisons that appear in the text pages of the 1982 annual report of Digicon Inc. The company is engaged above all with geophysical equipment and measuring devices. (USA)

■ 125, 126 Computer-designed bar graphs to compare statistics of three color-indicated factors. From the Employee Benefit Services report issued by *MTrust.* (USA)

■ 124 Zusammenstellung verschiedener Fünfjahresvergleiche, die in den Textseiten des Geschäftsberichtes 1982 von Digicon Inc. enthalten sind. Die Firma befasst sich vor allem mit geophysikalischen Ausrüstungen und Messungen. (USA)

■ 125, 126 Mit dem Computer hergestellte Säulendiagramme für vergleichende Statistiken von jeweils drei, durch Farben gekennzeichneten Faktoren. Bericht von *MTrust.* (USA)

■ 124 Présentation de diverses comparaisons quinquennales du rapport annuel 1982 de la Digicon Ltd. Il s'agit d'une société spécialisée surtout dans les équipements géophysiques et les mesures concernant la physique du globe. (USA)

■ 125, 126 Graphiques d'ordinateur à bandes pour des comparaisons statistiques trifactorielles codées couleur. Rapport de *MTrust* sur les avantages concédés au personnel. (USA)

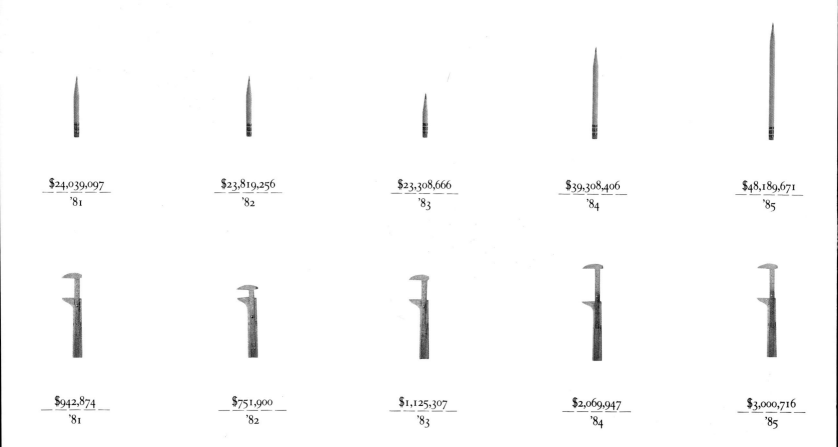

$24,039,097
'81

$23,819,256
'82

$23,308,666
'83

$39,308,406
'84

$48,189,671
'85

$942,874
'81

$751,900
'82

$1,125,307
'83

$2,069,947
'84

$3,000,716
'85

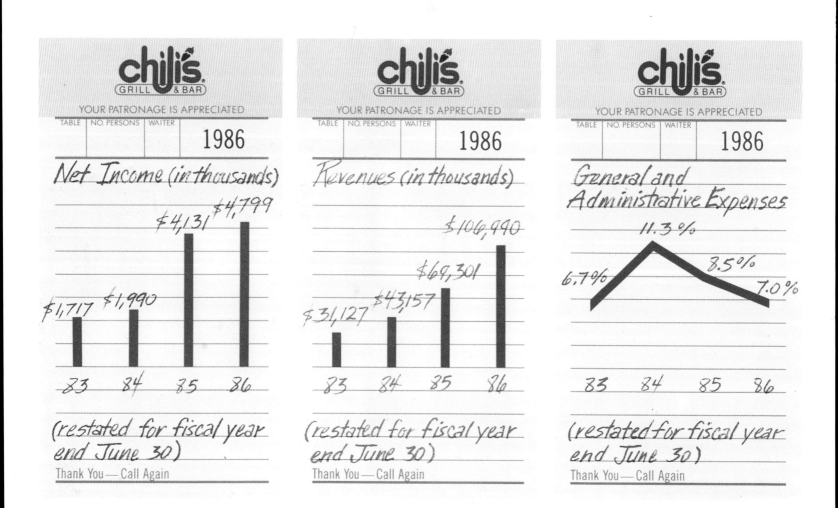

chili's
GRILL & BAR
YOUR PATRONAGE IS APPRECIATED
TABLE | NO. PERSONS | WAITER
1986

Net Income (in thousands)

$4,131 $4,799

$1,717 $1,990

83   84   85   86

(restated for fiscal year
end June 30)

Thank You — Call Again

chili's
GRILL & BAR
YOUR PATRONAGE IS APPRECIATED
TABLE | NO. PERSONS | WAITER
1986

Revenues (in thousands)

$106,990

$69,301

$43,157
$31,127

83   84   85   86

(restated for fiscal year
end June 30)

Thank You — Call Again

chili's
GRILL & BAR
YOUR PATRONAGE IS APPRECIATED
TABLE | NO. PERSONS | WAITER
1986

General and
Administrative Expenses

11.3%

8.5%
6.7%
7.0%

83   84   85   86

(restated for fiscal year
end June 30)

Thank You — Call Again

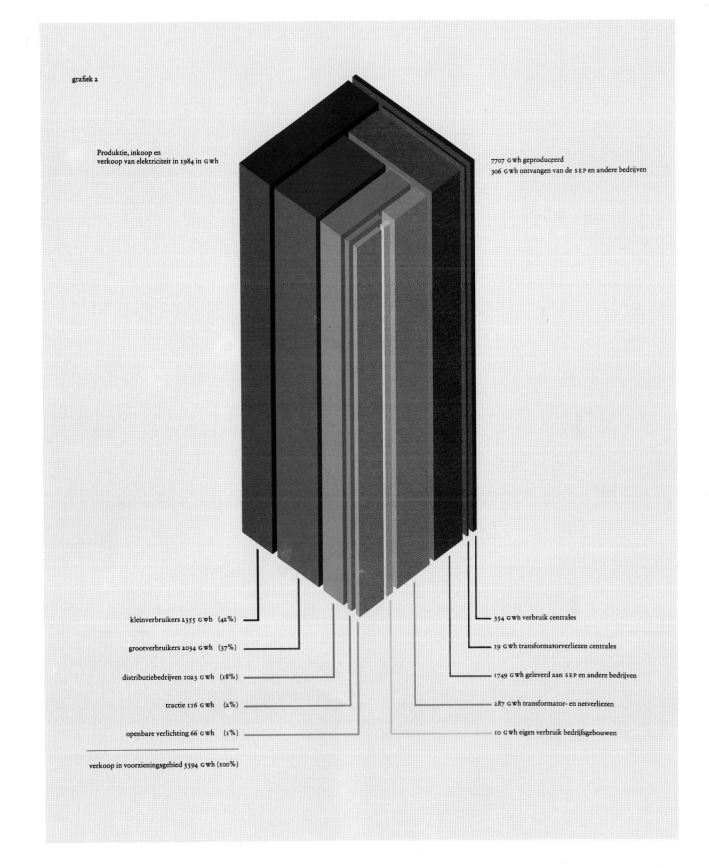

DESIGNER:
STEVEN TOLLESON/
NANCY PAYNTER
PHOTOGRAPHER:
HENRIK KAM
ART DIRECTOR:
STEVEN TOLLESON
AGENCY:
TOLLESON DESIGN
CLIENT:
MODULAIRE INDUSTRIES
◀■ 127, 128

grafiek 2

Produktie, inkoop en
verkoop van elektriciteit in 1984 in Gwh

7707 Gwh geproduceerd
306 Gwh ontvangen van de SEP en andere bedrijven

DESIGNER:
BRIAN BOYD
ART DIRECTOR:
BRIAN BOYD
AGENCY:
RBMM & A,
THE RICHARDS GROUP
CLIENT:
CHILI'S, INC.
◀■ 129-131

kleinverbruikers 2355 Gwh (42%)

grootverbruikers 2034 Gwh (37%)

distributiebedrijven 1023 Gwh (18%)

tractie 116 Gwh (2%)

openbare verlichting 66 Gwh (1%)

354 Gwh verbruik centrales

19 Gwh transformatorverliezen centrales

1749 Gwh geleverd aan SEP en andere bedrijven

287 Gwh transformator- en netverliezen

10 Gwh eigen verbruik bedrijfsgebouwen

DESIGNER:
MARTKEMPERS &
HANNIE PYNAPPELS
AGENCY:
MARTKEMPERS &
HANNIE PYNAPPELS
CLIENT:
P.G.E.M. ARNHEM
▶■ 132

verkoop in voorzieningsgebied 5594 Gwh (100%)

■ 127, 128 Business development in the allocation of immediate space for schools, emergency care facilities, and facto-
ries etc. in a 5-year period, shown with pencil and vernier
calliper. From the 1985 annual report of Modulaire Industries. (USA)

■ 129-131 Graphs showing development of business over
four years illustrated on an invoice form of Chilis Grill &
Bar. From the 1986 annual report. (USA)

■ 132 Diagram showing development of business of the
P.G.E.M. electricity plant, Arnhem, giving information about
consumers in percentage and kilowatt hours. (NLD)

■ 127, 128 Die Geschäftsentwicklung in der Bereitstellung
von Gebäuden für Gemeinden und für Industriezwecke in
einer Periode von fünf Jahren wird hier durch den Bleistift
und die Schublehre dargestellt. Aus dem Jahresbericht 1985
der Modulaire Industries. (USA)

■ 129-131 Auf den Rechnungsformularen von Chilis Grill &
Bar untergebrachte Darstellungen der Geschäftsentwicklung
über vier Jahre. Aus dem Jahresbericht 1986. (USA)

■ 132 Graphische Darstellung des Elektrizitätswerks P.G.E.M.
Arnhem, das hier Aufschluss über Abnehmer in Prozent
und Kilowattstunden gibt. (NLD)

■ 127, 128 L'évolution des commandes de constructions
provisoires pour les besoins communaux, scolaires, hospi-
taliers et industriels est représentée ici par un crayon et un
pied à coulisse. Rapport annuel 1985 de Modulaire Industries. (USA)

■ 129-131 Les formules de facturation de Chilis Grill & Bar
portent en surimpression ces diagrammes de l'évolution du
chiffre d'affaires sur quatre ans. Rapport annuel 1986. (USA)

■ 132 Pour la centrale électrique P.G.E.M. Arnhem renseignant sur la part des différents groupes de consommateurs
exprimée en pour-cent et en kilowattheures. (NLD)

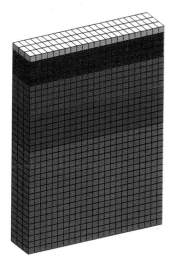
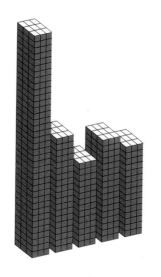
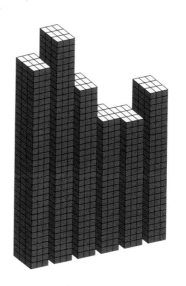
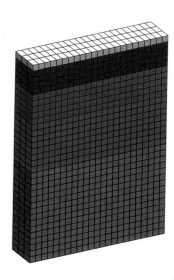

DESIGNER:
Kenton Lotz
ART DIRECTOR:
Ron Jefferies
AGENCY:
The Jefferies Association
CLIENT:
Fluor Corporation
■ 133

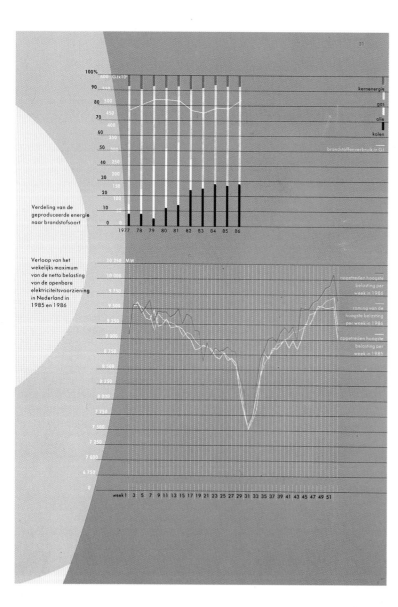

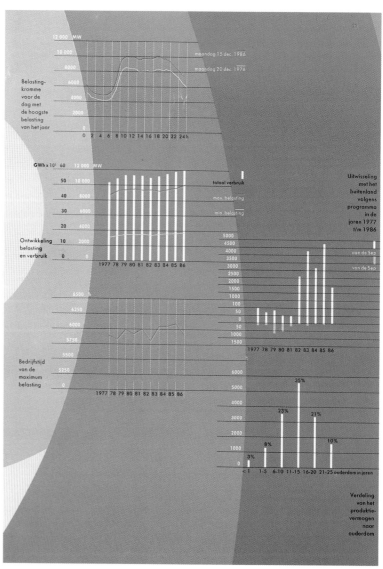

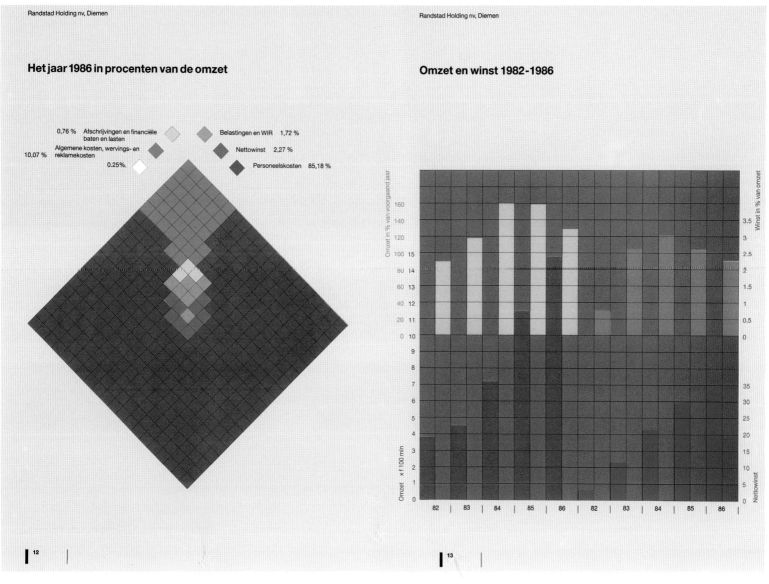

Randstad Holding nv, Diemen

Randstad Holding nv, Diemen

Het jaar 1986 in procenten van de omzet

Omzet en winst 1982-1986

0,76 % Afschrijvingen en financiële baten en lasten

Belastingen en WIR 1,72 %

Algemene kosten, wervings- en reklamekosten
10,07 %

Nettowinst 2,27 %

0.25% Personeelskosten 85,18 %

DESIGNER:
FRANS LIESHOUT
ARTIST:
JURJEN DRENTH
ART DIRECTOR:
FRANS LIESHOUT
AGENCY:
TOTAL DESIGN
CLIENT:
N.V. SAMENWERKENDE ELECTRICI-
TEITSPRODUKTIEBEDRIJVEN (SEP)
◄■ 134-135

DESIGNER:
BEN BOS
AGENCY:
TOTAL DESIGN
CLIENT:
RANDSTAD UITZENDBUREAU
■ 136

■ 133 Diagrams of the development in various sectors, from the annual report of the Fluor Corporation. The three-dimensional column diagrams relate to the main activities of the firm – engineering and construction services and natural resources management. (USA)

■ 134, 135 Typical pages from the 1986 annual report of a Dutch electricity works. The circular theme (the firm's symbol consists of three semi-circles) serves as background for the various diagrams, and it runs throughout the whole report. (NLD)

■ 136 Pages from the 1986 annual report of Randstad Holding NV. Left, cost segmented in percent of the turnover and net yield; right, turnover and profit development between the years 1982 and 1986, from four different points of view. (NLD)

■ 133 Darstellungen der Entwicklung in verschiedenen Bereichen, aus dem Jahresbericht der Fluor Corporation. Die dreidimensional wirkenden Säulendiagramme stehen im Einklang mit einem Haupttätigkeitsbereich des Unternehmens, dem Konstruktions- und Bauwesen. (USA)

■ 134, 135 Beispiele der Seiten aus dem Jahresbericht 1986 eines holländischen Elektrizitätswerkes. Das Kreisthema (das Firmenzeichen besteht aus drei Halbkreisen), das hier als Hintergrund für die verschiedenen Darstellungen dient, zieht sich durch den gesamten Bericht. (NLD)

■ 136 Seiten aus dem Jahresbericht 1986 der Randstad Holding NV. Links die Kostenanteile in Prozent vom Umsatz und der Nettoertrag, rechts Umsatz- und Gewinnentwicklung zwischen 1982 und 1986 nach vier verschiedenen Gesichtspunkten. (NLD)

■ 133 Représentation de l'évolution dans divers secteurs, dans le rapport annuel de la Fluor Corporation. Les graphiques à bandes à effet tridimensionnel se réfèrent à un secteur-clé du groupe, celui du bâtiment et de la construction mécanique. (USA)

■ 134, 135 Pages spécimens du rapport d'une centrale électrique néerlandaise pour 1986. Le motif circulaire (l'emblème de l'entreprise se compose de trois demi-cercles) se retrouve ici à l'arrière-plan de divers graphiques comme partout ailleurs dans ce rapport. (NLD)

■ 136 Pages du rapport annuel 1986 de la Randstad Holding NV. A gauche, la ventilation des coûts en pour-cent du chiffre d'affaires et le produit net, à droite l'évolution du C.A. et du bénéfice dans les années 1982–1986 dans quatre optiques différentes. (NLD)

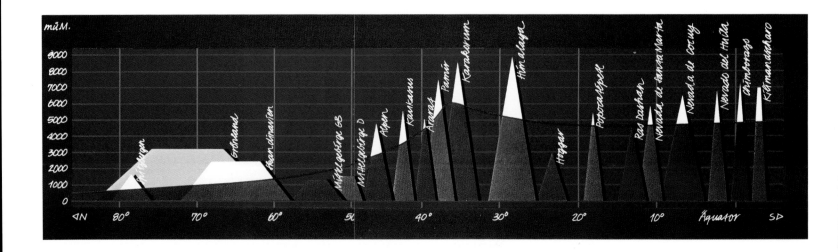

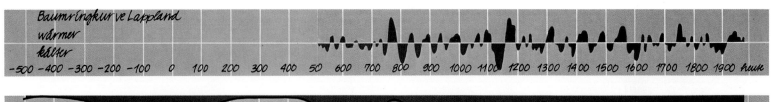

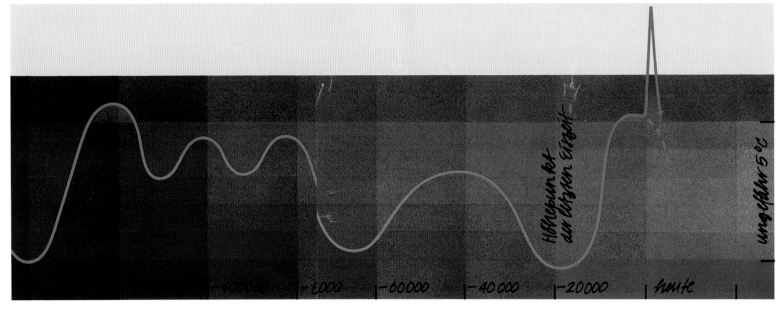

DESIGNER:
ROBERTO RENFER, SCHULE FÜR
GESTALTUNG BERN
ART DIRECTOR:
PETER ANDERMATT/
CLAUDE KUHN-KLEIN
PUBLISHER:
KÜMMERLY + FREY
CLIENT:
CC – SCHWEIZ. KOMMISSION FÜR
KLIMA- + ATMOSPHÄREN-
FORSCHUNG
■ 137, 139

DESIGNER:
SILVIA BRÜHLHARDT, SCHULE FÜR
GESTALTUNG BERN
ART DIRECTOR:
PETER ANDERMATT/
CLAUDE KUHN-KLEIN
PUBLISHER:
KÜMMERLY + FREY
CLIENT:
CC – SCHWEIZ. KOMMISSION FÜR
KLIMA- + ATMOSPHÄREN-
FORSCHUNG
■ 138

DESIGNER:
AGNES WEBER, SCHULE FÜR
GESTALTUNG BERN
ART DIRECTOR:
PETER ANDERMATT/
CLAUDE KUHN-KLEIN
AGENCY:
KÜMMERLY + FREY
CLIENT:
CC – SCHWEIZ. KOMMISSION FÜR
KLIMA- + ATMOSPHÄREN-
FORSCHUNG
■ 140

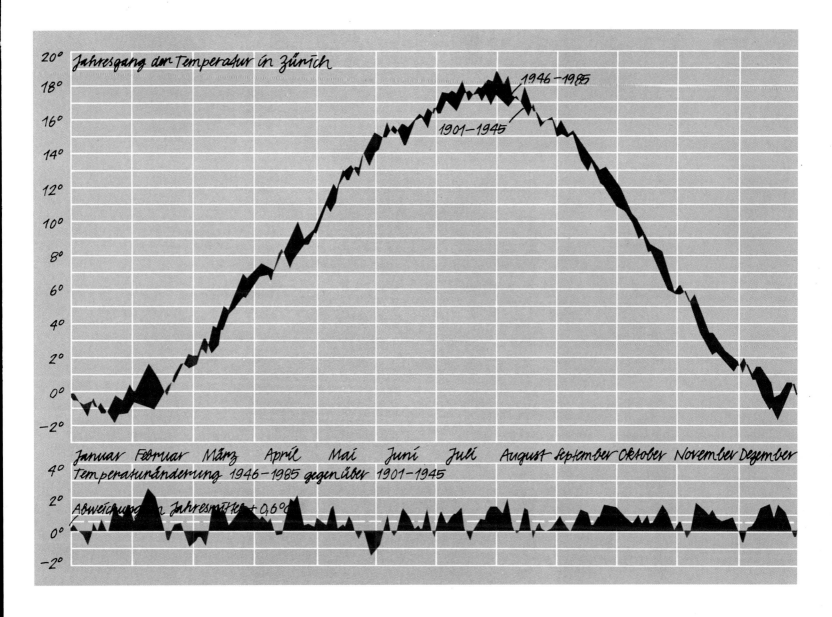

■ 137 Schematic diagram of the distribution of the snow-line – largely determined by rainfall and temperature – from the North Pole to the Equator. (SWI)

■ 138 Diagrams of the temperature variations in Lapland on the basis of the reaction of sensitive trees in this region over fifteen centuries, and the changes in the Aletsch glacier (lower section) in Switzerland over twenty-five centuries (the green bars represent tree trunks felled by the advancing glacier). (SWI)

■ 139 Estimated temperature course over the last 140 000 years and the future. The estimated global warming up lies between 1.5° and 4.5°C. (SWI)

■ 140 Temperature curve of a year in comparison with two periods. Below: difference in the year's average. (SWI)

■ 137 Schematische Darstellung des Verlaufs der Schneegrenze vom Nordpol bis zum Äquator, die im wesentlichen von Niederschlag und Temperatur bestimmt wird. (SWI)

■ 138 Darstellungen der Temperaturschwankungen in Lappland auf der Basis der Reaktion sensibler Bäume in dieser Region über eineinhalb Jahrtausende und der Schwankungen des Aletschgletschers (im unteren Teil) in der Schweiz über zweieinhalb Jahrtausende (die grünen Balken stehen für Baumstämme, die bei Gletschervorstössen fielen). (SWI)

■ 139 Geschätzter Temperaturablauf in den letzten 140 000 Jahren und der Zukunft. Die geschätzte globale Erwärmung liegt zwischen 1,5 und 4,5°C. (SWI)

■ 140 Temperaturkurve eines Jahres mit Vergleich zweier Perioden. Unten: Abweichung im Jahresdurchschnitt. (SWI)

■ 137 Tracé schématisé de la limite des neiges du pôle Nord à l'équateur, influencée principalement par les précipitations et la température. (SWI)

■ 138 Représentation des écarts de température en Laponie sur quinze siècles calculés d'après la thermosensibilité de certaines essences indigènes; en bas, variations du glacier suisse de l'Aletsch sur vingt-cinq siècles: les bandes vertes représentent des arbres arrachés par l'avance périodique du glacier. (SWI)

■ 139 Variations de température dans les 140 000 dernières années et perspectives d'avenir. Le réchauffement global est estimé à une fourchette de 1,5 à 4,5°C. (SWI)

■ 140 Courbe de température annuelle comparée à deux autres périodes. En bas: écarts en moyenne annuelle. (SWI)

DESIGNER:
DONALD RYAN

ART DIRECTOR:
DONALD RYAN

AGENCY:
EARTH SURFACE GRAPHICS

CLIENT:
*STATE OF CALIFORNIA
GOVERNOR'S OFFICE OF
PLANNING & RESEARCH*

■ 141

■ 141 Survey of the streams of California and the stream-flow past a gauging station within one year. The diagram tinted in yellow shows the actual flow measured, the blue one shows the hypothetical virgin condition as it would have been without artificial regulations. Green tints have been used wherever the yellow and blue tints overlap or where an unimpaired flow is shown. (USA)

■ 141 Übersicht der Flüsse Kaliforniens und der in einem Jahr gemessenen Wassermengen. Die gelb gekennzeichneten Diagramme zeigen die gemessenen Wassermengen an, die blauen die hypothetischen Mengen, die sich ohne künstliche Eingriffe ergeben hätten. Grün wurde verwendet, wo sich Blau und Gelb überschneiden oder bei nicht künstlich regulierten Stömen. (USA)

■ 141 Carte synoptique des fleuves de Californie et de leur débit mesuré pendant une année. Les diagrammes marqués en jaune indiquent les débits annuels, ceux marqués en bleu les débits naturels si l'homme n'était intervenu dans l'économie hydraulique. Le vert sert à l'intersection du jaune et du bleu, ainsi que pour les cours d'eau laissés à l'état naturel. (USA)

SEQUENCE AND ORGANIZATION

ABLÄUFE UND GLIEDERUNGEN

ORGANIGRAMMES

The representation of sequences dealt with in this chapter (as well as organizational diagrams) is the oldest form of the diagram. Even cave paintings depict impressive, beautiful examples of this form of representation. They tell stories, report events or give very precise instructions in an often ingenious way. The organizational diagram too is a very old form of representation, which has been used since the time when hierarchies and society structures were first formed and which then had to be explained.

As in other forms of diagrams, the fields overlap, yet the classification of technical function diagrams (which also describe procedures) with technical diagrams seems logical because cut-away and expanded graphics also explain functions. In contrast to statistical diagrams, the recording of the information to be conveyed is, in most cases, not very complicated, and it offers a great number of possibilities for visual translation.

In an organization chart for Bell/AT&T *(Fig. 143)*, to show the state of their organization after a restructuring, components from the field of telecommunications were used; the origin and deviation of the Japanese lettering Kana from the Chinese lettering Kani is shown through simple lines *(Fig. 147)*; the life cycle of a film by Silver Screen Film Co. is described with the aid of a pictorial diagram *(Fig. 146)*; a purely typographically-solved diagram with code colors shows the development of the *Kartell* furniture line *(Figs. 154, 155)*; a model of the production sequence of newspaper production *(Fig. 156)* was photographed - and used as a diagram; photographed objects - rails and products - have a symbolic character in a diagram for the Consolidated Rail Corporation *(Figs. 158, 159)*.

Here too the form selected depends on the purpose for which the diagram is to be used, in any case an unequivocal clear statement that utilizes generally understandable symbols is one of the most essential prerequisites. Only in such cases can one speak of a universality of the graphic visualization of a process - and this is very often absolutely essential, particularly with regard to an international readership. Organizational diagrams are frequently used by firms in their brochures or annual reports when they wish to show their infrastructure as well as the technical and organizational correlation between their various company divisions. The organizational diagrams serve political publications too for a generally better understanding when for instance, the structure of the executive in a specific governmental form, the constitution of governments, etc. need to be explained.

In the field of flow charts, as in organizational diagrams, there are many pictorial renderings (welcome as eye-catchers) and they are an easily understandable means of explaining activities and procedures. There is a danger, though, that there will be an exaggeration, overloading the diagram or complicating the simplest processes.

A carefully thought out concept, an unambiguous statement, the right choice of typography, tasteful coloring and coding, appropriate proportions, generally understandable symbols, a perfect execution that is technically - and aesthetically - justifiable, all add up to guarantee a satisfactory result.

Die Darstellung von Abläufen, die in diesem Kapitel neben Gliederungsdiagrammen behandelt wird, ist die älteste Form des Diagramms. Schon die Höhlenmalereien zeigen eindrucksvolle, schöne Beispiele dieser Darstellungsform. Sie erzählen Geschichten, berichten von Ereignissen oder geben ganz bestimmte Anweisungen. Auch das Gliederungsdiagramm ist eine sehr alte Form der Darstellung, es wurde gebraucht, seit es Hierarchien und Strukturen gibt, die es zu erklären gilt.

Wie auch bei anderen Formen des Diagramms überschneiden sich hier die Gebiete, doch schien die Zuordnung der technischen Funktionsdiagramme, die auch Abläufe beschreiben, zu den technischen Darstellungen am sinnvollsten, denn auch Schnitte und Transparentdarstellungen erklären Funktionen.

Anders als bei den statistischen Diagrammen, ist hier die Erfassung von zu übermittelnden Informationen in den meisten Fällen nicht sehr kompliziert, und es bietet sich eine grosse Anzahl von Möglichkeiten für die visuelle Umsetzung: In einem Organigramm für die Darstellung der betrieblichen Organisation von Bell/AT&T *(Abb. 143)* nach einer Umstrukturierung werden Teile aus der Fernmeldetechnik verwendet; der Ursprung und die Ableitung der japanischen Schrift Kana von der chinesischen Schrift Kani wird durch einfache Linien dargestellt *(Abb. 147);* der Lebenslauf eines Films der Silver Screen Film Co. wird mit Hilfe eines Bilddiagramms verdeutlicht *(Abb. 146);* ein rein typographisch gelöstes Diagramm mit Code-Farben zeigt die Entwicklung des *Kartell*-Möbelprogramms *(Abb. 154, 155);* ein Modell des Produktionsprozesses der Zeitungsherstellung *(Abb. 156)* wurde photographiert und als Diagramm eingesetzt; photographierte Gegenstände – hier Schienen und Produkte – erhalten Symbolcharakter in einem Diagramm der Consolidated Rail Corporation *(Abb. 158, 159)*.

Auch hier hängt die gewählte Form davon ab, für welchen Zweck das Diagramm verwendet werden soll, in jedem Fall ist eine eindeutige, klare Aussage, die sich allgemeinverständlicher Symbole bedient, eine der wichtigsten Voraussetzungen. Nur in solchen Fällen kann man von einer Universalität der graphischen Visualisierung von Abläufen sprechen, die bei einer internationalen Leserschaft absolut erforderlich ist.

Gliederungsdiagramme werden häufig von Firmen eingesetzt, die in Broschüren oder Jahresberichten ihre Struktur oder die arbeitstechnischen und organisatorischen Zusammenhänge zwischen den verschiedenen Geschäftsbereichen verdeutlichen wollen. Auch politische Publikationen bedienen sich des Gliederungsdiagramms zur allgemein verständlichen Erläuterung, z.B. des Aufbaus der Exekutive.

Sowohl im Bereich des Ablauf- wie auch des Gliederungsdiagramms findet man viele Schaubilder, als eine leicht verständliche Form der Erläuterung von Tätigkeiten und Abläufen. Hier liegt allerdings auch eine Gefahr, zuviel des Guten zu tun, überflüssige Bildmittel einzusetzen und dadurch das Schaubild zu überladen. Ein sorgfältig ausgearbeitetes Konzept, eine unmissverständliche Aussage, die richtige Wahl der Typographie, geschmackvolle Farbgebung, angemessene Grössenverhältnisse, allgemeinverständliche Symbole, eine einwandfreie Ausführung, die sowohl den technischen als auch den aesthetischen Ansprüchen gerecht wird, garantieren ein befriedigendes Ergebnis.

La représentation de séquences de travail inscrite au sujet de ce chapitre en même temps que les diagrammes de structure constitue la forme la plus ancienne du diagramme. Les peintures rupestres comportent déjà de beaux exemples impressionnants de représentations séquentielles. On y conte des histoires, on y rend compte d'événements, on y édicte des instructions précises. Le diagramme de structure jouit quant à lui d'une ancienneté non moins remarquable, puisqu'il a été employé de tout temps partout où il s'agissait d'expliciter des relations hiérarchiques ou des structures.

Evidemment, les domaines se recouvrent partiellement comme dans le cas des autres catégories de diagrammes. Pourtant, nous avons jugé utile de renvoyer au chapitre technique les diagrammes fonctionnels techniques décrivant des opérations séquentielles, puisque les dessins en coupe et les représentations transparentes rendent également compte des fonctions.

Contrairement aux diagrammes statistiques, la saisie d'informations à transposer en images n'est généralement pas très compliquée. Les moyens mis en œuvre au plan visuel sont des plus variés. Qu'on en juge: dans un organigramme reproduisant les niveaux d'organisation au sein de Bell/AT&T après la restructuration de l'entreprise *(fig. 143)*, on a intégré des éléments de la technique des télécommunications; l'origine de l'écriture japonaise Kana dérivée de l'écriture chinoise Kani est représentée par de simples lignes *(fig. 147)*; la vie utile d'un film de la Silver Screen Film Co. est explicitée au moyen d'un diagramme illustré *(fig. 146)*; un diagramme ne mettant en œuvre que la typo avec un code couleur montre l'évolution du programme d'ameublements *Kartell (fig. 154, 155)*; le modèle du processus de fabrication d'un journal *(fig. 156)* a été photographié pour faire fonction de diagramme; des objets pris en photo – ici des rails et des produits – prennent valeur de symbole

dans un diagramme de la Consolidated Rail Corporation *(fig. 158, 159)*.

Ici encore, la forme choisie est fonction du but poursuivi. Dans tous les cas, l'exigence primordiale est celle d'un message clair et univoque faisant appel à des symboles généraux compris en tous lieux. Ce n'est que lorsque cette exigence est satisfaite qu'il peut être question d'universalité dans la visualisation graphique de processus séquentiels. Or, cette universalité est indispensable dans de nombreux cas, particulièrement au vu du public international.

Les diagrammes de structure sont fréquemment utilisés par des entreprises désireuses d'expliquer dans leurs publications, notamment dans leurs rapports annuels, leur structure interne ou les relations entre leurs divers secteurs d'activité au plan de la technique et de l'organisation du travail. Les publications politiques font également appel au diagramme de structure pour illustrer avec toute la clarté souhaitable la composition de l'exécutif communal, départemental, régional ou national, par exemple.

Tant les organigrammes que les diagrammes de structure sont souvent agrémentés de force illustrations très appréciées pour leur impact visuel et la simplification de la démonstration d'activités et de processus séquentiels. Le danger est évident: on risque de surcharger le diagramme d'éléments illustratifs superfétatoires et d'aller jusqu'à illustrer inutilement des opérations archisimples. Dans ce domaine, un résultat satisfaisant est obtenu par la conjonction des facteurs suivants: une conception établie avec soin, un message qui ne prête à aucune équivoque, une typographie choisie avec discernement, des coloris et codes couleurs sélectionnés avec un goût sans faille, un dimensionnement adéquat du graphique, des symboles faciles à interpréter; enfin, une exécution impeccable satisfaisant pleinement aux exigences techniques et esthétiques.

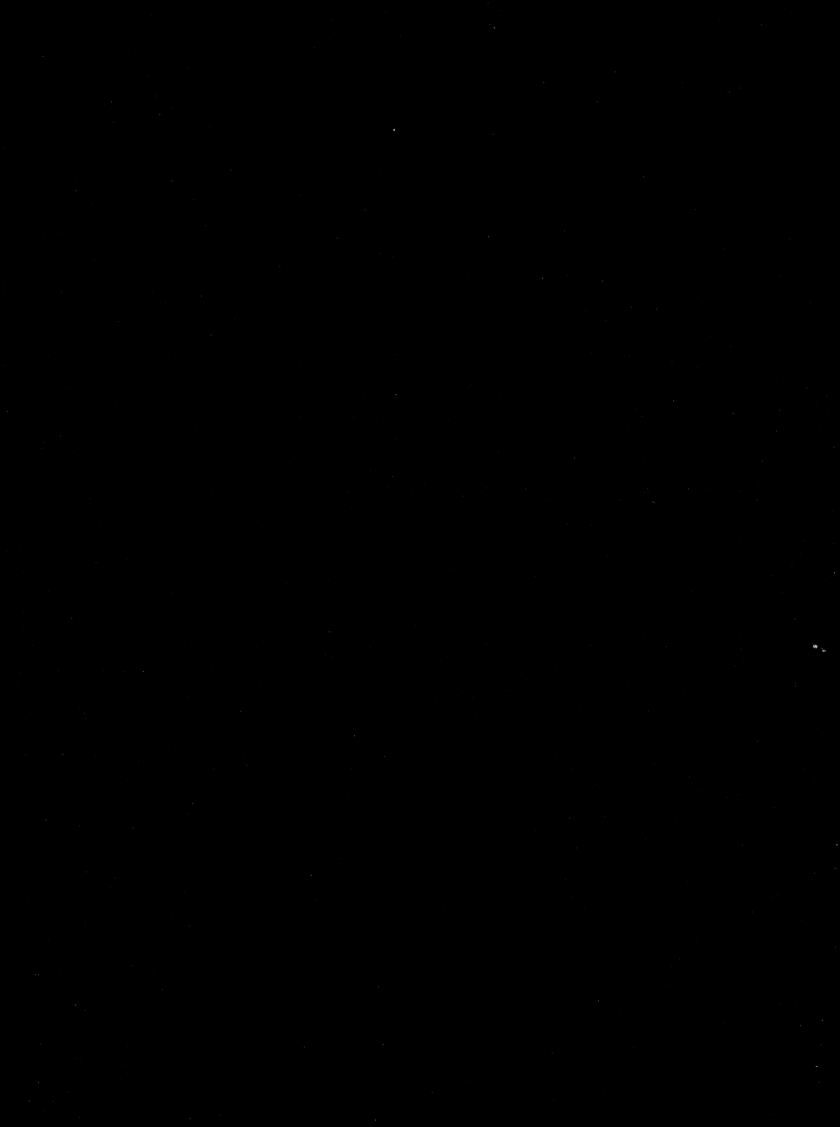

HOW BUILDING
MANAGEMENT
S Y S T E M S
O P E R A T E

Total solutions to building owner's problems — through sophisticated supervision and control — is provided by the MCC Powers System 600 Building Management System diagrammed at the right. By integrating the various building functions — including fire, security, lighting, maintenance management, and control of the building's heating, ventilating, and air conditioning system — the System 600 optimizes building performance and reduces both energy costs and operating costs. Fire and security systems protect both life and property assets, and software programs provide energy reports, inventory control, work orders, and alarms which help the building owner manage his building more efficiently.

The state-of-the-art technology diagrammed indicates the distributed control scheme which assigns control functions to control panels throughout the building. These control panels collect data on temperature, humidity, flow, pressure, and smoke from sensors within the control network. Based on this information, the control panels then implement control instructions programmed by the operator, thus providing control through local intelligence.

Control panels distributed throughout a building execute programmed sequences — operating, for example, motors, fans, and pumps. They also detect alarm conditions and activate alarms, and transmit information to the host computer and to other control panels on the local area network.

Though most direct control functions are distributed to control panels throughout the building, the host computer provides the vital supervisory functions which optimize the benefits of the total control scheme. By supervising multiple networks of control panels, the host computer assures the building owner that control decisions maximize benefits in terms of total building control, rather than in terms of individual local area networks.

In addition, the host computer stores data, generates reports, and allows the operator to set up data files for the entire system. Maintenance management is executed over the entire System 600 control network. The overall control functions executed by the host computer maximize the benefits of total building control by integrating the individual control decisions made by distributed control panels for their local area networks. MCC Powers engineers design the total system for each building, using state-of-the-art applications hardware and software to meet the unique needs of each building owner.

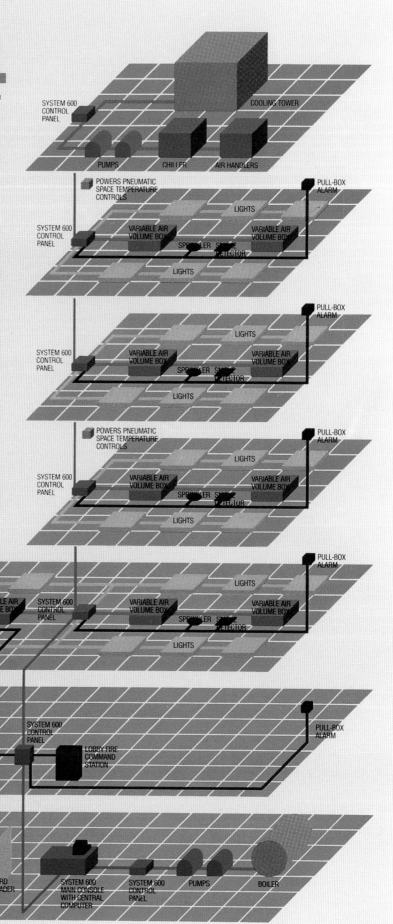

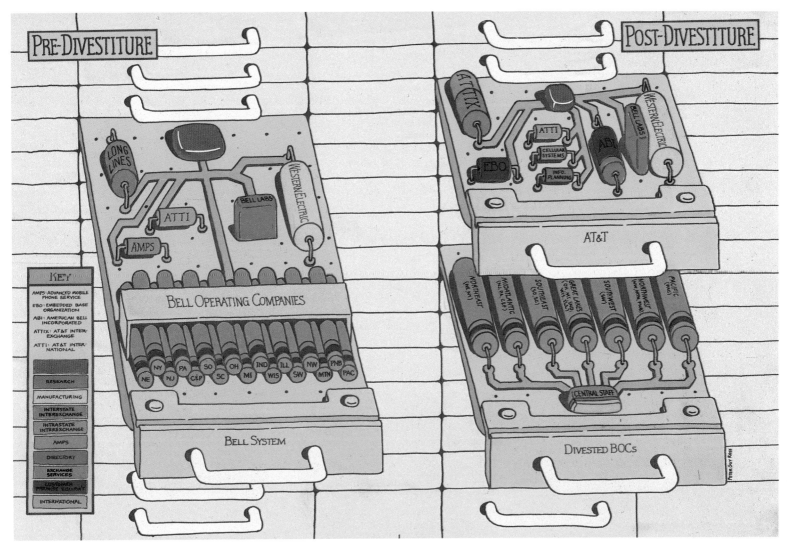

DESIGNER:
DOUG ARMSTRONG
ART DIRECTOR:
GEORGE KUBRICHT
AGENCY:
COM CORP, INC.
CLIENT:
MARK CONTROLS CORP.
◀■ 142

DESIGNER:
PETER ROSS
ART DIRECTOR:
PETER ROSS
AGENCY:
*ROSS CULPERT HOLLAND
& LAVERY, INC.*
CLIENT:
AT + T COMMUNICATIONS
■ 143

■ 142 Diagram showing the technology of "System 600" – a building control scheme (fire, security, lighting, heating, etc.). From a Mark Controls Corp. annual report. (USA)

■ 143 Managerial groups shown in diagrams – from the *Bell Telephone Magazine* issued by the telephone corporation AT&T. Shown is the managerial organization of the entities pre- and post-divestiture. (USA)

■ 142 Übersicht der elektrischen Anlagen, Sicherheits- und computerisierten Kontrollsysteme eines Gebäudes. Seite aus einem Jahresbericht der Mark Controls Corporation. (USA)

■ 143 Betriebsgruppen-Diagramme aus dem *Bell Telephone Magazine* der Telephongesellschaft AT&T. Dargestellt ist die betriebliche Organisation der Gruppe vor und nach einer Umstrukturierung. (USA)

■142 Plan général des fonctions électriques, de sécurité et de contrôle assurées dans un bâtiment par l'ordinateur central. Page d'un rapport annuel de la Mark Controls Corp. (USA)

■ 143 Diagrammes d'exploitation avant et après la réorganisation de la société des téléphones AT&T et sa séparation d'avec Bell System. Extrait du *Bell Telephone Magazine* publié par AT&T. (USA)

DESIGNER:
*BLUMENSTEIN, PLANCHEREL,
KRÜGEL*
AGENCY:
*BLUMENSTEIN, PLANCHEREL,
KRÜGEL*
CLIENT:
NESTEC SA
■ 144

DESIGNER:
WOLF SPOERL
ART DIRECTOR:
DAVID HILLMANN
AGENCY:
PENTAGRAM DESIGN, LONDON
CLIENT:
ERICSSON INFORMATION SYSTEMS
►■ 145

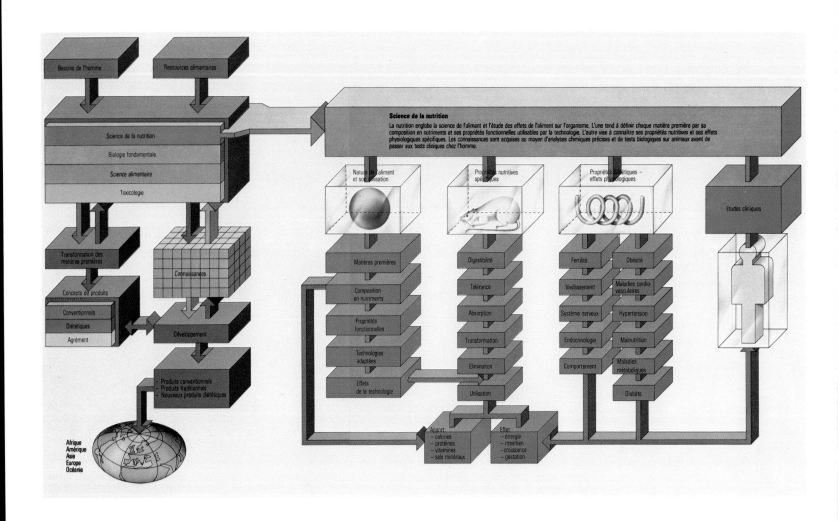

■ 144 Analysis of nutritional research, taken from the magazine *Recherche scientifique et Développement technologique* (Scientific Research & Technical Development) published by *Nestlé*. Diagrammed is the connection between man's need, the available natural resources, the related sciences, knowledge, development, processing of raw materials, and the final product groups. On the right the meaning of the term "nutritional science" as well as its functions, are explained. (SWI)

■ 145 Flow chart from the *Information Resource Management, - Human Factors & Information Systems,* a publication issued by Ericsson Information Systems. Shown is the conversion of the existing international telecommunications system to a digital system. This is planned in phases over a period of twenty years (1980-2000). (SWE)

■ 144 Aufgliederung der Ernährungsforschung aus der von *Nestlé* herausgegebenen Zeitschrift *Recherche scientifique et Développement technologique.* Dargestellt ist der Zusammenhang zwischen den Bedürfnissen des Menschen, den vorhandenen Rohstoffen, den damit verbundenen Wissenschaften, Erkenntnissen, Entwicklungen, der Verarbeitung der Rohstoffe und den endgültigen Produktgruppen. Im rechten Teil werden der Begriff der Ernährungswissenschaft und ihre Funktionen erläutert. (SWI)

■ 145 Ablaufdiagramm aus *Information Resource Management,* eine Publikation von Ericsson Information Systems. Dargestellt ist die in einem Zeitraum von 20 Jahren (1980-2000) geplante schrittweise Umstellung des bestehenden internationalen Telekommunikationssystems auf ein Digitalsystem. (SWI)

■ 144 Graphique donnant une vue d'ensemble de la recherche alimentaire, dans le périodique *Recherche scientifique et Développement technologique* de *Nestlé.* On y explicite les relations entre les besoins de l'homme, les matières premières disponibles, les sciences y relatives, leurs découvertes et développements, la transformation des matières premières et les groupes de produits finis en résultant. A droite, on définit la science de l'alimentation et en précise les fonctions. (SWI)

■ 145 Organigramme publié dans *Information Resource Management,* un périodique d'Ericsson Information Systems. On y présente la reconversion prévue du système international de télécommunications tel que nous le connaissons, pour passer en l'espace de 20 ans (1980-2000) à un système numérique. (SWE)

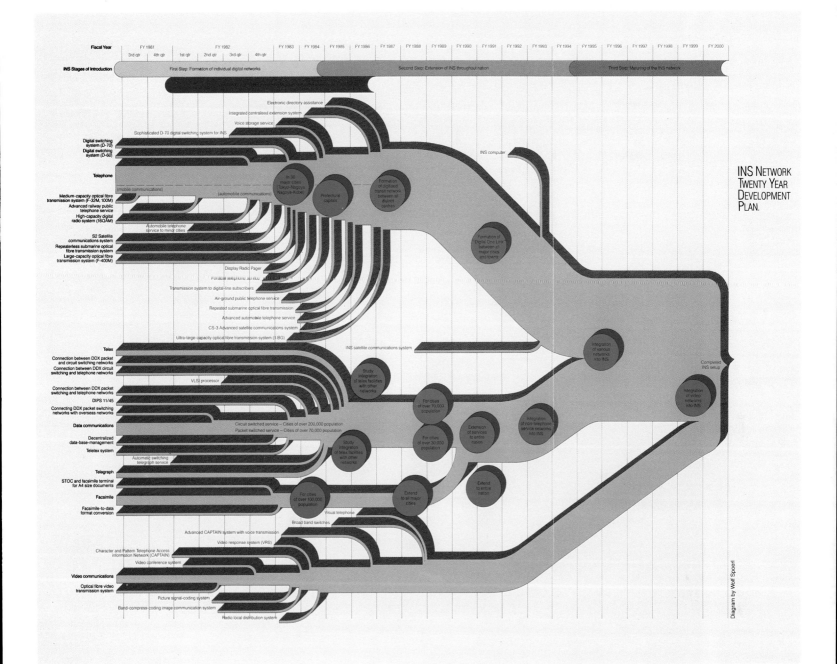

INS NETWORK
TWENTY YEAR
DEVELOPMENT
PLAN.

Diagram by Wolf Spoerl

■ 146 Illustration to show the life cycle of a film on the US market and abroad. From the annual report of the film distributors Silver Screen Partners II. (USA)

■ 147 Diagram showing the origin of the Japanese lettering Kana which was derived from the Chinese lettering Kanji – as is clearly depicted here. (JPN)

■ 148 The basic structure of the fifth computer generation is the subject of this diagram from *Information Resource Management*, a publication by Ericsson Information Systems. (SWE)

■ 146 Schaubild des Lebenslaufes eines Films auf dem US-Markt und im Ausland. Aus dem Jahresbericht des Filmverleihers Silver Screen Partners II. (USA)

■ 147 Darstellung des Ursprungs der japanischen Schrift Kana, die – wie hier verdeutlicht – von der chinesischen Schrift Kanji abgeleitet wurde. (JPN)

■ 148 Die Grundstruktur der fünften Computer-Generation ist Thema dieser Darstellung aus *Information Resource Management*, einer Publikation von Ericsson Information Systems. (SWE)

■ 146 Graphique montrant le cycle de vie d'un film sur le marché américain et à l'étranger. Rapport annuel du distributeur de films Silver Screen Partners II. (USA)

■ 147 Représentation de l'origine de la composante syllabique kana de l'écriture japonaise, dérivée, comme on le voit, de l'écriture chinoise Kanji. (JPN)

■ 148 Ce diagramme publié dans *Information Resource Management*, un périodique d'Ericsson Information Systems, a pour sujet la structure de base de la 5e génération d'ordinateurs. (SWE)

DESIGNER:
PETER HARRISON/
SUSAN HOCHBAUM
ARTIST:
PHILIP WEISBECKER
ART DIRECTOR:
PETER HARRISON/
SUSAN HOCHBAUM
AGENCY:
PENTAGRAM DESIGN, USA
CLIENT:
SILVER SCREEN PARTNERS II
■ 146

DESIGNER:
BABA YUJI
ART DIRECTOR:
BABA YUGJI
AGENCY:
UNI DESIGN
CLIENT:
LETRASET JAPAN
■ 147

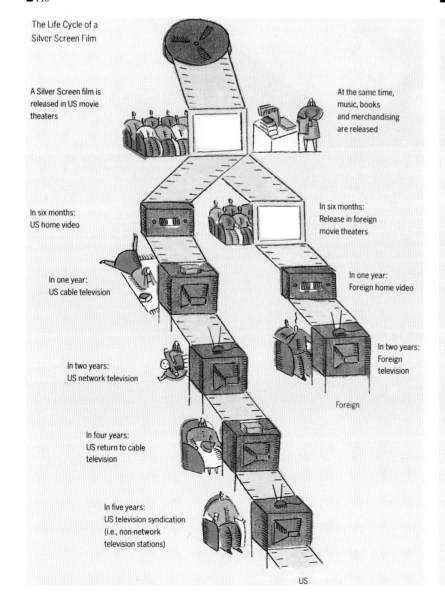

The Life Cycle of a Silver Screen Film

A Silver Screen film is released in US movie theaters

At the same time, music, books and merchandising are released

In six months: US home video

In six months: Release in foreign movie theaters

In one year: US cable television

In one year: Foreign home video

In two years: US network television

In two years: Foreign television

Foreign

In four years: US return to cable television

In five years: US television syndication (i.e., non-network television stations)

US

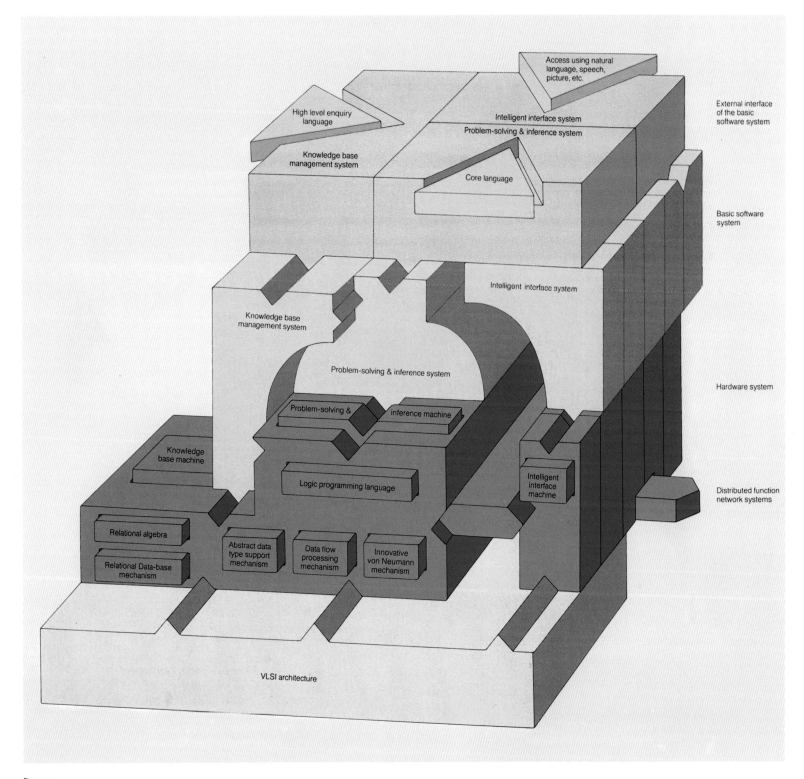

DESIGNER:
WOLF SPOERL & DAVID HILLMANN
ARTIST:
WOLF SPOERL
ART DIRECTOR:
DAVID HILLMANN
AGENCY:
PENTAGRAM DESIGN, LONDON
CLIENT:
ERICSSON INFORMATION SYSTEMS
■ 148

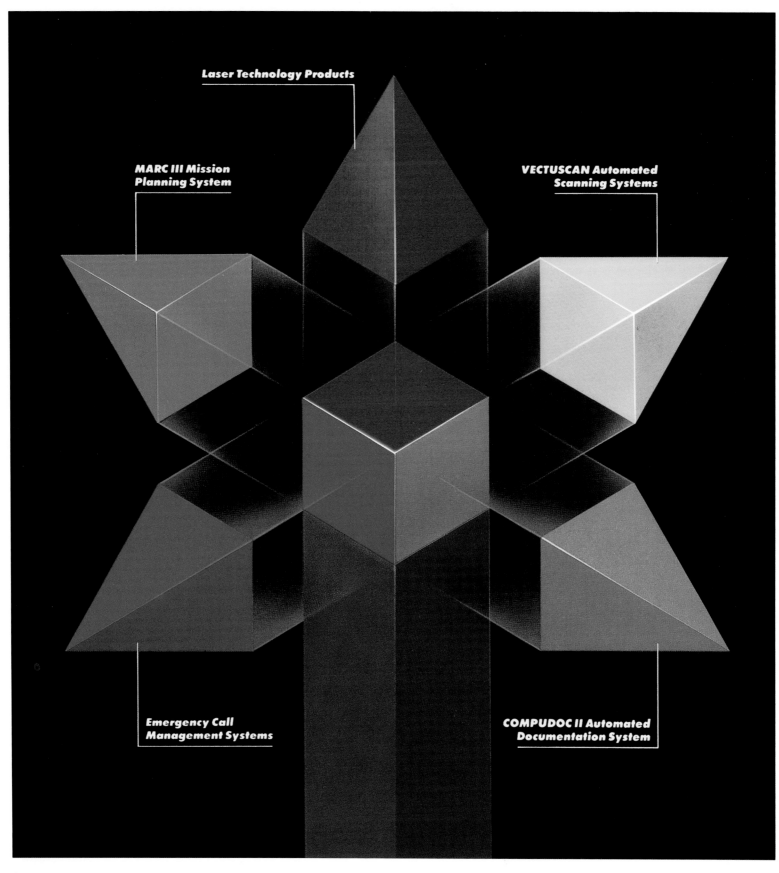

Laser Technology Products

MARC III Mission
Planning System

VECTUSCAN Automated
Scanning Systems

Emergency Call
Management Systems

COMPUDOC II Automated
Documentation System

DESIGNER:
CARL SELTZER
ARTIST:
GEORGE GRUBER
ART DIRECTOR:
CARL SELTZER
AGENCY:
CARL SELTZER DESIGN OFFICE
CLIENT:
COMARCO, INC.
■ 149-153

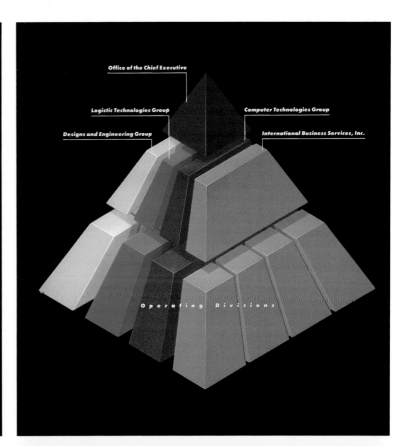

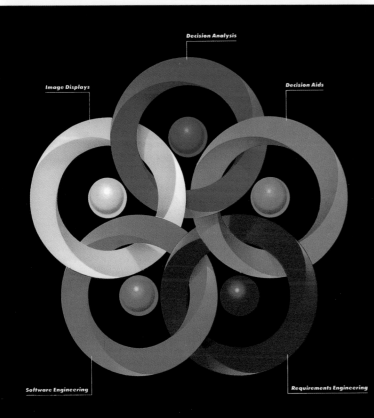

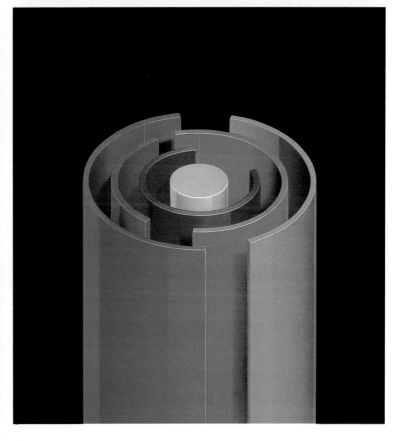

■ 149-153 Three-dimensional diagrams from the 1986 annual report of Comarco Inc. (weapons systems, logistics, software for government bases). It relates to product enhancement in the different groups, the upward trend (part of a cover diagram), structure for growth, special programs, and the most important figures (revenues, employees etc.) of International Business Services, a firm recently acquired by Comarco. (USA)

■ 149-153 Diagramme aus dem Jahresbericht 1986 der Comarco Inc. (Waffensysteme, Logistik und Software für Regierungsstellen). Hier geht es um Produktverbesserungen in den verschiedenen Bereichen, um den Aufwärtstrend (Teil eines Diagramms für die Umschlagseite), die Struktur der Firma, Spezialprogramme und um die wichtigsten Angaben (Einnahmen, Geschäftsbereiche, Angestellte etc.) über eine kürzlich übernommene Firma. (USA)

■ 149-153 Diagrammes à effet tridimensionnel dans le rapport annuel 1986 de Comarco Inc. (systèmes d'armes, logistique et logiciels pour les agences gouvernementales). Il s'agit de l'amélioration des produits dans divers secteurs, de la croissance (partie du diagramme en couverture), de l'organigramme, de programmes spéciaux et des données de base d'une société d'acquisition récente: revenus, activités, personnel, etc. (USA)

AGENCY:
CENTROKAPPA DESIGN
CLIENT:
KARTELL S.P.A.
■ 154, 155

■ 154, 155 Typographically-solved diagram that gives information about the development of the furniture manufacturers *Kartell.* Shown is the front and back of a foldout page from a company brochure. Easy readability and overview is achieved through the use of five code colors. (ITA)

■ 154, 155 Typographisches gelöstes Diagram, das über die Entwicklung des Möbel-produzenten *Kartell* Aus-kunft gibt. Hier die Vorder-und Rückseite der in einer Firmenbroschüre enthalte-nen, ausklappbaren Seite. Durch den Einsatz von fünf Code-Farben wird für leichte Lesbarkeit und Übersicht-lichkeit gesorgt. (ITA)

■ 154, 155 Diagramme amé-nagé typographiquement renseignant sur l'évolution du fabricant de meubles *Kartell:* recto et verso de la page dépliante encartée dans une brochure de l'entreprise. Le code couleur (cinq cou-leurs) augmente la lisibilité et la clarté de l'exposé. (ITA)

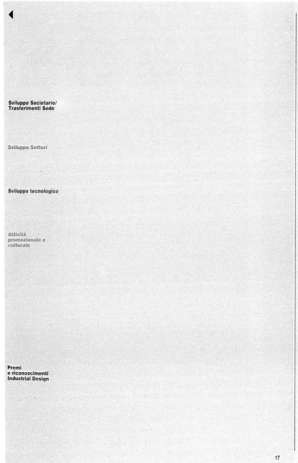

1954

onda il pool
… per lo
… di
…loni
…u u di
… sulle
plastiche

…ati alla
…izione del
Compasso

…i thermos

…lo
…bini
…ta
…accioli 1006
…o per
1088
…dura 1811

1955

Trasformazione della Kartell in S.r.l. con sede in Milano, Via Ripamonti 2

Nasce il nuovo marchio "Kartell Samco" per la vendita dei Casalinghi Kartell

Premio Compasso d'Oro al Secchio con coperchio KS 1146, design Gino Colombini

Selezionati i seguenti prodotti:
Bacinelle mondariso KS 1497
Caraffa termica KS 1432
Secchio quadro KS 1147
Lavacalze Shaklin KS 1074
Scatole per cucina KS 1095
Ciotola con beccuccio KS 1027

1956

Esce il primo numero della rivista Qualità (1956/60)

Selezionati per il Premio Compasso d'Oro i seguenti prodotti:
Bidone 36 lt. KS 1152
Tinozza con manici KS 1062
Scatola per cucina KS 1124

1957

Viene stampato il primo prodotto in nylon

Partecipazione alla XI Triennale di Milano nella Mostra di Industrial Design

Premio Compasso d'Oro alla Tinozza KS 1065, design Gino Colombini

Selezionati i seguenti prodotti:
Battipanni KS 1475
Ciotola KS 1032

1958

Nasce il Settore Illuminazione (1958/81)
Nasce il Settore Labware

1959

Inizia la produzione della prima lampada stampata a iniezione e della prima lampada in Raflon

Inizia la produzione di prodotti in poliestere

Premio Compasso d'Oro allo Spremilimone KS 1481, design Gino Colombini

Selezionati i seguenti prodotti:
Portaimmondizie con manico KS 1068
Lampada KD 4033
Portaprovette TS 130/136
Vasetto per bambini KS 1354

1960

Nasce il Settore Impianti Industriali (1960/68)

Partecipazione alla XII Triennale di Milano

Premio Compasso d'Oro allo Scolapiatti smontabile KS 1171/2/3/4, design Gino Colombini

Selezionati i seguenti prodotti:
Scolapasta KS 1036
Ciotole con coperchio KS 1190/5

1961

Medaglia d'argento alla XII Triennale di Milano

1962

Inizia la produzione di prodotti in polipropilene

Prima partecipazione al Salone del Mobile di Milano

Partecipazione alla Mostra di Villa Olmo

Medaglia d'oro alla produzione Kartell

1963

Inaugurazione dello stabilimento a Binasco

Nasce il Settore Habitat

1964

Trasferimento della Sede a Binasco

Inizia la produzione della prima sedia al mondo interamente in materiale plastico, stampata ad iniezione in polietilene: la Seggiolina per bambini 4999, design Marco Zanuso e Richard Sapper

Partecipazione alla XIII Triennale di Milano

Medaglia d'Oro della XIII Triennale di Milano e Premio Compasso d'Oro alla Seggiolina per bambini 4999, design Marco Zanuso e Richard Sapper

1965

Partecipazione alla 1ª Eurodomus

Design Award Interplast e Premio LGA Zentrum Baden Württemberg alla Seggiolina per bambini 4999, design Marco Zanuso e Richard Sapper

1966

1967

Trasformazione della Kartell in Società per Azioni. Acquisto del terreno e progetto per il nuovo stabilimento di Noviglio

Chiusura del Settore Autoaccessori

Inizia la produzione del primo mobile in abs, con gli Element componibili quadri 4970/72, design Anna Castelli Ferrieri

Nel Settore Labware, ricco ormai di 650 prodotti, viene stampato il primo prodotto in Teflon: i Becher 717/13

1° Premio Macef 1967 alla Pattumiera con pedale 8250/55, design Gino Colombini

16

1974

Inaugurazione del nuovo stabilimento di Noviglio, ampliato alla dimensione di 29.000 mq. coperti, su un'area di 110.000 mq.

Inizia la produzione dei primi mobili stampati in poliuretano strutturale, con la Sedia 4854, la Poltrona 4794 e il Tavolino 4894, design Gae Aulenti

Premio Casa Amica al Sistema cassetti componibili 4601/05, design Simon Fussel

1975

Sponsorizzazione della "Mostra Internazionale della sedia in materiale plastico", realizzata dal Centrokappa

I seguenti prodotti vengono inseriti nella Collezione permanente del Museum of Modern Art di New York:
Gettacarte 4663, design Gino Colombini
Sistema cassetti componibili 4601/05, design Simon Fussel

1976

Costituzione della Kartell Commercio e Representacao Ltda con sede a San Paolo, Brasile

Esce la prima edizione di "Idee per Abitare"

1977

Costituzione della Kartell Finanziaria S.p.A., con sede a Noviglio (Milano)

Sponsorizzazione della rivista "Modo"

Promozione e sponsorizzazione della "Mostra del Design Italiano degli Anni '50", realizzata dal Centrokappa

Alla Kartell viene assegnata la Medaglia d'Oro del Comune di Milano

Selezionato al Premio SMAU il Sistema Outline 5021/57, design Anna Castelli Ferrieri

1978

Inizia la pubblicazione del periodico periodica d'informazione "Kartellnews"

Sponsorizzazione dell'iniziativa "Colordinamo"

Primo Premio Interieur '78 al Sistema scuola 5300/40, design Centrokappa

1979

Costituzione della Kartell U.K Ltd, con sede a Cambridge, Gran Bretagna

Partecipazione nel Grupo T S.A., con sede a Barcellona, Spagna

Chiusura del Settore Casalinghi

Premio Compasso d'Oro alla Kartell, con la seguente motivazione: "Per la politica aziendale basata sulla coerenza della progettazione dei suoi prodotti e su una costante ricerca e immagine evolutiva"

Selezionati i seguenti prodotti:
Poltrona 4794 design Gae Aulenti
Apparecchio Labdryer 2220/21 design Centrokappa
Pronto Soccorso oculare 2384 design Centrokappa
Gancio 4702 design Olaf Von Bohr
Poltroncina 4820 design Masayuki Matsukaze e Centrokappa
Sgabelli 4822/44 design Anna Castelli Ferrieri

Sedia 4875 design Carlo Bartoli
Sistema scuola 5300/40 design Centrokappa
Struttura componibile 4760/65 design Giulio Polvara
Fioriere 4683/86 design Anna Castelli Ferrieri
Sistema Outline 5021/64 design Anna Castelli Ferrieri
Portacenere e cestino da muro 4663/65 design Centrokappa
Portacenere 4637/38 design Anna Castelli Ferrieri
Fermalibri 4909/10 design Giotto Stoppino
Specchi componibili 4732/36 design Anna Castelli Ferrieri
Zuppiere 5500/06 design Anna Castelli Ferrieri
Posate per insalata 5470 design Anna Castelli Ferrieri
Caraffa e bicchieri 5390/91 design Centrokappa
Vassoi frigo 9440/41 design Centrokappa
Ghiacciaia da tavolo 4624 design Giotto Stoppino

1980

Costituzione della Kappa Diseño S.A., con sede a Guadalajara, Messico

Partecipazione alla Mostra "Italienisches Moebel Design" allo Stadt Museum di Colonia, con lo sviluppo tecnologico progettuale dello Sgabello 4822/44 e con altri 5 prodotti:
Elementi componibili quadri 4970/84
Elementi componibili tondi 4953/60
Tavoli in poliestere 4991/4
Sistema scuola 5300/40
Poltroncina pieghevole 4820

Product Design Award del Resources Council Inc., USA a Sgabelli 4822/40, design Anna Castelli Ferrieri

Product Design Award del Resources Council Inc., USA al Sistema scuola 5300/40, design Centrokappa

1981

Costituzione della Kartell Japan Ltd, con sede a Tokio, Giappone

Costituzione della Kartell Holdings Ltd, con sede a Londra, Gran Bretagna

Costituzione della I&I Ltd. (Italian Design and International Contractors Ltd), con sede a Londra, Gran Bretagna

Chiusura del Settore Illuminazione

Selezionati al premio Compasso d'Oro i seguenti prodotti:
Sistema appendiabiti 4616/54 - 4788/90
Portacenere da tavolo 4639
Portacenere da tavolo 4640/41
Portacenere da tavolo 4642

Design Award American Societies of Industrial Design alla Poltroncina pieghevole 4820, design Masayuki Matsukaze e Centrokappa

Medaglia d'Oro della BIO9 di Lubiana a Sistema scuola 5300/40, design Centrokappa

1982

Istituzione del marchio "Kartell USA" per la divisione Habitat della ECP, con sede a Easly, South Carolina, USA

Costituzione della Kappa Diseño S.A., con sede a Barcellona, Spagna

Viene prodotto il primo tavolo completamente stampato a iniezione: il Tavolo 4300, design Anna Castelli Ferrieri

Partecipazione alla mostra "Italian Re-evolution, Design in Italian society in the Eighties" al La Jolla Museum of Contemporary Art, La Jolla, California, USA

Medaglia di Bronzo ICE al Salone del Mobile di Colonia alla Poltroncina 4855, design Anna Castelli Ferrieri

1983

Sponsorizzazione della "Casa per Vacanze" progettata da Michele De Lucchi, alla Triennale di Milano

Sponsorizzazione della mostra "Visual" alla Galleria del Sagrato di Milano

Partecipazione alla mostra "Design since 1945" al Philadelphia Museum of Art, Philadelphia USA

Partecipazione alla mostra "Möbel aus Italien" al Design Center Stuttgart, Baden Württemberg, Germania

Mostra "Kartell 1949-1983. Progetti per il presente", realizzata in occasione del Congresso ICSID Design '83 e progettata dal Centrokappa

ID Annual Design Award dell'Industrial Design Magazine, New York USA, al Tavolo 4300, design Anna Castelli Ferrieri

1984

Costituzione della Casakit S.A., con sede a Parigi, Francia

Partecipazione alla mostra "Design Furniture from Italy" al Sogetsu Kaikan, Tokio, Giappone

Sponsorizzazione della Mostra itinerante Achille Castiglioni

Partecipazione al Comitato Consultivo per Domus Academy del CISDI (Centro Italiano Studi Design per l'Industria)

21

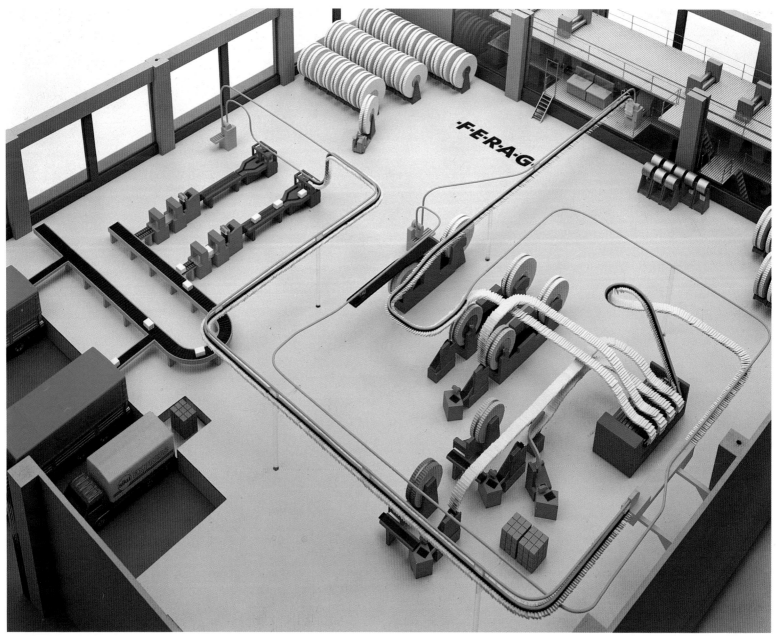

DESIGNER:
H. OBERHOLZER/H. P. HÖSLI
ARTIST:
CHRISTIAN OEHRLI
ART DIRECTOR:
U. FÜRER
AGENCY:
ADOLF WIRZ AG
CLIENT:
FERAG AG
■ 156

■ 156 Model of the production of a newspaper, from an ad portfolio issued by Ferag AG, producer of conveyors and processing systems for the printing industry. (SWI)

■ 157 Illustration showing the automated technology used in the sterile production and filling of lens solutions. Spread from the 1984 annual report of *Bausch & Lomb*. (USA)

■ 156 Modell des Produktionsprozesses einer Zeitung, aus einer Werbemappe der Ferag AG, Hersteller von Förder- und Verarbeitungs-Systemen für die Druckindustrie. (SWI)

■ 157 Schaubild über den Produktionsablauf in der sterilen Herstellung und Abfüllung von Linsen- und Augenwassern. Aus dem Jahresbericht 1984 von *Bausch & Lomb*. (USA)

■ 156 Modèle du processus de fabrication d'un journal. Dossier publicitaire de la Ferag AG, qui fabrique des systèmes de transport et de traitement pour l'industrie graphique. (SWI)

■ 157 Schéma opérationnel de la production et de l'embouteillage en atmosphère stérile de collyres (œil, cristallin). Du rapport annuel 1984 de *Bausch & Lomb*. (USA)

High-Quality Solutions From High-Speed Production

Our new solutions manufacturing plant in Greenville, South Carolina places Bausch & Lomb in the forefront of sterile-fill technology. This 100,000 square foot facility, the largest of its kind in the nation, is extensively automated to operate at high speed. It has the flexibility to produce all our lens solutions in any size container. The plant's advanced design and our high product volumes make Bausch & Lomb the most efficient producer of solutions in the industry.

Pallets are then stretch-wrapped in plastic film for protection.

Cases are automatically loaded onto pallets for shipping.

Filled cases move to an elevated tram which carries them across the plant.

Solutions are manufactured from various ingredients and purified water in 10,000 gallon mixing tanks, and routed to the filling area through stainless steel pipe.

Extensive computer controls have been designed into the plant. These systems assist in running the mixing and filling operations, as well as monitoring the critical environment of the facility.

Bottling occurs in this sterile area, in which workers must be fully gowned to avoid introducing contaminants. Even incoming air is carefully filtered.

Solutions are bottled and capped automatically, and move by conveyor out of the filling area. Automatic sensors pull imperfect or improperly filled bottles off the line.

Further down the conveyor, groups of cartons are packed in cases.

Bottles of solution, along with user instructions, are automatically inserted into cartons.

Labels are applied by a sophisticated, high speed device to each container of solution as it moves out of the filling area.

DESIGNER:
ROBERT MEYER
ART DIRECTOR:
FRANK JEPSON/ROBERT MEYER
AGENCY:
ROBERT MEYER DESIGN, INC.
CLIENT:
BAUSCH & LOMB
■ 157

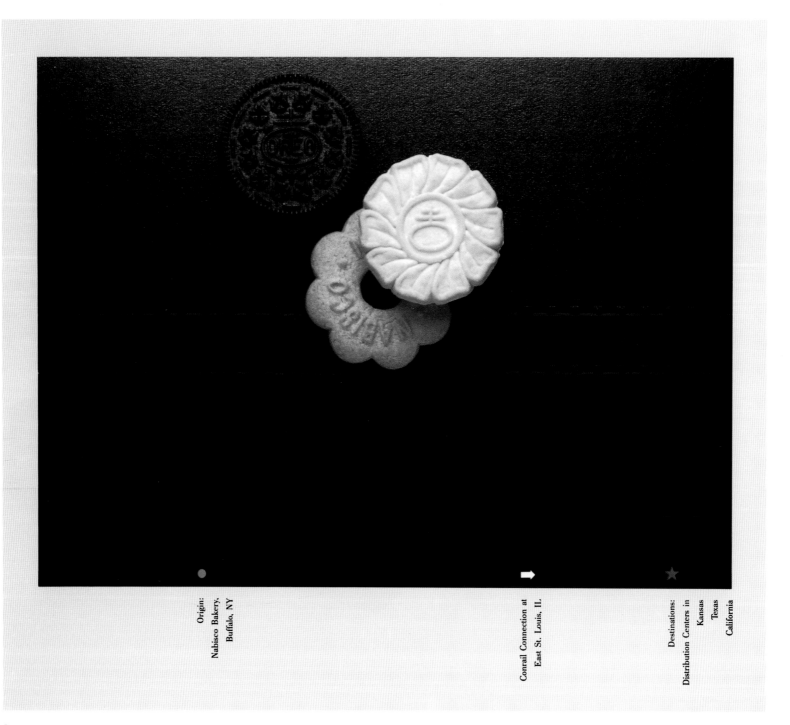

Origin:
Nabisco Bakery,
Buffalo, NY

Conrail Connection at
East St. Louis, IL.

Destinations:
Distribution Centers in
Kansas
Texas
California

DESIGNER:
ROGER COOK/DON SHANOSKY
PHOTOGRAPHER:
ARTHUR BECK
ART DIRECTOR:
ROGER COOK/DON SHANOSKY
AGENCY:
*COOK AND SHANOSKY
ASSOC., INC.*
CLIENT:
*CONRAI (CONSOLIDATED RAIL
CORPORATION)*
■ 158–159

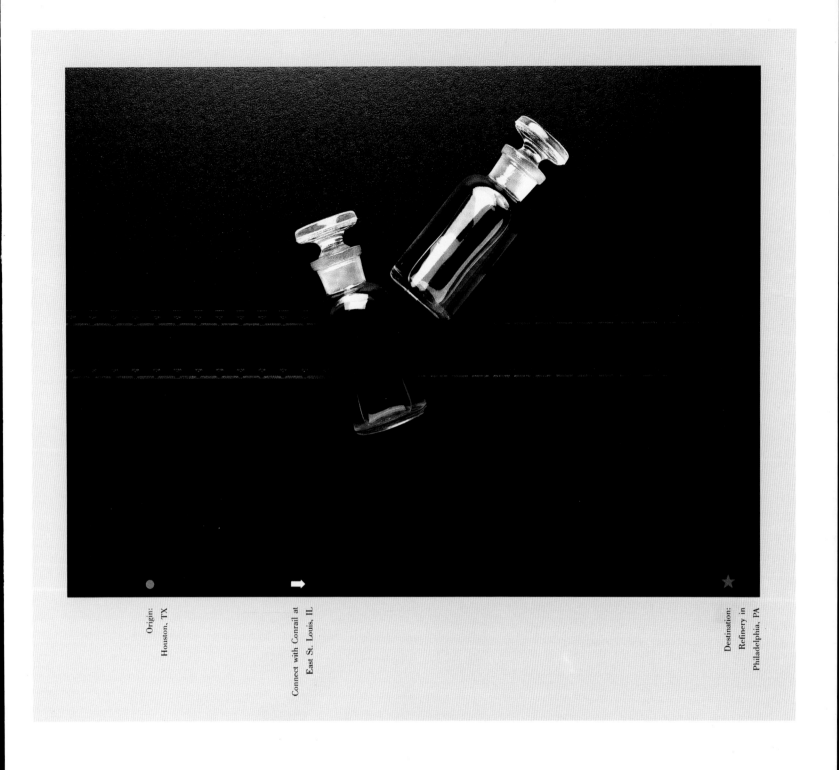

Origin:
Houston, TX

Connect with Conrail at
East St. Louis, IL

Destination:
Refinery in
Philadelphia, PA

■ 158, 159 Examples of diagrams from the 1986 annual report of the Consolidated Rail Corporation. This railway enterprise shows with photographic diagrams which freight is being carried and dispatched to its destinations and on which routes. Shown here are bakery wares and chemical products. (USA)

■ 158, 159 Beispiele der Darstellungen aus dem Jahresbericht 1986 der Consolidated Rail Corporation. Dieses Eisenbahnunternehmen zeigt anhand von photographischen Diagrammen, welche Güter sie auf welchen Strecken übernimmt und an ihren Bestimmungsort befördert, hier Gebäck und chemische Produkte. (USA)

■ 158, 159 Exemples de graphiques illustrant le rapport annuel de la Consolidated Rail Corporation pour 1986. Les diagrammes photo de cette entreprise ferroviaire montrent les catégories de fret qu'elle transporte et les destinations desservies. Ici, il s'agit de biscuits et de produits chimiques, symbolisés par les bouteilles. (USA)

DESIGNER:
BENNO WISSING/
JOHN STEGMEYER
ART DIRECTOR:
BENNO WISSING/
JOHN STEGMEYER
AGENCY:
THE WISSING
GENGLER GROUP, INC.
CLIENT:
THE CITY OF ROTTERDAM
■ 160

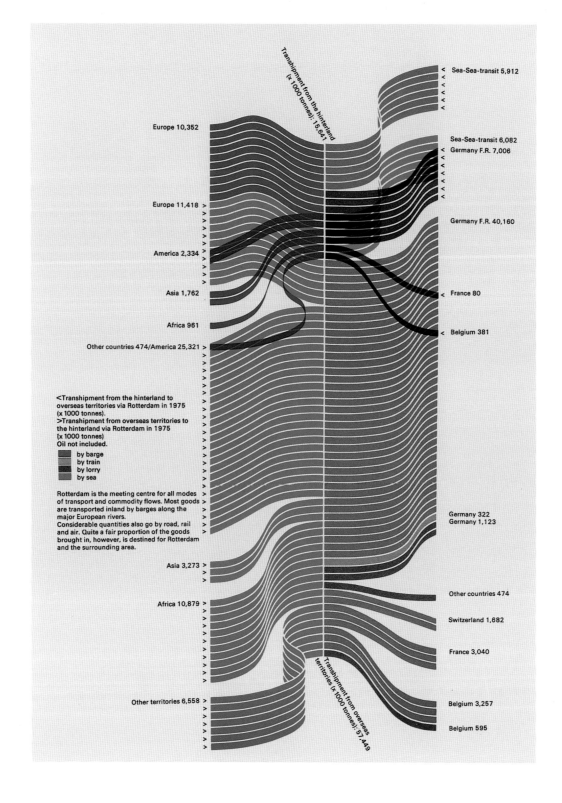

<Transhipment from the hinterland to overseas territories via Rotterdam in 1975 (x 1000 tonnes).
>Transhipment from overseas territories to the hinterland via Rotterdam in 1975 (x 1000 tonnes)
Oil not included.

■ by barge
■ by train
■ by lorry
■ by sea

Rotterdam is the meeting centre for all modes of transport and commodity flows. Most goods are transported inland by barges along the major European rivers. Considerable quantities also go by road, rail and air. Quite a fair proportion of the goods brought in, however, is destined for Rotterdam and the surrounding area.

Transhipment from the hinterland (x 1000 tonnes): 15,641
Transhipment from overseas territories (x 1000 tonnes): 57,449

Europe 10,352
Europe 11,418 >
America 2,334 >
Asia 1,762
Africa 961
Other countries 474/America 25,321 >
Asia 3,273 >
Africa 10,879 >
Other territories 6,558 >

Sea-Sea-transit 5,912
Sea-Sea-transit 6,082
Germany F.R. 7,006
Germany F.R. 40,160
France 80
Belgium 381
Germany 322
Germany 1,123
Other countries 474
Switzerland 1,682
France 3,040
Belgium 3,257
Belgium 595

■ 160 Diagram from a book presenting Rotterdam as a vital trans-shipment point for international freight traffic. The color coding relates to the way in which merchandise reaches Rotterdam – by barge, truck, train or ship. (NLD)

■ 160 Aus einem Buch über Rotterdam als Umschlagplatz für den internationalen Güterverkehr. Die Farbkodierung gibt an, ob die Waren per Frachtkahn, Lastwagen, Zug oder per Schiff nach Rotterdam gelangen. (NLD)

■ 160 Graphique illustrant un ouvrage sur le rôle de Rotterdam comme pivot des transports internationaux. Le code couleur se réfère aux moyens de transport utilisés: péniche, camion, train ou bateau. (NLD)

TECHNOLOGY

TECHNIK

TECHNIQUE

In the following chapter technical sequences of function, exploded and expanded diagrams, as well as cut-away drawings are presented. Common to each of them is the need to explain technical functions. The most frequent fields of assignment are assembly instructions; firms' publications; brochures for the training of staff and publications for sales purposes, or at least as an aid to decision making for professionals as well as the general public.

As in the other sections, the simplest forms of diagrams have purposely been omitted. Priority is given in this chapter to diagrams showing technical procedures that unfortunately in practice are all too often treated as second-class subjects and are generally found in large numbers to be less tastefully executed. Naturally the interpretation is dependent on the target reader and the purpose of use, but an unattractive graphic diagram will always miss the mark because it is simply disregarded.

The flow chart in Royal Zenith's brochure *(Figs. 161–165)* uses a printing process that shows, among other things, how an appealing result can be achieved by moderate means. Crucial to the aesthetics is also the positioning of a diagram on the page. For this reason full pages are also shown in this chapter, e.g. from the annual report of Automatix Inc. *(Figs. 166–168)*. How this form of diagram can be solved with the aid of a computer is shown by the transparent diagrams of a photocopying machine *(Figs. 177–179)*.

In the field of exploded and cut-away drawings the vital criterion is exact representation. This type of diagram affords the observer a view of the object that otherwise could not be seen.

The designer familiarizes himself with photographs – provided that the object to be drawn already exists – and with construction drawings. A good technical understanding and a lot of painstaking work is necessary, and yet in this section too, creative imagination is paramount. The choice of perspective makes a great difference in the end effect and statement. Added to which there are purely technical aspects to be considered. While for many exploded drawings the parallel perspective is chosen, a vanishing-point perspective offers the advantage of accommodating more details in the drawing. The diagram of a camera *(Fig. 184)* and a safety lock *(Fig. 201)* are examples of the vanishing-point perspective, which is, in comparison with the parallel perspective, much more difficult to produce.

In cut-away drawings the line technique allows the basic structure to be used as often as required – often called for in brochures using small overall views or partial views. The engine for the project "Rail 2000" *(Fig. 200)* is an example of this kind of diagram. The interior is done with a line/screen combination, while the exterior is done in a photographically realistic manner in airbrush technique. A combined technique with scratchboard too is evidently admirably suited to technical drawings, as the cut-away drawings of two automobiles *(Fig. 228)* prove.

Contrary to abstract and statistical diagrams, technical diagrams offer hardly any chance for manipulation. It is not only legitimate but also desirable that an aesthetically-appealing graphic catches the attention of the viewer. Even simple diagrams must never be boring, for they too can grip the viewer's attention, whether it be through coloration, the size of the diagrams, or the interplay with other illustrations. Even though the interest in this field may already exist (e.g. in operating instructions) this is no justification for unattractive graphics. Cut-away diagrams of automobiles, trains etc. easily attrack attention and frequently the creator of these, taking advantage of the (chiefly male) preference for them, offers them further as decorations in the form of posters. The amount of work and the care that is concealed in these graphics have more than earned their "extended lifespan".

Im folgenden Kapitel sind technische Funktionsabläufe, Explosions- und Phantomzeichnungen zusammengefasst. Ihnen allen gemeinsam ist das Thema Technik und die erklärende Funktion. Die häufigsten Einsatzgebiete sind Montageanleitungen, Gebrauchsanweisungen, Ersatzteillisten sowie auch Jahresberichte, Firmenpublikationen, Broschüren für die Personalschulung und Publikationen, die verkaufen sollen.

Wie auch in den anderen Sektoren wurde auf die einfachsten Formen dieser Diagramme bewusst verzichtet. An erster Stelle seien hier Diagramme technischer Funktionsabläufe erwähnt, die in der Praxis leider allzuoft stiefkindlich behandelt werden und entsprechend unsorgfältig und wenig geschmackvoll ausgeführt in grosser Anzahl zu finden sind. Natürlich hängt die Umsetzung vom Zielpublikum und dem Verwendungszweck ab, aber eine unattraktive Darstellung verfehlt ihren Zweck in jedem Fall, indem sie - wo immer möglich - nicht beachtet wird. Das im Prospekt von Royal Zenith *(Abb. 161-165)* verwendete Ablaufdiagramm eines Druckvorganges zeigt u.a., wie man mit sparsamen Mitteln ein ansprechendes Resultat erzielen kann. Für die ästhetische Darstellung ist selbstverständlich auch die Plazierung eines Diagramms auf einer Seite wichtig, deshalb sind in diesem Kapitel auch vollständige Seiten, z.B. aus dem Jahresbericht der Automatix Inc. *(Abb. 166-168)*, abgebildet. Wie diese Form der Darstellung mit Hilfe des Computers gelöst werden kann, zeigen die Transparentbilder eines Photokopierablaufes *(Abb. 177-179)*.

Im Bereich der Explosions- und Phantomzeichnungen geht es in erster Linie um eine exakte Darstellung und um die Herstellung einer Transparenz, die sich dem Betrachter beim Anblick des Objektes selbst nicht bietet. Der Designer orientiert sich an Photographien - sofern der Gegenstand der Darstellung bereits existiert - und an Konstruktionszeichnungen. Technisches Verständnis und sorgfältiges Arbeiten sind hier absolut erforderlich. Doch auch hier ist ein kreatives Mitwirken von

entscheidender Bedeutung. Zum Beispiel spielt die Wahl der Perspektive bei der Wirkung und Aussagekraft eine grosse Rolle. Während bei vielen Explosionszeichnungen die Parallelperspektive gewählt wird, bietet eine Fluchtpunktperspektive die Möglichkeit, mehr Einzelheiten in der Zeichnung unterzubringen. Beispiele für die im Vergleich zur Parallelperspektive sehr viel schwieriger herzustellende Fluchtpunktperspektive sind die Darstellungen einer Kamera *(Abb. 184)* und eines Sicherheitsschlosses *(Abb. 201)*.

Bei Phantomzeichnungen erlaubt die Darstellung des Grundgerüstes in Strichtechnik eine beliebig häufige Wiederverwendung. Die Lokomotive für das Projekt «Bahn 2000» *(Abb. 200)* ist ein Beispiel für diese Art der Darstellung: das Innere ist mit einer Strich/Rasterkombination dargestellt, während für das Äussere in photorealistischer Manier mit Spritztechnik gearbeitet wurde. Auch eine mit Schabkarton kombinierte Technik eignet sich hervorragend für technische Darstellungen, wie die Phantomzeichnungen von zwei Autos *(Abb. 228)* beweisen.

Anders als bei den abstrakten, statistischen Diagrammen, bietet das technische Diagramm kaum eine Möglichkeit zur Manipulation. Es ist nicht nur legitim, sondern wünschenswert, dass eine ästhetisch ansprechende Darstellung die Aufmerksamkeit des Betrachters auf sich zieht. Auch einfache Darstellungen müssen nicht langweilig wirken, sondern können den Betrachter durchaus in ihren Bann ziehen. Auch wenn das Interesse auf diesem Gebiet zwangsläufig vorhanden ist (z.B. bei Bedienungsvorschriften), ist dies keine Rechtfertigung für unattraktive Darstellungen. Besonders leicht haben es in dieser Hinsicht die Phantomdarstellungen von Autos, Bahnen usw., und häufig machen sich die Hersteller diese Vorliebe des vor allem männlichen Zielpublikums zunutze, indem sie die Zeichnungen auch als Plakate anbieten. Der Arbeitsaufwand und die Sorgfalt, die hinter diesen Darstellungen stecken, haben dieses «verlängerte Leben» mehr als verdient.

Le chapitre qui suit regroupe des représentations fonctionnelles séquentielles, des éclatés et des dessins fantômes relatifs au domaine technique, que ces graphiques entreprennent d'expliciter. Les secteurs d'application les plus fréquents sont les instructions de montage, les notices d'utilisation, les catalogues de pièces de rechange, mais aussi les rapports annuels, les publications d'entreprises, les brochures pour la formation du personnel, ainsi que les imprimés destinés à la force de vente ou censés faciliter la prise de décision lors des achats.

Tout comme pour les autres chapitres, nous avons délibérément renoncé à représenter les formes les plus simples de ce genre de diagrammes. Mentionnons en premier lieu les graphiques relatifs aux fonctions techniques séquentielles. Trop souvent traitées en parents pauvres dans la pratique, ces représentations abondent dans des versions hâtives et peu esthétiques. S'il est évident que la transposition de données techniques en images est tributaire du public-cible et du but poursuivi, ce but ne sera guère atteint si le graphique en question manque totalement d'attrait et ne retient donc pas l'attention du lecteur. Le diagramme séquentiel d'un processus d'impression utilisé dans le prospectus de Royal Zenith *(fig. 161-165)* démontre entre autres comment des résultats appréciables peuvent être obtenus avec des moyens limités. La position du diagramme sur la page contribue évidemment aussi à sa perception esthétique. C'est la raison pour laquelle nous reproduisons également des pages complètes, ainsi celles tirées d'un rapport annuel de l'Automatix Inc. *(fig. 166-168)*. Les diagrammes transparents analysant le processus de la photocopie *(fig. 177-179)* ont été réalisés avec l'assistance de l'ordinateur, ce qui montre l'apport de la CAO à la solution du problème de la représentation imagée technique.

Dans le domaine des éclatés et des dessins fantômes, l'accent est naturellement mis avant tout sur la précision rigoureuse du dessin et sur l'obtention d'une transparence qui n'est pas inhérente à l'objet, donc sur un acte de visibilisation. Le designer consulte des photos (pour autant que l'objet à représenter existe déjà), des plans de construction. Il y faut de réelles capacités techniques et une grande minutie. Pourtant, dans ce domaine également, la réalisation du diagramme ne va pas sans un

effort de créativité. C'est ainsi que le choix de la perspective influe grandement sur l'impact et la puissance expressive de l'éclaté. Il s'y ajoute des considérations purement techniques: alors que beaucoup d'éclatés observent la perspective en vue de face, la perspective cavalière permet d'introduire un plus grand nombre de détails dans le dessin. La perspective cavalière est plus difficile à établir que la vue de face; on en jugera par la représentation d'un appareil photo *(fig. 184)* et d'une serrure de sûreté *(fig. 201)*.

Dans le cas des dessins fantômes, la représentation de la structure fondamentale au trait autorise le réutilisation sans fin du dessin, comme c'est souvent nécessaire dans les prospectus exigeant des vues totales réduites et des vues partielles. La locomotive pour le projet «Rail 2000» *(fig. 200)* exemplifie ce genre de représentation: l'intérieur y figure dans une combinaison de traits et de trame, tandis que l'extérieur prend l'aspect réaliste d'une photo avec recours à l'aérographe. Même une technique mixte faisant appel à la manière noire s'avère parfaitement adaptée aux représentations techniques; on s'en rend compte en prenant connaissance de deux dessins fantômes d'automobiles *(fig. 228)*.

Autrement que pour ce qui est des diagrammes statistiques abstraits, le diagramme technique n'offre guère de prise à la manipulation. Il n'est pas seulement légitime, mais souhaitable qu'une représentation parée d'un certain attrait esthétique capte l'attention du lecteur. Même des graphiques simples ne doivent pas forcément respirer l'ennui, mais peuvent fort bien captiver le lecteur par leurs couleurs, leurs dimensions ou leur intégration dans un ensemble illustratif. Même en escomptant de la part de l'utilisateur un intérêt soutenu, par exemple dans les notices d'utilisation, il ne convient pas de renoncer à l'attrait du dessin. Les dessins fantômes sont à cet égard une mine de trouvailles esthétiques lorsqu'ils mettent en scène des autos, des trains, etc. Les fabricants exploitent du reste fréquemment la faveur dont ces dessins jouissent notamment auprès du public-cible masculin en les offrant également sous forme de décorations, voire d'affiches. La somme de travail et la minutie investies dans ces diagrammes justifient largement leur prolongation de vie.

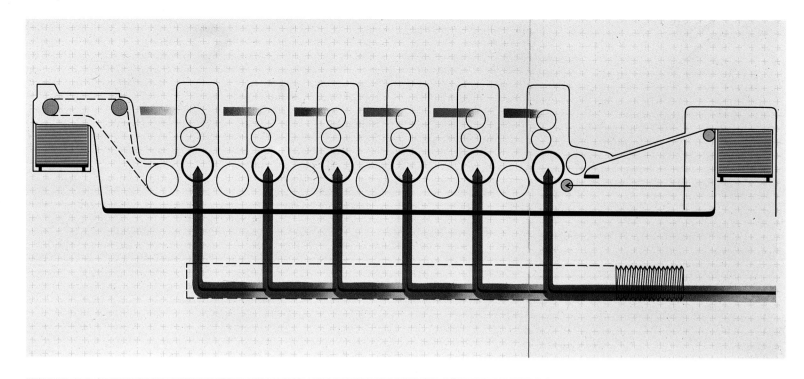

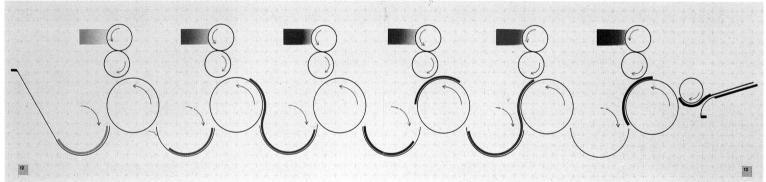

DESIGNER:
LOU FIORENTINO
ART DIRECTOR:
LOU FIORENTINO
AGENCY:
FIORENTINO LEIBE ASSOCIATES
CLIENT:
ROYAL ZENITH CORPORATION
■ 161–163

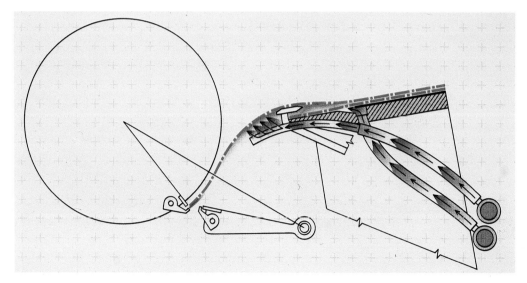

■ 161–165 Diagrams showing methods of paper transportation, from brochures for two printing presses of Royal Zenith Corporation. *161, 162* show the differential drive system with double-size cylinders, grippers, and *(163)* the air-controlled feeding. *164, 165* are full pages showing the pneumatic sheet guidance system and two-sided printing, *165* shows a photo and diagram of the controlled, consistent inking. (USA)

■ 161–165 Ablaufdiagramme zur Verdeutlichung des Papiertransports mit doppeltgrossen Transportwalzen *(161, 162)* und der Funktion der mit Luftsog arbeitenden Papierzufuhr *(163)*. *164* und *165* zeigen vollständige Seiten mit einem Ablaufdiagramm der mit einem pneumatischen System arbeitenden Papierführung bei beidseitigem Druck *(164)* und Aufnahme und Diagramm der Druckfarbenverteilung *(165)*. Aus Prospekten für zwei Druckpressen. (USA)

■ 161–165 Organigrammes montrant le transport du papier par doubles cylindres d'alimentation *(161, 162)* et le fonctionnement du système d'introduction du papier par appel d'air *(163)*. *164, 165:* Pages complètes avec l'organigramme de l'alimentation pneumatique en papier en cas d'impression recto-verso *(164)*, la photo et le diagramme de la répartition des encres *(165)*. Prospectus relatifs à deux presses de Royal Zenith Corp. (USA)

DESIGNER:
STANSILAW FERNANDES
ART DIRECTOR:
LOU FIORENTINO
AGENCY:
FIORENTINO LEIBE ASSOCIATES
CLIENT:
ROYAL ZENITH CORPORATION
■ 164, 165

Fast, one-side printing to perfecting

Controlled, consistent inking

The Royal Zenith 40″ Planeta can be converted to perfecting...in just a matter of minutes. The conversion requires no extra space or changes in press output and drive power.

Quality, two-sided printing. The unique pneumatic sheet guidance system of the 40″ Planeta provides high-quality, two-sided printing. In addition, at the beginning of the procedure, a sheet is seized entirely flat at its rear edge directly from the printing cylinder—to further assure the consistency and quality of the press run.

The Royal Zenith 40″ Planeta's sheet perfecting sequence:

1. The tail of the sheet is seized by the suction system.

2. The sheet is held in place as the suction and gripper systems swing into place.

3. The sheet is transferred from the suction system to the gripper system.

4. The sheet is guided by the gripper system.

5. The rear edge of the sheet is held by the gripper edge for the following printing cylinder.

One of the main advantages of the Royal Zenith 40″ Planeta Super Variant is its ability to quickly reach and maintain optimum ink feeding. In just a few sheets, this press can achieve an even ink flow across the entire cylinder. It produces consistent, high-quality work throughout any length press run.

Precise inking. The Royal Zenith 40″ Planeta's inking unit has four form rollers—each a different diameter to minimize ghosting and to distribute the ink. Four vibrator rollers spread the ink film with a smooth and even motion.

In addition, ink form vibrator rollers are coated with a special wear-resistant substance to improve ink accep-

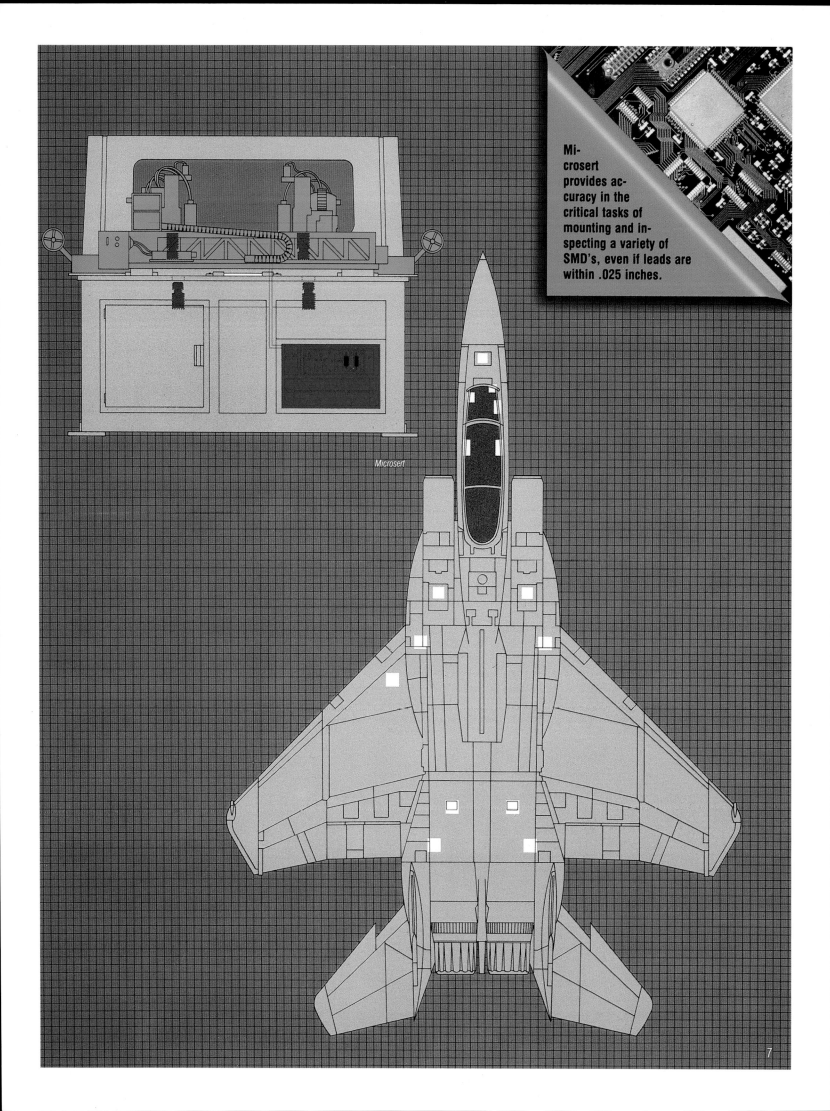

Microsert

Mi-
crosert
provides ac-
curacy in the
critical tasks of
mounting and in-
specting a variety of
SMD's, even if leads are
within .025 inches.

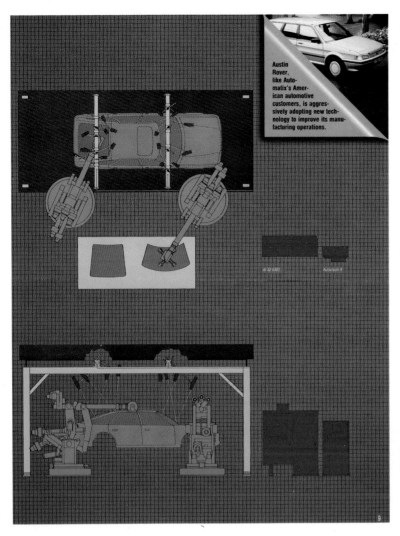

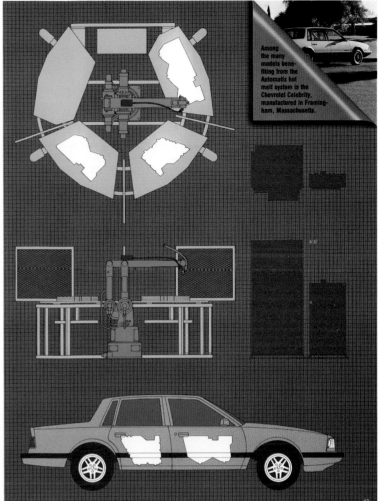

DESIGNER:
MICHAEL BENES
ARTIST:
DAVE HANNUM
ART DIRECTOR:
MICHAEL BENES
AGENCY:
MICHAEL BENES
COMMUNICATIONS
CLIENT:
AUTOMATIX INC.
■ 166–168

■ 166–168 Technical diagrams from the 1985 annual report of Automatix Incorporated, producers of remote control and vision-guided surface robots, used for assembly and inspection in many branches of industry, including the aerospace and automobile industries. (USA)

■ 166–168 Technische Diagramme aus dem Jahresbericht 1985 der Automatix Inc.: Roboterherstellung und -kontrolle elektronischer Anlagen, wie sie z.B. in Flugzeugen verwendet werden und um die Roboterherstellung von Windschutzscheiben und Türpolsterungen für Autos. (USA)

■ 166–168 Diagrammes techniques du rapport annuel 1985 d'Automatix Inc. Il s'agit de la production de robots et de systèmes robotisés de contrôle de fabrications pour l'industrie automobile par exemple, avec l'assemblage précis des pare-brise et du capitonnage des portières. (USA)

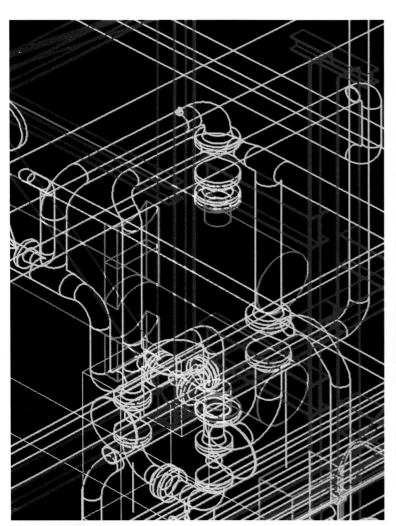
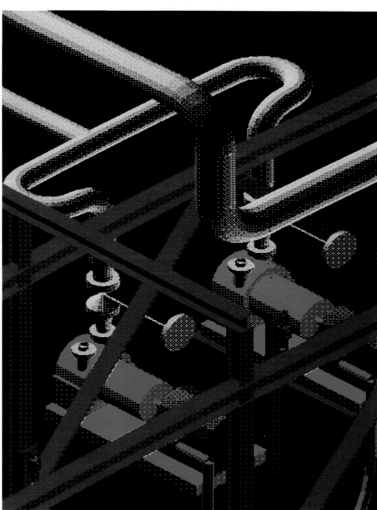

DESIGNER:
C. CLAUDIA JEFFERIES
ARTIST:
STEVE ALLEN
ART DIRECTOR:
RON JEFFERIES
AGENCY:
THE JEFFERIES ASSOCIATION
CLIENT:
FLUOR CORPORATION
■ 169–171

■ 169–171 Excerpts from technical cut-away drawings produced with the aid of a computer, and variations of the
firm's symbol. From an annual report for Fluor Corp. (USA)

■ 172, 173 Full-page illustrations from the annual report for
National Semiconductor: a chip and a 25 enlargement of a
microprocessor. (USA)

■ 169–171 Ausschnitte aus Phantomzeichnungen, die mit
Hilfe des Computers hergestellt wurden, und Varianten des
Firmensymbols. Jahresbericht der Fluor Corp. (USA)

■ 172, 173 Ganzseitige Abbildungen aus dem Jahresbericht
von National Semiconductor: ein Chip und eine 25fache
Vergrösserung eines Mikroprozessors. (USA)

■ 169–171 Détails de dessins techniques fantômes réalisés en
CAO et variations sur le dessin de l'emblème de la société.
Rapport annuel de la Fluor Corporation. (USA)

■ 172, 173 Illustrations pleine page pour un rapport annuel
de National Semiconductor: puce et agrandissement d'un
microprocesseur (25 x l'original). (USA)

DESIGNER:
RIK BESSER
ART DIRECTOR:
ROBERT MILES RUNYAN
AGENCY:
ROBERT MILES RUNYAN & ASSOC.
CLIENT:
*NATIONAL SEMICONDUCTOR
CORPORATION*
■ 172, 173

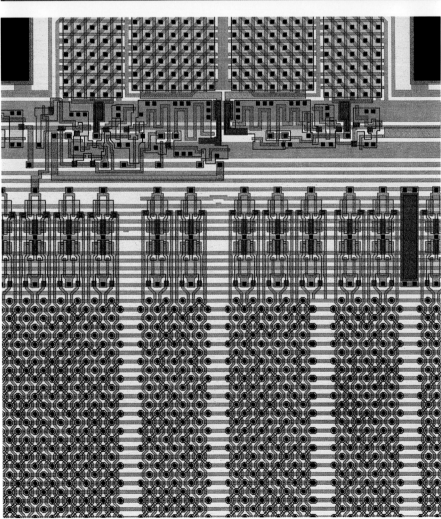

■ 174, 175 Technical diagrams showing a system for useful energy through clean combustion of coal *(174)* and of a safety relief valve *(175)*. Taken from the 1980 annual report of the Curtiss Wright Corporation, entitled "Technical Perspectives". (USA)

■ 176 Diagram of the jet engine of a civil aircraft from a brochure for *Wyman-Gordon* who supply forgings for critical jet engine components e.g. compressor, turbine, fan disks, and welded rings. (USA)

■ 174, 175 Technische Diagramme zur Erläuterung eines Systems für die Energiegewinnung durch saubere Kohleverbrennung *(174)* und eines Sicherheitsventils *(175)*. Darstellungen aus dem Jahresbericht 1980 der Curtiss Wright Corporation. (USA)

■ 176 Darstellung des Düsentriebwerkes eines Verkehrsflugzeugs zur Verdeutlichung des Einsatzes der von *Wyman-Gordon* produzierten Maschinenteile. Aus einer Firmenbroschüre des Unternehmens. (USA)

■ 174, 175 Diagrammes techniques expliquant un système de production d'énergie au moyen de la combustion sans déchets du charbon *(174)* et d'une soupage de sécurité *(175)*. Graphiques tirés du rapport annuel 1980 de la Curtiss Wright Corp. (USA)

■ 176 Graphique représentant le réacteur d'un avion commercial afin de mettre en évidence le rôle des éléments de machine *Wyman-Gordon* dans la construction aéronautique. Brochure commerciale de l'entreprise. (USA)

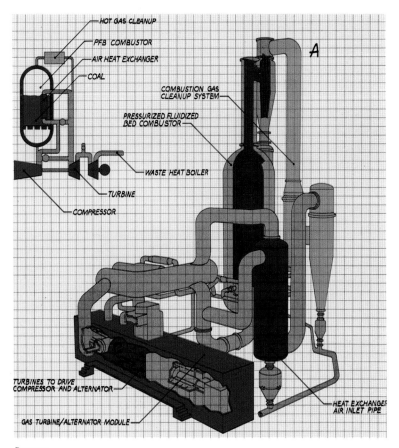

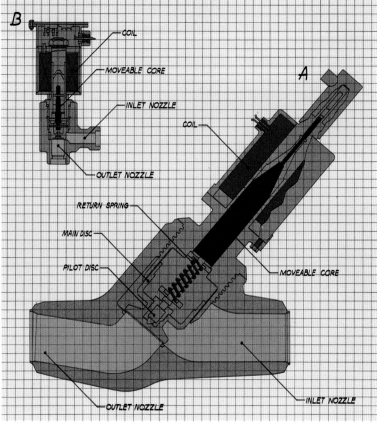

DESIGNER:
CLINT MORGAN
ARTIST:
BOB BILEK
ART DIRECTOR:
JOHN WATERS
AGENCY:
JOHN WATERS ASSOCIATES
CLIENT:
CURTISS-WRIGHT CORP.
■ 174-175

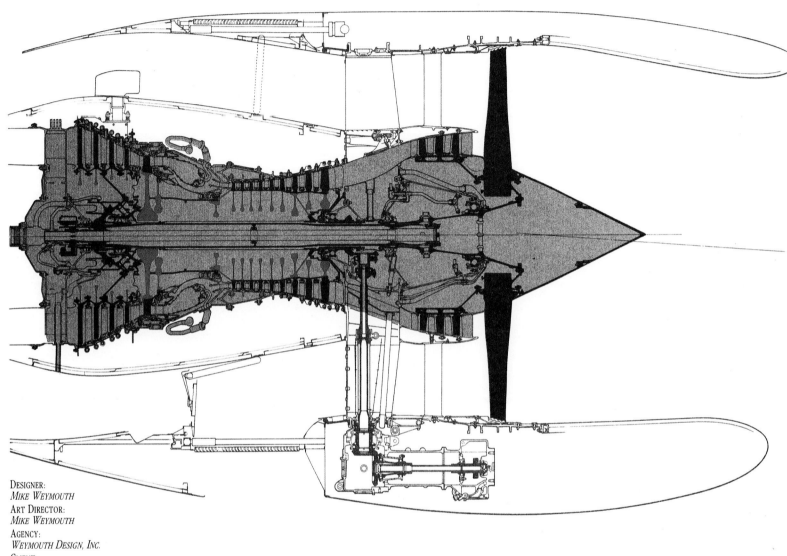

DESIGNER:
MIKE WEYMOUTH
ART DIRECTOR:
MIKE WEYMOUTH
AGENCY:
WEYMOUTH DESIGN, INC.
CLIENT:
WYMAN-GORDON COMPANY
■ 176

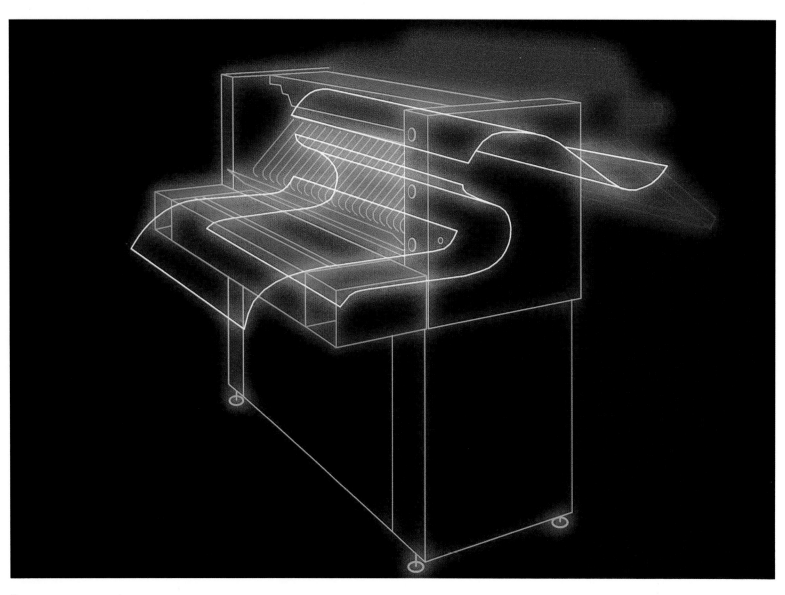

DESIGNER:
Klaas Wertenbroek
ART DIRECTOR:
Klaas Wertenbroek
CLIENT:
R. Sauter AG
■ 177–179

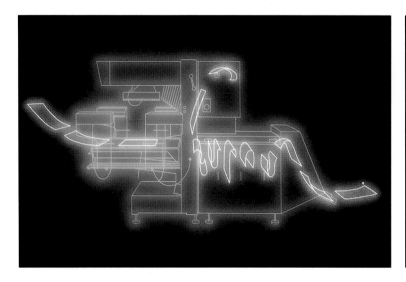

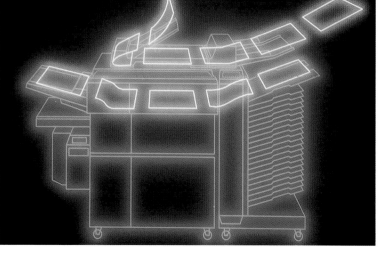

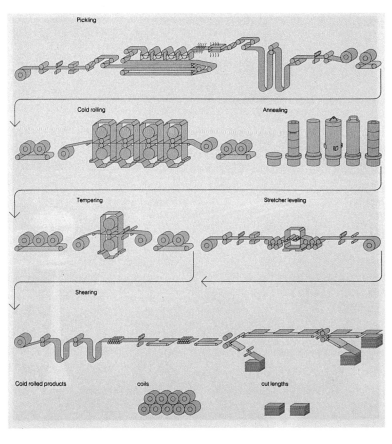

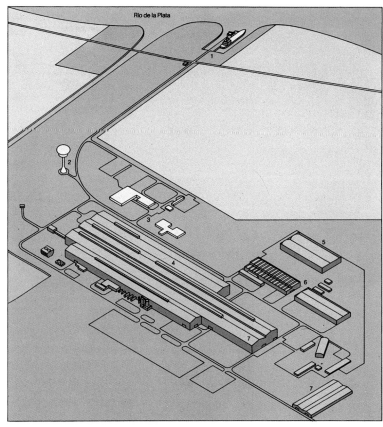

DESIGNER:
RUBEN FONTANA
ART DIRECTOR:
RUBEN FONTANA
CLIENT:
PROPULSORA SIDERURGICA
■ 180, 181

■ 177–179 Computer-aided transparent pictures of the photo-copying procedure in various copier machines. (SWI)

■ 180, 181 Illustrations showing production procedure in the manufacture of rolled sheet steel, and a plan of the works of Propulsora Siderurgica. (ARG)

■ 177–179 Mit Hilfe des Computers hergestellte Transparentbilder des Photokopierablaufs in verschiedenen Geräten. (SWI)

■ 180, 181 Darstellung des Produktionsablaufes in der Herstellung von Walzstahl und der Plan der Industrieanlage von Propulsora Siderurgica. (ARG)

■ 177–179 Vues transparentes du processus séquentiel de photocopie réalisées par ordinateur. (SWI)

■ 180, 181 Organigramme de la production d'acier laminé et plan du laminoir industriel correspondant de la Propulsora Siderurgica. (ARG)

■ 182-187 Technical illustrations of the *Polaroid Spectra/ Image* system, from the 1985 annual report of *Polaroid. 182* shows a section of the electronics and *184* the 21-part detector camera. *183* is a diagram of a production line with seven robots engaged on the Spectra (Image) system. *185-187* show the camera, here closed, opened and as cutaway, to elucidate on the lighting system and the aperture. (USA)

■ 182-187 Technische Darstellungen des *Polaroid-Image*-Systems, aus dem Jahresbericht 1985 von *Polaroid. 182* zeigt einen Teil der Elektronik und *184* die aus 21 Teilen bestehende Sucherkamera. *183* ist eine Darstellung einer mit sieben Robotern arbeitenden Produktionslinie für die *Image*-Kamera. *185-187* sind Darstellungen der Kamera, hier geschlossen, geöffnet und aufgeschnitten gezeigt, zur Erläuterung des Belichtungssystems und der Blende. (USA)

■ 182-187 Diagrammes techniques relatifs au système *Pola-roïd Image,* dans le rapport annuel de *Polaroïd* pour 1985. *182:* Vue partielle de l'électronique, *184:* le viseur composé de 21 éléments. *183:* Chaîne de production du système *Image* équipée de sept robots. *185–187:* Vues de l'appareil fermé, ouvert et éclaté, ce qui permet de comprendre les raffinements du système optique et de sa lentille frontale asphérique. (USA)

DESIGNER:
MICHAEL BENES
ARTIST:
DAVE HANNUM
ART DIRECTOR:
MICHAEL BENES
AGENCY:
POLAROID IN HOUSE
CLIENT:
POLAROID CORPORATION
■ 182-187

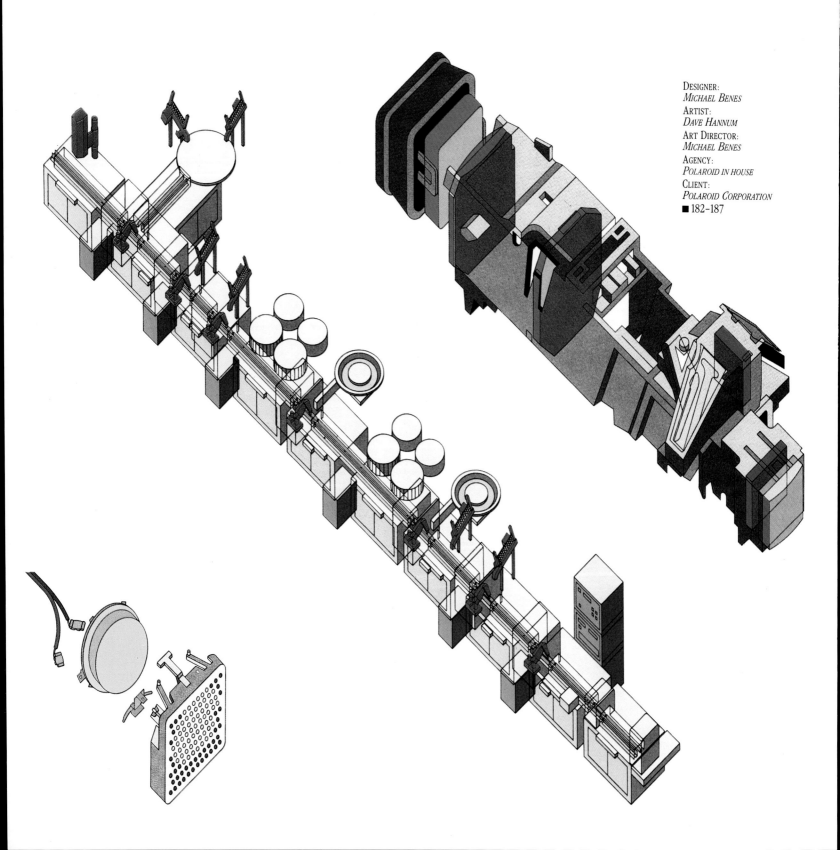

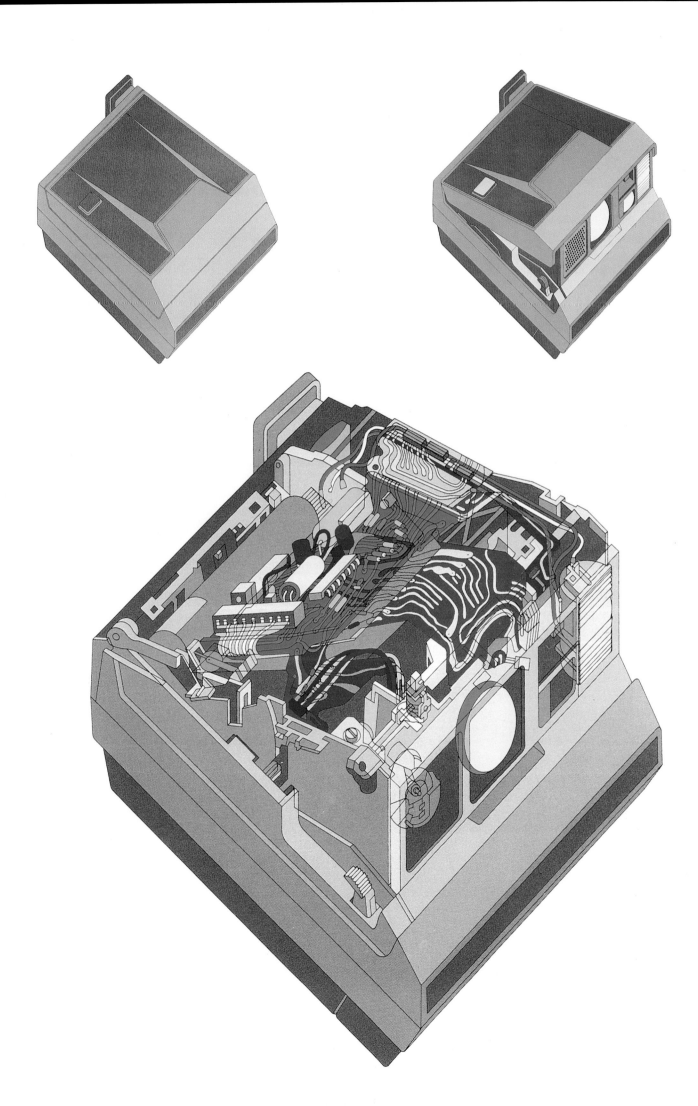

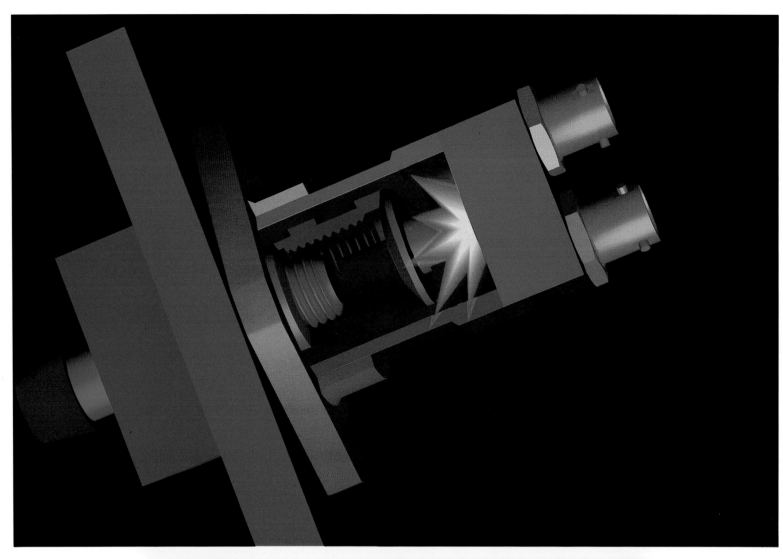

DESIGNER:
TOM CROFT/STEPHEN FERRARI

ARTIST:
RON SCOTT

ART DIRECTOR:
STEPHEN FERRARI

AGENCY:
THE GRAPHIC EXPRESSION, INC.

CLIENT:
HI-SHEAR INDUSTRIES, INC.

■ 188–192

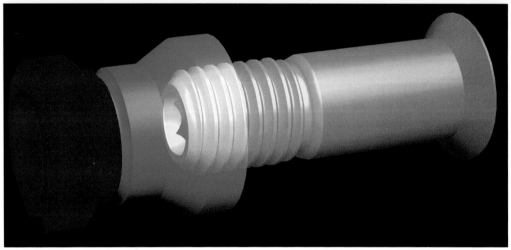

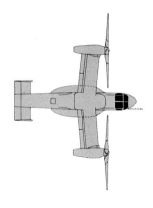

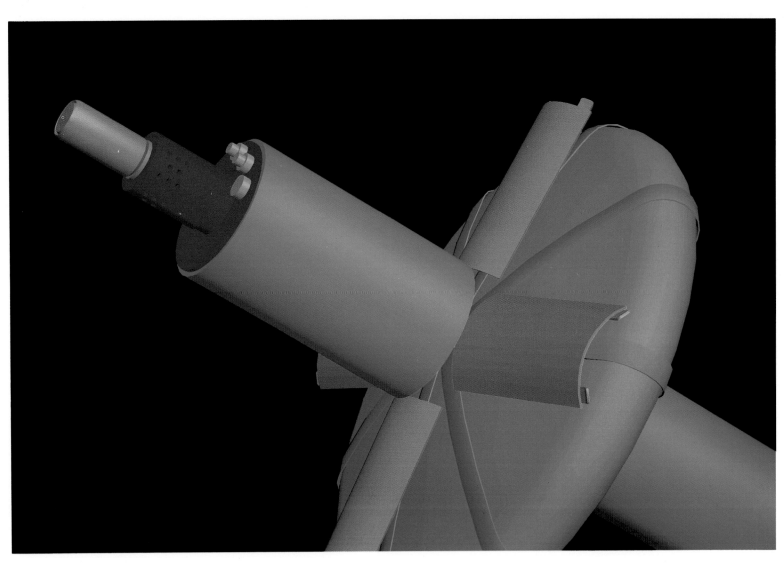

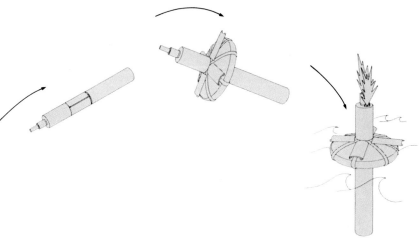

■ 188-192 From the annual report of the Hi-Shear Industries, producers of high-tech products for aircraft and space defense e.g. aerospace fastening systems. Shown are blind bolts, a weight-saving shortened threaded pin *(188, 189)* and a "torch" - an infrared decoy used in the defense of naval surface vessels *(191, 192)*. (USA)

■ 188-192 Illustrationen aus einem Jahresbericht der Hi-Shear-Industries, Hersteller von hochtechnisierten Produkten für die Raum-/Luftfahrt und Verteidigung. Hier spezielle Bolzen und Schrauben für den Flugzeugbau *(188, 189)* und ein «Fackel»-Köder, der auf Wärme ausgerichtete Raketen von Kriegsschiffen ablenken soll *(191, 192)*. (USA)

■ 188-192 Illustrations d'un rapport annuel de Hi-Shear Industries, fournisseur de technologie de pointe pour l'aéro- et l'astronautique et les forces armées: boulons et vis pour la construction aéronautique *(188, 189);* leurre en torche, mesure contre-électronique visant à protéger les bâtiments de guerre contre les missiles thermoguidés *(191, 192)*. (USA)

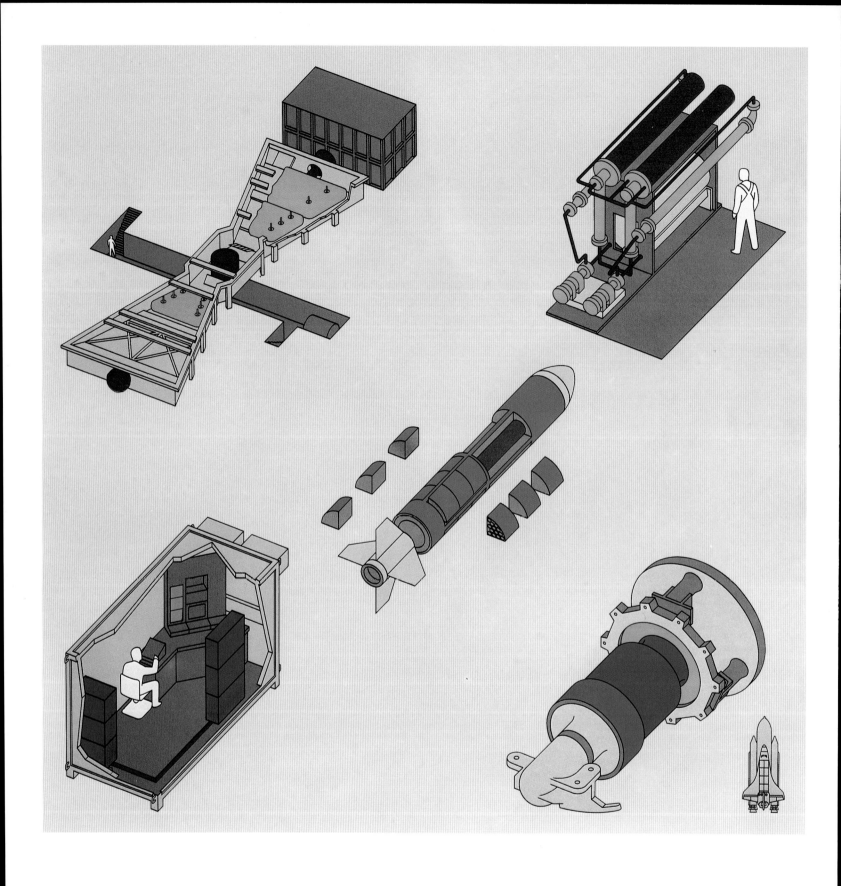

■ 193-197 Explanatory illustrations from the 1984 annual report of Rockcor Inc., a company dealing in highly developed technology for interplanetary space, defense, energy etc. Shown is a radiation simulator, the prototype of a chemical heat pump, an airbag dispersing submunitions (from carrier missiles), a portable telephone exchange and a gas generator for booster nozzles on the Space Shuttle. (USA)

■ 198 From Tylan Corp.'s 1983 annual report. Used in the semiconductor industry, it is a mass flow controller, with gas fittings, flow sensor, valve, and electronics. (USA)

■ 193-197 Aus dem Jahresbericht 1985 der Rockcor Inc., einer Firma, die sich mit hochentwickelter Technologie für Raumfahrt, Verteidigung, Energie etc. befasst. Hier ein Simulator für radioaktive Strahlung, der Prototyp einer chemischen Wärmepumpe, eine Rakete mit Luftsackauslöser für den Sprengstoff, eine bewegliche Telephonstation für das Militär und ein Zusatztriebwerk für die Raumfahrt. (USA)

■ 198 Darstellung eines Kontrollgeräts, das in der Herstellung von Halbleitern verwendet wird. Aus dem Jahresbericht 1983 der Tylan Corporation. (USA)

■ 193-197 Du rapport annuel 1984 de Rockcor Inc., société spécialisée dans la technologie de pointe pour l'astronautique, les forces armées, la production d'énergie, etc. On voit ici un simulateur de radiations, le prototype d'une pompe à chaleur, un missile à airbag disséminant les munitions embarquées, une station téléphonique mobile militaire, un réacteur auxiliaire de fusée spatiale. (USA)

■ 198 Représentation d'un appareil de contrôle utilisé dans la fabrication de semi-conducteurs. Extrait du rapport annuel de la Tylan Corporation pour 1983. (USA)

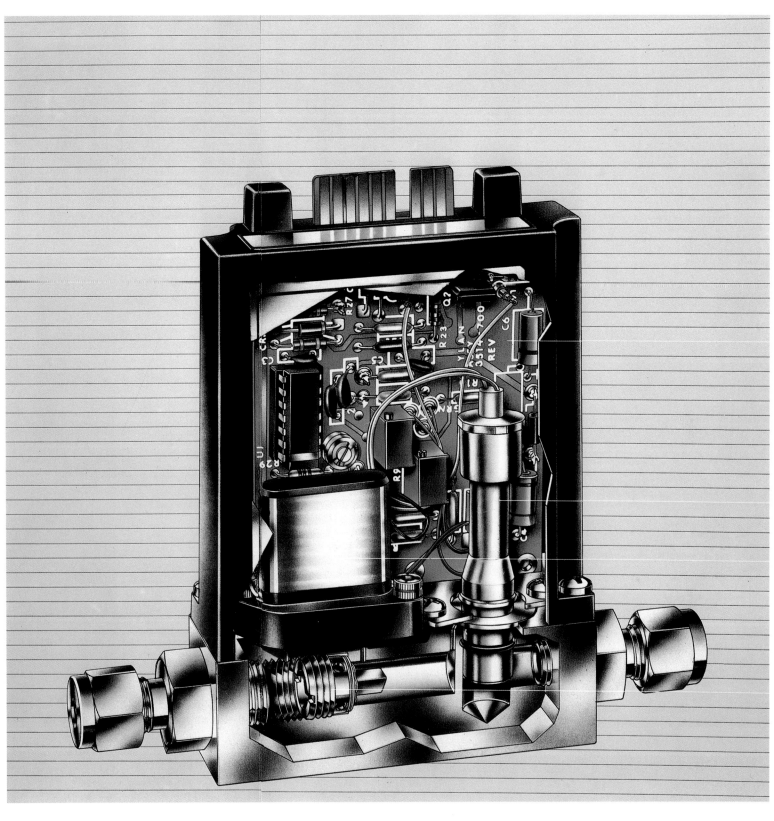

DESIGNER:
JOHN VAN DYKE
ARTIST:
LARRY JOST
ART DIRECTOR:
JOHN VAN DYKE
AGENCY:
VAN DYKE COMPANY
CLIENT:
ROCKCOR, INC.
◀■ 193–197

DESIGNER:
DOUG JOSEPH
ARTIST:
DAVID KIMBLE
ART DIRECTOR:
DOUG JOSEPH
AGENCY:
BESSER JOSEPH PARTNERS
CLIENT:
TYLAN CORPORATION
■ 198

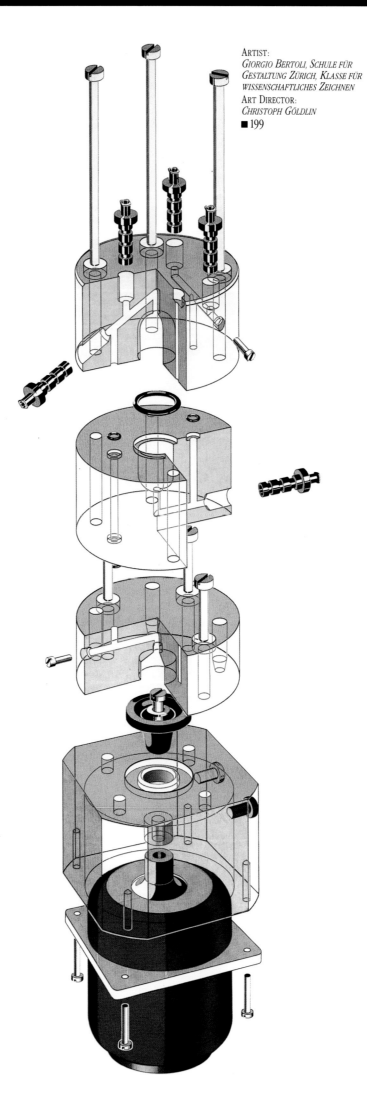

ARTIST:
*GIORGIO BERTOLI, SCHULE FÜR
GESTALTUNG ZÜRICH, KLASSE FÜR
WISSENSCHAFTLICHES ZEICHNEN*
ART DIRECTOR:
CHRISTOPH GÖLDLIN
■ 199

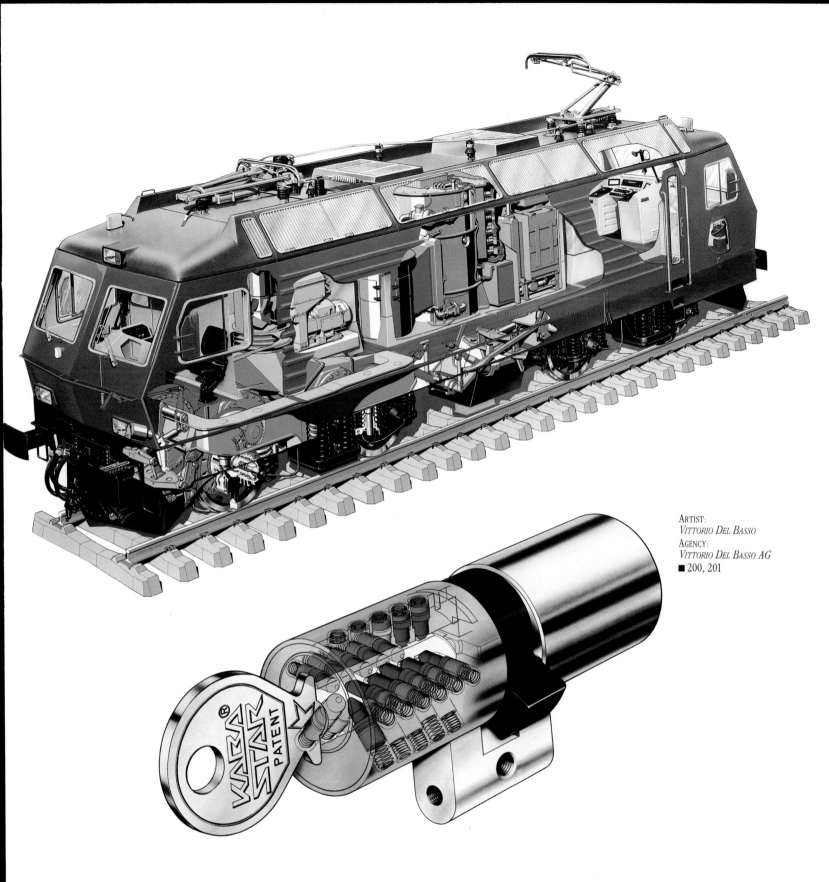

ARTIST:
VITTORIO DEL BASSO
AGENCY:
VITTORIO DEL BASSO AG
■ 200, 201

■ 199 Exploded drawing (pen, rapidograph, and rub-on transfer) of a hydraulic pressure-gauge system based on the Wiederhielm method. (SWI)

■ 200 Cut-away drawing of the electric engine Re 4/4 IV for the "Rail 2000" project being undertaken by the Swiss Federal Railways. (Airbrush and line technique.) (SWI)

■ 201 Exploded drawing of a safety lock with key, in airbrush and line technique. For *Kaba*. (SWI)

■ 199 Explosionszeichnung (Reissfeder, Rapidograph, Haftdruckfolien) einer Hydraulik zum Druckmess-System nach Wiederhielm. (SWI)

■ 200 Phantomzeichnung der elektrischen Lokomotive Re 4/4 IV für das Projekt Bahn 2000 der Schweiz. Bundesbahnen. Es wurde mit Airbrush und Strich gearbeitet. (SWI)

■ 201 Explosionsdiagramm eines Sicherheitsschlosses mit Schlüssel in Airbrush- und Strich-Technik. Für *Kaba*. (SWI)

■ 199 Eclaté (tire-ligne, rapidographe, feuils adhésifs) du système hydraulique d'un manomètre d'après le système Wiederhielm. (SWI)

■ 200 Dessin fantôme de la locomotive électrique Re 4/4 IV pour le projet Rail 2000 des Chemins de Fer Fédéraux Suisses, réalisé à l'aérographe et au trait. (SWI)

■ 201 Eclaté d'une serrure de sûreté et de sa clé. Technique à l'aérographe et au trait. Pour *Kaba*. (SWI)

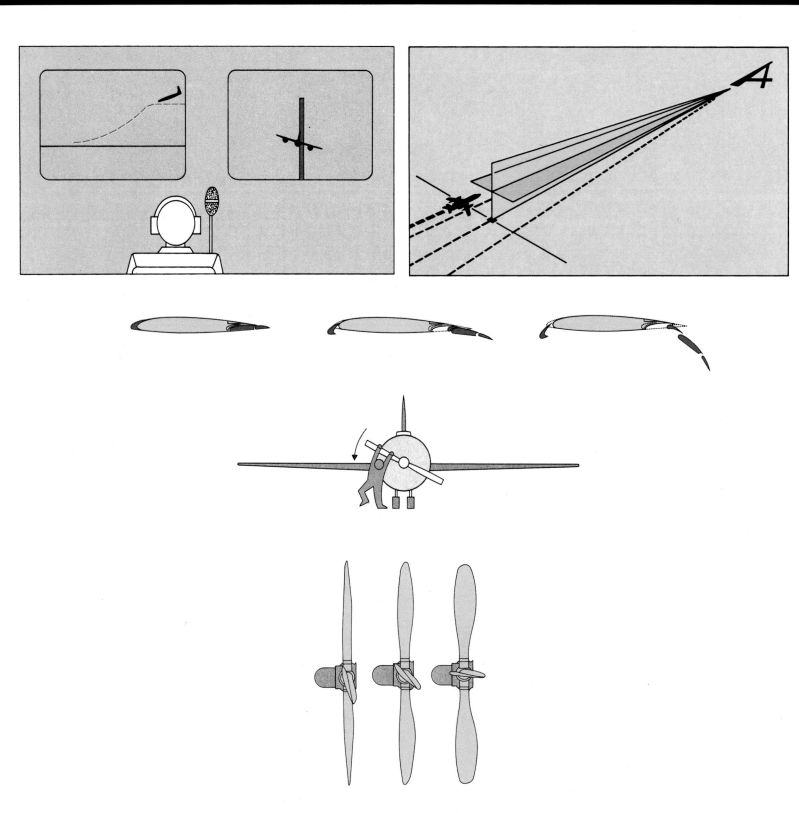

■ 202-211 The history and development of the airplane is the subject of these elementary diagrams from an annual report for Charles Stark Draper Laboratories, one of the scientific institutions employed by the government. It deals above all in monitoring, control and navigational instruments. Shown is the ground control approach during a blind landing; the instrument landing system in bad visibility; the function of the wing flaps; self-starting propellers; propeller types. On the right page: two versions of gas turbines; a combination of both (used today in most of the large jet-engined commercial planes), as well as a modified version for military planes and a lightweight power source for high speed aerial vehicles such as drones or missiles. (USA)

■ 202-211 Geschichte und Entwicklung des Flugzeuges sind Gegenstand dieser elementaren Darstellungen aus einem Jahresbericht der Charles Stark Draper Laboratories, eines für die Regierung tätigen wissenschaftlichen Instituts, in dessen Bereich vor allem Leit-, Kontroll- und Navigationsgeräte fallen. Hier die Bodenkontrolle bei Blindlandung; die Instrumentenlandung bei schlechter Sicht; die Funktion von Flügelklappen; manuelle Betätigung des Propellers; Propellertypen. Auf der rechten Seite: Zwei Versionen von Gasturbinen; eine Kombination aus beiden (der heute in den meisten grossen Transportflugzeugen verwendete Düsenantrieb) sowie eine abgeänderte Version für Militärmaschinen und ein leichtgewichtiges Antriebssystem für Hochgeschwindigkeitsobjekte. (USA)

■ 202-211 L'histoire et le développement de l'aviation sont interprétés sous cette forme élémentaire dans un rapport annuel des Charles Stark Draper Laboratories, un institut de recherche scientifique au service du gouvernement et qui s'occupe surtout de dispositifs de guidage, de contrôle et de navigation. On voit ici le contrôle au sol en cas d'atterrissage sans visibilité; l'atterrissage aux instruments à visibilité réduite; la fonction des volets d'ailes; le maniement manuel de l'hélice; les types d'hélices. Page de droite: deux versions de turbines à gaz; une combinaison des deux types dans la propulsion à réaction de la plupart des grands avions-cargos; une version légèrement modifiée pour appareils militaires; et un système de propulsion pour avions et fusées téléguidés. (USA)

DESIGNER:
ROBERT L. STEINLE
ART DIRECTOR:
ROBERT L. STEINLE
AGENCY:
ADVERTISING DESIGNERS, INC.
CLIENT:
THE CHARLES STARK DRAPER
LABORATORY, INC.
■ 202–211

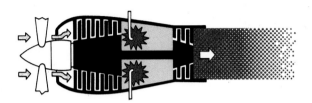

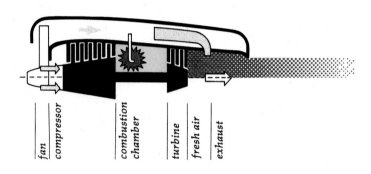

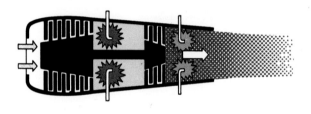

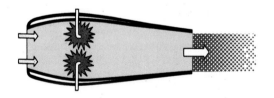

■ 212 Part of the surge barrier at the Oosterschelde, Holland. To prevent seabed erosion sand-and-gravel mattresses were laid. On these stand the 18 000 metric ton piers and a traffice beam with hydraulic and electronic equipment to operate the gates. To withstand the enormous lateral force the superstructure was buttressed with mountains of rock. From an article in *National Geographic.* (USA)

■ 213-215 Examples of diagrams used to illustrate various product sectors, from the 1984 annual report of *Fluorocarbon*. Shown: for the Fluid Sealing Group (aerospace), for the Plastics Group (forming, molding and fabricating engineered resins) and for the Rubber Group (oil field and valve markets etc). (USA)

■ 212 Teil eines aus Dämmen, Deichen und Kanälen bestehenden Projekts zum Schutz des Deltas von Oosterschelde (Holland), wo 1953 bei einer Sturmflut 1800 Menschen ums Leben kamen. Diese Sperre besteht aus mehreren Millionen Tonnen Zement, Felsbrocken und Stahl sowie aus Seebett-Matratzen aus Sand und Schotter. Aus einem Artikel in *National Geographic.* (USA)

■ 213-215 Beispiele der für die Erläuterung der verschiedenen Produktionsbereiche eingesetzten Darstellungen aus dem Jahresbericht 1984 von *Fluorocarbon*. Hier geht es um Flüssigkeitsverschlussschrauben für die Luftfahrt, um Kunstharze für technische Zubehörteile und um Gummiprodukte für Ventile. (USA)

■ 212 Vue partielle d'un projet intégrant des digues, jetées et canaux pour la protection du delta d'Oosterschelde en Hollande où le raz de marée de 1953 coûta la vie à 1800 personnes. Ce barrage comprend des millions de tonnes de ciment, de rochers et d'acier, ainsi que des matelas de sable et de pierres concassées déposés au fond de la mer. Tiré du *National Geographic.* (USA)

■ 213-215 Exemples des graphiques expliquant divers domaines de production dans le rapport annuel de *Fluorocarbon* pour 1984. Il s'agit d'obturateurs hydrauliques pour la construction aéronautique, de résines synthétiques pour équipements techniques et de produits en fluorocarbone pour soupapes. (USA)

ARTIST:
WILLIAM H. BOND
ART DIRECTOR:
WILLIAM H. BOND
PUBLISHER:
NATIONAL GEOGRAPHIC
◄■ 212

DESIGNER:
KENTON LOTZ
ART DIRECTOR:
RON JEFFERIES
AGENCY:
THE JEFFERIES ASSOCIATION
CLIENT:
THE FLUOROCARBON COMPANY
■ 213–215

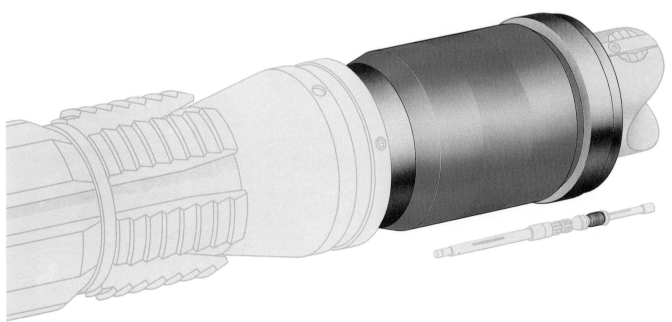

4 GARDNER/NEOTEC VISIBLE INSTRUMENTS

The Gardner/Neotec Division was created by the merger of Gardner Laboratory, acquired by Pacific Scientific in 1978, the Neotec Corp., acquired in 1981, and Computer Colour Systems in 1983.

Gardner, founded in 1917, was a pioneer in the field of color and appearance measurement instruments. Pacific Scientific's Industrial Sales Division had been Gardner's sales representative in the western United States for many years, so the association between the two companies was a long one.

Since the merger with Neotec, the combined Gardner/Neotec operation has been relocated into a 40,000 square foot facility in Silver Spring, Maryland. Gardner products are marketed by a network of approximately 80 independent sales representatives located worldwide.

Technology

Color of an object is determined by the amount of energy absorbed and reflected at selected wavelengths of light. A spectrophotometer is an instrument for measuring the reflected wavelengths. The surface of the diffusion sphere is illuminated by a lamp (A) which reflects "white light" on the sample (B). Depending on the color of the sample, certain wavelengths of light are reflected from the sample toward the holographic grating (C). The angle of the grating determines which wavelength of light is reflected on the photodetector (D). The signal level from the photodetector and the angle of the grating are processed by a computer to determine the distribution of the levels of various wavelengths of light which define the color of the sample.

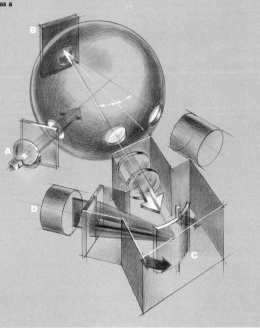

6 GARDNER/NEOTEC NEAR-INFRARED INSTRUMENTS

Neotec Corp. was acquired by Pacific Scientific in 1981 and merged with Gardner Laboratory to form the Gardner/Neotec Division. The combination was logical from both the standpoint of technology and geography. Both divisions were based in Maryland.

Neotec's technology in the field of near-infrared instruments was highly compatible with Gardner's expertise in quality control color measurement instruments.

The Gardner/Neotec line of near-infrared instruments is marketed through independent sales representatives and distributors worldwide, as is the line of color sensing instruments. In Europe, the representatives are supported by a wholly-owned subsidiary, Pacific Scientific, Ltd.

Technology

For many years, it has been known that various substances absorb certain near-infrared wavelengths and reflect others. However, it was not until the development of fast, economical computers that this technology became available to a wide cross-section of users. With near-infrared, it is possible to quickly determine the properties of a sample by measuring reflected energy. A light source (A) is projected up through a set of filters revolving on a wheel (B), which has the effect of tilting each filter as it passes through the beam of light. A key to Neotec's success is the exclusive and patented tilting filter, which produces a continuous spectrum of NIR energy over a broad range of wavelengths. The sample material in the cup (C) absorbs some wavelengths of the NIR energy and reflects others back toward the detectors (D). The reflected energy, in relationship to the position of the filter wheel, is processed by proprietary computer software which provides an analysis of the sample.

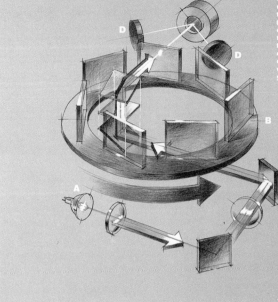

8 KIN-TECH RESTRAINTS

The Kin-Tech Division is the successor to a small aircraft products division acquired by Pacific Scientific in 1951. That operation, then located in Glendale, California, manufactured tensiometers — devices to measure the tension in aircraft control cables. This product is still produced by Pacific Scientific.

In subsequent years, the division developed the patented technology for restraint system components and restraints that enabled it to gain a dominant position in production of personnel restraint systems and, beginning in 1974, mechanical shock arrestors.

The Kin-Tech Division is located in two buildings encompassing 137,000 square feet in Anaheim, California.

Virtually all Kin-Tech products are sold directly to the original equipment manufacturer, both in the U.S. and overseas, by the division's own marketing organization.

Technology

Kin-Tech — a contraction of KINetic TECHnology — produces mechanisms which control motion. For example, this ballistic reel positions a pilot securely in his seat during emergency ejection sequence. Upon the pilot's command, a ballistic charge generates gas that drives the piston (A) down the ball screw (B) rotating the drive wheel (C). This wheel, through a mechanical connector, retracts the shoulder straps (D) positioning the pilot securely in his seat. The entire sequence is virtually instantaneous. An advanced recyclable system, now being tested, will replace the ballistic charge with a gas reservoir, permitting the pilot to use the system without ejection in the event of extreme turbulence or controlled high "g" flight maneuvers.

10 BELFAB COMPONENTS

The Belfab Division was acquired in 1981 and is located in a 34,000 square foot facility in Daytona Beach, Florida. Belfab has carved out an important niche in the production of welded metal bellows — its success due in large measure to sophisticated design engineering and automated manufacturing techniques developed by Belfab engineers. The division also produces an off-the-shelf line of seals under the Accuflex label.

Two acquisitions in 1983 have expanded the basic Belfab line of products, enhancing its overall competitive position. The Gits line of mechanical seals and a line of formed metal bellows have enabled Belfab to reach markets that previously were not open to it. Both of these product lines are now produced in the Daytona Beach plant.

Belfab's Accuflex seals and the Gits seals are sold through a nationwide network of distributors and original equipment manufacturer accounts. Since bellows are made to the specifications of original equipment manufacturers, they are marketed directly.

Technology

Metal bellows are convoluted, flexible devices that can also be extended and compressed. They function as accumulators, sensors or springs (A) as flexible conduits (B) or as connectors (C). Belfab fabricates bellows by welding convolutions in an automated process, or by mechanically forming bellows from metal tubing. Bellows are fabricated in diameters ranging from 1/8 inch to over 24 inches.

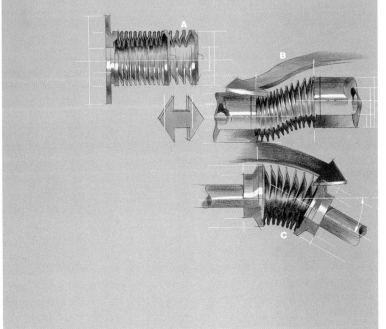

■ 216–220 Pages from the 1983 annual report for *Pacific Scientific*. The diagrams are colored in crayon to enable shareholders to understand the function of various instruments and procedures. Shown is a spectrophotometer for measuring the reflected wavelengths; a color sensing instrument for quality control; mechanisms which control motion, e.g. for placing a pilot securely in the ejector seat during emergencies (a ballistic charge generates gas to drive the piston); welded metal bellows; and particle counting instruments (with laser beam and photo cell) which measure contaminants in liquids, air or gases. (USA)

■ 216–220 Seiten aus dem Jahresbericht 1983 von *Pacific Scientific*. Die mit Farbstift gezeichneten Illustrationen von Prüfvorgängen und Funktionen sollen den Aktionären die Funktion verschiedener Geräte und Verfahren veranschaulichen. Hier geht es um ein Spektrophotometer für die Bestimmung von reflektierten Wellenlängen; um ein Farbmessgerät für die Qualitätskontrolle; eine Vorrichtung, die den festen Halt des Piloten im Schleudersitz gewährleisten soll; um bewegliche Metallverbindungsstücke und um ein Testverfahren, mit dem Giftstoffe in Luft oder Flüssigkeiten festgestellt werden. (USA)

■ 216–220 Pages du rapport annuel 1983 de *Pacific Scientific*. Ces représentations d'opérations de contrôle et de fonctions, faites au crayon couleur, renseignent les actionnaires sur le mode opératoire de divers appareillages et processus. Il s'agit ici d'un spectrophotomètre mesurant des longueurs d'ondes après réflexion; d'un colorimètre pour le contrôle de qualité; d'un dispositif ancrant solidement le pilote dans son siège éjectable; de raccords métalliques flexibles et d'un dispositif (avec rayon laser et cellule photoélectrique) de détection de substances toxiques dans un milieu aérien ou liquide. (USA)

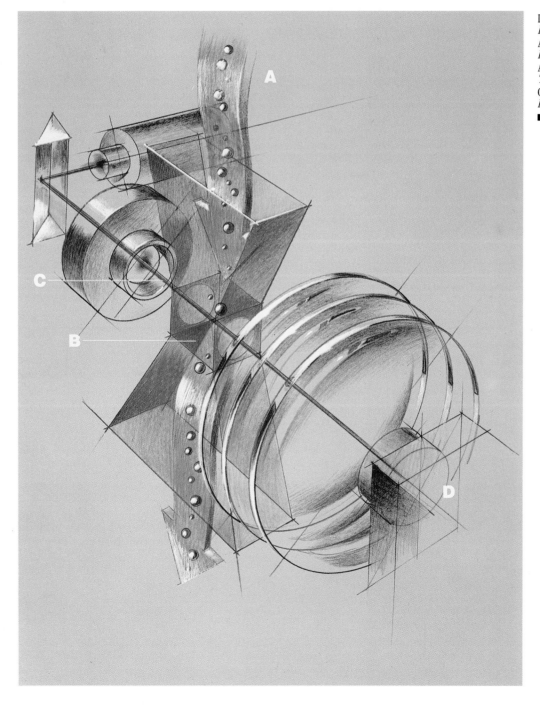

DESIGNER:
KENTON LOTZ
ART DIRECTOR:
RON JEFFERIES
AGENCY:
THE JEFFERIES ASSOCIATION
CLIENT:
PACIFIC SCIENTIFIC
■ 216–220

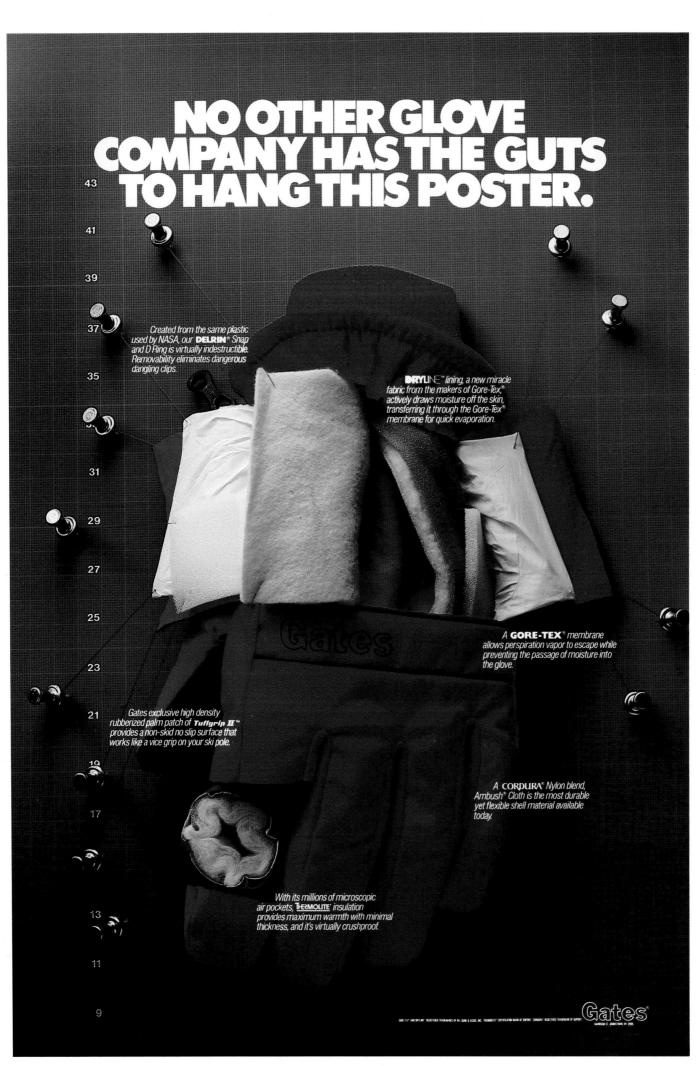

DESIGNER:
David Bender
ARTIST:
Gil Cope
ART DIRECTOR:
David Bender
AGENCY:
Janklow Bender
CLIENT:
Gates-Mills
■ 221

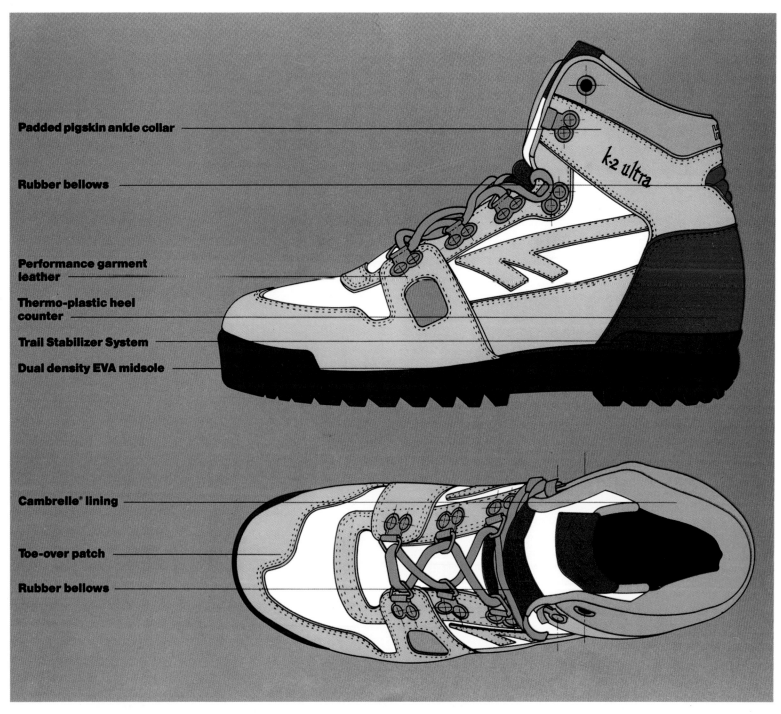

Padded pigskin ankle collar

Rubber bellows

Performance garment leather

Thermo-plastic heel counter

Trail Stabilizer System

Dual density EVA midsole

Cambrelle° lining

Toe-over patch

Rubber bellows

DESIGNER:
BOB ANKERS/DAN DOHERTY
ARTIST:
DAN DOHERTY
ART DIRECTOR:
DAVID GAUGER/BOB ANKERS
AGENCY:
GAUGA & SILVA, INC.
CLIENT:
HI-TEC SPORTS, INC.
■ 222

■ 221 Diagram showing the "inner life" of a glove (materials, fibers etc.), used on a poster for the *Gates Mills* glove company. (USA)

■ 222 Finely-detailed diagram of a *Hi-Tec* sports shoe to show the individual components, viewed from the side and from above. From a catalog for *Hi-Tec Sports.* (USA)

■ 221 «Kein anderer Hersteller hätte den Mut, dieses Plakat aufzuhängen.» Darstellung des «Innenlebens» eines Handschuhs. (USA)

■ 222 Detailgetreue Darstellung eines *Hi-Tec*-Sportschuhs zur Verdeutlichung der einzelnen Bestandteile, von der Seite und von oben gesehen. Katalog für *Hi-Tec Sports.* (USA)

■ 221 «Aucun autre gantier n'a le courage de placarder cette affiche.» Représentation de la «vie intérieure» d'un gant *Gates Mills.* (USA)

■ 222 Représentation détaillée d'une chaussure de sport *Hi-Tec* pour bien en faire saisir toutes les parties. Vues latérale et de dessus. Catalogue pour *Hi-Tec Sports.* (USA)

■ 223, 224 Transparent and cut-away diagrams of a part of a *Yamaha* motorcycle and a *Yamaha* boat engine. (JPN)

■ 223, 224 Phantomdarstellungen eines Teils eines *Yamaha*-Motorrads und eines *Yamaha*-Bootsmotors. (JPN)

■ 223, 224 Représentations fantômes partielles d'une moto *Yamaha* et d'un moteur *Yamaha* pour bateaux. (JPN)

ARTIST:
Makoto Ouchi
CLIENT:
Yamaha Motor Co., Ltd.
■ 223, 224

ARTIST:
GORO SHIMAOKA
AGENCY:
DENTSU
CLIENT:
OLYMPUS OPTICAL CO., LTD.
◀■ 225

ARTIST:
YOSHIHIRO INOMOTO
ART DIRECTOR:
YOSHIHIRO INOMOTO
AGENCY:
YOSHIHIRO INOMOTO
CLIENT:
MINOLTA CAMERA
■ 226

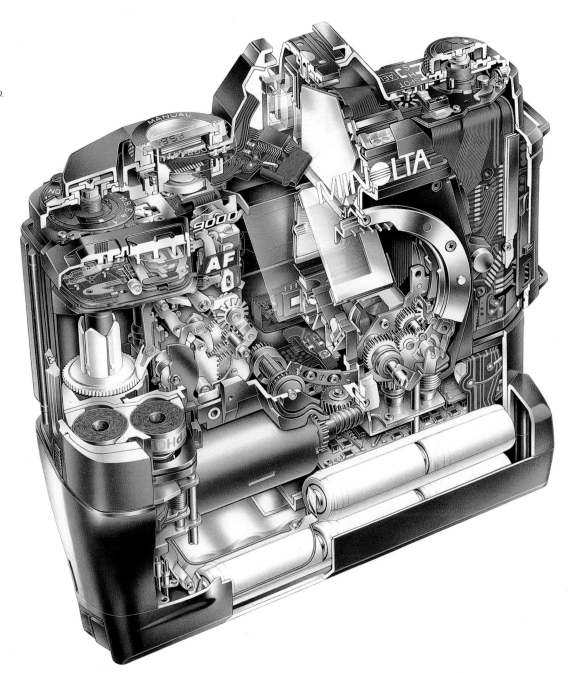

■ 225 Technical drawing with transparent diagram of the *Olympus* OM System, for catalogs and posters. (JPN)

■ 226 Transparent drawing of a *Minolta* camera. (JPN)

■ 225 Technische Zeichnungen mit Transparentdarstellung des *Olympus*-OM-Systems, für Kataloge und Plakate. (JPN)

■ 226 Phantomzeichnung einer *Minolta*-Kamera. (JPN)

■ 225 Dessin technique montrant en transparence le système *Olympus OM*, pour catalogues et affiches. (JPN)

■ 226 Dessin fantôme d'un appareil photo *Minolta*. (JPN)

ARTIST:
HIDEO HATSUJAI
CLIENT:
VICTOR COMPANY OF JAPAN
■ 227

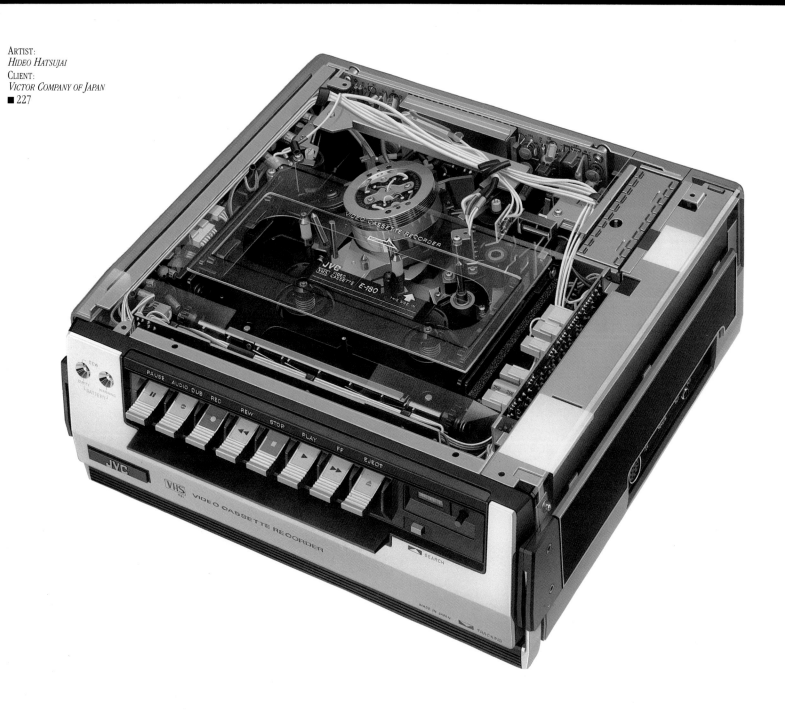

■ 227 Transparent diagram showing a partial view of a JVC video tape recorder. For a sales catalog. (JPN)

■ 228 Black-and-white diagrams (combination technique with scratchboard) of an *Alfa Romeo P 2* of 1925 and an *MG K3 Magnette* of 1934. (JPN)

■ 227 Transparentdiagramm eines Teils eines JVC-Video-kassettengerätes, für einen Katalog. (JPN)

■ 228 Schwarzweissdarstellungen (Mischtechnik mit Schabkarton) eines *Alfa Romeo P2* von 1925 und eines *MG K3 Magnette* von 1934. (JPN)

■ 227 Diagramme transparent donnant une vue partielle d'un magnétoscope JVC, dans un catalogue. (JPN)

■ 228 Représentations en noir et blanc (technique mixte et manière noire): *Alfa Romeo P2* de 1925, *MG K3 Magnette* de 1934. (JPN)

ARTIST:
F. YANO
CLIENT:
RYU TSUSHIN CO., LTD.
■ 228

154

ARTIST:
GORO SHIMAOKA
CLIENT:
CBS/SONY PUBLISHING INC.
■ 229

■ 229 Realistic drawing with cutaway diagram of a section
of a space shuttle, for a book published by CBS/Sony
Publishing Inc., Tokyo. (JPN)

■ 229 Realistische Zeichnung mit Transparentdarstellung
eines Teils einer Raumfähre, für ein Buch von CBS/
Sony Publishing Inc., Tokyo. (JPN)

■ 229 Illustration technique donnant par transparence une
vue partielle d'une navette spatiale, dans un ouvrage publié
par CBS/Sony Publishing Inc. à Tokyo. (JPN)

KARTEN UND PLÄNE

The illustrations shown in the chapter "Cartographic Diagrams" serve – as those of all other sections – the visualization of the not visible, or not so apparent conditions and procedures. In the first chapter, the "Comparative Diagrams" are mainly calculated values, nothing material, nothing tangible, arranged in a coordinated system – in the main with the aid of columns, circles, and curves. In the chapter "Scientific and Popular Science Diagrams" the investigating draftsman penetrates deep in the human body, the earth and rock strata to record the cosmos of microscopic activity and infinitesimal particles. To produce architectural diagrams it requires in most cases an elevated view as from a tall building or the top of a tower. Finally, to produce cartographic diagrams the draftsman must be – at least in theory – so far removed from the earth that his vantage point might be an airplane or even a satellite.

In the first pages of this chapter representations of the world are shown – a world that appears to be viewed from another planet. The diagrams, for instance, that companies produce for their own self-promotion and frequently include in their annual reports are of this ilk. The presentation of worldwide markets, the multi-continental sales, in short the internationality of a firm, whether it be an insurance corporation or a news agency, is the aim and purpose of such diagrams. And, in spite of some overlapping of intentions, individual diagrams in their end result turn out to be considerably different. The world (or an individual country) is either portrayed as round as a globe *(Fig. 232)* or as flat as in a normal geographic atlas *(Figs. 230, 231, 239)*. Sometimes the diagram is underscored by an enormous continental pedestal *(Figs. 238, 242, 253)* or one gives the earth an arithmetic sheet *(Fig. 237)* and with it submits the diversity and organic growth of the continents and their boundaries to a mathematical assessment, meaning the whole world. The globe holds no mysteries any longer; everything has been revealed. The earth is subject to the frailties of humanity, even to the strength (or weakness?) of societies and corporations created by man. The world is measured, calculated, chopped up, and distributed. Some firms show the earth (instead of being adapted to the sterile computer) romantically, swathed in nocturnal darkness *(Figs. 230, 239, 244)*. The lighter color dots by which production or processing plants are marked, illuminate like lights in the surrounding twilight, like glowing lifespots in contrast to an oppressive sleep. From this artistically formulated and esoteric information, one can deduce that the company itself, through its

own products, is a beacon in the gloomy darkness, which is to say that the firm offers life, knowledge, and civilization.

The chemical corporation Lydall *(Figs. 233, 234)* shows the world carved up on the sides of a transparent cube. This graphic cleverly relates to the firm's symbol – Lydall and the world are one.

The news agency Reuters *(Fig. 244)* shows the earth radiating with light spots from space – as seen from their satellite stations.

If the focal point is to demonstrate movement, transportation by air or water, then the presentation of the continent retreats to the background in favor of the various interests of a shipping line or airline. The world is reduced to simple black-and-white contour drawings. *(Figs. 250, 251)*.

After the companies' geographic maps there are those that must fulfill the special demands merely as orientation. The diversity of the aspects under which a city can be observed and presented, appears almost limitless. Whether it be concerning work and utilitarian areas (offices, schools, industry, etc.) as in *Fig. 245*, or tourist routes and cultural sights *(Fig. 267)*, leisure amenities *(Fig. 272)*, various city districts *(Figs. 255-264)* or only a special row of distinguished high-rise towers *(Fig. 273)*, the most concise forms of expression are searched for, and those that appear unimportant for this special purpose are cast aside.

Isometric diagrams, best suited to show the contours of the greatest number of buildings in a strictly limited space, are greatly preferred *(Figs. 114, 245, 273, 281, 284)*. Also sequence presentations, as if the observer were looking through a camera with a zoom lens and wished to crystallize singly each phase of movement, or as if the observer were approaching earth, slowly, from outer space – these are not seldom. *(Figs. 246-249, 285-288)*.

There are traffic schemes used in a rather general sense, such as the S-Bahn (rapid transit) and Metro diagrams *(Figs. 252, 266, 267, 268)*, all well known to us and therefore here rather less represented than those under specific categories like detours and departure notices *(Figs. 253, 254)*.

Cartographic and architectural diagrams are often seen in connection with each other and partly overlap. Here we refer the reader to the visitors' brochure for the former Alcatraz prison. *(Fig. 274-276)*. More about this brochure can be gleaned in the following chapter.

Die im Kapitel «Kartographische Diagramme» gezeigten Abbildungen dienen – wie die aller anderen Abschnitte – der Visualisierung nicht sichtbarer oder, besser, so nicht sichtbarer Zustände und Vorgänge. Im ersten Kapitel, den «Vergleichenden Diagrammen», werden vor allem errechnete Werte, nicht Materielles, nicht Sichtbares in ein Koordinatensystem eingespannt – grösstenteils mit Hilfe von Säulen-, Kreis- oder Kurvendiagrammen. Im Kapitel der «Wissenschaftlichen und populärwissenschaftlichen Diagramme» dringt der forschende Zeichner zur Erstellung zum Beispiel medizinischer oder geologischer Zeichnungen quasi in den menschlichen Körper oder in die Erde und Gesteinsschichten ein und versucht, den Kosmos der kleinen und kleinsten Teilchen zu erfassen. Um architektonische Diagramme anzufertigen, bedarf es in den meisten Fällen eines Blickwinkels, der erhöht liegt, wie von einem hohen Haus oder einem Aussichtsturm aus gesehen. Zur Erstellung der «Kartographischen Darstellungen» schliesslich müsste sich der Zeichner theoretisch so weit von der Erde entfernen, dass ein Flugzeug, wenn nicht gar eine Raumsonde als Blickpunkt zu empfehlen wäre.

Auf den ersten Seiten dieses Kapitels werden ebensolche, wie von einem anderen Stern aus gesehene Weltdarstellungen gezeigt, die Firmen zum Zweck der Eigenwerbung, meist in ihren Jahresberichten, anfertigen liessen. Die Darstellung der weltweiten Produktion, des Kontinente überschreitenden Verkaufs, kurz, der Internationalität einer Firma ist Ziel und Zweck solcher Diagramme. Die einzelnen Darstellungen sind trotz übergreifend gleicher Absicht dennoch recht unterschiedlich. Die Welt oder einzelne Länder werden rund wie ein Globus gezeichnet *(Abb. 232)* oder auch wie in einem normalen geographischen Atlas *(Abb. 230, 231, 239)*. Manchmal unterstellt man einen enormen Kontinentalsockel *(Abb. 238, 242, 253)*, oder man passt die Erde einem Rechenblatt an *(Abb. 237)* und unterwirft damit die Vielfalt und organische Gewachsenheit der Kontinente und ihrer Begrenzungen, das heisst hier die ganze Welt, dem rechnerischen Kalkül. Der Globus birgt keine Mysterien mehr, alles ist erschlossen und bekannt. Die Erde ist dem Menschen, einer Firma untertan. Sie ist ausgemessen, berechnet, eingeteilt. Andere zeigen die Erde romantischer, in nächtliches Dunkel getaucht *(Abb. 230, 239, 244)*. Die helleren, farbigen Punkte, mit denen die Produktions- oder Verarbeitungsstätten gekennzeichnet werden, leuchten wie Lichter in einer umgebenden Dämmerung, wie glitzerndes Leben gegenüber einem dumpfen Schlaf. Die aus derartiger bildneri-

scher Formulierung ablesbare unterschwellige Information kann man wohl dahingehend formulieren, dass mit den Firmenprodukten, der Firma selbst Licht ins Dunkle kommt, was soviel heisst wie: die Firma bringt Leben, Wissen und Zivilisation.

Der Chemiekonzern Lydall *(Abb. 233, 234)* zeigt die Welt zerlegt auf den Wänden eines transparenten Kastens. Die äussere Form dieser Graphik entspricht dem Firmensignet, Lydall und die Welt sind eins.

Die Nachrichtenagentur Reuters *(Abb. 244)* zeigt die Erde wie mit Lichtspots vom All aus angestrahlt – wie von ihren Satellitenstationen aus gesehen und von dort organisiert.

Liegt das Schwergewicht im Aufzeigen von Bewegungen, Transporten zu Luft und zu Wasser, dann tritt die Darstellung der Kontinente zurück zugunsten der unterschiedlichen Spannungsbögen einer Schiffs- oder Fluglinie. Die Welt wird reduziert auf einfache schwarzweisse Umrisszeichnungen. *(Abb. 250, 251)*.

Auf die firmenbezogenen geographischen Karten folgen solche, die speziellen Ansprüchen genügen sollen. Die Vielfalt der Aspekte, unter denen etwa eine Stadt betrachtet und also dargestellt werden kann, scheint schier uferlos. Ob es sich um Arbeitsbereiche handelt (Büros, Schulen, Industrie usw.) *(Abb. 245)* oder um Touristenrouten und kulturelle Sehenswürdigkeiten *(Abb. 267)*, um Freizeitangebote *(Abb. 272)*, um verschiedene Stadtviertel *(Abb. 255-264)* oder um einen speziellen Strassenzug mit seinen höchst markanten Hochhäusern *(Abb. 273)*, immer werden die prägnantesten Ausdrucksmittel gesucht und das für diesen speziellen Zweck Unwichtige weggelassen.

Isometrische Darstellungen, bestens geeignet, um auf begrenztem Raum die Formen möglichst vieler Gebäude zu zeigen, erfreuen sich grosser Beliebtheit *(Abb. 114, 245, 273, 281, 284)*. Auch Darstellungsabfolgen, als ob der Betrachter durch eine Kamera mit einem Zoom-Objektiv schaue und sämtliche Stadien der Bewegung einzeln herauskristallisiert wären, oder als ob sich der Betrachter aus dem All langsam der Erde nähere, sind nicht selten. *(Abb. 246-249, 285-288)*.

Kartographische und architektonische Diagramme werden oft in Verbindung miteinander gebracht und gehen zum Teil ineinander über. Hier sei auf den Prospekt verwiesen, der für Besucher des ehemaligen Alcatraz-Gefängnisses hergestellt wurde *(Abb. 274-276)*. Im nächsten Kapitel, Architektonische Diagramme, soll noch einmal die Rede davon sein.

Les illustrations présentées dans ce chapitre consacré aux Cartogrammes servent, tout comme celles des autres chapitres, à visualiser des états et processus invisibles ou, si l'on veut, invisibles tels quels. Au premier chapitre, celui des «diagrammes comparatifs», il s'agissait surtout d'insérer des valeurs calculées, soit immatérielles, invisibles dans un système de coordonnées, principalement à l'aide de graphiques ordinaires ou à bandes ou à secteurs. Au chapitre des «diagrammes scientifiques et de vulgarisation», le dessinateur créatif qui veut par exemple réaliser des représentations médicales ou géologiques se lance dans l'exploration en profondeur du corps humain ou du globe terrestre en ses strates successives et cherche à appréhender l'univers des constituants infimes de la matière vivante ou inanimée. La réalisation de diagrammes architecturaux exige dans la plupart des cas un point fixe de référence supérieur au plan étudié, équivalant au toit-terrasse d'un immeuble ou à un belvédère. Si l'on voulait en appliquer le principe à la représentation cartographique, le dessinateur devrait se trouver tellement éloigné de la surface de la Terre qu'il faudrait le situer sur un aéronef ou un engin spatial.

Les premières pages de ce chapitre présentent effectivement des représentations de la Terre vues, semble-t-il, depuis une autre planète, telles que des entreprises soucieuses d'autopromotion en font confectionner généralement pour leur rapport annuel. Ce genre de diagrammes a pour but de documenter la production à l'échelle mondiale, la commercialisation intercontinentale, bref le caractère international d'une entreprise, d'une compagnie d'assurances, d'une société de télécommunications. Si l'intention générale est identique, les divers graphiques présentent néanmoins des différences notables. Le monde, voire certains pays affectent une forme sphérique *(fig. 232)* ou obéissent au principe de la projection cartographique telle qu'on la connaît dans nos atlas *(fig. 230, 231, 239)*. Parfois on ajoute la dimension d'un énorme socle continental *(fig. 238, 242, 253)*, ou bien on adapte la Terre aux deux dimensions d'une feuille de statistique *(fig. 237)*, ce qui soumet au calcul la diversité et le devenir organique des continents et de leurs limites, soit le monde entier. Le globe terrestre n'a plus de taches blanches, tout y est connu, répertorié. La Terre est soumise à l'homme, à l'entreprise. Elle est arpentée, calculée, divisée. D'autres sociétés montrent la Terre sans intervention de l'ordinateur, plongée dans une obscurité propice au romantisme *(fig. 230, 239, 244)*. Les points couleur caractérisant les lieux de production ou de transformation étincellent ainsi telles des lumières dans la pénombre ambiante, évoquant une impression de vie rutilante sur un fond de sommeil obtus. L'information subliminale qui se dégage d'une telle représentation visuelle est à peu près celle-ci: les produits de l'entreprise même ont un rôle civilisateur éminent qui fait surgir, la vie, le savoir, la lumière des ténèbres environnantes.

Le groupe chimique Lydall *(fig. 233, 234)* déploie le monde sur les parois d'une boîte transparente. La forme extérieure de ce graphique fait allusion à l'emblème de l'entreprise: Lydall et le monde, c'est bonnet blanc et blanc bonnet.

L'agence de presse Reuters *(fig. 244)* montre la Terre prise dans le faisceau de spots lumineux venus de l'espace, tout comme si sa représentation se créait et s'organisait à partir des satellites de télécommunications utilisés par l'agence.

Lorsque l'accent est mis sur la cinétique des transports par air ou par mer, la représentation des continents s'estompe au profit des arcs de tension introduits par le tracé des lignes aériennes ou maritimes. Le monde n'est plus alors que silhouetté en noir et blanc *(fig. 250, 251)*.

Outre les cartogrammes adaptés aux besoins des entreprises, on en rencontre qui se contentent de satisfaire à des besoins d'orientation spécifiques. Il ne semble y avoir aucune limite à la diversité des points de vue régissant la présentation d'une ville par exemple, et aux moyens mis en œuvre pour la réaliser. Qu'il s'agisse de zones de travail (bureaux, écoles, usines, etc.) *(fig. 245)* ou de routes touristiques et de sites culturels à visiter *(fig. 267)*, d'activités de loisirs *(fig. 272)*, de différents quartiers *(fig. 255-264)* ou d'une seule rue avec ses gratte-ciel caractéristiques *(fig. 273)*, on a toujours recours aux moyens d'expression les plus frappants, reléguant dans l'oubli les détails sans importance du point de vue adopté.

Les représentations isométriques parfaitement adaptées au regroupement sur une surface restreinte d'un grand nombre d'immeubles de forme variée connaissent actuellement une vogue certaine *(fig. 114, 245, 273, 281, 284)*. Même les représentations séquentielles évoquant le départage au zoom des phases successives du mouvement ou l'approche lente de la planète depuis l'espace se retrouvent assez fréquemment *(fig. 246-249, 285-288)*.

Quant à la schématisation graphique générale des réseaux de métro et de trains de banlieue *(fig. 252, 266, 267, 268)*, elle est tellement connue que nous n'en donnons pas beaucoup d'exemples, au contraire des indications de déviation et de sortie d'autoroute *(fig. 253, 254)*.

Les cartogrammes et les diagrammes d'architecture sont souvent associés et vont jusqu'à se recouvrir partiellement. Nous en voulons pour exemple le prospectus réalisé à l'intention des visiteurs de l'ancienne prison d'Alcatraz *(fig. 274-276)*. Nous y reviendrons dans le prochain chapitre, consacré aux diagrammes d'architecture.

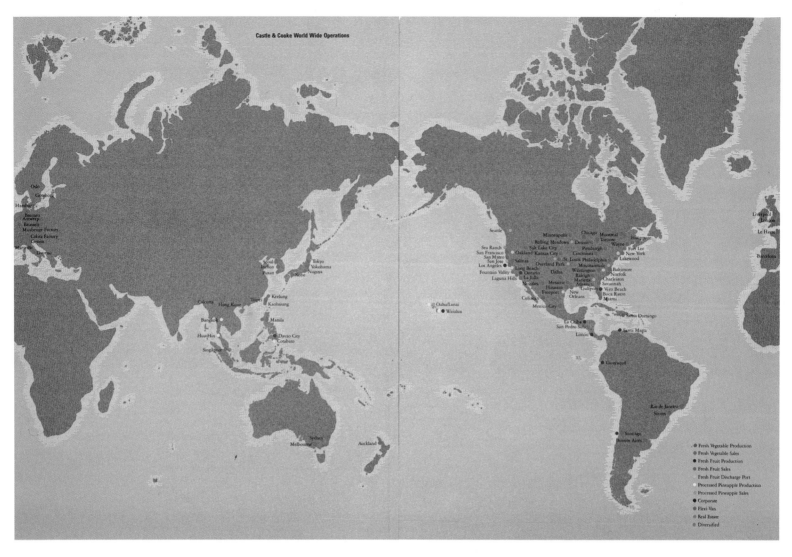

Castle & Cooke World Wide Operations

DESIGNER:
DOUGLAS JOSEPH
ART DIRECTOR:
ROBERT MILES RUNYAN
AGENCY:
*ROBERT MILES RUNYAN
& ASSOC.*
CLIENT:
CASTLE & COOKE, INC.
■ 230

■ 230 World map showing production and sales outlets of the *Castle & Cooke* company who are active mainly in the cultivation and sales of fruit and vegetables. Double spread from the company's annual report for 1985. (USA)

■ 231 Stylized world map illustrating the various business sectors in America, Europe, and the Pacific countries. From an annual report of the Sealed Power Corporation. (USA)

■ 232 Typographic diagram (ideogram) listing the locations of *Lloyds of London* agents. (GBR)

■ 230 Weltkarte zur Veranschaulichung der Produktions- und Verkaufsstellen der Firma *Castle & Cooke*, die sich vor allem mit dem Anbau und Verkauf von Obst und Gemüse befasst. Doppelseite aus dem Jahresbericht 1985. (USA)

■ 231 Stilisierte Weltkarte zur Verdeutlichung der Geschäfts- bereiche in Amerika, Europa und Pazifikländern. Aus einem Jahresbericht der Sealed Power Corporation. (USA)

■ 232 Typographisches Diagramm, aus dem alle Agenturen von *Lloyds of London* ersichtlich sind. (GBR)

■ 230 Planisphère où sont reportés les centres de produc- tion et de ventes de la société *Castle & Cooke*, spécialisée surtout dans la production et la commercialisation de fruits et légumes. Double page du rapport annuel pour 1985. (USA)

■ 231 Planisphère stylisée des divers secteurs d'activité d'une société en Amérique, en Europe et dans le Pacifique. D'un rapport annuel de la Sealed Power Corporation. (USA)

■ 232 Diagramme typographique énumérant toutes les agences du *Lloyd* de Londres. (GBR)

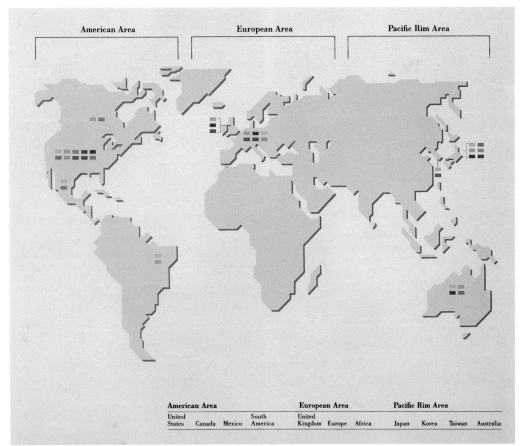

American Area				European Area			Pacific Rim Area			
United States	Canada	Mexico	South America	United Kingdom	Europe	Africa	Japan	Korea	Taiwan	Australia

DESIGNER:
THOM DAWSON + COMPANY
ART DIRECTOR:
THOM DAWSON + COMPANY
AGENCY:
THOM DAWSON + COMPANY
CLIENT:
SEALED POWER CORPORATION
■ 231

DESIGNER:
PENNY HOWARTH
ART DIRECTOR:
ALAN FLETCHER
AGENCY:
PENTAGRAM DESIGN, LONDON
CLIENT:
LLOYDS OF LONDON
■ 232

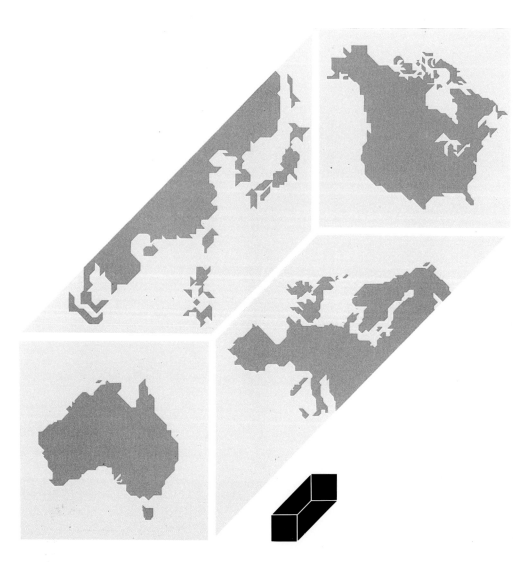

DESIGNER:
ROBERT APPLETON
ARTIST:
NATALIE VASA
ART DIRECTOR:
ROBERT APPLETON
AGENCY:
APPLETON DESIGN, INC.
CLIENT:
LYDALL, INC.
■ 233

DESIGNER:
ROBERT APPLETON
ARTIST:
JOHN EARLE/TIM NIGHSWANDER
ART DIRECTOR:
ROBERT APPLETON
AGENCY:
APPLETON DESIGN, INC.
CLIENT:
LYDALL INC.
■ 234

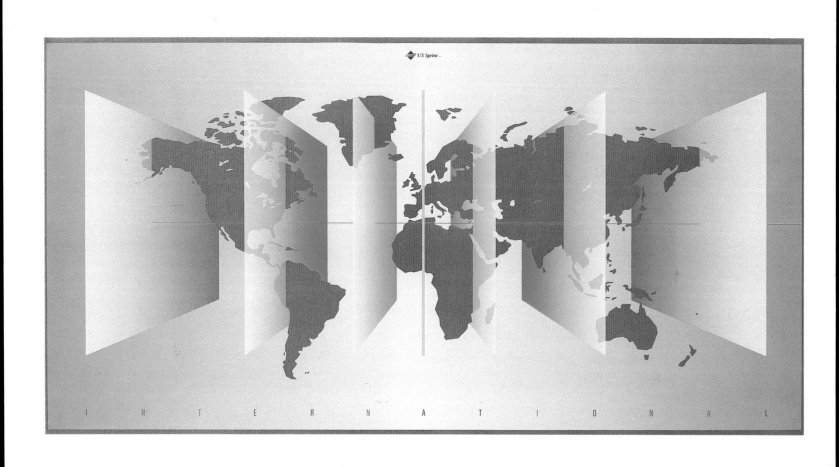

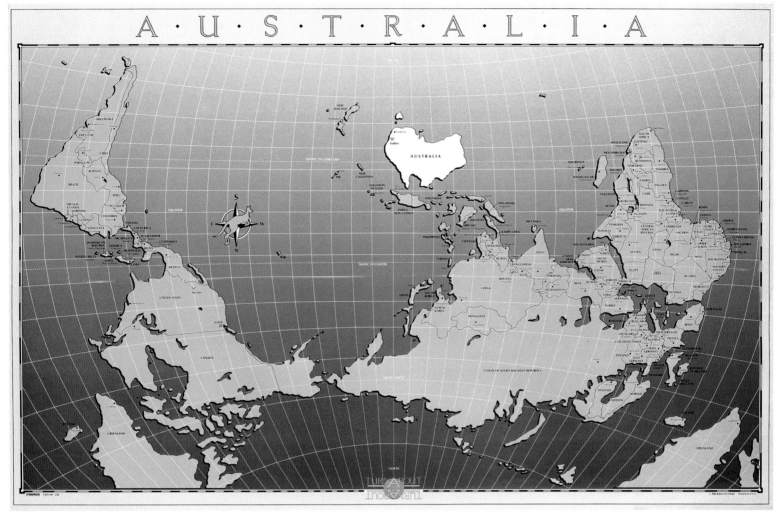

DESIGNER:
EARL GEE
ARTIST:
EARL GEE
ART DIRECTOR:
TONY MILNER/MARK ANDERSON
AGENCY:
MARK ANDERSON DESIGN
CLIENT:
*US SPRINT COMMUNICATIONS
CORPORATION*
◀■ 235

DESIGNER:
ROBERT PECKHAM
ARTIST:
ROBERT PECKHAM
ART DIRECTOR:
AIMEE MacDONALD
AGENCY:
SAFECO MARKETING
CLIENT:
SAFECO INSURANCE COMPANY
■ 236

■ 233, 234 The symbol of the *Lydall* company forms the basis of the design for these stylized maps of the Far East, the USA, Europe, and Australia. From a brochure on the firm's products and markets. (USA)

■ 235 Poster for the US Sprint Communications Corp. with information about which areas of the earth the various satellites are responsible for. (USA)

■ 236 An upside-down world with "down under" Australia now "up over", offering itself as a holiday country. (AUS)

■ 233, 234 Das Signet der Firma *Lydall* bildet die Grundform für die Anordnung der stylisierten Karten des Fernen Ostens, der USA, Europas und Australiens. Aus einer Broschüre über Produkte und Märkte der Firma. (USA)

■ 235 Plakat für die US Sprint Communications Corp. Hier wird verdeutlicht, für welche Gebiete der Erde die verschiedenen Satelliten zuständig sind. (USA)

■ 236 Die Welt auf den Kopf gestellt, dominiert von Australien, das sich hiermit als Ferienland anbietet. (AUS)

■ 233, 234 L'emblème de la société *Lydall* fournit la conception de base de la disposition des cartes stylisées d'Extrême-Orient, des Etats-Unis, d'Europe et d'Australie. Brochure présentant les produits et marchés de l'entreprise. (USA)

■ 235 Affiche pour la US Sprint Communications Corp. On y voit la répartition des zones géographiques arrosées par les divers satellites en orbite autour du globe. (USA)

■ 236 Le monde à l'envers, dominé par l'Australie qui se présente ainsi comme pays de vacances. (USA)

MAC Gateways to World Trade

DESIGNER:
INFIELD + D'ASTOLFO
ART DIRECTOR:
INFIELD + D'ASTOLFO
AGENCY:
INFIELD + D'ASTOLFO
CLIENT:
MARUBENI AMERICA
CORPORATION
■ 237

■ 237 Stylized world map of the vertically-oriented concern, Marubeni America Corporation. The colors serve as
codes for the various business sectors, e.g. gray for the textile sector, blue for the machine sector etc. Double spread
from the 1984 annual report. (USA)

■ 238 Stylized map of the USA drawn with color pencils,
with direct allusion to the subject of the diagram – the
wood reserves of the paper producers Champion International. From the company's 1985 annual report. (USA)

■ 239 Map as overview of various projects, establishments
and plants of the Fluor Corporation, illustrated through different colored squares. The countries in which the firm is
active are again emphasized by the flags. From the company's annual report. (USA)

■ 237 Stilisierte Weltkarte des vertikal ausgerichteten Unternehmens Marubeni America Corporation. Die Farben dienen
als Codes für die verschiedenen Geschäftszweige, z.B. Grau
für den Textilsektor, Blau für den Maschinensektor etc. Doppelseite aus dem Jahresbericht für 1984. (USA)

■ 238 Mit Farbstiften gezeichnete, stilisierte Karte der USA,
eine direkte Anspielung auf den Gegenstand der Darstellung,
die Holzreserven des Papierherstellers Champion International. Aus dem Jahresbericht der Firma für 1985. (USA)

■ 239 Karte als Übersicht der verschiedenen Projekte, Niederlassungen und Anlagen der Fluor Corporation, dargestellt durch verschiedenfarbige Quadrate. Die Länder, in
denen die Firma tätig ist, werden nochmal durch die Flag-
gen vor Augen geführt. Aus einem Jahresbericht. (USA)

■ 237 Planisphère stylisée montrant l'implantation verticale
de la Marubeni America Corporation. Les couleurs codent
les différents secteurs d'activités. C'est ainsi que le gris
désigne l'industrie textile, le bleu la construction mécanique, etc. Double page du rapport annuel 1984. (USA)

■ 238 Carte stylisée des Etats-Unis réalisée au crayon couleur, une allusion directe au sujet traité: les réserves de bois
du groupe papetier Champion International. Extrait du rapport annuel du groupe pour 1985. (USA)

■ 239 Carte donnant un aperçu des divers projets, succursales et usines de la Fluor Corporation symbolisés par des car-
rés de couleur différente. Les drapeaux rappellent les pays
où se déroulent les activités du groupe. Extrait d'un rapport
annuel de la Fluor Corporation. (USA)

DESIGNER:
THOMAS D. MORIN
ARTIST:
PAUL GIOUANOPOULOS
ART DIRECTOR:
THOMAS D. MORIN
AGENCY:
JACK HOUGH ASSOCIATES, INC.
CLIENT:
CHAMPION INTERNATIONAL
■ 238

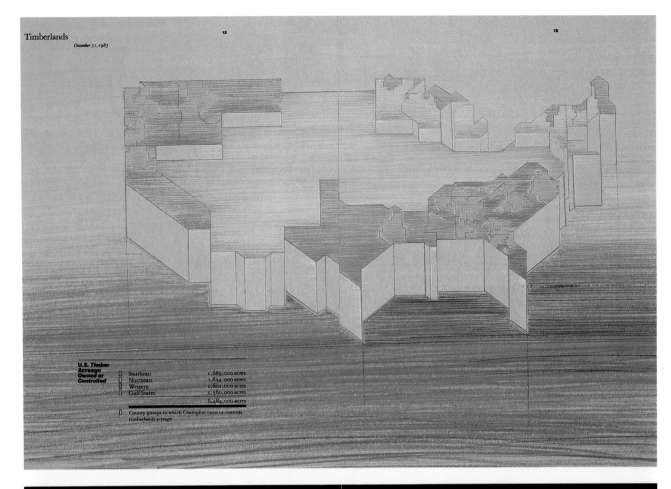

DESIGNER:
C. CLAUDIA JEFFERIES
ART DIRECTOR:
RON JEFFERIES
AGENCY:
THE JEFFERIES ASSOCIATION
CLIENT:
FLUOR CORPORATION
■ 239

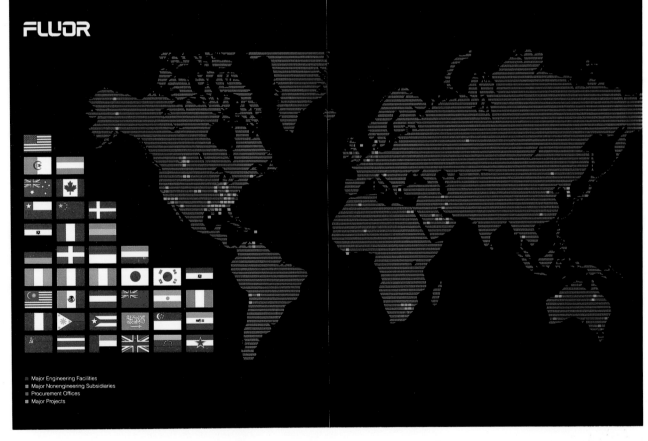

Understanding Maps and Scale

An overview of the most common maps published by the USGS

The U.S. Geological Survey (USGS) publishes a wide variety of maps over a range of different scales. This poster can help you understand the kinds of maps produced and it shows which are available at the most common scales.

Map Scale

The scale of a map describes the relationship between a distance on the map and the corresponding distance on the ground. Scale is usually expressed as a ratio. For example 1:24,000 is the scale of USGS standard quadrangle maps—1 inch on the map represents 24,000 inches on the ground.

The USGS publishes maps ranging in scale from 1:20,000 (1 inch represents about 1,600 feet) to 1:7,500,000 (1 inch represents about 120 miles).

The most common USGS map scales are listed in the column below. The colored dots in the columns to the right show the kinds of maps currently available at each scale.

Map Types

Planimetric Maps

Planimetric maps show the positions of features without showing the hills and valleys of the land. They usually include rivers, lakes, roads, transportation routes, and boundaries. The common road map is an example of a planimetric map.

Topographic Maps

Topographic maps show the positions of features and also represent their vertical position in a measurable form.

Contour maps are the most common method of representing the shape and elevation of the land. A contour is a line of equal elevation above or below a specific reference elevation—usually sea level.

Shaded-relief maps are pictorial. They are shaded to simulate sunlight on the terrain. This shadow effect accentuates the shape of the physical features.

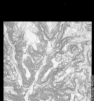

Slope maps show terrain by using a progression of colors or shades to indicate steepness of zones or similar slope zones.

Photoimage Maps

Photoimage maps are based on photographs taken from the air. They show details that are not usually represented by conventional map symbols.

Orthophotoquads are prepared from high-resolution black and white aerial photographs which have been corrected to eliminate the displacements of perspective, camera-tilt and terrain relief. They are scale-true, that is, they permit you to make accurate linear or area measurements.

Orthophotomaps are a further refinement of the orthophotoquad which also include contour lines and names. Orthophotomaps are color-enhanced to improve their readability. Like the orthophotoquads, they are related to standard quadrangle formats and reference systems.

Thematic Maps

Thematic maps are designed to show information about a specific topic such as geology, rainfall, population, etc. The entire map is devoted to presenting the distribution or concentration of the subject.

Geologic maps show the position, structure, and composition of geologic features such as types of rock, faults, and slope of mineral deposits.

Hydrologic maps display information about water resources. They are used to identify flood-prone areas and analyze water resources.

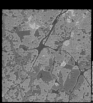

Land-Use maps display information about how land is being used. They depict many different categories of specific uses such as agricultural, recreational and urban lands.

US GeoData

US GeoData tapes are computer tapes which contain cartographic data in digital form.

Tapes are used in conjunction with special computer programs to automatically plot either complete maps or maps which contain only selected categories of information. Because the data for producing the map is in digital form, it is also possible to change the projection and scale of the map plot.

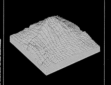

Terrain models are created from special US GeoData tapes, and they use different software to create contour bases as well as perspective drawings of the terrain.

Scale		Planimetric Maps	Topographic Maps			Photoimage Maps		Thematic Maps			US GeoData Tapes
			Contour	Shaded-relief	Slope	Orthophotoquads	Orthophotomaps	Geologic	Hydrologic	Land-Use	
1:24,000	7.5-minute series		●	●	●	●	●	●			●
1:25,000	7.5×15-minute metric series		●								
1:50,000	County Map and Quadrangle series		●								
1:62,500	15-minute series		●	●				●			
1:63,360	15-minute Alaska series		●	●				●			
1:100,000	30×60-minute series		●					●		●	
1:250,000	1×2-degree series		●		●			●	●	●	●
1:500,000	State Map series	●	●	●				●	●		
1:1,000,000	International Map of the World (IMW) series		●								
1:2,000,000	National Atlas Sectional Map series	●									●
1:7,500,000	United States	●						●	●		

Detail versus Area

Your choice of map scale depends on how you intend to use the map. A large-scale map shows more detail but less land area, while a small-scale map shows less detail but a larger land area.

Large-scale Maps: More detail, less area.
1:24,000 – 1:25,000

Intermediate-scale Maps
1:50,000 – 1:100,000

Small-scale maps: Less detail, more area.
1:250,000 – 1:7,500,000

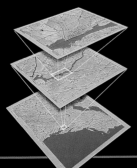

Minutes and Degrees

A minute is a unit of angular measurement equal to one-sixtieth of a degree. The entire globe contains 360 degrees.

A line of latitude across the United States from Richmond, Virginia, to San Francisco, California, spans 46 degrees of longitude—a distance covered by 368 quadrangle maps, each 7.5 minutes wide. At that latitude, a standard 7.5-minute quadrangle map represents an area approximately 7 miles from east to west and 8 miles north to south.

More Information

To find out if a map of a specific place is available or for detailed information about other maps not published by the U.S. Geological Survey, contact the National Cartographic Information Center.

US Maps are available from your local USGS map dealer and directly from the U.S. Geological Survey at the addresses shown below:

Eastern Distribution Branch
U.S. Geological Survey
1200 South Eads Street
Arlington, Virginia 22202

Western Distribution Branch
U.S. Geological Survey
Box 25286 Denver Federal Center
Denver, Colorado 80225

or the following office:

U.S. Department of the Interior
Geological Survey
National Mapping Program

DESIGNER:
AGNEW MOYER SMITH, INC.
ART DIRECTOR:
AGNEW MOYER SMITH, INC.
CLIENT:
U.S. GEOLOGICAL SURVEY
◀■ 240

DESIGNER:
JOHN & MARY CONDON
CLIENT:
*THE NEW YORK CONVENTION
& VISITORS BUREAU*
■ 241

■ 240 Poster with an overview and explanation of the most common maps scale published by the U.S. Geological Survey. (USA)

■ 241 Maps of the boroughs of New York: Manhattan, Bronx, Queens, Brooklyn, and Staten Island, specially drawn up for tourists. Cultural institutions, places of interest, railway stations, and airports etc. are indicated by the incorporation of the white numbers. (USA)

■ 240 Plakat mit einer Übersicht der gebräuchlichsten kartographischen Diagramme, die vom U.S. Geological Survey herausgegeben werden. (USA)

■ 241 Pläne für New Yorks Stadtteile Manhattan, Bronx, Queens, Brooklyn und Staten Island, speziell ausgerichtet auf Touristen. Kulturelle Einrichtungen, Sehenswürdigkeiten sowie Bahnhöfe, Flughäfen usw. sind hier durch die weissen Zahlen besonders deutlich hervorgehoben. (USA)

■ 240 Affiche présentant les principaux cartogrammes publiés par l'U.S. Geological Survey, les Services nationaux américains de géodésie. (USA)

■ 241 Plans des quartiers new-yorkais de Manhattan, du Bronx, de Queens, de Brooklyn et de Staten Island pour l'usage des touristes. Les hauts lieux de la culture, les sites, les gares, les aéroports, etc. sont signalés de façon particulièrement voyante par les chiffres blancs. (USA)

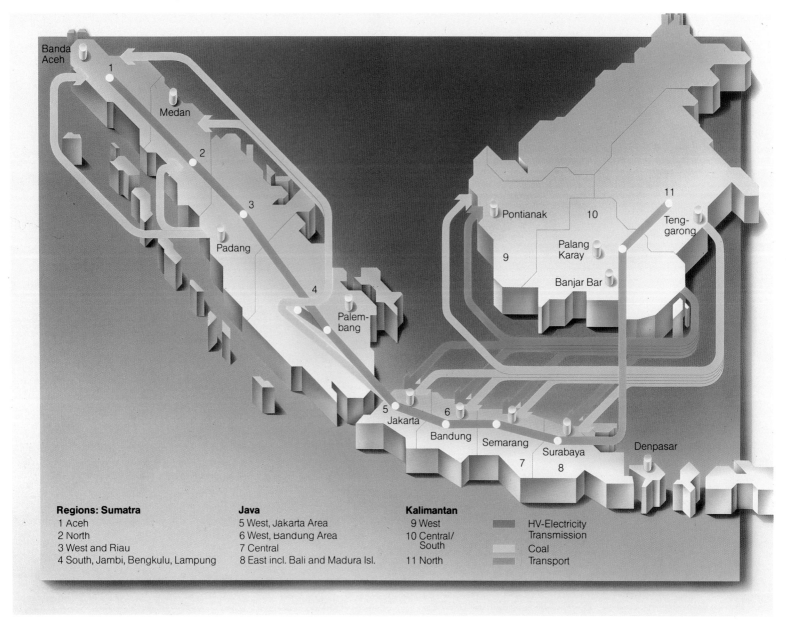

Regions: Sumatra
1 Aceh
2 North
3 West and Riau
4 South, Jambi, Bengkulu, Lampung

Java
5 West, Jakarta Area
6 West, Bandung Area
7 Central
8 East incl. Bali and Madura Isl.

Kalimantan
9 West
10 Central/South
11 North

■ HV-Electricity Transmission
■ Coal
■ Transport

DESIGNER:
HEINZ HENKEL
ARTIST:
WINFRIED FRASE
ART DIRECTOR:
PETER RADOWITZ
CLIENT:
SIEMENS AG
■ 242

DESIGNER:
JAMES CROSS
ART DIRECTOR:
JAMES CROSS
CLIENT:
AGI CONFERENCE ITINERARY
►■ 243

■ 242 Stylized map (airbrush graphic) of Sumatra, Java and Kalimantan (Borneo) showing the energy supply/transport routes. (GER)

■ 243 Program of the AGI conference giving duration of the journey by air, train, and car from various places in California to San Francisco, the venue. (USA)

■ 242 Stilisierte Karte (Spritzgraphik) der Inseln Sumatra, Java und Kalimantan (Borneo) zur Verdeutlichung der Energieversorgung und Transportwege. (GER)

■ 243 Tagungsprogramm der AGI mit Angabe der Reisedauer per Flug, Bahn und Auto von verschiedenen Orten in Kalifornien nach San Francisco, dem Ort des Treffens. (USA)

■ 242 Carte stylisée (airbrush) des îles de Sumatra, Java et Kalimantan (Bornéo): approvisionnement énergétique, voies de transport. (GER)

■ 243 Programme d'un congrès de l'AGI à San Francisco, avec l'indication de la durée du trajet en avion, par la route ou le train depuis différents points de la Californie. (USA)

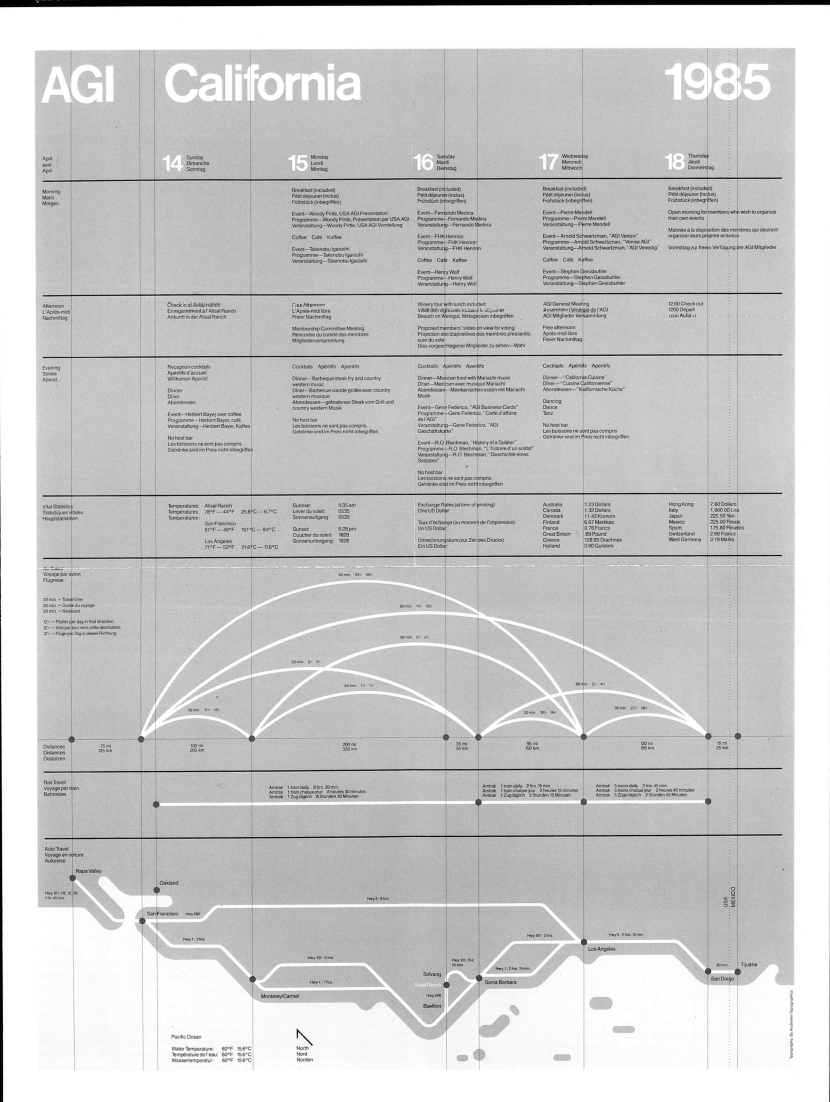

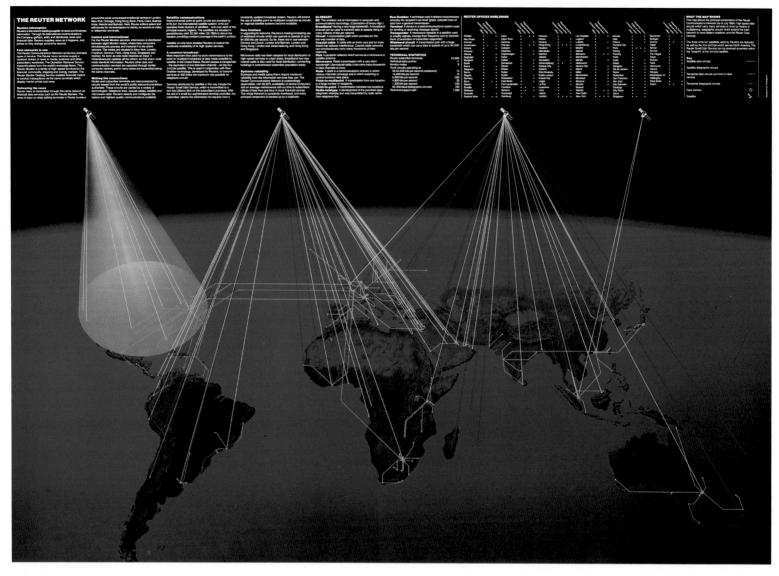

DESIGNER:
*MERVYN KURLANSKY/
BOB MAUDE*

ARTIST:
*RICHARD CLIFTON-DEY/
ROBERT TAYLOR*

ART DIRECTOR:
MERVYN KURLANSKY

AGENCY:
PENTAGRAM DESIGN, LONDON

CLIENT:
REUTERS
■ 244

■ 244 Geographic diagram of *Reuters,* the international news agency, giving information about data exchange and telegraph connections via satellites and overland, and also through their branches. (GBR)

■ 245 Map of the city published by the *San Francisco Business Times* depicting real estate development and showing the ages of the various buildings and their uses. (USA)

■ 244 Geographisches Diagramm der Nachrichtenagentur *Reuters,* das Aufschluss über die Datenvermittlung und die telegraphischen Verbindungen via Satelliten und auf dem Landweg sowie über die Niederlassungen gibt. (GBR)

■ 245 Von der *San Francisco Business Times* herausgegebene Karte der City, aus der das Baujahr und die Nutzung der Gebäude nach Kategorien ersichtlich sind. (USA)

■ 244 Diagramme géographique de l'agence de presse *Reuters* renseignant sur la transmission informatisée de données et les communications télégraphiques via satellite et par voie de terre, ainsi que sur les succursales de Reuters. (GBR)

■ 245 Carte du centre de San Francisco publiée par le *San Francisco Business Times:* année de construction et affectation des divers immeubles par catégories. (USA)

DESIGNER:
JACK & GAY REINECK

ARTIST:
JACK & GAY REINECK

ART DIRECTOR:
JACK & GAY REINECK

AGENCY:
REINECK & REINECK

CLIENT:
SAN FRANCISCO BUSINESS TIMES
■ 245

DESIGNER:
*KARTOGRAPHIEBÜRO
FRANZ HUBER*
AGENCY:
*KARTOGRAPHIEBÜRO
FRANZ HUBER*
PUBLISHER:
*FREMDENVERKEHRSAMT
MÜNCHEN*
■ 246–249

■ 246–249 Maps of Europe,
West Germany, and Bavaria
lead to a Munich city map
and finally to a map of the
inner city, with tourist information on the most impor-
tant buildings. From the
manual issued by the Tourist Authority Board of
Munich, 1987. (GER)

■ 246–249 Die Karten Europas, der Bundesrepublik
Deutschland und Bayerns
führen zu einem Stadtplan
Münchens und schliesslich
zu einem Plan des Zentrums
der Stadt mit Angabe der für
Touristen wichtigsten Bau-
werke. Aus dem Verkaufs-
handbuch des Fremdenver-
kehrsamtes der Landeshaupt-
stadt München, 1987. (GER)

■ 246–249 Ces cartes d'Europe, de la RFA et de Bavière
acheminent progressive-
ment le lecteur vers un plan
de la ville de Munich suivi
d'un plan du centre ville où
sont signalés les principaux
sites d'intérêt touristique.
Edition 1987 du Guide
d'agences de l'Office du tou-
risme de Munich. (GER)

Europa

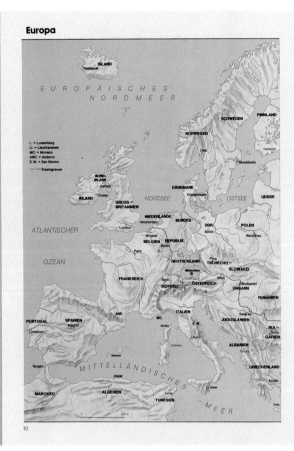

10

Bundesrepublik Deutschland

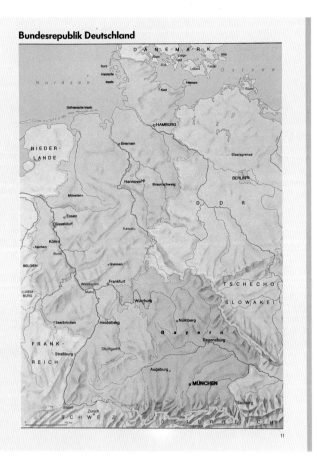

11

Bayern

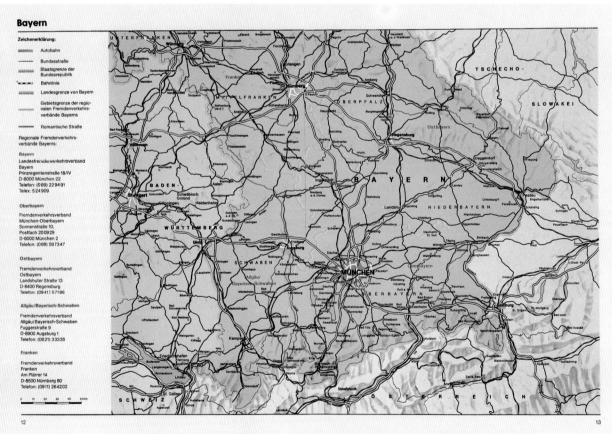

12

13

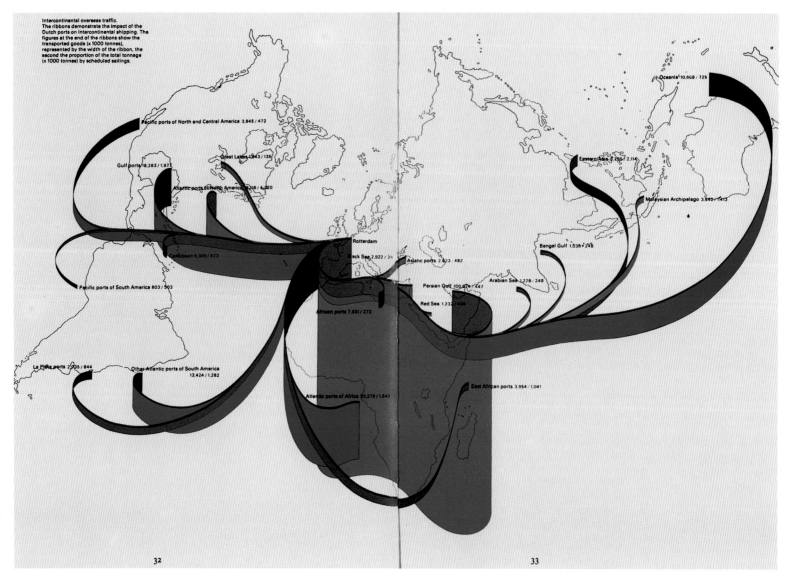

Intercontinental overseas traffic.
The ribbons demonstrate the impact of the
Dutch ports on intercontinental shipping. The
figures at the end of the ribbons show the
transported goods (x 1000 tonnes),
represented by the width of the ribbon, the
second the proportion of the total tonnage
(x 1000 tonnes) by scheduled sailings.

Pacific ports of North and Central America 3,845 / 472

Gulf ports 18,263 / 1,973

Great Lakes 1,343 / 135

Atlantic ports of North America 9,218 / 4,320

Caribbean 6,309 / 873

Pacific ports of South America 803 / 503

La Plata ports 2,035 / 844

Other Atlantic ports of South America
13,424 / 1,282

African ports 7,931 / 272

Atlantic ports of Africa 30,279 / 1,643

Rotterdam

Black Sea 2,922 / 34

Asiatic ports 2,023 / 482

Persian Gulf 100,976 / 447

Red Sea 1,232 / 408

East African ports 3,954 / 1,041

Arabian Sea 1,278 / 248

Bengal Gulf 1,036 / 248

Malaysian Archipelago 3,845 / 1,413

Eastern Asia 7,285 / 2,116

Oceania 10,668 / 725

32   33

DESIGNER:
BENNO WISSING/
JOHN STEGMEYER
ARTIST:
ART DIRECTOR:
AGENCY:
THE WISSING GENGLER
GROUP, INC.
CLIENT:
THE PORT OF ROTTERDAM
AUTHORITY
■ 250, 251

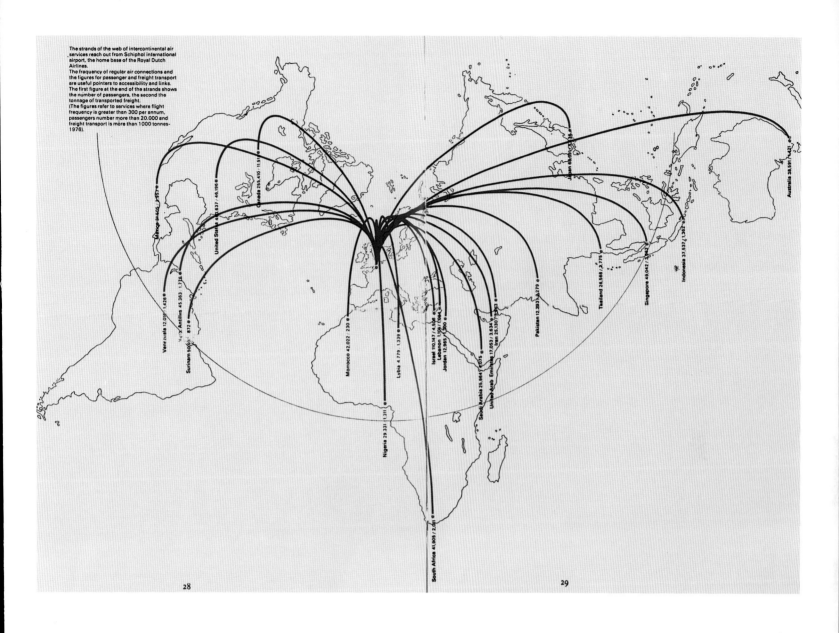

The strands of the web of intercontinental air
services reach out from Schiphol international
airport, the home base of the Royal Dutch
Airlines.
The frequency of regular air connections and
the figures for passenger and freight transport
are useful pointers to accessibility and links.
The first figure at the end of the strands shows
the number of passengers, the second the
tonnage of transported freight.
(The figures refer to services where flight
frequency is greater than 300 per annum,
passengers number more than 20,000 and
freight transport is more than 1000 tonnes-
1976).

28　　　　　　　　　　　　　　29

■ 250, 251 Maps of the world showing departure routes from Rotterdam for shipping and air transportation. The width of the stripes in *250* corresponds to the amounts of cargo transported by sea. The figures are given at the ends (in 1000 tons). The lines in *251* show the inter-continental destinations of the air traffic routes from Schipol International Airport, and figures are given of passenger and cargo traffic. The diagrams are taken from a book to publicize the importance and development potential of the port of Rotterdam, Holland. (NLD)

■ 250, 251 Weltkarten mit von Rotterdam ausgehenden Schiffs- und Flugrouten. Die Breite der Bänder in *250* richtet sich nach der Menge der auf dem Seeweg transportierten Güter. Die Werte sind in 1000 Tonnen an den Enden angegeben. Die Linien in *251* zeigen die interkontinentalen Destinationen, die vom Schipol International Airport aus angeflogen werden, mit Angabe der Passagier- und Frachtgutzahlen. Diagramme aus einem Buch über die Bedeutung Rotterdams für den internationalen Verkehr und über die Entwicklungsmöglichkeiten. (NLD)

■ 250, 251 Planisphères montrant les voies de communication maritimes et aériennes au départ de Rotterdam. La largeur des bandes de *250* est fonction du volume des marchandises transportées par mer. Les chiffres sont exprimés en milliers de t. Les lignes de *251* relient les destinations intercontinentales à l'aéroport international de Schipol; on trouve sur cette carte le nombre des passagers et le volume du fret. Diagrammes tirés d'un ouvrage qui met en évidence le rôle présent et les possibilités d'avenir de la plaque tournante internationale qu'est Rotterdam. (NLD)

Montgomery County

Points of interest
1 Valley Forge National Historical Park
2 Philadelphia Zoo
3 Civic Center
4 Museum of Art
5 City Hall
6 Independence National Historical Park
7 Penn's Landing
8 Sports Complex
9 Airport

I-276 PA Tpke

PA 9

Exit 25

Chemical Rd

Germantown Pk

Ridge Pike

US 202

I-476

Philadelphia

Exit 24

South Gulph Rd

I-76 Schuylkill Expwy

Lincoln Dr

Henry Ave

US 202

PA 320

Spring Mill Rd

PA 23

I-76 Schuylkill Expwy

Ridge Ave

US 1 Roosevelt Blvd

I-95

US 30 Lancaster Ave

PA 320

Conshohocken State Rd

Belmont Ave

US 1

Huntington Park Ave

PA 611 Broad St

Montgomery Ave

US 30 Lancaster Ave

PA 23

Monument Rd

Belmont Ave

Kelly Dr

Ridge Ave

US 1 City Ave

The Parkway

I-676–US 30–Vine St

Benj Franklin Br

NJ 38

Girard Ave

Spring Garden St

34th St

Arch St

I-676

Market St

22nd St

18th St

15th St

Market St

PA 291 Broad St

I-95

Spruce St

South St

Civic Center Blvd

West Whitman Br

Schuylkill River

I-76 Schuylkill Expwy

I-95

Delaware River

■ 253 View of the highway network and alternative routes necessary in the district of Philadelphia during highway building works. From a folded tourist prospectus issued by the Pennsylvania Department of Transportation. (USA)

■ 254 Maps of the detours and exit routes during construction works on a fast highway, parts of which are closed. From a brochure of the Pennsylvania Department of Transportation issued for regular and occasional users of the fast highway. (USA)

■ 253 Übersicht des Strassennetzes und der durch Strassenbau erforderlichen Ausweichmöglichkeiten in der Umgebung von Philadelphia. Aus einem Faltprospekt des Pennsylvania Department of Transportation. (USA)

■ 254 Übersichtspläne von Umleitungen und Ausfahrten während der Bauarbeiten an einer Schnellstrasse, von der jeweils Teilstrecken geschlossen werden. Aus einer Broschüre des Pennsylvania Department of Transportation für Benutzer der Schnellstrasse. (USA)

■ 253 Plan du réseau routier et des voies de déviation permettant de contourner les chantiers routiers dans les environs de Philadelphie. Dépliant du Pennsylvania Department of Transportation destiné aux touristes. (USA)

■ 254 Plans de situation des voies de détournement et des sorties d'autoroutes durant les travaux de réfection affectant des tronçons fermés à la circulation. Brochure du Pennsylvania Department of Transportation destinée aux usagers réguliers ou occasionnels de l'autoroute en question. (USA)

DESIGNER:
JOEL KATZ
ART DIRECTOR:
JOEL KATZ
AGENCY:
KATZ WHEELER DESIGN
CLIENT:
PENNSYLVANIA DEPARTMENT OF TRANSPORTATION
■ 253, 254

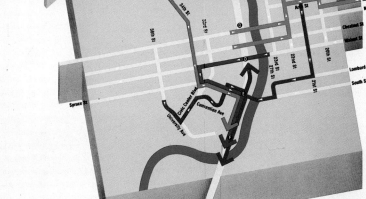

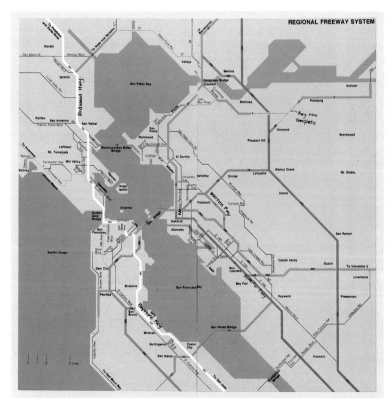

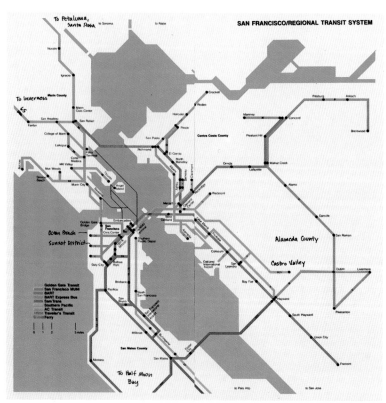

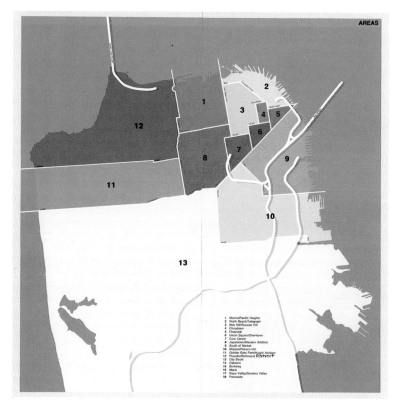

DESIGNER:
RICHARD SAUL WURMAN
ART DIRECTOR:
MICHAEL EVERITT
PUBLISHER:
ACCESS PRESS LTD.
■ 255-259

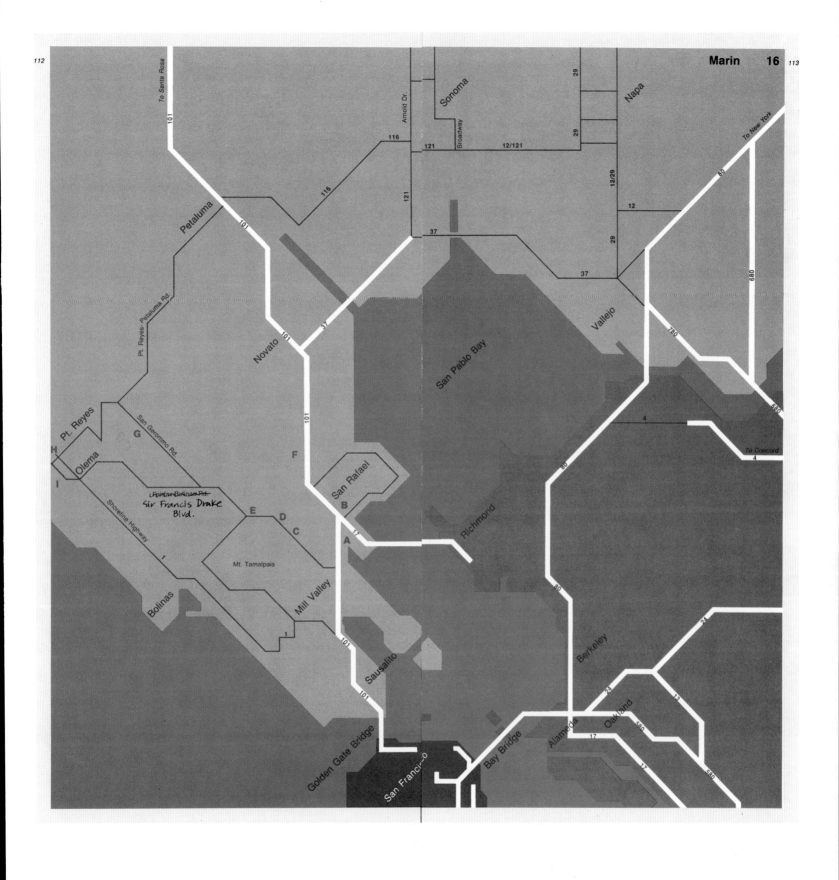

■ 255-259 Cartographic diagrams from a city guide to San Francisco - one of the *Access* series. Shown are overviews of the regional road networks, the transit system, city districts, the city's bus and tramcars, and the "Marin" - the peninsula north of the Golden Gate Bridge. (USA)

■ 255-259 Kartographische Diagramme aus einem in der *Access*-Reihe erschienenen Stadtführer für San Francisco. Hier Übersichten des regionalen Strassennetzes, des Transit-systems, der Stadtteile, der Stadt mit Bus und Strassenbah-nen und der «Marin» genannten Halbinsel. (USA)

■ 255-259 Cartogrammes figurant dans un guide *Access* de San Francisco. Ils représentent le réseau routier régional, le système de transit, les différents quartiers de la ville, le réseau des transports publics - autobus et tramways - et la presqu'île Marin au nord du pont du Golden Gate. (USA)

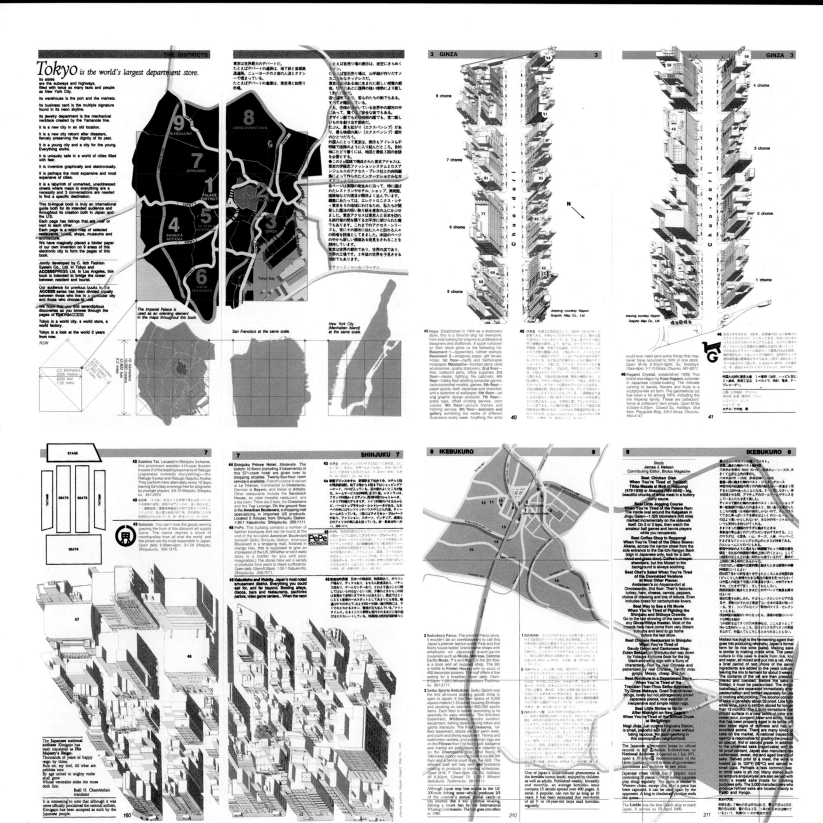

DESIGNER:
RICHARD SAUL WURMAN
ART DIRECTOR:
RICHARD SAUL WURMAN
PUBLISHER:
ACCESS PRESS LTD.
■ 260, 263, 264

DESIGNER:
RICHARD SAUL WURMAN
ARTIST: *HARUHIKU GRAPHIC*
PUBLISHER:
ACCESS PRESS LTD.
■ 261, 262

■ 260-264 Double spreads from a city guide to Tokyo (Access Press). Shown is a map indicating various areas of the city, below with special emphasis on the Emperor's Palace, which serves as size comparison on all maps; on the same scale also a comparison with San Francisco and Manhattan. *261* shows the blocks of houses in the shopping area, *262* the area Shinjuku with cinema and theater, *263* a plan of the new shopping and leisure area Ikebukuro located on the city outskirts, and *264* a view of two subway lines and their connections. (USA)

■ 260-264 Doppelseiten aus einem Stadtführer für Tokio (Access Press). Hier eine Karte mit den verschiedenen Stadtteilen, unten mit besonderem Gewicht auf dem kaiserlichen Palast, der auf allen Karten als Vergleichsgrösse dient; ausserdem im gleichen Massstab ein Vergleich mit San Francisco und Manhattan. *261* zeigt die Häuserblocks des Einkaufsviertels, *262* den Stadtteil Shinjuku mit Kino und Theater, *263* einen Übersichtsplan des am Stadtrand gelegenen neuen Einkaufs- und Unterhaltungsdistrikts Ikebukuro und *264* eine Übersicht von zwei U-Bahnlinien. (USA)

■ 260-264 Doubles pages d'un guide de Tokyo édité par Access Press. 260: carte des différents quartiers; dans la partie inférieure, l'accent est mis sur le Palais impérial qui sert d'unité de référence pour les surfaces; à la même échelle, comparaison avec San Francisco et Manhattan. 261: les pâtés de maisons du quartier commercial; 262: quartier de Shinjuku (cinémas et théâtres); 263: plan d'ensemble du nouveau quartier périphérique d'Ikebukuro (commerces et divertissements); 264: plan de réseau de deux lignes de métro, avec les correspondances. (USA)

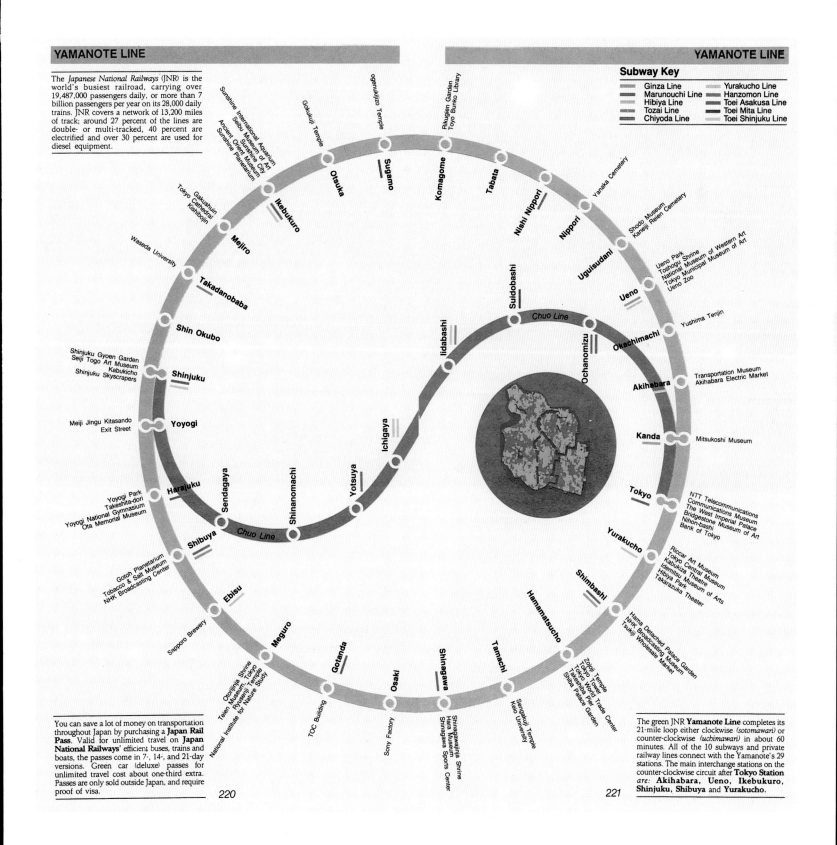

YAMANOTE LINE

The *Japanese National Railways* (JNR) is the world's busiest railroad, carrying over 19,487,000 passengers daily, or more than 7 billion passengers per year on its 28,000 daily trains. JNR covers a network of 13,200 miles of track; around 27 percent of the lines are double- or multi-tracked, 40 percent are electrified and over 30 percent are used for diesel equipment.

YAMANOTE LINE

Subway Key

Ginza Line	Yurakucho Line
Marunouchi Line	Hanzomon Line
Hibiya Line	Toei Asakusa Line
Tozai Line	Toei Mita Line
Chiyoda Line	Toei Shinjuku Line

You can save a lot of money on transportation throughout Japan by purchasing a **Japan Rail Pass**. Valid for unlimited travel on **Japan National Railways'** efficient buses, trains and boats, the passes come in 7-, 14-, and 21-day versions. Green car (deluxe) passes for unlimited travel cost about one-third extra. Passes are only sold outside Japan, and require proof of visa.

The green JNR **Yamanote Line** completes its 21-mile loop either clockwise (*sotomawari*) or counter-clockwise (*uchimawari*) in about 60 minutes. All of the 10 subways and private railway lines connect with the Yamanote's 29 stations. The main interchange stations on the counter-clockwise circuit after **Tokyo Station** are: **Akihabara, Ueno, Ikebukuro, Shinjuku, Shibuya** and **Yurakucho**.

■ 265 Stylized map of the United States with various symbols that give information about the location, energy, transport routes, and activities of the companies belonging to the energy concern Union Pacific Corporation. Double spread from the group's annual report. (USA)

■ 266 Plan of the underground railway of Baghdad. (IRQ)

■ 265 Stilisierte Karte der Vereinigten Staaten mit verschiedenen Symbolen, die über die Lage, Energie, Transportwege und Aktivitäten der zu dem Energie-Konzern Union Pacific Corporation gehörenden Firmen Aufschluss gibt. Doppelseite aus dem Jahresbericht der Firmengruppe. (USA)

■ 266 Plan des U-Bahnnetzes von Bagdad. (IRQ)

■ 265 Carte stylisée des Etats-Unis dont les symboles renseignent sur l'implantation et les activités des sociétés affiliées au groupe énergétique Union Pacific Corporation, ainsi que sur le réseau de transport de l'énergie produite. Double page d'un rapport annuel du groupe. (USA)

■ 266 Plan du métro de Bagdad. (IRQ)

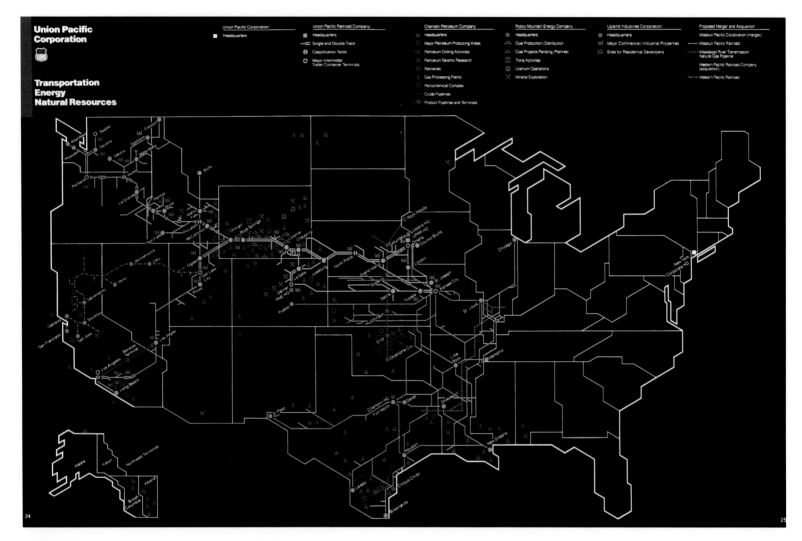

DESIGNER:
STEFF GEISSBUHLER/
OLIVER JOHNSTON
ART DIRECTOR:
TOM GEISMAR/
STEFF GEISSBUHLER
AGENCY:
CHERMAYEFF & GEISMAR
CLIENT:
UNION PACIFIC CORP
■ 265

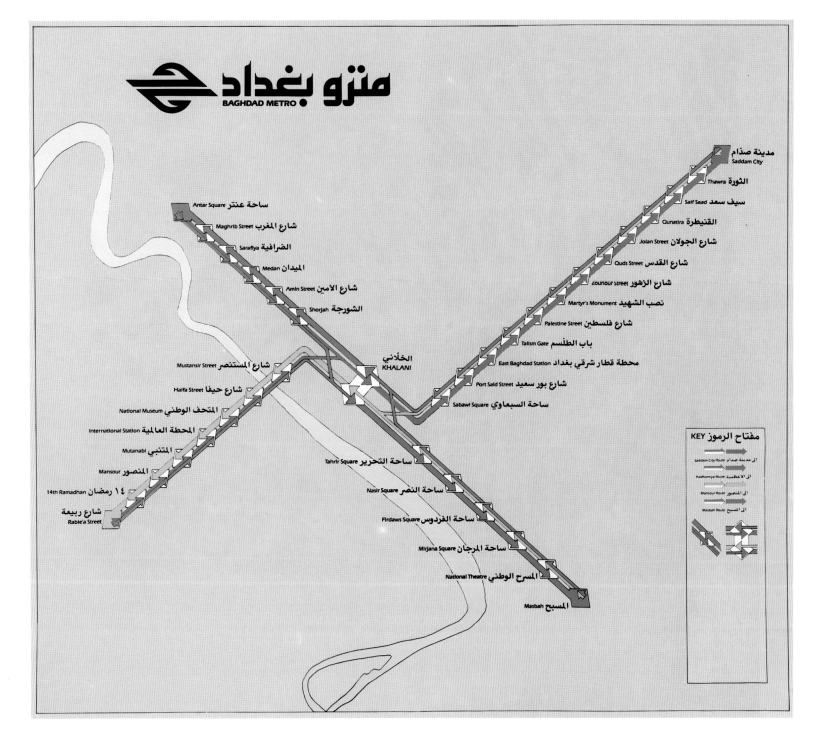

DESIGNER:
RICHARD DRAGUN
ART DIRECTOR:
RICHARD DRAGUN
AGENCY:
DESIGN RESEARCH UNIT LONDON
CLIENT:
*BAGHDAD RAPID
TRANSIT AUTHORITY*
■ 266

WEGWIJZER

HIER BEVINDT U ZICH
XYZ BEGIN/EINDPUNT VAN HOOFDROUTE
XYZ BESTEMMING
HOOFDROUTE
ZIJTAK ROUTE
■ INFO-ZUIL MET STRATEN- EN
BESTEMMINGENREGISTER

DIRECTION SIGN

YOU ARE STANDING HERE
XYZ START/END OF MAIN ROUTE
XYZ DESTINATION
MAIN ROUTE
BRANCH ROUTE
■ INFO PILLAR WITH STREET AND
DESTINATION REGISTER

WEGWEISER

HIER BEFINDEN SIE SICH
XYZ ANFANG/ENDPUNKT DER HAUPTROUTE
XYZ BESTIMMUNGSORT
HAUPTROUTE
ROUTEABZWEIGUNG
■ INFO-SAULE MIT STRASSEN- UND
BESTIMMUNGSORTSVERZEICHNIS

POTEAU INDICATEUR

VOUS ETES ICI
XYZ DEBUT/FIN DE L'ITINERAIRE PRINCIPAL
XYZ DESTINATION
ITINERAIRE PRINCIPAL
ITINERAIRE SECONDAIRE
■ COLONNE INFORMATION AVEC REGISTRE
DES RUES ET DES DESTINATIONS

6 MIN/500 M

A
B2/C1 ACHTERBURGWAL, OUDEZIJDS
B2 ALLARD PIERSON MUSEUM
B2/C3 AMSTEL
BC2 AMSTELSTRAAT
B3 AMSTELVELD
B2 AMSTERDAMS HISTORISCH MUSEUM
A1 ANNE FRANKHUIS
C2 ANTONIESBREESTRAAT, SINT
D2 ARTIS ZOO

B
A3 BAERLESTRAAT, VAN
B2 BEGIJNHOF
B2 BIJBELS MUSEUM
B2 BLOEMENMARKT
A1 BLOEMGRACHT
B3 BOLSTRAAT, FERDINAND
A3 BROUWERSPLEIN, J.W.

C
C3 CARRE
C3 CEINTUURBAAN
C1 CENTRAAL STATION
A3 CONCERTGEBOUW
B3 CUYPSTRAAT, ALBERT

D
B1 DAM
B1 DAMRAK
B2 DAMSTRAAT
B2 DOELENSTRAAT, OUDE

E
A1 EGELANTIERSGRACHT
A2 ELANDSGRACHT

F
A1 FRANKHUIS, ANNE
C2 FRANKSTRAAT, ANNE
C3 FREDERIKSPLEIN

G
C1 GELDERSEKADE
A3 GOGHMUSEUM, VAN

H
B1 HAARLEMMERSTRAAT
BC1/C3 HENDRIKKADE, PRINS
B1-2/C2 HERENGRACHT
C2 HERENGRACHT, NIEUWE
CD1 HET IJ
B3 HOBBEMAKADE
B3 HOBBEMASTRAAT
A3 HOOFTSTRAAT, P.C.
C2 HOOGSTRAAT, NIEUWE
B2 HOOGSTRAAT, OUDE
D2 HOOGTE KADIJK
C2 HORTUS BOTANICUS

J
C2 JODENBREESTRAAT
C2 JOODS HISTORISCH MUSEUM (OPEN AS FROM MAY 1987)

K
B2 KALVERSTRAAT
B1-2-3 KEIZERSGRACHT
C2 KEIZERSGRACHT, NIEUWE
CD2 KERKLAAN, PLANTAGE
C1/B2 KLOVENIERSBURGWAL
B2 KONINGSPLEIN
B1 KONINKLIJK PALEIS

L
A2 LAURIERGRACHT
AB2 LEIDSEGRACHT
A2-3 LEIDSEPLEIN
AB2 LEIDSESTRAAT
A1-2/B3 LIJNBAANSGRACHT
AB1 LINDENGRACHT
D3 LINNAEUSSTRAAT
A2 LOOIERSGRACHT

M
C3 DE MAGERE BRUG
A1-2 MARNIXSTRAAT
C3-4/D2 MAURITSKADE
C2 MEIJERPLEIN, JONAS DANIEL
CD2 MIDDENLAAN, PLANTAGE
B2 MUNTPLEIN
B2 MUSEUM FODOR
A3 MUSEUM OVERHOLLAND
A3 MUSEUMPLEIN
C2 MUSEUM WILLET HOLTHUYSEN
C2 MUZIEKTHEATER/STADHUIS

N
A1-2 NASSAUKADE
B1 NIEUWE KERK, DE
B1 NIEUWENDIJK
B1-2 NIEUWEZIJDS VOORBURGWAL
C2 NIEUWMARKT

O
C1 ONS' LIEVE HEER OP SOLDER
C1 OOSTERDOKSKADE
D3 OOSTERPARK
BC1 OUDE KERK
B2/C1 OUDEZIJDS ACHTERBURGWAL
B1-2/C1 OUDEZIJDS VOORBURGWAL
A3 OVERTOOM

P
CD2 PLANTAGE KERKLAAN
CD2 PLANTAGE MIDDENLAAN
C2 PLANTAGE PARKLAAN
A2 POLITIEBUREAU LIJNBAANSGRACHT
B1 POLITIEBUREAU WARMOESSTRAAT
A3 POTTERSTRAAT, PAULUS
AB1-2/BC3 PRINSENGRACHT
C2-3 PRINSENGRACHT, NIEUWE
B1 PTT POSTKANTOOR

R
B1 RAADHUISSTRAAT
B2 REGULIERSBREESTRAAT
B2-3 REGULIERSGRACHT
B2 REMBRANDTHUIS
B2 REMBRANDTPLEIN
B3 RIJKSMUSEUM
C2-3 ROETERSSTRAAT
B2 ROKIN
A1 ROZENGRACHT
BC1 RUIJTERKADE, DE

S
C3/D2-3 SARPHATISTRAAT
C2 SCHEEPVAARTMUSEUM
C1 SCHREIERSTOREN
B1-2 SINGEL
B2-3 SPIEGELSTRAAT, NIEUWE
B2 SPUI
B1-2 SPUISTRAAT
ABC3 STADHOUDERSKADE
C2 STADHUIS/MUZIEKTHEATER
A2 STADSSCHOUWBURG
BC1 STATIONSPLEIN
A3 STEDELIJK MUSEUM

T
B1 THEATERMUSEUM
B2 THORBECKEPLEIN
TOURIST INFORMATION
A2 - VVV-III LEIDSESTRAAT
BC1 - VVV-III STATIONSPLEIN
D3 TROPENMUSEUM

V
C2 VALKENBURGERSTRAAT
A3 VAN GOGHMUSEUM
B3 VEILIGHEIDSINSTITUUT
B3 VIJZELGRACHT
B2-3 VIJZELSTRAAT
A3 VONDELPARK
B1-2 VOORBURGWAL, NIEUWEZIJDS
B1-2/C1 VOORBURGWAL, OUDEZIJDS
A2 VVV-III LEIDSESTRAAT
BC1 VVV-III STATIONSPLEIN

W
B1 WARMOESSTRAAT
C2 WATERLOOPLEIN
C2-3 WEESPERSTRAAT
C3 WESTEINDE
AB1 WESTERMARKT
B3 WETERINGPLANTSOEN
B3 WETERINGSCHANS
C3 WIBAUTSTRAAT
C3 WOUSTRAAT, VAN

Z
D2 ZOOLOGISCH MUSEUM

BC1

AMSTERDAM TOURIST OFFICE
POSTBUS 3901
1001 AS AMSTERDAM

COLOPHON
SYSTEEM: VIA VERKEERSADVIESBURO, VUGHT
ONTWERP: PAUL MERTZ/MARGREEN BOSMA, TOTAL DESIGN
KAART: PAUL LÄUDERMAN

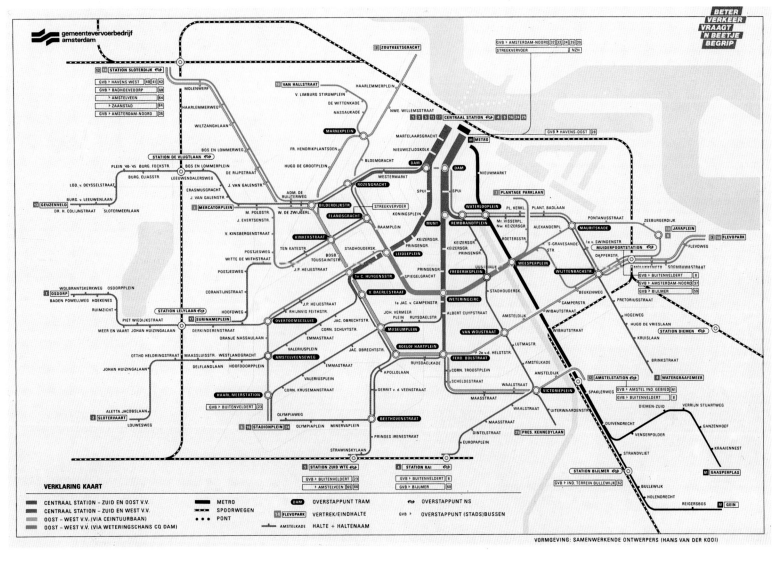

DESIGNER:
Rijk Boerma/Paul Mijksenaar
AGENCY:
Total Design
CLIENT:
VVV, Amsterdam
◄■ 267

DESIGNER:
Hans van der Kooi
ART DIRECTOR:
Hans van der Kooi
AGENCY:
Samenwerkende Outwerpers
CLIENT:
City of Amsterdam
■ 268

■ 267 Plan for visitors to the city of Amsterdam. The red lines show the route to the various tourist sights. (NLD)

■ 268 Plan with the railway and underground network of the city of Amsterdam. (NLD)

■ 267 Für Besucher von Amsterdam gestalteter Plan. Die rote Linie weist den Weg zu Sehenswürdigkeiten. (NLD)

■ 268 Plan mit dem Strassenbahn- und U-Bahnnetz der Stadt Amsterdam. (NLD)

■ 267 Plan réalisé à l'intention des touristes visitant Amsterdam. La ligne rouge relie les sites touristiques. (NLD)

■ 268 Plan du réseau des transports publics de la ville d'Amsterdam - tramways et métro. (NLD)

QUICK REFERENCE TO SERVICES

Services	Terminal A	Terminal B	Terminal C	North Terminal
Bank	C	C		C
Barber	C	C		
Book/Gift Shop	C	C		C
Cafeteria	C	C	D	
Car Rental Counters/Phones	A	A		C
Cash Machine	C			
Cocktails	C/S	C/S	D	C
Coffee/Snacks	C/S	C/S	D	C
Duty Free Shop		C	D	C
Elevator for Disabled (For assistance call 961-2154)	A/D/C	A/D/C		
Foreign Currency Exchange		C		C
Hotel Reservations Phones	A	A		
Ice Cream	C	C		C
Information Counter	A	A	A	C
Limo Counters/Phones	A	A		
Lockers		S		
Mail Slots	C	C		C
Newsstand/Smoke Shops	C/S	C/S	D	C
Nursery	C	C		C
Pay TV			D	
Pharmacy	C			
Stamp Machines	C	C		C
Shoeshine	C			C
Telegram	C	C		
Ticketing	D	D	D	C
Travelers Checks/Vending Machine	C	C		
Travel Insurance	C/S	C		C

A = Arrivals Area
D = Departures Area
C = Concourse
S = Satellite Area

14   15

QUICK REFERENCE TO SERVICES

Services	International Arrivals Building (Bus Stops #2, 6, 8)	American Airlines Terminal (Bus Stop #16)	United Airlines Terminal (Bus Stop #18)	Eastern Airlines Terminal (Bus Stop #20)	Northwest/Delta Terminal (Bus Stop #22)	Pan American Airlines Terminal (Bus Stops #24A, 24)	TWA International Terminal A (Bus Stop #10)	TWA Domestic Terminal B (Bus Stop #12)	British Airways Terminal (Bus Stop #14)
Bank									
Barber/Beauty Shop									
Book/Gift Shop									
Cafeteria									
Car Rental Counter/Phones									
Cash Machine									
Cocktails									
Coffee/Snacks									
Duty Free Shops									
Foreign Currency Exchange									
Free Limo Phones									
Gourmet Shops									
Hotel Reservations									
Ice Cream									
Information Counter									
Locker/Baggage Storage									
Newsstand/Smoke Shop									
Nursery									
Pay Television									
Pharmacy									
Postal Stamp Vending Machine									
Post Office									
Shoeshine									
Telegrams									
Travelers Checks Vending Machines									
Travel Insurance									

14   15

Central Terminal Building

Finger 1 Gates 1 to 10
Finger 2 Gates 11–21
Finger 3 Gates 22–29
Finger 4 Gates 30–36
To Parking Garage
NY Helicopter

Second Floor
Ticketing

Lobby
Ramp

First Floor
Baggage Claim

Bus to Eastern Air Terminal
Bus to Parking Lots DELTA NORTHWEST Q33 and Q48 Buses Carey Coaches to NYC
Carey Coaches to NYC and Kennedy Int'l Airport
Bus to Marine Air Terminal
Bus to Eastern Shuttle

Central Terminal Building Key

American Express Machine	Duty Free	Liquor Bar	Restrooms
Barber	Elevator	Lobster	Shoe Shine
Bank	Facilities for Handicapped	Mail Box	Taxi
Books	Fruit & Nuts	Manufacturers Hanover Trust	Terrace Restaurant—4th Floor
Bus	Gift/Toys	Money Exchange	TV Chairs/Coin Operated
Car Rental	Hotel Reservations	Newsstand	Snack Bars in All Fingers
Coffee Shop	Insurance	Nursery	
Drug Store	Limousine Service	Post Office	

DESIGNER:
PAM AHERN
ART DIRECTOR:
ROSS HUDSON
AGENCY:
OGILVY & MATHER PROMOTIONAL CAMPAIGNS, INC.
CLIENT:
PORT AUTHORITY OF NEW YORK & NEW JERSEY
■ 269–270a

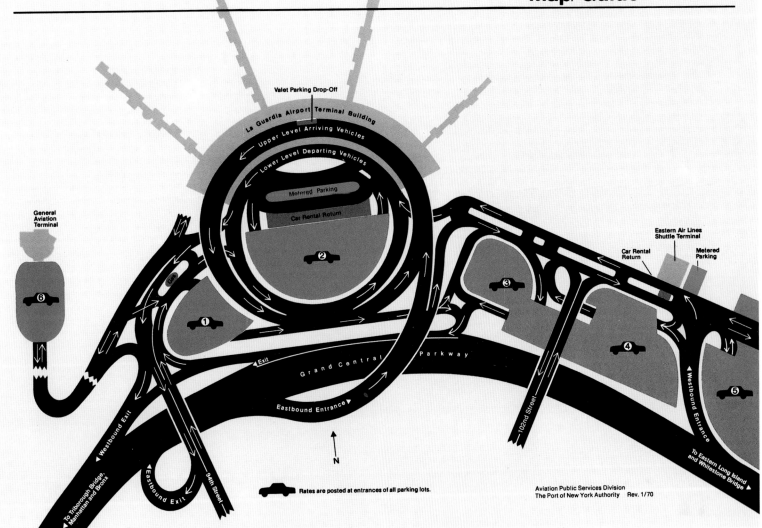

La Guardia
Airport
Map/Guide

Valet Parking Drop-Off

La Guardia Airport Terminal Building

Upper Level Arriving Vehicles

Lower Level Departing Vehicles

Metered Parking

Car Rental Return

General
Aviation
Terminal

Eastern Air Lines
Shuttle Terminal

Car Rental
Return

Metered
Parking

Grand Central Parkway

Exit

Eastbound Entrance ▶

Westbound Exit

▼ Westbound Exit

▲ Eastbound Exit

94th Street

▲ To Triborough Bridge,
Manhattan and Bronx

N

102nd Street

Westbound Entrance

To Eastern Long Island
and Whitestone Bridge ▲

Rates are posted at entrances of all parking lots.

Aviation Public Services Division
The Port of New York Authority   Rev. 1/70

■ 269 Charts with overviews of the public service areas in various buildings of Newark and JFK international airports. The color coding helps identify different buildings and assists the distinguishing of them. (USA)

■ 270, 270a Overview of two floors of La Guardia Airport, New York, from a brochure for the handicapped; and a folder showing the airport grounds and access roads, which serves as a guide for air passengers and visitors. (USA)

■ 269 Tabellen mit Übersichten der Dienstleistungsbetriebe in den verschiedenen Gebäuden der internationalen Flughäfen Newark und JFK, New York. Die Farbkodierung nach Gebäuden unterstützt die klare Aufteilung. (USA)

■ 270, 270a Übersicht von zwei Stockwerken des La Guardia Airports aus einem Prospekt für Behinderte und eine Faltkarte, die als Führer dieses Flughafens dient und das Flughafengelände und die Zufahrtsstrassen zeigt. (USA)

■ 269 Tableaux énumérant les entreprises de services installées dans les aéroports internationaux de Newark et J.F. Kennedy de New York. Le code couleur attribué aux bâtiments permet de s'y retrouver facilement. (USA)

■ 270, 270a Vue d'ensemble de deux étages de l'aéroport La Guardia de New York, dans un prospectus pour handicapés; carte dépliante servant à l'orientation des passagers et visiteurs de l'aéroport avec indication des voies d'accès. (USA)

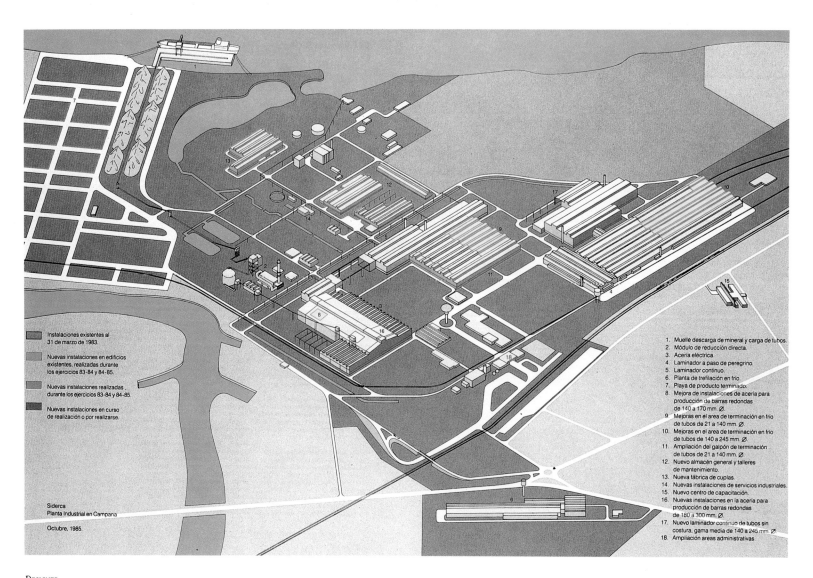

1. Muelle descarga de mineral y carga de tubos.
2. Módulo de reducción directa.
3. Acería eléctrica.
4. Laminador a paso de peregrino.
5. Laminador continuo.
6. Planta de trefilación en frío.
7. Playa de producto terminado.
8. Mejora de instalaciones de acería para producción de barras redondas de 140 a 170 mm. Ø.
9. Mejoras en el area de terminación en frío de tubos de 21 a 140 mm. Ø.
10. Mejoras en el area de terminación en frío de tubos de 140 a 245 mm. Ø.
11. Ampliación del galpón de terminación de tubos de 21 a 140 mm. Ø.
12. Nuevo almacén general y talleres de mantenimiento.
13. Nueva fábrica de cuplas.
14. Nuevas instalaciones de servicios industriales.
15. Nuevo centro de capacitación.
16. Nuevas instalaciones en la acería para producción de barras redondas de 180 a 300 mm. Ø.
17. Nuevo laminador continuo de tubos sin costura, gama media de 140 a 245 mm. Ø.
18. Ampliación areas administrativas.

Instalaciones existentes al 31 de marzo de 1983.

Nuevas instalaciones en edificios existentes, realizadas durante los ejercicios 83-84 y 84-85.

Nuevas instalaciones realizadas durante los ejercicios 83-84 y 84-85.

Nuevas instalaciones en curso de realización o por realizarse.

Siderca
Planta Industrial en Campana

Octubre, 1985.

DESIGNER:
RUBÉN FONTANA
AGENCY:
RUBÉN FONTANA
CLIENT:
SIDERCA
■ 271

■ 271 Plan for a proposed extension of a factory. (ARG)

■ 272 Folded prospectus with diagram to show the planning of a new community near the Japanese town of Yokohama. (JPN)

■ 273 Pictorial diagram of 53rd Street, Manhattan, with the most important buildings marked. From one of the area's tourist folders. (USA)

■ 271 Plan für den projektierten Ausbau einer Fabrik. (ARG)

■ 272 Faltprospekt mit Bilddiagramm, das Auskunft über die Planung einer neuen Gemeinde in der Nähe Yokohamas gibt. (JPN)

■ 273 Bilddiagramm der 53. Strasse in Manhattan, mit Bezeichnungen der wichtigsten Gebäude. Aus einem für Touristen bestimmten Faltprospekt. (USA)

■ 271 Plan du projet d'extension d'une usine. (ARG)

■ 272 Dépliant comportant un diagramme illustré: information sur le projet d'établir une cité-satellite près de Yokohama. (JPN)

■ 273 Diagramme illustré de la 53e Rue de Manhattan, avec l'indication des principaux bâtiments. Dépliant de quartier destiné aux touristes. (USA)

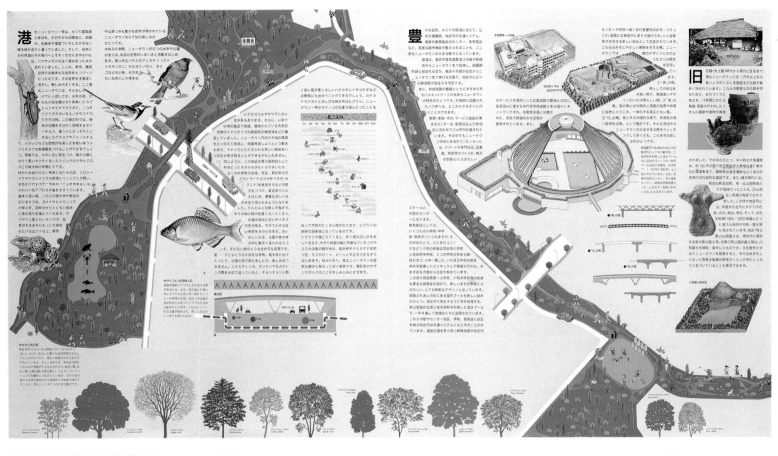

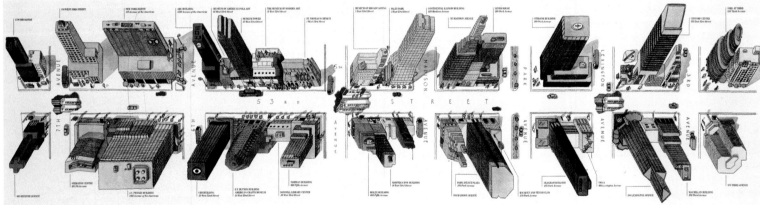

DESIGNER:
Isao Kusumi/Tokihiro Okuda/
Kenzo Nakagawa
ARTIST:
Isao Kusumi/Tokihiro Okuda/
Kenzo Nakagawa
ART DIRECTOR:
Isao Kusumi/Tokihiro Okuda/
Kenzo Nakagawa
AGENCY:
RIV Associates
CLIENT:
Housing and Urban
Development
▲■ 272

DESIGNER:
Michael Gericke/
Kaspar Schmid
ARTIST:
Steven Guarnaccia
ART DIRECTOR:
Colin Forbes
AGENCY:
Pentagram Design, USA
CLIENT:
53rd Street Associates, NYC
■ 273

ALCATRAZ

Alcatraz sits alone in the middle of San Francisco Bay, a small, rocky island sometimes barely visible through the fog. It is only 1¼ miles from Fisherman's Wharf—yet for years it seemed as inaccessible as if it were a thousand miles out to sea. Because the island appeared so uninviting, it played a vivid role in California history. It was the site of a powerful fortress, a military prison, and a federal prison whose inmates were isolated by a ring of water and a barricade of mystery created by the island's tight security.

Today Alcatraz is no longer a forbidding and forbidden place but a national park, open to anyone who wants to retrace its many interesting years. You can join a ranger-guided walk or explore the island on your own, following the sequence in this Map and Guide.

The National Park Service welcomes you to Alcatraz.

Alcatraz wharf

Dock Tower
"Your constant vigilance insures safety." The wharf was guarded by the dock tower during the federal-prison era. Three towers were strategically located on the island, where tower guards kept a lonely watch. Today, the dock tower is the last of the guard towers still standing.

Wharf
"The first glimpse of Alcatraz fills a convict with grim forebodings," noted Bryan Conway. From the wharf, the island's only safe boat landing, the men got the first glimpse of their new home. The original wharf was built in 1854, when Alcatraz was a military fort; it has been repaired and enlarged over the years.

Fortified Barracks/Exhibit Area/Theater/Bookstore
The ground floor of the fortified barracks, built between 1865 and 1867, originally served to bastion the wharf. When Alcatraz was a military fortress, the building was intended to house both soldiers and cannon. The guns, however, were technically obsolete before they were ever mounted. In 1905, a three-story apartment building for soldiers was constructed atop the brick fortifications. Today, the armored enclosures, or "casemates," meant for cannons are occupied by an exhibit area, theater, and bookstore.

Temporary barracks atop fortified brick casemates, ca. 1900

Guardhouse/Sally Port
Alcatraz was the most highly fortified military site on the West Coast during the 1860s. This guardhouse with its "sally port," or armed gate, was built in 1857 and is the oldest standing building on the island. A dry moat once stretched across the road and had a drawbridge that could be pulled up to block entry.

Sally port, ca. 1900

Attackers who got beyond these would have been met by a barrage of bullets fired through the rifle-slit windows in the thick brick walls of the entry way.

During the Civil War, wooden walls transformed the gun rooms into cells for Confederate agents and other enemies of the Union. After the Civil War, other structures were built to enlarge the Army prison complex.

Chapel
In the 1920s the Army built a two-story addition atop the guardhouse, in the graceful mission-revival style of architecture. The first floor became employee living quarters, and the upper floor served as a school and occasional chapel for military families.

Military chapel, ca. 1920

Post Exchange (Ruins)
Throughout the last half of the nineteenth century and until 1933, the post was occupied not only by soldiers and military prisoners but

also by soldiers' families. The Post Exchange, built in 1910, sold food and domestic articles, contained a gymnasium and a bowling alley. Later, the Exchange was turned into a recreation hall and club for correctional officers and their families. The Post Exchange was destroyed by fire in 1970.

Post exchange, ca. 1910

Warden's House (Ruins)
Once an imposing residence with spacious rooms and high windows opening onto spectacular views of the Bay, the warden's house was reduced to a charred ruin after a 1970 fire. The house had been built in 1929 for Col. G. Maury Cralle, commandant of the island military prison. Tough as well as fair, Cralle ended a 1926 mass-escape threat by announcing to the assembled prisoners, "Go ahead—swim!" The house was later occupied in 1934 by James A. Johnston, the first warden of the new federal penitentiary, and by all subsequent wardens.

Warden's house, 1934

Officer's row, 1893

Officers' Quarters (Ruins)
On the harsh, rockbound fortress, life had its pleasanter side. Military officers and their families lived in handsome 1880s Victorian cottages surrounded by flower gardens. Though the cottages themselves were demolished in 1940, the brick basements and stairways of three homes are still visible in the dense foliage.

First U.S. lighthouse on the Pacific coast, built 1854

Second lighthouse, built in 1909 to tower above the new prison

Lighthouse
In 1854, the first U.S. lighthouse on the Pacific coast was built on Alcatraz. The lightkeepers lived in a cottage at the base and climbed into the high tower to clean the lens of the light and keep the oil lamp full. In 1909 the old lighthouse was replaced by an 84-foot tower, high enough to be seen above the recently completed cellblock. The oil lamp gave way to an electric light, but the lightkeepers remained on Alcatraz after the prison closed in 1963. The light is now automated.

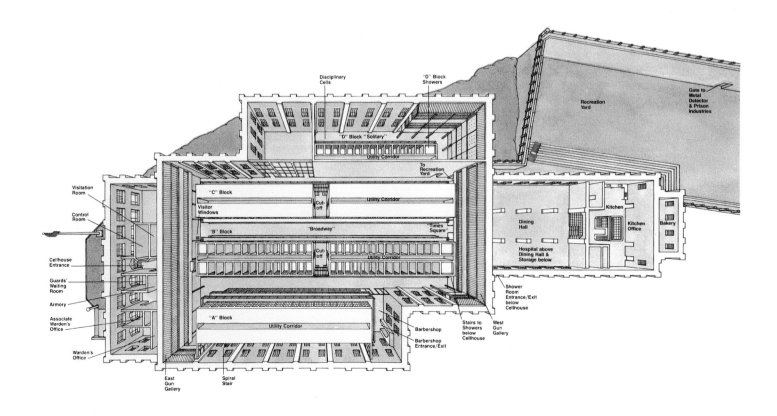

Visitation Room · Control Room · Cellhouse Entrance · Guards' Waiting Room · Armory · Associate Warden's Office · Warden's Office · East Gun Gallery · Spiral Stair · "A" Block · Utility Corridor · "B" Block · "Broadway" · "C" Block · Visitor Windows · Cut-Off · Utility Corridor · Disciplinary Cells · "D" Block "Solitary" · "D" Block Showers · Recreation Yard · Gate to Metal Detector & Prison Industries · Times Square · To Recreation Yard · Kitchen · Dining Hall · Kitchen Office · Bakery · Hospital above Dining Hall & Storage below · Shower Room Entrance/Exit below Cellhouse · West Gun Gallery · Stairs to Showers below Cellhouse · Barbershop · Barbershop Entrance/Exit

DESIGNER:
JACK & GAY REINECK
ARTIST:
JACK & GAY REINECK
ART DIRECTOR:
JACK & GAY REINECK
AGENCY:
REINECK & REINECK
CLIENT:
*GOLDEN GATE NATIONAL PARK
ASSOCIATION*
◄■ 274-276

DESIGNER:
*ALAN FLETCHER/
PENNY HOWARTH*
ARTIST:
RON SANDFORD
ART DIRECTOR:
ALAN FLETCHER
AGENCY:
PENTAGRAM DESIGN, LONDON
CLIENT:
LLOYD'S OF LONDON
■ 277

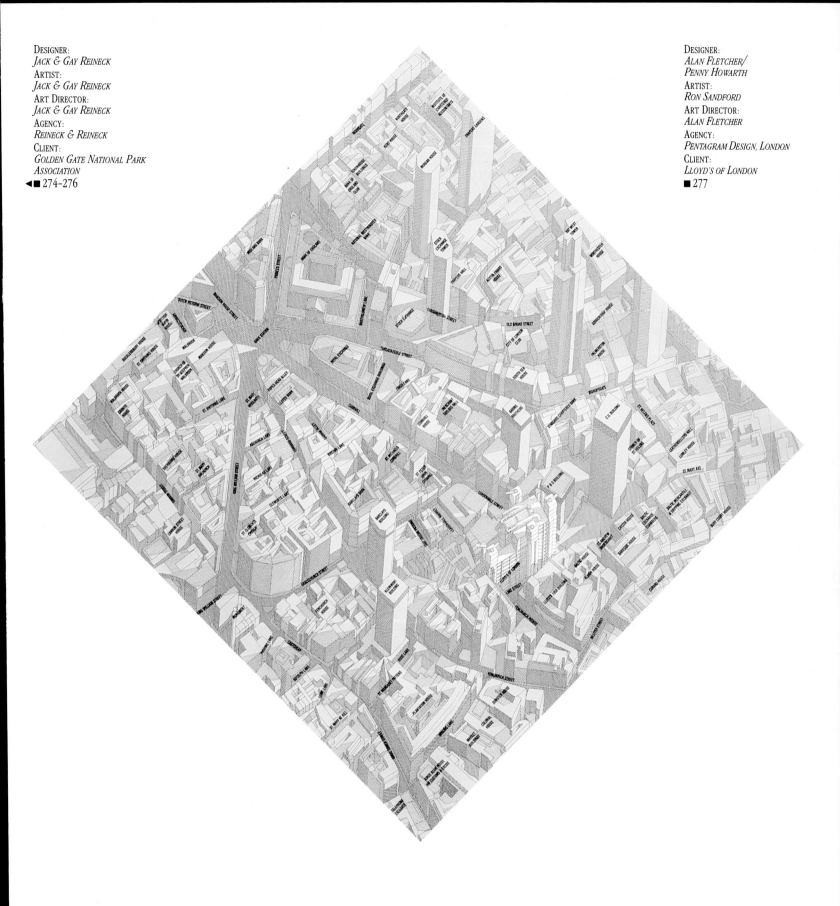

■ 274-276 Plans of the notorious island of Alcatraz and its equally infamous prison, which is now a national park and popular tourist attraction. *275* shows the front and inside pages of a folder for visitors. (USA)

■ 277 A bird's eye view and pictorial map of the new *Lloyds* building in London. (GBR)

■ 274-276 Pläne der berühmt-berüchtigten Insel Alcatraz und des Gefängnisses, heute Nationalpark und beliebtes Ausflugsziel. *275* zeigt die Vorderseite und die Innenseite des für Besucher bestimmten Faltprospekts. (USA)

■ 277 Bildkarte der Umgebung eines neuen Gebäudes von *Lloyds* London aus der Vogelperspektive. (GBR)

■ 274-276 Plans de la célèbre île d'Alcatraz et de sa prison aujourd'hui transformées en parc national et site d'excursion très prisés des touristes. Recto et pages intérieures du dépliant destiné aux visiteurs. (USA)

■ 277 Dessin cartographique représentant à vol d'oiseau les alentours d'un bâtiment du *Lloyds* de Londres. (GBR)

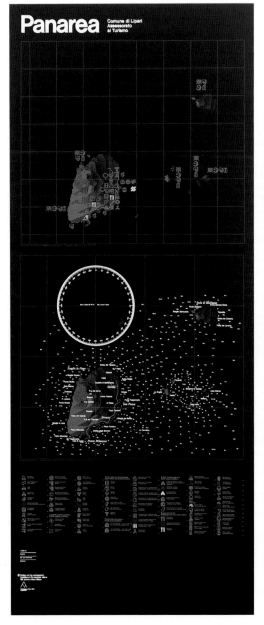

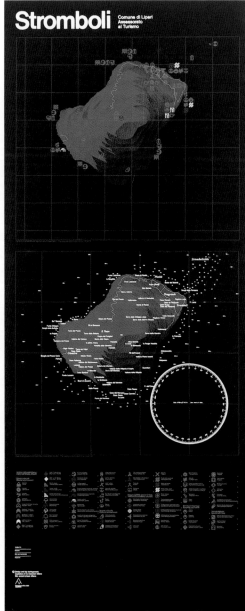

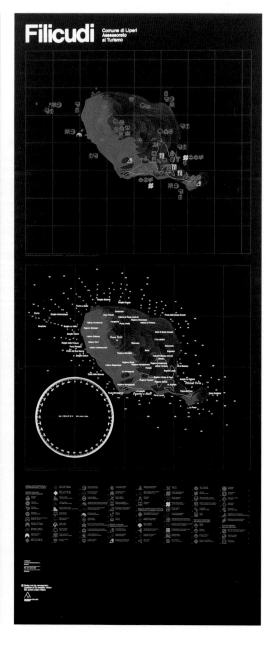

DESIGNER:
MIMMO CASTELLANO
ART DIRECTOR:
MIMMO CASTELLANO
AGENCY:
MIMMO CASTELLANO
& CO. ASSOCIATI
CLIENT:
COMUNE DI LIPARI
■ 278–280

■ 278–280 Three examples from a series of tourist brochures for the Lipari Islands. A version of the maps uses symbols to show the topographic and climatic conditions as well as various establishments and offices that are of interest to tourists. (ITA)

■ 281 Isometric diagram of the center of Seattle. This form of diagram allows the tourist to recognize buildings by their shape. Restrained coloring adds to the tastefulness and effectiveness of this map. (USA)

■ 278–280 Drei Beispiele aus einer Serie von Touristik-Prospekten für die Lipari-Inseln. Eine Version der Karten zeigt jeweils anhand von Symbolen topographische und klimatische Gegebenheiten sowie verschiedene Einrichtungen und Behörden, die für Touristen von Interesse sind. (ITA)

■ 281 Isometrische Darstellung des Zentrums von Seattle. Diese Form der Darstellung erlaubt dem Touristen, Gebäude anhand ihrer Form zu erkennen. Zurückhaltende Farben lassen diese Karte geschmackvoll und elegant wirken. (USA)

■ 278–280 Trois exemples de prospectus touristiques dans une série réalisée pour les îles Eoliennes. Une version des cartes fait état des données topographiques et climatiques par le truchement de symboles et renvoie à diverses institutions et autorités intéressant le touriste. (ITA)

■ 281 Représentation isométrique du centre de Seattle, qui permet aux touristes de reconnaître les bâtiments d'après leur forme. Les coloris atténués sont censés conférer à cette carte un caractère d'élégance de bon loi. (USA)

Sponsoring Hotels:
(48)Alexis Hotel & Restaurant, 1st at Madison
(7)The Best Western Executive Inn, 200 Taylor N.
(9)Edgewater Inn, Pier 67
(40)Four Seasons Olympic Hotel, 411 University
(39)Holiday Inn Crowne Plaza, 6th at Seneca
(42)The Madison Hotel, 6th at Madison
(23)Mayflower Park Hotel, 4th at Olive
(41)The Pacific Plaza, 4th at Spring
(37)The Seattle Hilton, 6th at University
(34)Seattle Sheraton Hotel, 6th at Pike
(16)The Warwick Hotel, 4th at Lenora
(36)Washington Athletic Club, 1325 6th
(18)The Westin Hotel, Seattle, 1900 5th

Antiques:
(27)The Globe Antiques, 6th at Pine
(26)Wide World Shop, 5th at Pine

Apparel:
(Also see Department Stores)
(27)Frank More Shoes, 511 Pine
(28)I. Magnin, Pine at 6th
(40)John Doyle Bishop, 411 University
(B-84)Littler, Rainier Square
(B-84)Polo/Ralph Lauren Shop, Rainier Square

Art:
(51-H)Flury & Co., 1st S. at S. Jackson
(26)Foster White Gallery, Frederick & Nelson
(48)Legacy, Ltd., 1st at Madison
(40)R31, 411 University
Seattle Art Museum, Volunteer Park (See Inset)
(6-D)Seattle Art Museum Pavilion, Seattle Center
(26)Steuben Gallery, Frederick & Nelson

Booksellers:
(B-84)B. Bailey Books, Rainier Square
(51-H)Elliott Bay Book Company, 1st So. at So. Main
(26)International News & Books, Frederick & Nelson
(43-C)Peter Miller Architecture & Design Books, 1909 1st
(34)Seattle Book Center, 2nd at Bell

Department Stores:
(24)The Bon, 4th at Pine
(26)Frederick & Nelson, 5th at Pine
(29)Nordstrom, 5th at Pine

Florists:
(B-84)Crissey Flowers & Gifts, Rainier Square
(40)Topper's English Floral Design, 411 University

Gifts for the Home:
(45)A Cook's Tour, Pier 56
(43-E)Sur la Table, 84 Pine

Jewelry:
(32)Rivkin's Jewelers, 4th at Pike
(33)Ben Bridge Jeweler, 409 Pike

Legal Services:
(B-84)Davis Wright, Todd, Riese & Jones, Sea-First Bldg.

Luggage:
(19)Bergman Luggage Company, Third at Virginia

Music:
(6-F)Seattle Opera, Seattle Center Opera House
(6-F)Seattle Symphony, Seattle Center Opera House

Northwest Gifts:
(21)The Emerald Fox, 410 Stewart
(22)Exclusively Northwest, 415 Stewart
(50)Ye Olde Curiosity Shop, Pier 51

Oriental Rugs:
(51-G)The Golden Horn, 317 1st St.

Outdoors:
(B-25)Eddie Bauer, Rainier Square
(17)Yak Works, 2004 Westlake

Photography:
(B-25)Olympic Camera Rainier Square
One Hour Film Stop:
(2)508 3rd W.
(3)506 Pike
(B-82)708 3rd

Public Houses:
(43-D)Kell's, 1916 Post Alley
(48)The Mark Tobey, Madison at Post

Restaurants:
(48)Alexis Restaurant, First at Madison
(23)Clipper's, Mayflower Park Hotel, 409 Olive
(43-F)Copacabana, Pike Place Market
(26)Frederick & Nelson, 5th at Pine
(34)Fuller's, Sheraton Hotel, 6th at Pike
(40)The Georgian, Four Seasons Olympic Hotel, 411
University
(43-G)Gill Bistro, Pike Place Market
(47)Italia, 1010 Western
(46)Ivar's Acres of Clams, Pier 54
Ivar's Captain's Table, 333 Elliott W.
Ivar's Salmon House, North Lake Union (See Inset)
(49)Metropolitan Grill, 2nd at Marion
(20)1904 Restaurant; Bar, 1904 3rd
(51-H)Occidental Grill, Occidental S. at S. Main
Osteria Mitchelli, 2040 Westlake N.
(43-H)Place Pigalle, Pike Place Market
(42)Prego, Madison Hotel, 6th at Madison
(49)Shuckers, Four Seasons Olympic Hotel, 4th at Seneca
(51)Le Tastevin French Restaurant, 19 W. Harrison
(10)Trade Winds, 1st at Wall
(51-B)Trattoria Mitchelli, Yesler at Post

Shopping Arcades:
(6-A)Center House, Seattle Center
(B-88)First Interstate Center Plaza, 2nd at Marion
(51-F)Grand Central Arcade, 214 1st S.
(B-34, 25)Rainier Square, 4th at Union

Specialty Foods:
Aplets & Cotlets at fine stores everywhere
(26)Arcade Deli & Bakery, Frederick & Nelson
(51-C)Geppetto's Gelateria, 1st at Yesler
(29)See's Candies, 1623 Westlake

Specialty Gifts:
(43-C)Bazaar des Bears, 1927 1st
(45)Trident Imports, Pier 56

Tours & Attractions:
(39)Freeway Park
(45)Harbor Tours, Pier 56
(5)International District
(52)King Street Station, AMTRAK
(MR)Monorail
(4)Myrtle Edwards Park
(6-C)Pacific Science Center, Seattle Center
(43)Pike Place Market
(51)Pioneer Square
(44)Seattle Aquarium, Waterfront Park
(8)Tillicum Tours to Victoria and Vancouver, B.C.,
departing Pier 69
(45)Tillicum Village on Blake Island, departing Pier 56
(51-A)Underground Tour, Pioneer Square
(WT)Waterfront Trolley

Toys:
(22)Christopher House, 4th at Stewart

Travel Residences:
Chelsea Green: 451-0707
Condominium Rentals of Seattle: 454-2800

Visitors Information:
(B-21)Downtown Seattle Association, 1402 3rd: 623-0340
(B-19)Seattle-King County Convention & Visitors Bureau,
1807 7th: 447-7273
The Weekly, Seattle's Newsmagazine, on sale everywhere.
Seattle Best Places, at better bookstores

Wine Merchants:
(40)Chatwin's Wine Merchants, 411 University

● Major Office Buildings:
The following major office buildings are listed in the
Seattle Business Journal's Downtown Office Building
Directory. Note that office buildings are keyed separately
from Commercial Sponsors—look for the special color
code.
(9) Aetna Plaza, 2201-6th
(5)Airborne Building, Western at Bay
(46)Alaska Building, 618-2nd
(42)Arctic Building, 700-3rd
(35)Bank of California Center, 900-4th
(15)Broadacre Building, 1601-2nd
(45)Broderick Building, 619-2nd
(39)Colman Building, 811-1st
(36)Columbia Center, 5th at Columbia
(16)A. E. Doyle Building, 119 Pine
(30)111 Third Avenue, 1111-3rd
(1)Elliott Bay Office Park, 300 Elliott W.
(38)First Interstate Center, 999-3rd
(8)Fourth & Battery Building, 2401-4th
(10)Fourth & Blanchard Building, 4th at Blanchard
(7)Fourth & Vine Building, 2615-4th
(44)Hoge Building, 705-2nd
(43)Dexter Horton Building, 710-2nd
(22)Jones Building, 1333-3rd
(12)Lloyd Building, 603 Stewart
(14)Marsh & McLennan Building, 720 Olive
Metropolitan Tract:
(27)IBM Building, 1200-5th
(24)Rainier Bank Tower (Rainier Square), 1301-5th
(25)Skinner Building (Rainier Square), 1326-5th
(26)Unigard Financial Center, 1215-4th
(23)Washington Building, 1325-4th
(13)Northern Life Building, 1100-3rd
(40)Norton Building, 801-2nd
(17)Olympic Tower, 217 Pine
(3)One Hundred West Harrison Plaza, 100 W. Harrison
(4)One Ninety Queen Anne Building, 190 Queen Anne
(28)One Union Square, 600 University
(41)Pacific Building, 720-3rd
(29)Park Place Building, 1200-6th
(11)Plaza 600 Building, 600 Stewart
(37)Seafirst Fifth Avenue Plaza, 800-5th
(42)Seattle First National Bank Building, 1001-4th
(33)Sixth & Pike Building, 6th at Pike
(47)Smith Tower, 506-2nd
(19)Stimson Center, 1420-5th
(6)Third & Broad Building, 3rd at Broad
(13)Tower Building, 1807-7th
(2)Two Hundred West Thomas Building, 200 W. Thomas
(21)Joseph Vance Building, 1402 3rd
(20)Washington Federal Building, 5th at Pike
(14)Waterfront Place Building, Western at Madison
(31)Watermark Tower, 1st at Spring

Art Gallery Guide:
This guide to downtown art galleries featuring
contemporary Northwest, American and international
artists is courtesy of the Weekly, Seattle's Newsmagazine, and
Seattle Best Places, the authority on greater Seattle's
best restaurants, stores and attractions.
(43-D)Clay Occasion (ceramics), Stewart House, 343-5992
(51-C)Davidson Galleries (etchings and woodcuts), 87
Yesler, 624-7684
(51-C)Donnally/Hayes, 85 Yesler, 622-7669
(51-J)Linda Farris Gallery, 320 2nd S., 623-1110

(51-H)Flying Shuttle, Ltd. (fiber arts), 310 1st S., 343-9762
(51-F)Foster/White Gallery, 311½ Occidental S., 622-2833
(51-K)Gallery mack Northwest, 123 S. Jackson, 623-1464
(43-D)The Glass Eye (art glass), 1902 Post Alley, 682-5929
(51-G)The Hodges/Banks Gallery, 319 1st S., 624-3034
(51-C)Manolides Gallery, 89 Yesler, 622-3204
(30)Nancy Reque Gallery, 1512 5th, 447-9166
(51-H)Native Design (ethnic crafts), 108 S. Jackson,
624-9985
(43-B)Penryn Gallery, 1920½ 1st, 632-6533
(51-H)Pioneer Square Gallery, 314 1st S., 625-9753
(51-K)Sacred Circle Gallery of American Indian Art, 2223
4th, 223-0072
(15)Sander-Crichton Gallery, 2134 3rd, 621-0001
(51-C)Silver Image (photography), 92 S. Washington,
623-8116
(51-C)Stone Press Gallery, 91, Yesler, 624-6752
(42)Assomington Gallery, 2030 1st, 621-1108
(15)Traver Sutton Gallery, 2219 4th, 622-4234
(12)Two Bells Tavern (Scheduled exhibitions), 4th at Bell,
345-9203
(43-C)The Virginia Inn (occasional exhibitions), 1st at
Virginia, 624-3173

Theatre Guide:
This guide to live theatre in downtown Seattle is courtesy
of the law firm of Davis, Wright, Todd, Riese & Jones.
(1)ACT—A Contemporary Theatre, 100 W. Roy, 285-5110
(10)City Stage (Opening Summer, 1984), 2318 4th, 622-0251
The Empty Space Theatre, 919 E. Pike on Capitol Hill,
325-4443; Opening October, 1984, at First S. at S. Jackson
(B-25)The Fifth Avenue Theatre, Skinner Building, Rainier
Square, 625-1900
(35)Intiman Theatre (at Second Stage), 8th between Pike
and Union, 587-5766
(51-D)Pioneer Square Theatre,107 Occidental S. in Pioneer
Square, 682-2346
(6-F)Seattle Repertory Theatre, Bagley Wright Theatre,
Seattle Center, 447-2222

DESIGNER:
DOUG FAST

ARTIST:
ROBERT PECKHAM

ART DIRECTOR:
DOUG FAST

AGENCY:
JAY ROCKEY PUBLIC RELATIONS

PUBLISHER:
ROCKET CONCIERGE PUBLISHING

■ 281

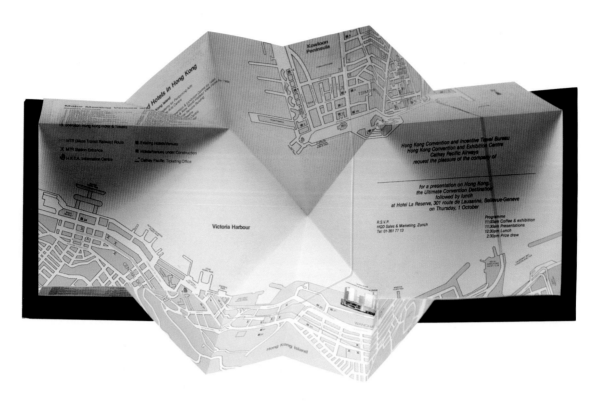

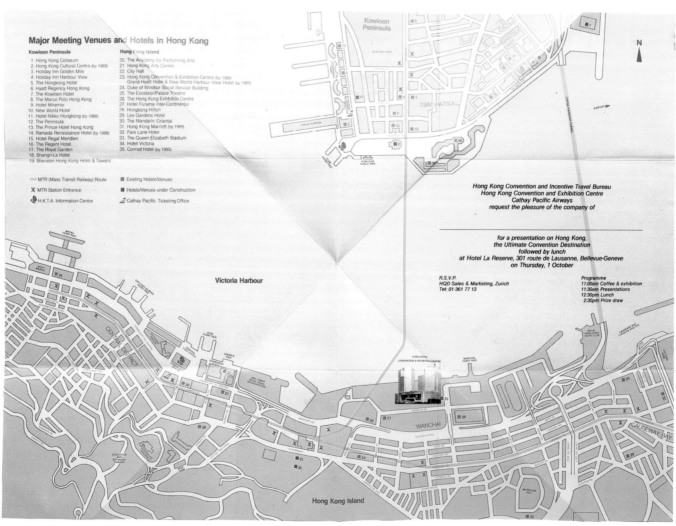

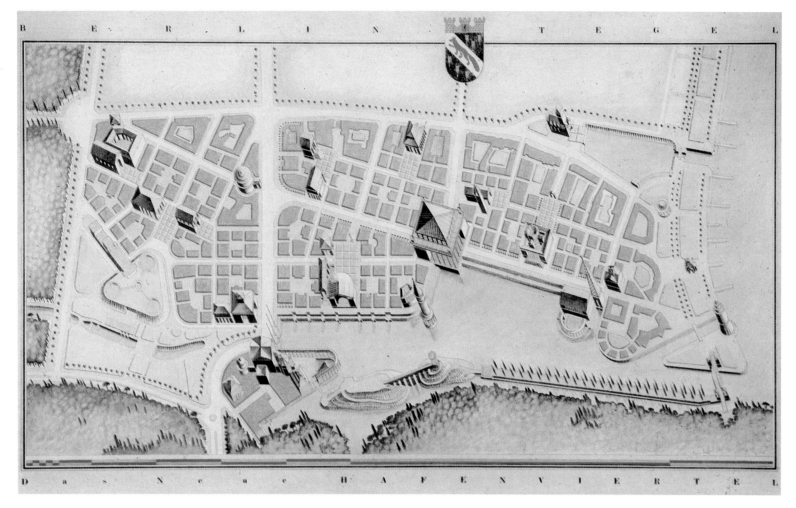

DESIGNER:
HELEN LAI
CLIENT:
*HONG KONG CONVENTION
& INCENTIVE TRAVEL BUREAU*
◀■ 282, 283

ARTIST:
LEON KRIER
PUBLISHER:
KLETT-COTTA
CLIENT:
*DEUTSCHES ARCHITEKTUR-
MUSEUM FRANKFURT*
■ 284

■ 282, 283 Half opened and fully opened map showing a part of Hongkong. It was sent by the Society of Exhibitions and Trade Fairs as an invitation to a conference. Shown are the public transport services, the tourist center and the existing and planned hotels. (HKG)

■ 284 "The New Harbor District". This design on the theme "Living and Leisure in Tegel Harbor" was submitted to the International Building Exhibition, Berlin, 1987, and won an award. It is in the form of a tourist plan (color pencil on paper, scale 1:2000). From the book *Internationale Bauausstellung Berlin 1987*, Klett-Cotta-Verlag. (GER)

■ 282, 283 Halb und ganz geöffnete Karte von Hongkong, die von der Gesellschaft für Messen und Ausstellungen als Einladung zu einer Tagung verschickt wurde. Es sind die öffentlichen Verkehrsmittel, das Touristenzentrum sowie die vorhandenen und geplanten Hotels eingezeichnet. (HKG)

■ 284 «Das neue Hafenviertel.» Zur Internationalen Bauausstellung Berlin 1987 eingereichter und prämierter Entwurf zum Thema «Wohnen und Freizeit am Tegeler Hafen», in Form eines Touristenplans (Buntstift auf Papier, Massstab 1:2000). Aus dem Buch *Internationale Bauausstellung Berlin 1987*, Klett-Cotta-Verlag. (GER)

■ 282, 283 Carte de Hong Kong mi-dépliée et ouverte, expédiée comme invitation à un congrès par l'organisme responsable des foires et expositions. Le visiteur y trouve les transports publics, le centre touristique, les hôtels existants, mais aussi le site des hôtels en construction. (HKG)

■ 284 «Le nouveau quartier portuaire.» Projet urbanistique sur le thème de «l'habitat et les loisirs dans le port de Tegel» primé lors de l'Exposition internationale du Bâtiment 1987 à Berlin. Crayon couleur sur papier, au 1/2000. Tiré de l'ouvrage *Internationale Bauausstellung Berlin 1987*, Ed. Klett-Cotta. (GER)

DESIGNER:
Doug Joseph
ARTIST:
Kenji Matsumoto/
Doug Joseph
ART DIRECTOR:
Doug Joseph
AGENCY:
Runyan & Associates
CLIENT:
Maguire Thomas Partners
■ 285-288

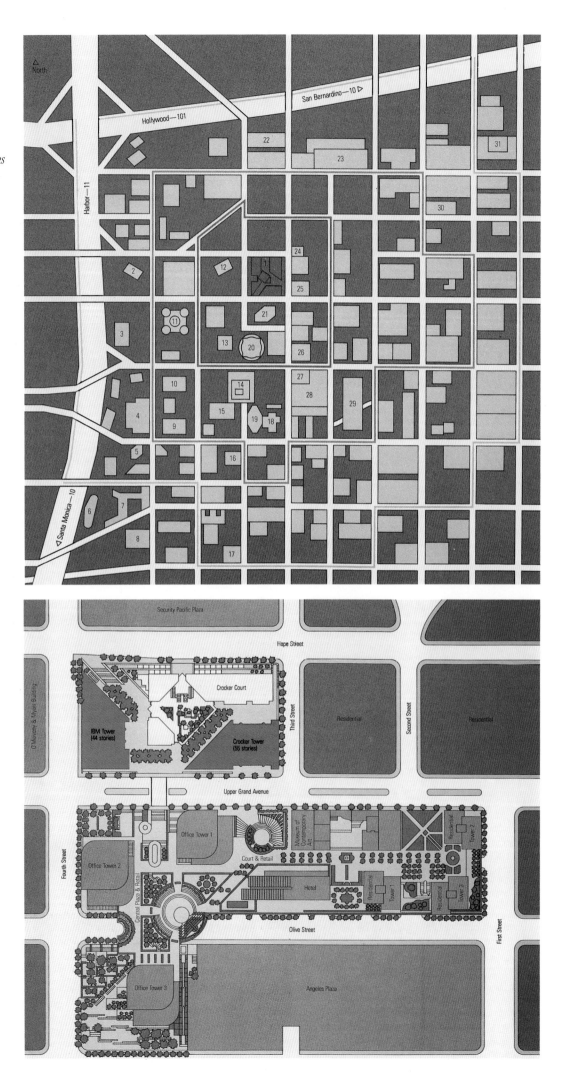

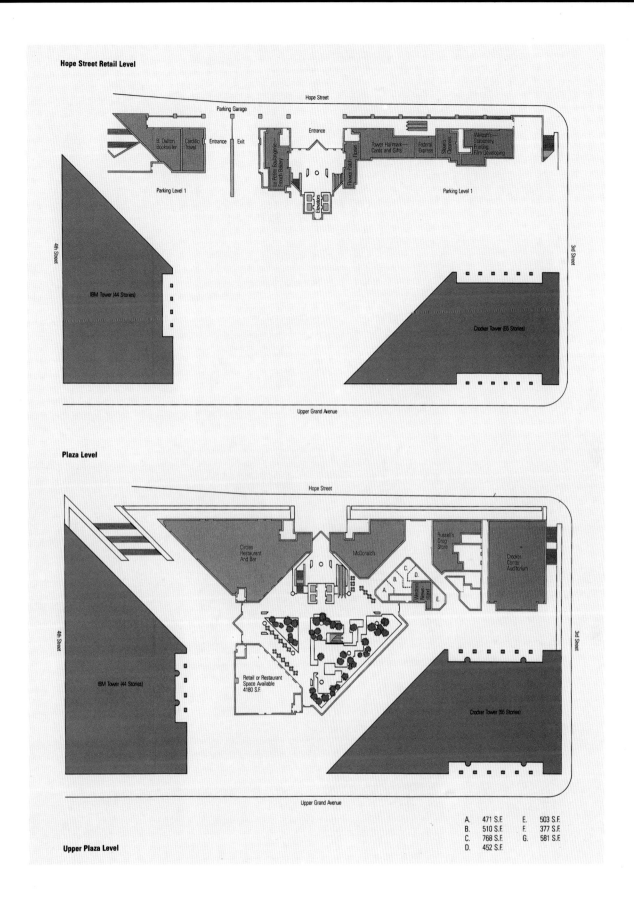

Hope Street Retail Level

Plaza Level

Upper Plaza Level

A.	471 S.F.	E.	503 S.F.
B.	510 S.F.	F.	377 S.F.
C.	768 S.F.	G.	581 S.F.
D.	452 S.F.		

■ 285-288 Plans to illustrate the location, the environs and the design of a building complex to be erected. Here a phasewise approximation with overview of the complex in Los Angeles, its vicinity, and two floors of the building. From a folder issued by the building project planners. (USA)

■ 285-288 Pläne der Lage, Umgebung und Gestaltung eines neu zu erstellenden Gebäudekomplexes. Hier eine stufenweise Annäherung mit Übersicht des Quartiers in Los Angeles, der Umgebung und von zwei Ebenen des Gebäudes. Aus einem Faltprospekt für das Bauprojekt. (USA)

■ 285-288 Plans montrant l'implantation d'un projet immobilier dans le quartier, son environnement, sa conception. On y procède par étapes en présentant d'abord le quartier de Los Angeles, l'environnement immédiat et deux niveaux du bâtiment projeté. Dépliant du promoteur. (USA)

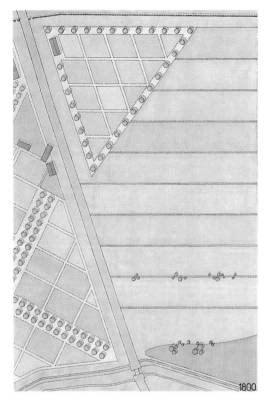

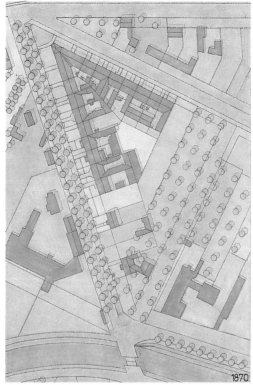

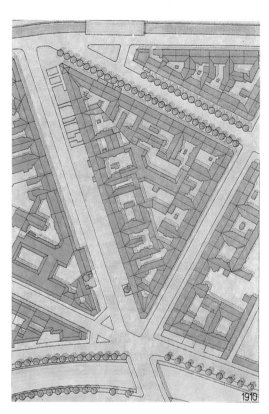

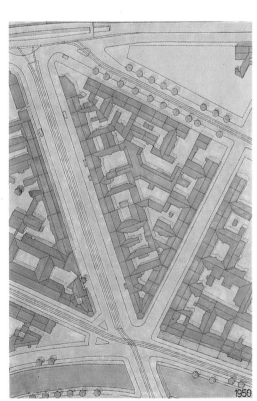

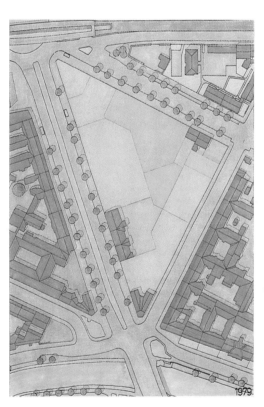

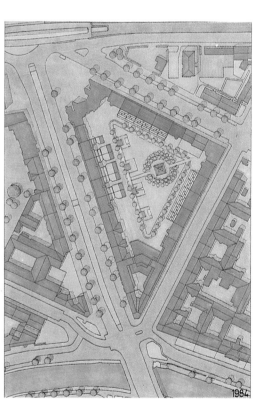

ARTIST:
M. Gies/F. Mossmann/
F. Rau/M. Wuttig
PUBLISHER:
Klett-Cotta
CLIENT:
Deutsches Architektur-
museum Frankfurt
■ 289–294

ARTIST:
O. M. Ungers/M. Dudler
PUBLISHER:
Klett-Cotta
CLIENT:
Deutsches Architektur-
museum Frankfurt
►■ 295

■ 289–294 Series of six site plans, giving information about the planning, building and utilization of a Kreuzberg building complex. (Felt pen and pencil on paper, colored with felt pen; scale 1:5000.) (GER)

■ 295 Design for a competition: "Culture Forum Berlin", organized for the occasion of the International Building Exhibition Berlin 1987. Shown is an isometric graph, scale 1:1000, ink on transparent paper. (GER)

All illustrations on this double spread are taken from the book *Internationale Bauausstellung Berlin 1987,* Klett-Cotta-Verlag.

■ 289–294 Serie von sechs Lageplänen, die über Planungs-, Bau- und Nutzungsgeschichte eines Kreuzberger Baublocks Auskunft geben. (Filzstift und Bleistift auf Papier, mit Filzstift koloriert; M 1:5000.) (GER)

■ 295 Entwurf für einen Wettbewerb unter dem Thema «Kulturforum Berlin», vorgestellt anlässlich der Internationalen Bauausstellung Berlin 1987. Hier eine Isometrie, M 1:1000, Tusche auf Transparentpapier. (GER)

Alle Abbildungen auf dieser Doppelseite stammen aus dem Buch *Internationale Bauausstellung Berlin 1987,* Klett-Cotta-Verlag.

■ 289–294 Série de six plans de situation renseignant sur l'histoire de la mise en chantier, de la construction et de l'exploitation d'un pâté d'immeubles à Kreuzberg. Feutre et crayon sur papier, colorié au feutre, au 1/5000. (GER)

■ 295 Projet de concours sur le thème du «Forum culturel de Berlin» présenté lors de l'Exposition internationale du Bâtiment 1987 à Berlin: représentation isométrique au 1/1000, encre de Chine sur papier-calque. (GER)

Toutes les illustrations de cette page double sont tirées de l'ouvrage *Internationale Bauausstellung Berlin 1987,* Ed. Klett-Cotta.

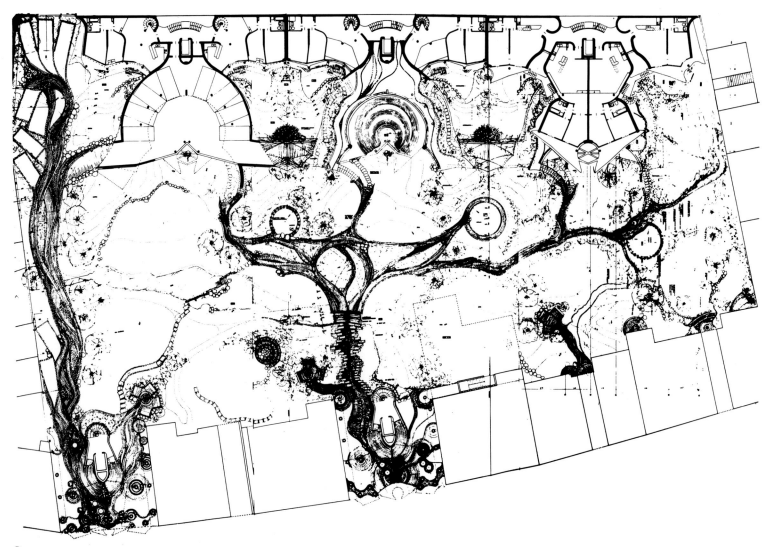

DESIGNERS:
INKEN & HINRICH BALLER
PUBLISHER:
KLETT-COTTA
CLIENT:
*DEUTSCHES ARCHITEKTUR-
MUSEUM FRANKFURT*
■ 296

■ 296 A design for the garden planning of the housing development on the Fraenkelufer in Berlin. (Ink on transparent paper, scale 1:50). From the Klett-Cotta book *Internationale Bauausstellung Berlin 1987.* (GER)

■ 296 Für die Wohnbebauung am Berliner Fraenkelufer erstellter Entwurf für die Gartenplanung. (Tusche auf Transparentpapier, M 1:50). Aus dem bei Klett-Cotta erschienenen Buch *Internationale Bauausstellung Berlin 1987.* (GER)

■ 296 Projet d'aménagement des jardins de l'ensemble résidentiel berlinois de Fraenkelufer. Encre de Chine sur papier-calque, au 1/50. Tiré de l'ouvrage *Internationale Bauausstellung Berlin 1987* paru aux Ed. Klett-Cotta. (GER)

ARCHITECTURE

ARCHITECTURE

ARCHITEKTUR

ARCHITECTURE

ARCHITECTURE

The diversity of ways to view a whole city is clearly demonstrated in the chapter "Cartographic Diagrams". Looking at the contributions in the architectural section, it is obvious that individual buildings can also be perceived and represented from many viewpoints and with many different objectives in mind. Figures *304–309* present a company's newly-erected headquarters. In sketches of almost childlike simplicity as well as in very precise geometric drawings, in color diagrams and in black-and-white renderings, this building is wonderfully presented. The use of the most varied artistic media and techniques, and the impressions that result from them, are symbolic of the many requirements imposed on such high-rise towers, and of how these requirements are met.

Architectural diagrams are used for the design of complete buildings *(Figs. 312–315)* as well as for single floors, apartments and rooms *(Figs. 297–303, 311–315)* offered for sale or rent. A diagram can also accent historical or traditional building elements *(Figs. 332, 334);* it can be used in an architect's self-promotion *(Fig. 329)* or in the depiction of the restoration of a building over the course of the years *(Figs. 329, 333).*

The architect's main tool is the diagram. Sketches are used to visualize his basic concepts, to arrange his thoughts, and finally to crystallize his final idea in detail. They are put before prospective developers, clients, or quite often, as in *Figs. 316, 325–327,* a competition jury.

The descriptions of architectural diagram methods are numerous, which is not really surprising since they fall within the jargon of the everyday activities of one of the most ancient, richest, and noble of all the arts – the vernacular of which must be constantly brought up to date. Apart from the isometric representations (already encountered in the chapter "Cartographic Diagrams"), there are design studies that incorporate a loosely defined form almost bordering on the picturesque, and in addition there are the most varied diagrammatic representations of views, cross-sections, perspectives, floor plans, layouts, and location guides. Apart from the factual information that each diagram offers (and they all serve a specific purpose and must state the facts concisely) and setting aside the diagram's aesthetics for a moment, what is interesting to note are the concealed messages, the esoteric statements. Leslie A. Segal writes in his preface to the first GRAPHIS DIAGRAMS book, published in 1983, that a really good and convincing diagram must put across a feeling such as "Why on earth didn't I think of that?" And, as in advertising (in whose service diagrams also play a role) information and intention are far more impressive, the more emotional, consistent, and manipulative the formulation.

Therefore the brilliant blue color behind the beach houses that are for rent *(Fig. 315)* immediately ushers in the additional subconscious promise of sunshine and holiday contentment with it. As the grain and pigmentation increase towards the lower edge of the picture, so the impression is created of a beach merging with the ocean. Potential tenants are subconsciously promised quality on a higher plane than that inherent in just a beautiful house.

Another clear example of a hidden statement is apparent in the drawing of the Library Tower *(Figs. 297–301).* The contour of this building is organic and circular and this does much to its enhancement in contrast to the surrounding high-rise buildings. This natural structure radiates warmth and security, and these elements are accentuated by the choice of paper – a finely structured, soft paper, and also by the warm gray tones in which the elevators and utilitarian cells, depicted in color, are nestled. The illustrations in the middle of the page seem to be held in suspense like so many small creatures; the building breathes life – not with heart and soul, but with elevators and utilitarian cells. By placing the emphasis on the organic, the warm and corporal in a cool and rectangular area, confidence is awakened – and the guarantee of a well-functioning and pleasant working atmosphere is offered.

The visitors' brochure for the former Alcatraz prison *(Fig. 274–276)* is an exceptionally good example of the harmony of compressed information with a stimulating, reflective mood. While the drawing of the whole island emits an aura almost of charm (shown by the soft and delicate watercolors, and the joy in minute details, while the whole is bathed in a blue sea) the starkness of the prison – itself captured and intensified in gray-green tones – has the shock effect of a nightmare. The viewer's perspective is central, hovering over the all-too regular buildings. It is as if a bird were arrested in mid flight. The walls appear to stretch out in front of the bird, waiting to devour it. The viewer feels inexorably sucked into the gravitational pull of this desperate and desolate place. Even though there is some land around the main prison building – as can be seen in the accompanying map – the prison is drawn as if there were none, as if this edifice of captivity extended right into the sea – and was doomed by it. Through this manner of representation the feeling of captivity is at once doubled: no escape from the cell and no way off the island, a frightening demonstration. The only exit from the hermetically-sealed building with its gigantic outer walls seems to be upwards. The escape, the rescue, can only come from heaven. The impossibility of ever fleeing this gloomy fate is so clearly and dramatically illustrated in this diagram that one is happy to turn the page.

Die Vielfältigkeit möglicher Stadtansichten ist im Kapitel «Kartographische Diagramme» gezeigt worden. Beim Betrachten der Beiträge des architektonischen Teils wird deutlich, dass auch einzelne Häuser unter verschiedensten Aspekten gesehen und gezeichnet werden können und so den unterschiedlichsten Zielen gerecht werden. Um das Vorstellen eines kürzlich fertiggestellten neuen Firmensitzes geht es in den Abbildungen *304-309*. In kindlich anmutenden Entwurfsskizzen oder exakt geometrischen Zeichnungen, in schwarzweissen oder farbigen Darstellungen wird immer wieder derselbe Gebäudekomplex anvisiert. Mit der Unterschiedlichkeit der bildnerischen Mittel wird auf die Vielfalt der Ansprüche hingewiesen, die an derartige Hochhäuser gestellt werden und die sie erfüllen müssen.

Architektonische Diagramme entstehen weiterhin in der Absicht, ganze Häuser *(Abb. 312-315)* oder nur einzelne Etagen und Räume *(Abb. 297-303, 311-315)* zur Vermietung oder zum Verkauf anzubieten. Die Betonung von historischen oder traditionellen Bauaspekten kann ein weiterer Anlass für ein Diagramm sein *(Abb. 332, 334)*, die Eigenwerbung eines Architekten *(Abb. 329)* oder das Aufzeigen von Veränderungen eines Gebäudes im Laufe der Jahre *(Abb. 329, 333)*.

Die Bezeichnungen für die architektonischen Darstellungsmethoden sind ungewöhnlich differenziert, was nicht weiter erstaunlich ist, da es sich hier um die täglichen, mehr oder minder feststehenden Arbeitsprogramme eines regen Berufsstandes handelt. Neben den isometrischen Darstellungen, die schon aus dem Kapitel der «Kartographischen Diagramme» bekannt sind, gibt es zum Beispiel Entwurfsstudien, die fast immer eine lockerere Linienführung, eine geradezu malerische Komponente haben, und weiterhin die verschiedensten Arten von Ansichten, Querschnitten, Perspektiven, Grundrissen und Lageplänen.

Neben der sachlichen Information, die jedes Diagramm zu liefern hat, denn sie alle stehen ja im Dienst von etwas und sollen einen Sachverhalt zum Ausdruck bringen – und neben dem ästhetischen Aspekt – interessieren hier die versteckten Mitteilungen, die unterschwelligen Aussagen. Leslie A. Segal formulierte 1983 im Vorwort zum ersten Band von GRAPHIS DIAGRAMS, dass ein wirklich gutes und einleuchtendes Design ein Gefühl vermitteln müsse wie – «Warum ist das mir nicht eingefallen?» Wie in der Werbung, in deren Dienst Diagramme ja zum Teil auch stehen, prägt sich eine Information und Intention um so mehr ein, je stimmiger und einheitlicher, je manipulativer und unbewusster eine auch noch mitgelieferte Aussage formuliert wird.

So wird zum Beispiel das strahlende Blau hinter den zur Vermietung angebotenen Strandhäusern *(Abb. 315)* zu einem Versprechen von Sonnenschein und Ferienglück. Das Körnigwerden des Farbtons, die zunehmende Pigmentierung zum unteren Bildrand hin verstärkt diesen Eindruck, sie bringt die Assoziation von Strand, der sich im Meer verliert. Den möglichen Mietern werden so unterschwellig viel weitreichendere Qualitäten versprochen als nur die eines schönen Hauses.

Ein weiteres Beispiel einer mitgelieferten, versteckten Aussage ist die Zeichnung vom Library Tower *(Abb. 297-301)*. Der Umriss des Gebäudes ist organisch und rund und hebt sich betont ab von den umgebenden Hochhäusern. Diese organische, warme Ausstrahlung wird nochmals hervorgehoben durch das Papier – es ist fein strukturiert und weich statt glatt und hochglänzend – und durch den warmen Grauton, in den die farbig gekennzeichneten Lifte und sanitären Anlagen eingebettet sind. Wie kleine Lebewesen scheinen die Darstellungen in der Mitte des Blattes zu schweben, das Gebäude, belebt nicht von Herz, Lunge und Nieren, sondern von Liften und sanitären Anlagen. Die Betonung des Organischen, des Warmen und Lebendigen in einer coolen, rechteckigen Umgebung soll Vertrauen erwecken, soll ein gutes Funktionieren und eine gute Arbeitsatmosphäre garantieren.

Die Broschüre für Besucher des ehemaligen Alcatraz-Gefängnisses *(Abb. 274-276)* ist ein besonders gutes Beispiel dafür, wie neben der eigentlichen Information eine sehr dominante Stimmung mitgeliefert wird. Während die Zeichnung der ganzen Insel eine fast liebliche Ausstrahlung hat, da sie in zarten Aquarellfarben gehalten ist, mit Freude am Detail und viel blauem Meer drumherum, wirkt das Gefängnis selbst, in grün-gräulichen Tönen gehalten, geradezu wie ein Alptraum. Die Betrachterperspektive liegt zentral über dem allzu regelmässigen Gebäude, es ist, als ob ein Vogel im Flug verharre. Die Mauern scheinen sich ihm entgegenzustrecken, ihn umschlingen zu wollen. Der Sog hinab ist gewaltig. Obwohl, wie auf der zugehörigen Übersichtskarte der ganzen Insel ersichtlich, durchaus noch Land um das Hauptgebäude herum gegeben ist, wird auf der Zeichnung des Gefängnisses allein der Bau so dargestellt, als hätte er kaum Raum um sich, als würde er unmittelbar vom Meer bedrängt. Durch diese Art der Darstellung wird das Eingesperrtsein gleichsam verdoppelt, indem neben der assoziierten Vorstellung einer Zelle die Ausweglosigkeit auch an der kleinen Insel demonstriert wird. Die einzige Öffnung des hermetisch verschlossenen Gebäudes mit seinen riesigen Aussenmauern weist gen Himmel, in die Vertikale. Ein Ausweg, eine Rettung ist nur von dort zu erwarten. Die verdoppelte Situation des Eingesperrtseins, die Unmöglichkeit, diesem düsteren Schicksal zu entfliehen, wird hier so klar veranschaulicht, dass man sich gerne wieder vom Blatt abwendet.

La multiplicité des points de vue en cause lorsqu'il s'agit de faire le portrait d'une ville a été évoquée au chapitre des Cartogrammes. En considérant les dessins d'architecture, on réalise qu'un immeuble peut également être vu sous un grand nombre d'aspects différents qui se reflètent dans la représentation qu'on en fait et rendent compte des buts fort divers poursuivis par les illustrateurs. Les *fig. 304-309* nous renseignent sur l'achèvement d'un immeuble destiné au siège social d'une entreprise. Des croquis d'étude au caractère quasiment enfantin, des dessins à la précision géométrique et des représentations noir-blanc ou en couleur viennent éclairer le bâtiment sous des jours divers. La variété de l'approche artistique et la diversité des impressions qui en résultent modulent les exigences variées imposées à de tels immeubles-tours et auxquelles ce genre de construction doit satisfaire.

Les diagrammes d'architecture servent aussi à présenter soit des immeubles entiers *(fig. 312-315)*, soit des étages, appartements ou locaux *(fig. 297-303, 311-315)* mis en vente ou en location. Un diagramme peut aussi servir à mettre en évidence les aspects historiques ou traditionnels d'une construction *(fig. 332, 334)*, à faire la promotion d'un architecte *(fig. 329)* ou à documenter les étapes de la transformation d'un bâtiment au fil des années *(fig. 329, 333)*.

Les architectes ont évidemment une ample production de diagrammes destinés à visualiser leurs idées, puis à les ordonner et à les formuler. Ce genre d'esquisse aboutit finalement sur la table des intéressés, clients potentiels, maîtres de l'ouvrage ou - comme ici - membres d'un jury *(fig. 316, 325-327)*.

Les désignations sous lesquelles se rangent les différentes méthodes de représentation en architecture sont très diverses, ce qui ne saurait étonner si l'on se rappelle qu'il s'agit là des programmes de travail quotidiens plus ou moins invariables d'une profession fort active. Les représentations isométriques que nous avons déjà rencontrées au chapitre des Cartogrammes côtoient des études de projets caractérisées dans presque tous les cas par un tracé souple, une composante quasi picturale, mais aussi des projections, coupes, perspectives, plans d'ensemble et plans de situation de tout genre.

Chaque diagramme est tenu de fournir un certain volume d'informations objectives puisqu'il est au service de quelque chose et est censé exprimer un ensemble de faits; il a également un aspect esthétique indéniable; finalement, il sert de véhicule à des messages indirects, subliminaux. Dans la préface qu'il a contribuée en 1983 au premier volume de GRAPHIS DIAGRAMS, Leslie A. Segal affirmait qu'un design de qualité incontestable et vraiment convaincant doit communiquer une impression du genre «Mais pourquoi est-ce que je n'en ai pas eu l'idée, moi?», par exemple en voyant la carte du Texas découpée dans un bifteck. Qu'il s'agisse de publicité ou d'architectonique - et le diagramme

sert l'une comme l'autre -, une information et une intention s'impriment d'autant mieux à l'esprit que le message qui les accompagne est formulé de manière pertinente et homogène, et qu'il est chargé de tonalités manipulatives qui en appellent à l'inconscient.

C'est ainsi que le ciel bleu éclatant qui surplombe les bungalows de plage mis en location *(fig. 315)* est riche de promesses de soleil et de vacances réussies. La granulation accrue de la couleur au fur et à mesure que l'on s'approche du bord inférieur de l'image renforce encore cette impression en suggérant par association la présence de la mer au-delà de la plage. Les locataires potentiels se voient ainsi offrir bien davantage que les seules qualités de construction d'une belle maison.

Un autre exemple évident d'un message caché concomitant, c'est le dessin de la Library Tower *(fig. 297-301)*. Le plan organique, tout en rondeur du bâtiment tranche sur les buildings environnants. La chaleur que dégage la Library Tower est encore soulignée par la qualité du papier choisi, qui offre une structure fine et souple au lieu d'un couché lisse brillant, ainsi que par le gris chaud où sont insérés en couleur les ascenseurs et les sanitaires. Ces taches couleur donnent l'impression d'être de vivantes inclusions dans le dessin, comme si sanitaires et ascenseurs faisaient figure du cœur, des poumons et des reins d'un être humain. L'accent mis sur l'organique, la chaleur de la vie au sein d'un environnement rectangulaire et froid en appelle à la confiance en un fonctionnement adéquat et une atmosphère de travail rassurante.

La brochure réalisée à l'intention des visiteurs de l'ancienne prison d'Alcatraz *(fig. 274-276)* témoigne admirablement de la capacité de l'artiste à fournir en même temps que l'information proprement dite une ambiance qui saisit à la gorge. L'île même a un caractère idyllique renforcé par les teintes délicates de l'aquarelle, le soin du détail et l'étendue de mer bleue tout autour, tandis que la prison vert grisâtre a l'air franchement sinistre. Le point de vue de l'observateur se situe au-dessus du centre du bâtiment construit avec une régularité de proportions extrême: on a l'impression de voir la prison par les yeux d'un oiseau en vol plané que les murs cherchent à enserrer pour l'attirer au sol, dans un irrésistible mouvement d'aspiration. La carte synoptique de l'île a beau faire état de terres non bâties autour du bâtiment principal, le dessinateur a campé sa prison comme si elle était baignée d'eau de toutes parts. Ce mode de représentation accroît la sensation de claustrophobie dégagée par le régime cellulaire en y ajoutant l'idée d'un site sans issue. La seule ouverture visible du bâtiment scellé hermétiquement aux murs extérieurs gigantesques est au niveau du toit, à la verticale. Ce n'est que de là que peuvent venir les secours d'ailleurs improbables. La double expérience de la claustration, l'impossibilité d'échapper à ce sort funeste sont mises en image de manière tellement parlante que c'est avec un réel soulagement que l'on passe à autre chose.

DESIGNER:
DOUG JOSEPH
ARTIST:
KENJI MATSUMOTO/DOUG JOSEPH
ART DIRECTOR:
DOUG JOSEPH
AGENCY:
RUNYAN & ASSOCIATES
CLIENT:
MAGUIRE THOMAS PARTNERS
■ 297–303

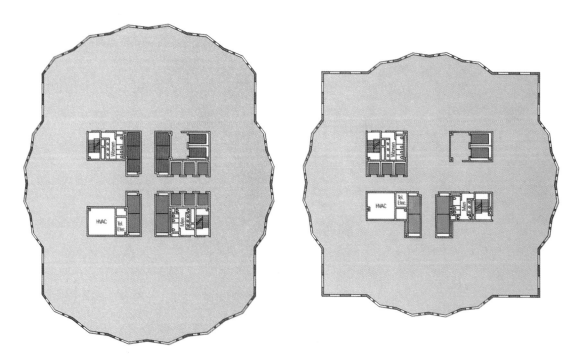

Library Tower   The Center of Downtown

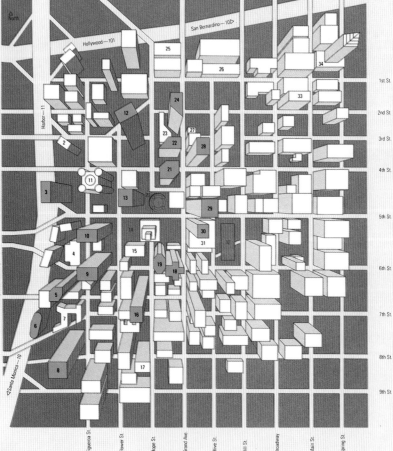

Library Tower . . . the 100 percent location in downtown Los Angeles.

Adjacent to the historic Central Library, the true heart of downtown . . .

A bridge between the traditional city center and the new financial district on Bunker Hill.

Library Tower is at the core of the city's business and civic life. Institutional quality office buildings, luxury hotels and important clubs surround the Library Tower site. The city's major office centers are in close proximity: Crocker Center, ARCO Plaza, Wells Fargo Bank, Security Pacific Plaza and others. This grouping of important buildings with more than 10 million square feet of space within two blocks of the Central Library establishes the center of Los Angeles.

Library Tower with its Bunker Hill Steps becomes the gateway to Bunker Hill, where one encounters the cosmopolitan elegance of the Music Center and Museum of Contemporary Art. A total community with urban vitality 24 hours a day, Bunker Hill's prime residential developments co-exist with corporate headquarters and government centers that include the County Courthouse.

1 Library Tower
2 Sheraton Grande Hotel
3 Union Bank Square
4 Jonathan Club
5 Mitsui Development
6 Coast Federal Bldg.
7 Los Angeles Hilton
8 Citicorp Plaza
9 Bank of America
10 Arco
11 Bonaventure Hotel
12 Security Pacific Plaza
13 Wells Fargo
14 Central Library
15 California Club
16 First Interstate Tower
17 Hyatt Regency Hotel
18 AT&T Building
19 Lincoln Properties
20 Bunker Hill Steps
21 O'Melveny & Myers Bldg.

22 IBM Tower
23 Crocker Court
24 Crocker Tower
25 Music Center
26 County Courthouse
27 Museum of Contemporary Art
28 California Plaza
29 Grand Place Tower
30 Biltmore Place
31 The Biltmore Hotel
32 Pershing Square
33 Los Angeles Times
34 City Hall

Major Office Buildings

■ 297–303 Survey of the stories and location plans of a highrise building (Library Tower) in Los Angeles, in which space is offered for rent. *297–301* illustrate the various ground plans, the existing elevators, and sanitary facilities. *302, 303* show plans of the immediate and close surroundings of the building. Its extraordinary contours are marked in red. (USA)

■ 297–303 Stockwerkübersichten und Lagepläne eines Wolkenkratzers (Library Tower) in Los Angeles, in dem Mietfläche angeboten wird. In *297–301* geht es um die Darstellung verschiedener Grundrisse und der vorhandenen Aufzüge und sanitären Anlagen. *302, 303* zeigen Pläne der näheren und ganz nahen Umgebung des Gebäudes, dessen ungewöhnlicher Umriss hier rot eingezeichnet ist. (USA)

■ 297–303 Plans d'étages et de situation d'un gratte-ciel de Los Angeles, le Library Tower, où des surfaces de bureaux sont à louer. *297–301:* Représentations de divers plans d'ensemble, des systèmes d'ascenseurs et des installations sanitaires. *302, 303:* Plans de l'environnement lointain et immédiat de l'immeuble, dont le plan de construction insolite apparaît en rouge. (USA)

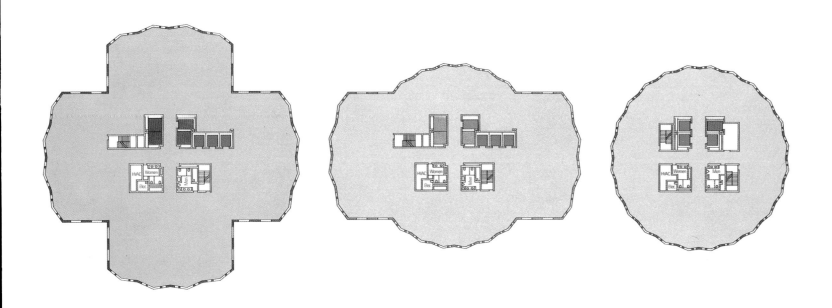

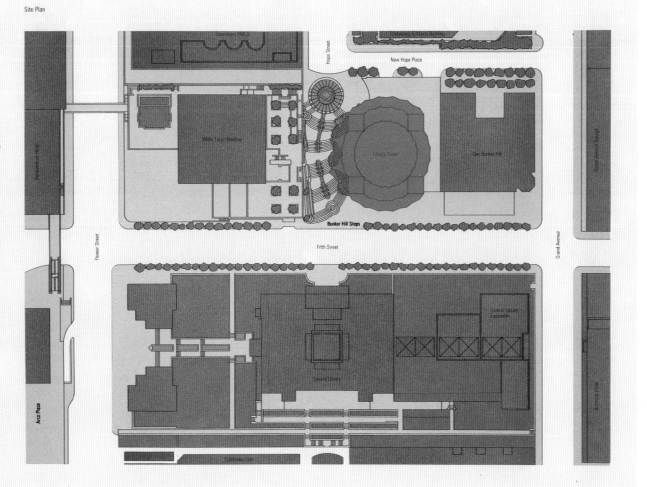

Library Tower   Site Plan

The Library Tower masterplan solves a number of downtown's most pressing urban planning problems. To eliminate a downtown bottleneck, the plan calls for rerouting two blocks of Hope Street to create New Hope Place between Library Tower and the O'Melveny & Myers Building. Creation of the new street makes possible the Bunker Hill Steps, a sweeping watergarden–stairway that will connect the traditional city center and Bunker Hill.

A spectacular fountain marks the main entrance to Library Tower on New Hope Place and the auto entrance to a 500-car garage. The main pedestrian entrance opens onto Fifth Street directly across from the Central Library.

To enhance the Central Library's attractiveness as a downtown gathering place, the West Lawn will be developed into an inviting landscaped park. A 600-car garage will be constructed beneath the park for use by Library patrons and Library Tower tenants and visitors.

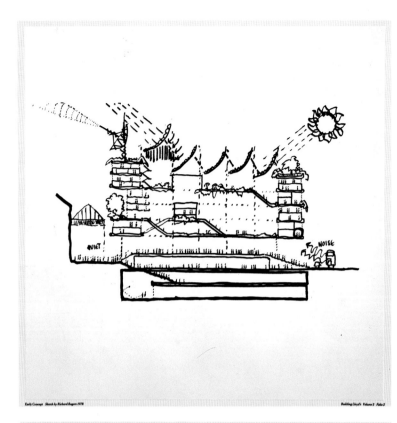

Early Concept Sketch by Richard Rogers 1978

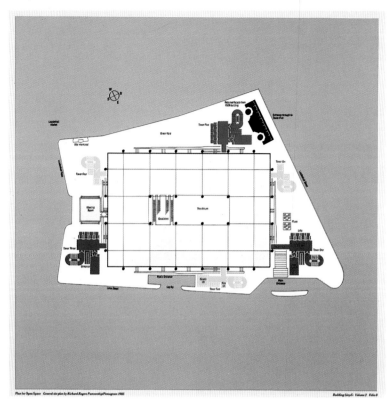

Plan for Open Space General site plan by Richard Rogers Partnership/Pentagram 1985

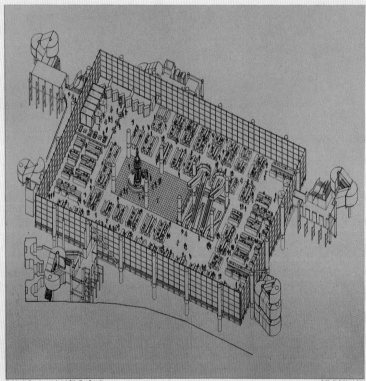

The Underwriting Room Axonometric drawing by Richard Rogers Partnership

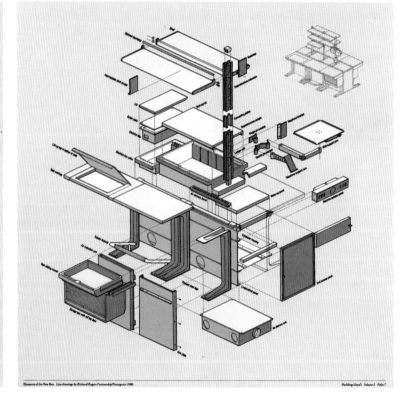

Elements of the New Box Line drawings by Richard Rogers Partnership/Pentagram 1986

■ 304-309 Loose sheets from a comprehensive portfolio for *Lloyd's of London,* dedicated to the newly erected head-quarters of the firm. Shown here is an early concept of the building, with plans for open space (general site plan); a plan of the square site made possible through the towers for the lifts and washroom facilities; the underwriting room; an illustration of part of a central base with computer connections, telephones, video equipment, and air conditioners; an axonometric representation of the building and elements of the New Box, Lime Street 1986. (GBR)

■ 304-309 Blätter aus einer Kassette für *Lloyd's of London,* die dem neu erstellten Firmensitz der Firma gewidmet ist. Hier ein früher Entwurf des Gebäudes; ein Plan des rechteckigen Grundrisses, der durch den Einsatz von Türmen für die Lifts, Waschräume etc. ermöglicht wird; der Raum für den Publikumsverkehr der Versicherungsgesellschaft; eine Darstellung der Elemente einer Zentrale mit Computeranschlüssen, Telephonen, Videogeräten und Air Conditioning; eine axonometrische Darstellung des Gebäudes und die Gebäudeansicht von der Lime Street. (GBR)

■ 304-309 Feuilles volantes figurant dans un important dossier sous emboîtage pour le *Lloyd's* de Londres voué au nouveau siège du groupe: première version du projet; vue en plan du bâtiment carré, les ascenseurs, toilettes, etc. étant rejetés dans les tours; la salle des guichets de cette compagnie d'assurances; représentation des éléments de la centrale avec les raccordements d'ordinateurs, les téléphones, les systèmes vidéo, la climatisation, le même bâtiment en vue axonométrique (les droites faisant entre elles des angles de 120°); vue de l'immeuble depuis Lime Street. (GBR)

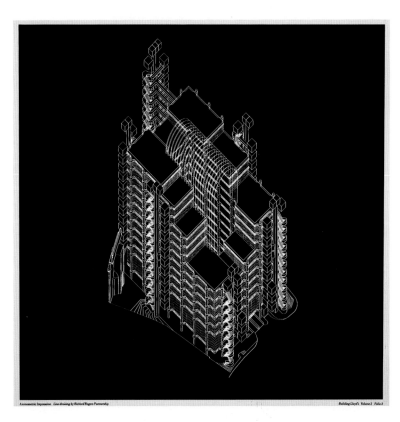

DESIGNER:
ALAN FLETCHER/
PENNY HOWARTH
ARTIST:
RICHARD ROGERS
ART DIRECTOR:
ALAN FLETCHER
AGENCY:
PENTAGRAM DESIGN, LONDON
DESIGN:
LONDON
CLIENT:
LLOYD'S OF LONDON
■ 304-308

DESIGNER:
ALAN FLETCHER/
PENNY HOWARTH
ARTIST:
ALAN STANTON
ART DIRECTOR:
ALAN FLETCHER
AGENCY:
PENTAGRAM DESIGN, LONDON
DESIGN:
LONDON
CLIENT:
LLOYD'S OF LONDON
■ 309

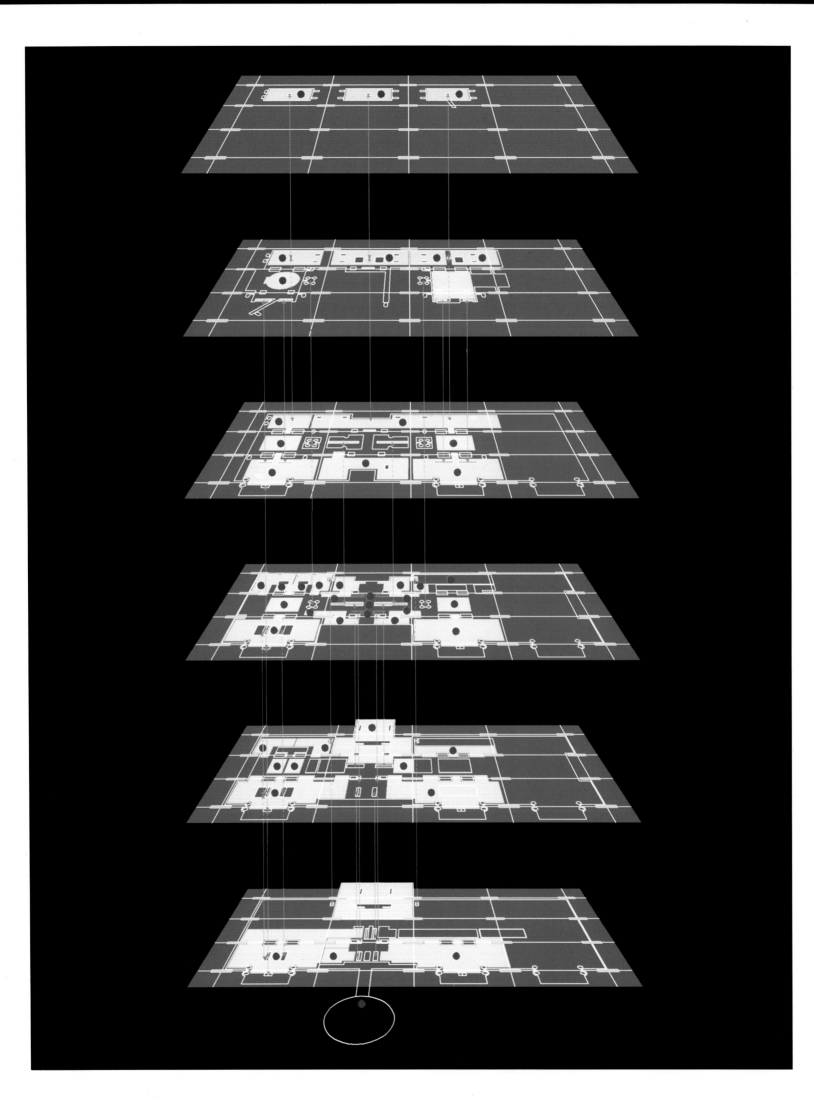

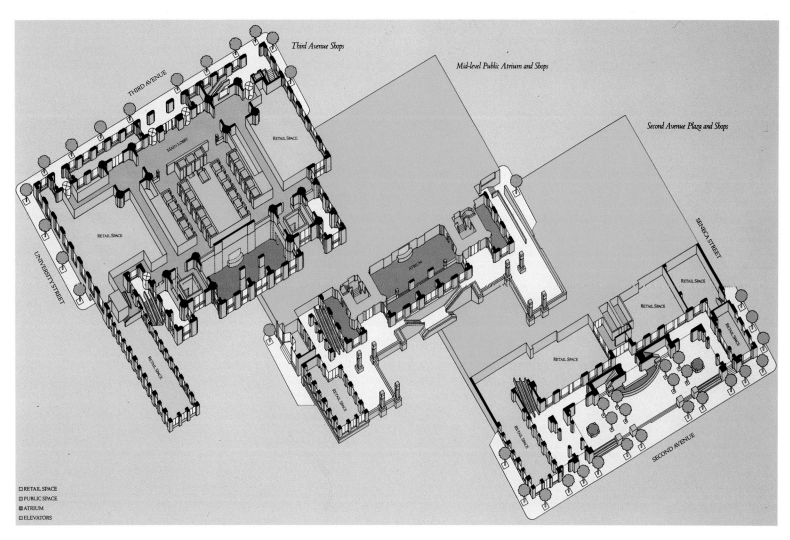

THIRD AVENUE

Third Avenue Shops

Mid-level Public Atrium and Shops

RETAIL SPACE

MAIN LOBBY

RETAIL SPACE

Second Avenue Plaza and Shops

SENECA STREET

UNIVERSITY STREET

ATRIUM

RETAIL SPACE

RETAIL SPACE

RETAIL SPACE

RETAIL SPACE

RETAIL SPACE

RETAIL SPACE

RETAIL SPACE

SECOND AVENUE

☐ RETAIL SPACE
☐ PUBLIC SPACE
▣ ATRIUM
☐ ELEVATORS

DESIGNER:
JOLIJN VAN DE WOUW/
GIJSBERT DIJKER
AGENCY:
TOTAL DESIGN
CLIENT:
ETABLISSEMENT PUBLIQUE PARC
DE LA VILETTE, PARIS
◀■ 310

DESIGNER:
KATHY EITNER
ARTIST:
ROBERT PECKHAM
ART DIRECTOR:
KATHY EITNER
AGENCY:
JAY ROCKEY PUBLIC RELATIONS
CLIENT:
WRIGHT RUNSTAD & CO.
■ 311

■ 310 Floor plans as part of the signalization system of the Museum Cité des Sciences et de l'Industrie in Paris. (FRA)

■ 311 Plans of the ground floor and between floors of a new office block in which sales areas are offered for leasing. Taken from a building prospectus. (USA)

■ 310 Stockwerkpläne als Teil des Signalisierungssystems des Museums Cité des Sciences et de l'Industrie. (FRA)

■ 311 Pläne des Parterres und Zwischen-Parterres eines neuen Bürogebäudes, in dem Verkaufsflächen zur Miete angeboten werden. Aus einem Prospekt. (USA)

■ 310 Plans d'étages intégrés dans le système de signalisation du musée Cité des Sciences et de l'Industrie. (FRA)

■ 311 Plans du rez-de-chaussée et de l'entresol d'un nouvel immeuble de bureaux où des surfaces de vente sont offertes à la location. Prospectus du promoteur. (USA)

DESIGNER:
NORITSUGU ODA
AGENCY:
ODA ILLUSTRATION OFFICE
CLIENT:
PHP INSTITUTE INC.
■ 312–314

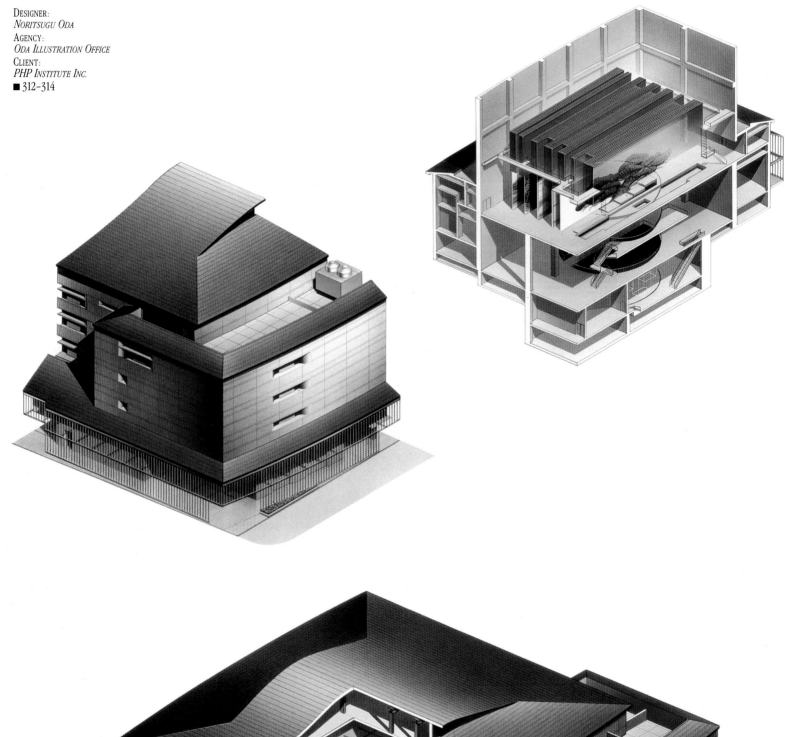

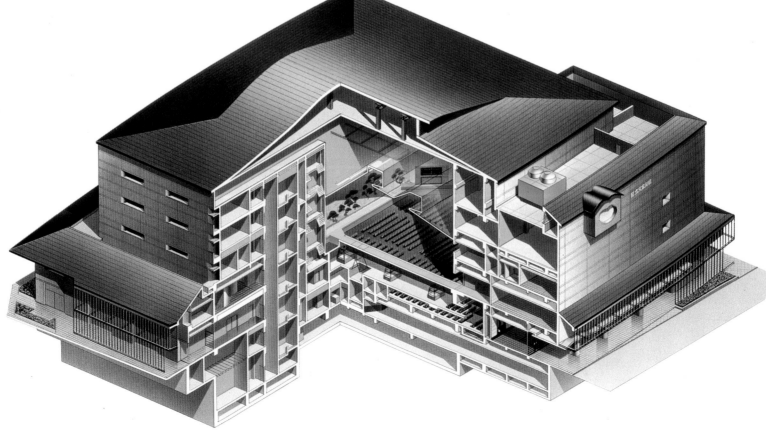

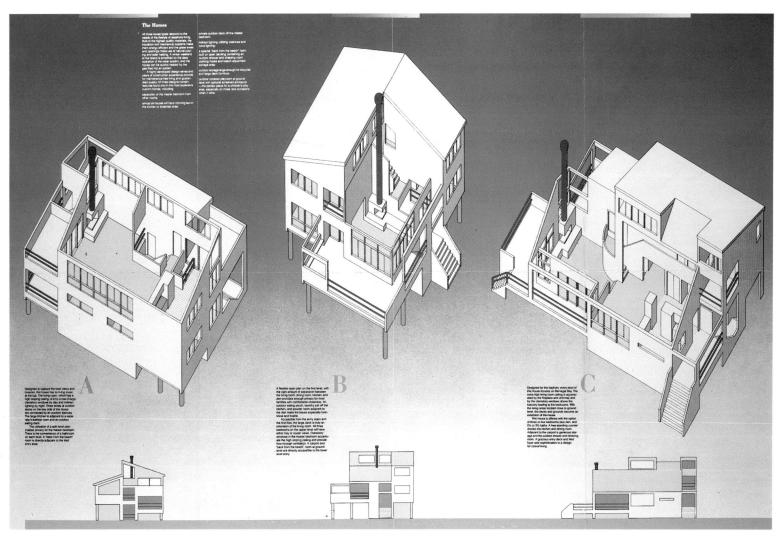

DESIGNER:
JEROME CLOUD

ARTIST:
LAURINDA STOCKWELL

ART DIRECTOR:
JOEL KATZ

AGENCY:
KATZ WHEELER DESIGN

CLIENT:
LBI ASSOCIATES

■ 315

■ 312–314 Partial view and cut-away drawings of a
Japanese Opera House. (JPN)

■ 315 Graphics from a sales brochure for beach houses
inhabitable throughout the whole year. (USA)

■ 312–314 Teilansicht und Aufriss-Diagramme eines Opern-
hauses. (JPN)

■ 315 Darstellungen aus einem Verkaufsprospekt für Strand-
häuser, die das ganze Jahr über bewohnbar sind. (USA)

■ 312–314 Vue partielle et diagrammes éclatés d'un Opéra
japonais. (JPN)

■ 315 Représentations graphiques dans un prospectus pour
des maisons de plage habitables toute l'année. (USA)

■ 316–318 Plans submitted to a competition for the development of Wilhelmstrasse, Berlin. *316:* perspective with ground plans overlayered. It shows the view from the inner court towards the outer building. (Blueprints, with different tracings and collages). *317:* Street view with normal story floor plan (felt pen and crayon on blueprint). *318:* perspective with overlayered ground plan and facade sketches (pencil and ink on transparent paper). From the book *Internationale Bauausstellung Berlin 1987,* published by Klett-Cotta. (GER)

■ 316–318 Im Rahmen eines Wettbewerbs für die Überbauung der Wilhelmstrasse, Berlin, erstellte Pläne. *316:* Perspektive mit überlagertem Grundriss. Sie zeigt den Blick vom Innenhof gegen die Randbebauung (Lichtpausen, unterschiedlich gepaust und collagiert). *317:* Strassenansicht mit Normalgeschossgrundriss (Filzstift und Ölkreide auf Lichtpause). *318:* Perspektive mit überlagertem Grundriss und Fassadenskizzen (Bleistift und Tusche auf Transparentpapier). Aus dem bei Klett-Cotta erschienenen Buch *Internationale Bauausstellung Berlin 1987.* (GER)

■ 316–318 Plans établis dans le cadre d'un concours d'urbanisation de la Wilhelmstrasse à Berlin. *316:* Perspective, avec plan d'ensemble superposé. Vue de la cour intérieure vers les immeubles (photocalques tirés différemment et montés par collage). *317:* Vue de la rue avec plan d'ensemble d'un étage type (feutre et craie grasse sur calque). *318:* Perspective avec plan d'ensemble superposé et croquis de façades (crayon et encre de Chine sur papier-calque). Tiré de l'ouvrage *Internationale Bauausstellung Berlin 1987,* Ed. Klett-Cotta. (GER)

ARTIST:
HANSJÜRG ZEITLER/
HELMUT BIER/HANS KORN
CLIENT:
DEUTSCHES ARCHITEKTUR-
MUSEUM FRANKFURT
PUBLISHER:
KLETT-COTTA
■ 316

ARTIST:
ALDO ROSSI/GIANNI BRAGHIERI
CLIENT:
DEUTSCHES ARCHITEKTUR-
MUSEUM FRANKFURT
PUBLISHER:
KLETT-COTTA
■ 317, 318

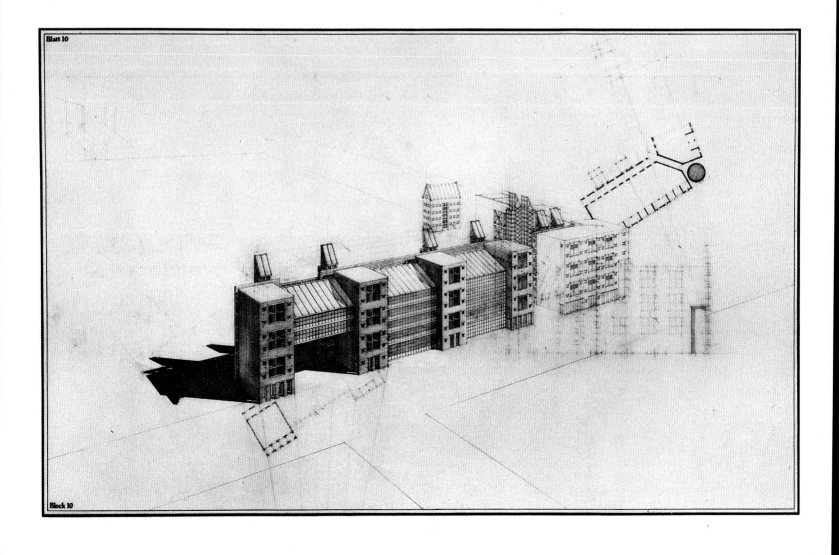

ARTIST:
ALDO ROSSI/GIANNI BRAGHIERI
CLIENT:
DEUTSCHES ARCHITEKTUR-
MUSEUM FRANKFURT
PUBLISHER:
KLETT-COTTA

DESIGNER:
GARY BLAKELEY
ARTIST:
MULKERN RUTHERFORD
ART DIRECTOR:
GARY BLAKELEY
AGENCY:
AITKEN BLAKELEY
CLIENT:
*THE QEEN ELIZABETH II
CONFERENCE CENTRE*
■ 319–324

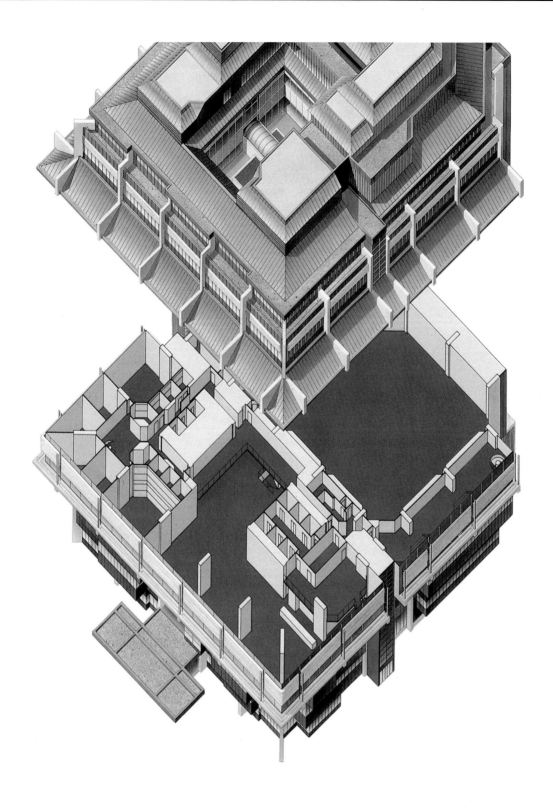

■ 319–324 Plans from a brochure about the Queen Elizabeth II Conference Centre in London. *319* shows illustrations (used for the cover) of the roof construction and one of the stories (see also *323, 324*). *320–322:* various floors of the building. The plans are, in each case, supplemented by a photograph of one of the rooms. (GBR)

■ 319–324 Pläne aus einer Broschüre über das Queen-Elizabeth-II-Konferenzzentrum in London. *319* zeigt die für den Umschlag verwendeten Darstellungen der Dachkonstruktion und eines Stockwerkes (s. auch *323, 324*), *320–322* verschiedene Stockwerke des Gebäudes. Die Pläne werden jeweils von einer Photographie eines Raumes ergänzt. (GBR)

■ 319–324 Plans tirés d'une brochure descriptive du Centre de conférences Queen-Elizabeth-II à Londres. *319:* Vues de la construction du toit et d'un étage pour la couverture (voir aussi *323, 324*). *320–322:* Divers étages de l'immeuble. Tous ces plans sont judicieusement complétés par la photo de l'un des locaux en question. (GBR)

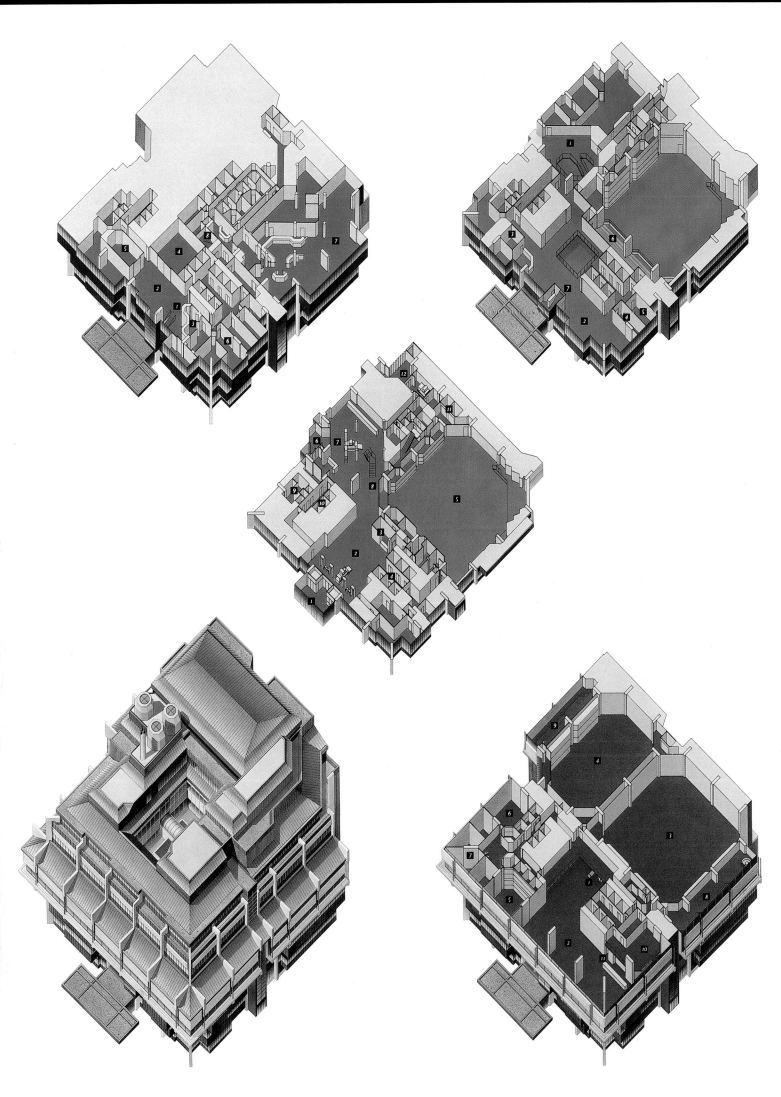

ARTIST:
Oswald Mathias Ungers
CLIENT:
*Deutsches Architektur-
museum Frankfurt*
PUBLISHER:
Klett-Cotta
■ 325, 326

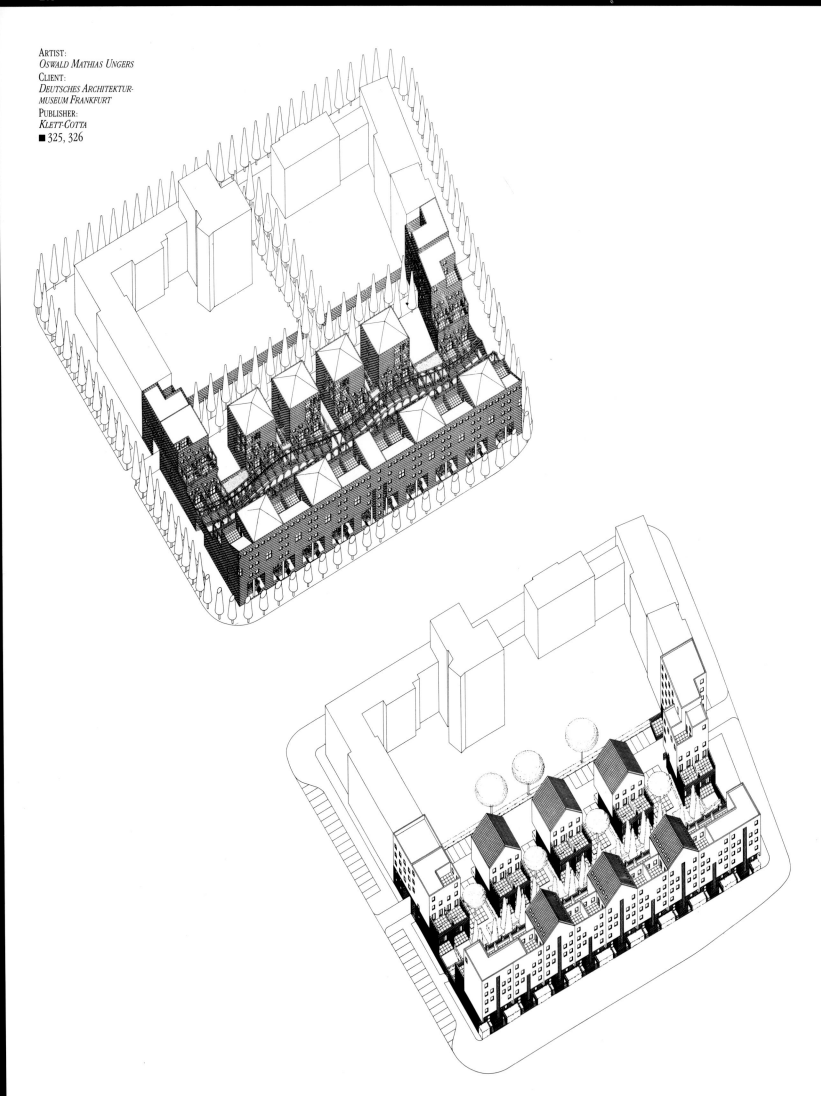

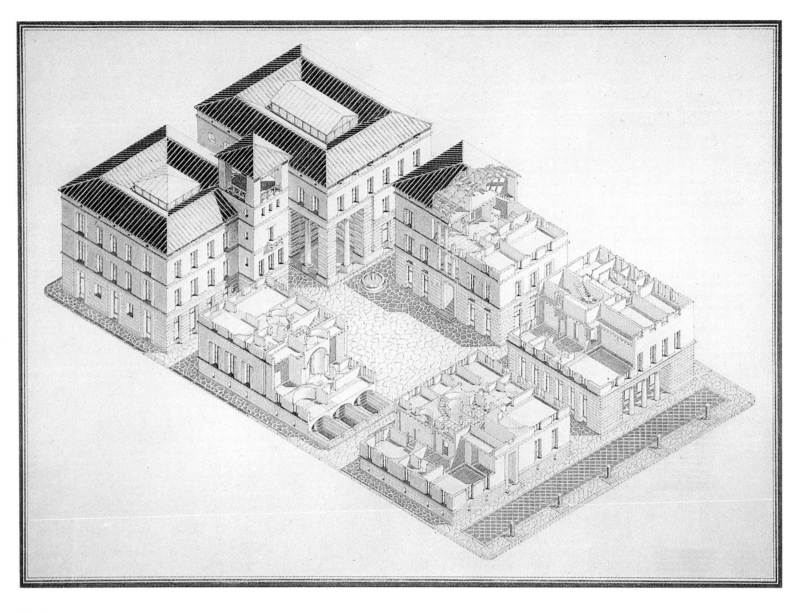

ARTIST:
LEON KRIER
CLIENT:
DEUTSCHES ARCHITEKTUR-
MUSEUM FRANKFURT
PUBLISHER:
KLETT-COTTA
■ 327

■ 325, 326 Isometric presentations of a design and the constructed housing development at Lützowplatz, Berlin. (Ink on transparent paper, scale 1:100). (GER)

■ 327 Isometric design of the project "Living and Leisure in Tegel Harbor" (color pencil on paper, scale 1:200), shown at the Berlin Architecture Exhibition 1987. (GER)

All illustrations on this double spread are from the *Internationale Bauausstellung Berlin 1987,* Klett-Cotta-Verlag.

■ 325, 326 Isometrische Darstellungen eines Entwurfs und des gebauten Projektes der Wohnanlage Lützowplatz, Berlin. (Tusche auf Transparentpapier, M 1:100.) (GER)

■ 327 Isometrischer Entwurf zum Projekt «Wohnen und Freizeit am Tegeler Hafen» (Buntstift auf Papier, M 1:200), für die Berliner Architekturausstellung 1987. (GER)

Alle Abbildungen auf dieser Doppelseite aus *Internationale Bauausstellung Berlin 1987,* Klett-Cotta-Verlag.

■ 325, 326 Représentations isométriques d'un projet d'immeubles place Lützow, à Berlin, et du projet une fois réalisé. Encre de Chine sur papier-calque, au 1/100. (GER)

■ 327 Etude isométrique pour le projet «l'habitat et les loisirs dans le port de Tegel» (crayon couleur sur papier, au 1/200). Exposition internationale du Bâtiment 1987. (GER)

Toutes les illustrations de cette page double sont de *Internationale Bauausstellung Berlin 1987,* Klett-Cotta. (GER)

■ 328 Technical drawing of the Brazo Largo Bridge in Argentina. (ARG)

■ 329 Diagrams of the various building phases of a barn. Self promotion for architect/illustrator R. Peckham. (USA)

■ 330, 331 Double spreads from "Human dimensions" – a brochure issued by the magazine *Interiors* targeted at professional interior designers of offices, hotels, private practices etc. (USA)

■ 328 Technische Zeichnung der Brazo-Largo-Brücke in Argentinien. (ARG)

■ 329 Diagramme der Bauetappen einer Scheune. Eigenwerbung des Architekten/Illustrators R. Peckham. (USA)

■ 330, 331 Doppelseiten aus «Die Masse des Menschen», eine von der Zeitschrift *Interiors* herausgegebene Broschüre, die sich an professionelle Designer von Inneneinrichtungen von Büros, Hotels, Praxisräumen etc. richtet. (USA)

■ 328 Dessin technique représentant le pont sur le Brazo Largo, en Argentine. (ARG)

■ 329 Diagrammes des étapes de construction d'une grange. Autopromotion de R. Peckham, architecte/illustrateur. (USA)

■ 330, 331 Doubles pages de la brochure «Dimensions humaines» publiée par la revue *Interiors,* dont les lecteurs se recrutent parmi les décorateurs de bureaux, hôtels, cabinets médicaux, etc. (USA)

DESIGNER:
GUSTAVO PEDROZA
ARTIST:
GUSTAVO PEDROZA
ART DIRECTOR:
GUSTAVO PEDROZA
AGENCY:
GUSTAVO PEDROZA
CLIENT:
TECHINT
■ 328

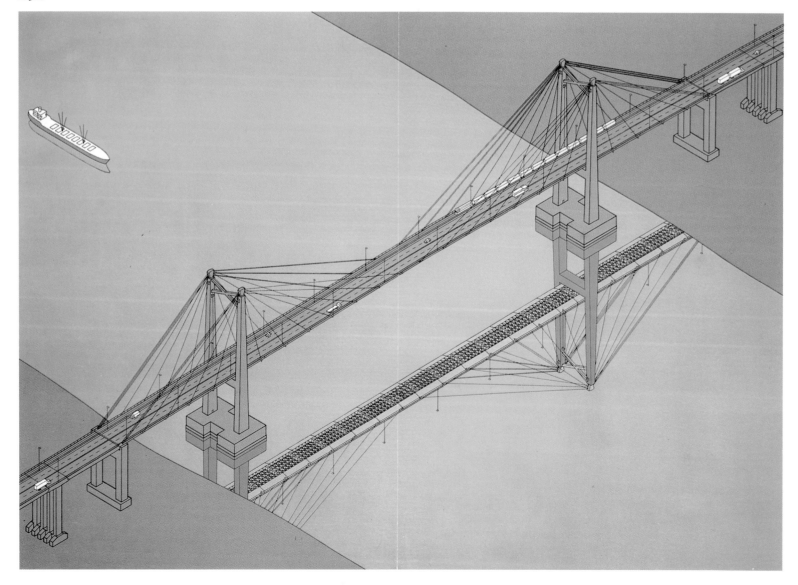

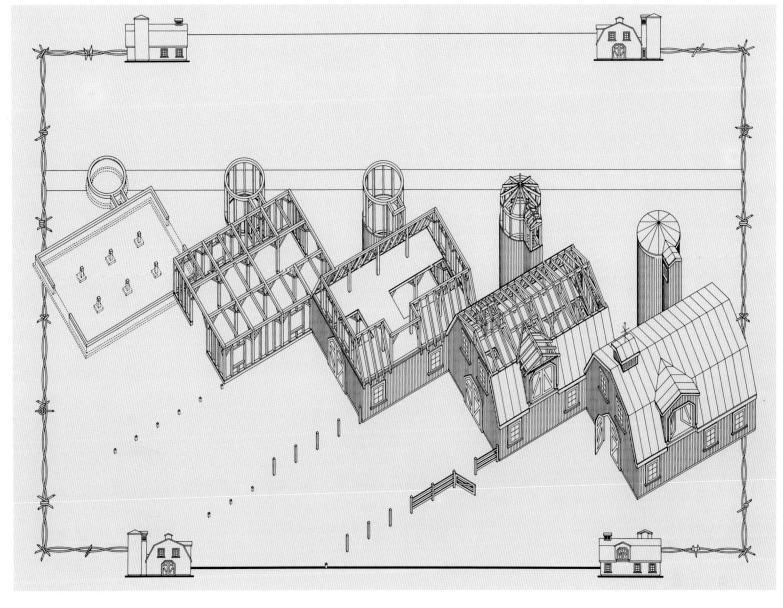

DESIGNER:
ROBERT PECKHAM
ARTIST:
ROBERT PECKHAM
AGENCY:
ROBERT PECKHAM
CLIENT:
ROBERT PECKHAM
■ 329

DESIGNER:
MARYANN LEVESQUE
ART DIRECTOR:
COLIN FORBES
AGENCY:
PENTAGRAM DESIGN, USA
PUBLISHER:
WATSON-GUPTILL
▼■ 330, 331

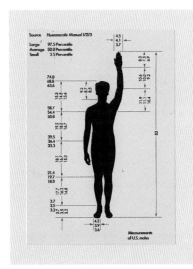

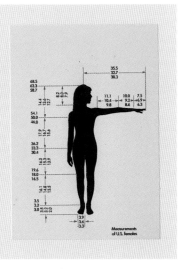

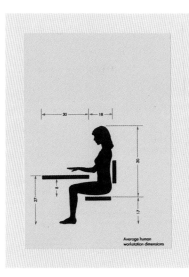

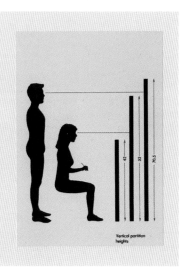

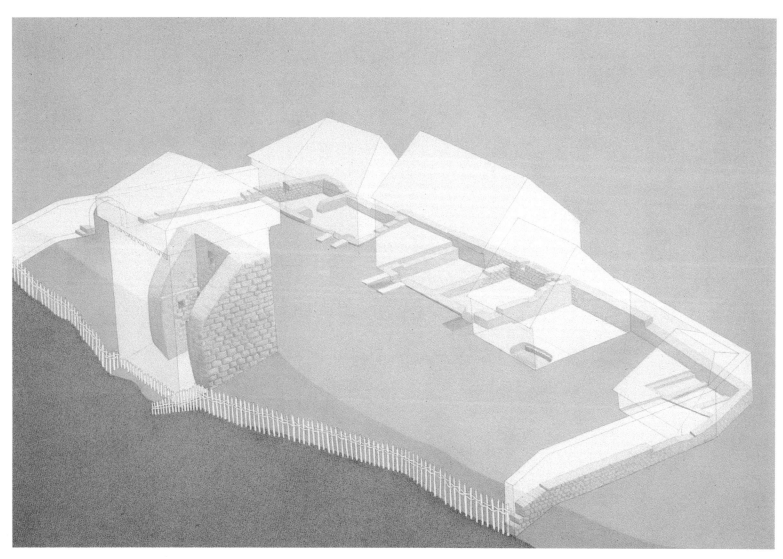

ARTIST:
SABINA NÜSSLI, SCHULE FÜR
GESTALTUNG ZÜRICH, KLASSE FÜR
WISSENSCHAFTLICHES ZEICHNEN
ART DIRECTOR:
CHRISTOPH GÖLDLIN
■ 332

■ 332 Reconstruction of the Freudenau castle ruins (Switzerland). Ink, wash and watercolor. (SWI)

■ 333 Reconstruction of the construction phases of a farmhouse in Zurich from the 15th to the 20th century (ink drawing). (SWI)

■ 332 Rekonstruktion der Burgruine Freudenau (Schweiz). Tusche laviert, Aquarell. (SWI)

■ 333 Rekonstruktion der verschiedenen Bauphasen eines Bauernhauses in Zürich vom 15. bis zum 20. Jahrhundert (Federzeichnung). (SWI)

■ 332 Reconstruction du château fort de Freudenau en ruine (Suisse). Encre de Chine au lavis, aquarelle. (SWI)

■ 333 Reconstruction des différentes étapes de construction d'une ferme à Zurich du XVe au XXe siècle. Dessin à la plume. (SWI)

Abb. 1: Zustand um 1500

ARTIST:
*CHRISTOPH FREY, SCHULE FÜR
GESTALTUNG ZÜRICH, KLASSE FÜR
WISSENSCHAFTLICHES ZEICHNEN*
ART DIRECTOR:
CHRISTOPH GÖLDLIN
■ 333

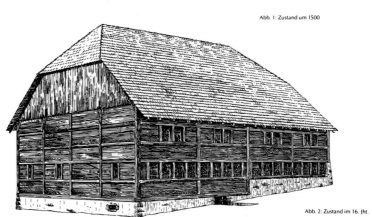

Abb. 2: Zustand im 16. Jht.

Abb. 4: Zustand im 18. Jht.

Abb. 5: Zustand im 19. Jht.

Abb. 6: Zustand im 20. Jht.

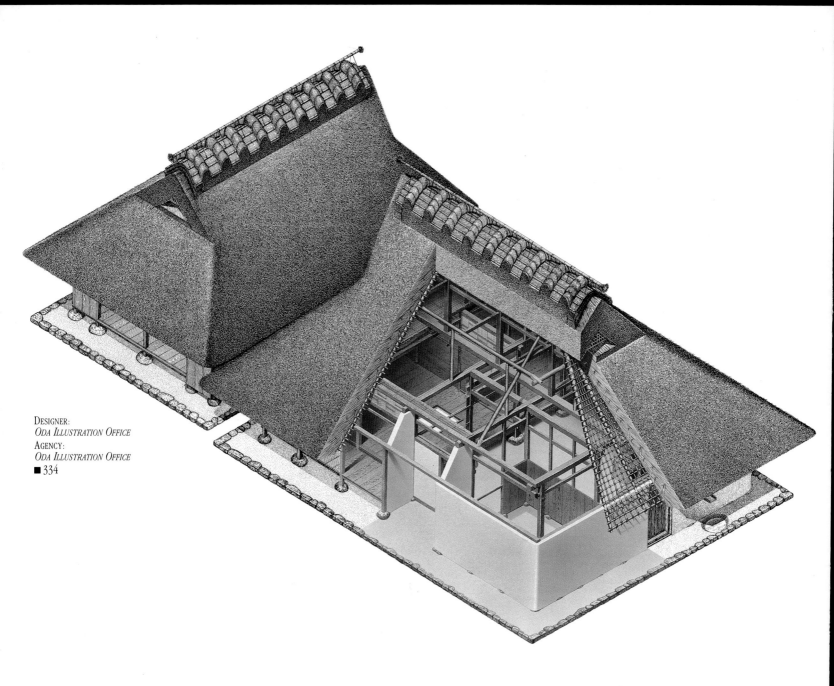

DESIGNER:
ODA ILLUSTRATION OFFICE
AGENCY:
ODA ILLUSTRATION OFFICE
■ 334

■ 334 Portrayal of a part of a traditional Japanese reed-roof construction and view of the exterior. (JPN)

■ 334 Transparentdarstellung eines Teils einer traditionellen japanischen Reetdachkonstruktion und Aussenansicht. (JPN)

■ 334 Vue en transparence d'une partie d'un toit japonais traditionnel en roseaux, et vue extérieure. (JPN)

SCIENCE

WISSENSCHAFT

Both true scientific and popular scientific diagrams are found predominantly in specialist books, textbooks, and magazines, where they generally serve to describe natural conditions and processes, e.g. in such fields as medicine, biology, geology, meteorology, and even geography. They must therefore elucidate sometimes complex facts, and the resulting visualizations are accordingly diverse. In addition to exploded and expanded diagrams, charts with three-dimensional appearance, transparent and "cut-away" illustrations, an almost endless spectrum of representative styles and possibilities is opened up. Parallels to the fine arts are sometimes striking – easy comparisons can be made to the New Objectivity of the 1920's, surrealism, or storybook painting across the board to pop art. It is perhaps worth mentioning though that there are practically no diagrams bearing any similarity to baroque art or impressionism. The true essence and components of fine art – the merging of colors, of forms and objects; a dissolving of precise borders; the imagery needed to portray the atmospheric; the dependence of all objects on cosmic phenomena, on light, on the sun – this is not the goal of a diagram. Its task is to inform in the simplest way about conditions and circumstances, or processes with precise beginnings and ends.

A diagram is in any case a reduction of reality. Trivia and unimportant facts are disregarded; illusory surroundings are omitted. The draftsman selects that which is visible to him, according to the assignment and his own sensitivity. The making of a good diagram lies in the possibility of generalizing and objectivizing. Complexity is reduced to such an extent that it finally becomes descriptive and comprehensible.

On the other hand, a diagram is for exactly this reason an extension of the visible. In a nutshell one could say: "The diagram designer does not illustrate what he sees but rather what he knows." The aim of a graphic diagram is not only to illustrate the object's surface – as does a photo, for example – but rather to make an entire organism understandable, with its complex interdependencies and interconnecting systems. The "innermost essence" of an object must be grasped and expressed. The "grasping" is as important as the "expressing": very often a diagram must illustrate structures or interrelationships which have never been seen by the naked eye, but only revealed by experimentation, or never even revealed, but merely hypothesized!

In order to reach the goal of an increased, if possible universal readability, many scientific diagrams have adopted a set of uniform signs and colors, e.g. the red of arterial blood versus the blue of venal blood. In fact, diagrammatical convention in the field of medicine has reached a very high degree; not only is oxygenated blood red and de-oxygenated blood blue, but the gall bladder is almost always green, fatty tissues are yellow, etc. – the graphic artist is left with the aesthetic decision of deciding how bright the blue should be or how dark the red. The advantage of having such a convention is the quick recognition by a reader who has already been exposed to the same conventions in the past, predisposing him to recognize the various colors as international "codes" for the substances which they almost universally represent.

But maybe a clear visual signal to the expert, however, could be beyond the layman's comprehension – and this is the disadvantage of convention. Reduction and abstraction can lead to an inability to recognize what is being represented. Diagrams meant for a more general public, as for example in *National Geographic,* tend to be less reduced to the abstract and at the same time more colorful and "artistic". More room is left for imagination. Nature thus appears manifold and unexplored, like a miracle, a mystery, a strange cosmos. The unfathomable is expressed to the same extent as the latest scientifically founded facts, and in spite of all the documented knowledge the visualization shows clearly that there are still more fascinating secrets in store, as yet not fully unveiled.

The spectrum of readers for whom scientific diagrams must be understandable is very broad. In the field of medicine alone, for example, it reaches from highly educated specialists to the absolute layman. The extraordinarily differentiated histological representations by Peter Roth *(Figs. 350–352)* were developed during and after operations in constant contact with a highly qualified surgeon and partly in collaboration with a neuro-radiologist. Decades of experience and the latest medical discoveries are conveyed in three dimensions, often from the special vantage point of the surgeon as he is peering into the body. In this respect, the diagrams have the additional function of serving as a kind of "user's manual" for the neuro-surgeon.

Contrast these with the diagrams by R. S. Wurmann *(Figs. 341–348),* which were created for quick consumption by a lay public. Complex processes are very strongly reduced in content, especially through the use of simplified forms and colors. The representations of the human body in *Medical Access* appear as formulaic as mathematical equations, as if there were no more questions unanswered, as if every aspect and problem of the human organism had been solved. This book is not so much involved with the diversity of natural processes, or the unfathomable, or the enigmatic. Man and nature are reduced here to the simplest denominations. Imagination is left very little scope. Man has become a more-or-less well functioning machine. As *Medical Access* however is intended for a public wanting to be informed about diseases and their cures, it is nevertheless appropriate to allow no room for fantasies and elaborations.

In the following chapter a whole range of representations between these two extremes are shown which prove equally illuminating to both the scientist and the layman.

Wissenschaftliche und populärwissenschaftliche Diagramme gibt es vorrangig in Fachbüchern, Schulbüchern und Zeitschriften. Da sie meistens der Veranschaulichung von naturhaften Zuständen und Prozessen dienen, zum Beispiel aus den Bereichen der Medizin, Biologie, Geographie, Geologie und der Meteorologie, das heisst sehr komplexe Tatbestände zum Ausdruck bringen sollen, sind ihre Erscheinungsbilder entsprechend vielfältig. Neben Explosions-, Block-, Transparentoder Phantom-Diagrammen eröffnet sich ein unendliches Spektrum von Darstellungsmöglichkeiten.

Parallelen zur bildenden Kunst, Vergleiche unter anderem mit der Malerei der Neuen Sachlichkeit, dem Surrealismus oder der Historienmalerei bis hin zur Pop-Art bieten sich an. Aufschlussreich und bedenkenswert bezüglich der Aussage eines Diagramms ist indessen die Tatsache, dass sich Ähnlichkeiten zu barocker oder impressionistischer Kunst so gut wie nie ergeben. Wirklich malerische Komponenten, das heisst ein Ineinanderfliessen der Farben, der Formen und der Gegenstände, eine Auflösung der präzisen Umgrenzungen, die Darstellung des Atmosphärischen, der Gebundenheit aller Objekte an kosmische Phänomene, an das Licht, die Sonne, zum Beispiel, und wie sie die Erscheinung eines Gegenstandes verändern kann - das kann nicht Ziel und Zweck eines Diagramms sein. Seine Aufgabe ist es, auf möglichst einfache Art und Weise über Zustände oder klar überschaubare Prozesse mit präzisem Anfang und Ende zu informieren.

Ein Diagramm ist in jedem Fall eine Reduktion von Wirklichkeit. Unwichtiges wird vernachlässigt, der illusionistische Umraum meist weggelassen. Der Zeichnende sortiert das ihm Sichtbare entsprechend der gestellten Aufgabe und seinem Empfinden. Es geht um die Möglichkeit der Verallgemeinerung und der Versachlichung. Die Komplexität wird soweit reduziert, dass sie verständlich und anschaulich wird.

Andererseits ist ein Diagramm genau deshalb auch eine Erweiterung des Sichtbaren. Überspitzt kann man sagen: «Der Zeichnende bildet nicht ab, was er sieht, sondern was er weiss.» Nicht nur die Darstellung der Objektoberfläche, wie sie ein Photo leistet, ist Ziel einer graphischen Darstellung, sondern das Verständlichmachen eines ganzen Organismus und seiner Zusammenhänge. Das «innerste Wesen» eines Gegenstandes muss erfasst sein und zum Ausdruck kommen.

Um das Ziel der erhöhten, möglichst international gültigen Lesbarkeit einer diagrammatischen Zeichnung besser zu erreichen, ist man bestrebt, einheitliche Signaturen und Farben für die dargestellten Materialien zu bestimmen. Im medizinischen Bereich ist das in recht hohem Masse erreicht. Arterienblut wird rot dargestellt, Venenblut blau - für welchen Ton Rot oder Blau sich der Zeichnende dann entscheiden will und für welchen Helligkeits- oder Dunkelwert, das bleibt seinem eigenen ästhetischen Empfinden überlassen -, die Galle sollte grün sein, das

Fett gelb etc. Vorteil solch genauer Vorgaben ist, wie gesagt, die erhöhte allgemeine schnelle Lesbarkeit. Allerdings wird andererseits vorausgesetzt, dass der Betrachter die Zeichen entziffern kann, folglich schon ein gewisses Vorwissen hat. Was sich für den Fachmann also positiv darstellt, kann sich für den Laien unter Umständen erschwerend auswirken. Zu grosse Reduktion und Abstraktion kann zu Unkenntlichkeit führen. So ist auch generell zu bemerken, dass Diagramme in ihrer Aufmachung oft umso reduzierter und unspektakulärer sind, je höher der wissenschaftliche Anspruch ist. Wird andererseits explizit für ein grosses umfassendes Publikum gezeichnet, wie zum Beispiel in *National Geographic,* dann sind die Darstellungen meist weniger reduziert angelegt, stattdessen vielfarbiger und malerischer. Der Phantasie wird mehr Spielraum gewährt. Die Natur erscheint vielfältig und unerschlossen - wie ein Wunder, ein Mysterium, ein fremder Kosmos. Das Nichtergründbare wird ebenso zum Ausdruck gebracht wie neueste wissenschaftliche Erkenntnisse, und trotz allem dargestellten Wissen wird bildnerisch deutlich gemacht, dass sie noch weitere faszinierende Geheimnisse birgt, noch keineswegs völlig verfügbar und erschlossen ist.

Das Spektrum derjenigen, die angesprochen werden sollen, ist sehr gross. Es reicht zum Beispiel im medizinischen Bereich von Fachleuten bis zu absoluten Laien. Die ausserordentlich differenzierten histologischen Darstellungen von Peter Roth *(Abb. 350–352)* entstehen während und nach Operationen in ständiger Auseinandersetzung mit dem hochqualifizierten Chirurgen und zum Teil sogar noch in Zusammenarbeit mit einem Neuroradiologen. Jahrzehntelange Erfahrungen und die neuesten Erkenntnisse werden ins Dreidimensionale übertragen, oft unter spezieller Berücksichtigung der Optik des in den Körper hineinschauenden Chirurgen. Die Diagramme haben so unter anderem auch die Funktion von Handlungsanleitungen für den Neurochirurgen.

Demgegenüber sind die Darstellungen von R.S. Wurmann *(Abb. 341-348)* für die schnelle Konsumierbarkeit durch ein Laienpublikum geschaffen. Komplexe Vorgänge werden inhaltlich sehr stark reduziert, wie auch bezüglich ihrer Form- und Farbgebung. Formelhaft wie mathematische Gleichungen erscheinen die Menschendarstellungen in *Medical Access,* als blieben keine Fragen mehr offen, als seien sämtliche Aspekte durchschaut und die Probleme gelöst. Hier geht es nicht mehr um die Vielfalt natürlicher Prozesse, um das Nichtergründbare, das Wunderbare, sondern hier werden der Mensch und die Natur auf einfachste Zusammenhänge reduziert. Der Phantasie wird wenig Spielraum zugestanden. Der Mensch wird zu einer mehr oder minder gut funktionierenden Maschine. Da es sich bei *Medical Access* jedoch um eine Publikation handelt, die über Krankheiten und deren Heilung Auskunft geben will, scheint es angebracht, möglichen Phantasien und Ausschmückungen keinen Raum zuzugestehen.

Les diagrammes scientifiques et de vulgarisation se rencontrent surtout dans les ouvrages spécialisés, les manuels scolaires et les périodiques. Leur présentation est d'autant plus diverse qu'ils servent la plupart du temps à expliciter des états et processus naturels dans les domaines de la médecine, de la biologie, de la géographie, de la géologie, de la météorologie, etc. Ils affectent donc non seulement la forme d'éclatés, de blocs-diagrammes, de diagrammes transparents ou fantômes, mais celle d'une infinité de représentations graphiques créatives.

Un parallélisme s'y affirme avec les arts plastiques, notamment avec la peinture des nouveaux réalistes, le surréalisme, la peinture historique ou le pop art. Phénomène révélateur et remarquable, l'art baroque, l'impressionnisme ne sont pratiquement jamais mis à contribution. De toute façon, le but d'un diagramme ne peut pas consister en une transposition picturale qui fait fusionner les coloris, les formes et les objets, annule les délimitations précises, rend compte de sensations atmosphériques, rattache tous les objects figurés à des phénomènes cosmiques, à la lumière, au soleil qui peut modifier l'apparence d'un objet. Un diagramme a pour tâche de fournir des renseignements aussi simples que possible sur des états ou des processus parfaitement compris qui connaissent un point de départ et une fin définis avec précision.

Dans tous les cas, un diagramme constitue une réduction du réel. Les éléments sans importance sont supprimés, l'entourage illusionniste soustrait. Le dessinateur trie ce qu'il voit en fonction de la tâche posée et de l'idée qu'il s'en fait. Pour la multiplicité des formes, il cherche une forme idéale. Il ne s'agit en effet pas de représenter un état momentané, mais d'étudier la possibilité d'une généralisation et d'une objectivation loisibles. La complexité du sujet est réduite au point qu'elle en devient compréhensible et expressive.

Par ailleurs, et précisément pour cette raison, le diagramme élargit le domaine du visible. En forçant un peu les choses, on pourrait soutenir que «le dessinateur ne reproduit pas ce qu'il voit, mais ce qu'il sait». Une photo est apte à représenter la surface d'un objet; la représentation graphique, elle, veut faire davantage: rendre accessible à la compréhension le fonctionnement d'un organisme entier et de ses structures. L'«être intime» de l'objet étudié doit être perçu et traduit dans les faits. Un diagramme réalise la concrétisation de données structurelles déterminées par la théorie ou analysées par des instruments.

Afin d'obtenir une lisibilité accrue qui ait si possible une validité internationale, on cherche à codifier de manière uniforme les caractéristiques et coloris des matériaux représentés. Dans le domaine médical, on y est déjà parvenu dans une large mesure. Le sang artériel apparaît en rouge, le sang veineux en bleu. Il est vrai que le dessinateur est libre de choisir l'intensité du bleu ou du rouge, sa luminosité ou son obscurcissement relatif, selon son bon plaisir esthétique. La bile devrait être verte, les graisses jaunes, etc. Dans d'autres domaines aussi, il existe des conventions universellement reconnues. Ainsi, dans une représentation géographique, un triangle représente le charbon, le sable est figuré par des points, l'argent par des hachures particulières, etc. L'avantage d'indications précises de ce genre, c'est leur lisibilité et donc un accès plus rapide à l'information souhaitée. Cela présuppose évidemment que le lecteur est capable de déchiffrer ces signes, donc qu'il dispose d'un certain savoir préalable. Ce qui peut s'avérer positif pour le spécialiste peut le cas échéant constituer un obstacle pour la compréhension de M. Tout-le-monde. Une réduction et une abstraction trop poussées peuvent rendre un dessin inintelligible. Dans cet ordre d'idées, il est intéressant de noter que la présentation des faits dans un diagramme est souvent d'autant plus réductrice et peu spectaculaire que son niveau scientifique est plus élevé. Inversement, le dessin qui s'adresse expressément au grand public, par exemple dans le magazine *National Geographic,* a recours à moins de réduction et souligne généralement les aspects chromatiques et picturaux. L'imagination peut alors davantage faire valoir ses droits, et la nature est parée de toute la séduction de la diversité, de l'inconnu, de la merveille, du mystère, d'un univers étrange. Ce qui se dérobe à l'investigation est représenté au même titre que les dernières découvertes scientifiques; et tout le savoir explicité n'empêche pas de faire comprendre au lecteur, par l'image, que les secrets fascinants à élucider sont légion et que la nature reste encore largement terra incognita.

L'éventail des publics visés est très large. Pour ne prendre que le domaine médical, on réalise des dessins aussi bien pour le médecin spécialisé que pour le lecteur vierge de toute information médicale. Les représentations histologiques extrêmement différenciées de Peter Roth *(fig. 350-352)* sont réalisées en cours d'opération ou immédiatement après en contact permanent avec le chirurgien qualifié, parfois même en collaboration avec un neuroradiologue. Une expérience de plusieurs décennies est mise en œuvre pour transposer les dernières données de la science dans une représentation tridimensionnelle en tenant souvent compte du regard que l'instrumentation moderne permet de plonger dans les arcanes du corps humain. Ces diagrammes revêtent alors entre autres la dignité d'instructions opératoires pour neurochirurgiens.

En comparaison, les graphiques de R.S. Wurman *(fig. 341-348)* sont destinés à la consommation rapide par un public non averti. La complexité des phénomènes y est fortement réduite, tant au plan du contenu qu'à celui des formes et des couleurs. La représentation de l'être humain se fait stéréotypée à la manière d'une équation mathématique dans *Medical Access,* donnant l'impression que toutes les questions sont résolues, tous les aspects compris, tous les problèmes résolus. Il n'est plus ici question de la multiplicité des phénomènes naturels, de ce qui ne saurait être appréhendé, de la merveilleuse machine vivante: l'homme et la nature sont réduits à leur plus simple expression. L'imagination n'a plus de libre cours. L'homme se mue en mécanisme plus ou moins fiable. Il est vrai que *Medical Access* est une publication qui entend renseigner d'une manière simple sur les maladies et les thérapies à leur appliquer, ce qui semble exclure l'imagination qui brode et les fioritures qui dénaturent.

DESIGNER:
David Pelham
ARTIST:
Harry Willock
ART DIRECTOR:
David Pelham
PUBLISHER:
Jonathan Cape Ltd.
■ 336–340

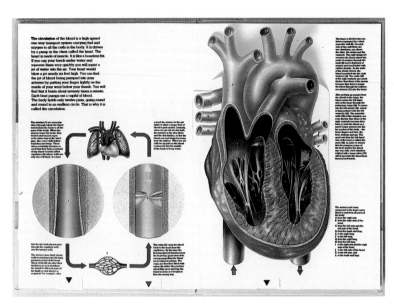

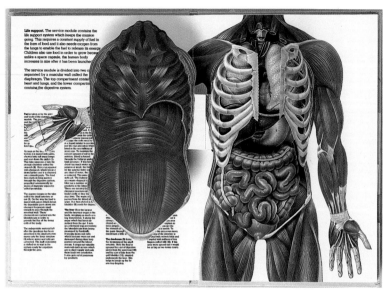

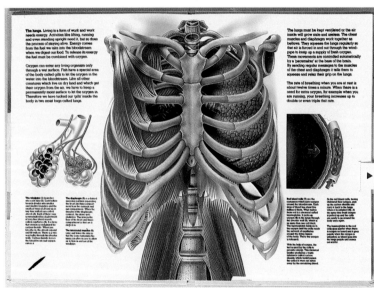

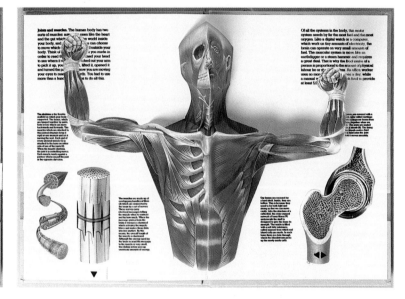

■ 336-340 Double spreads showing the three dimensional, moveable illustrations from the pop-up book *The Human Body* published by Jonathan Cape Ltd. The subjects shown here are: the circulation (arteries and heart) *(336)*; the process of nourishment as life support from the stage of consumption to digestion *(337)*; the lungs *(338)*; joints and muscles *(339)*, and the head *(340)*. (GBR)

■ 336-340 Doppelseiten mit dreidimensionalen, beweglichen Darstellungen aus dem Buch *Der menschliche Körper* (Jonathan Cape Ltd.). Die Themen: Die Blutzirkulation, d.h. Funktion und Aufbau von Arterien und Herz *(336)*; die Energiezufuhr durch Nahrungsmittelaufnahme und -umsetzung *(337)*; die Atmungsorgane *(338)*; Gelenke und Muskeln *(339)* und der Kopf *(340)*. (GBR)

■ 336-340 Doubles pages du livre *The Human Body* (Le Corps humain, Ed. Jonathan Cape Ltd.) comportant des représentations tridimensionnelles mobiles: la circulation, fonction et structure des artères et du cœur *(336)*; l'apport d'énergie par ingestion et assimilation de la nourriture *(337)*; les organes respiratoires *(338)*; muscles et articulations *(339)*; la tête *(340)*. (GBR)

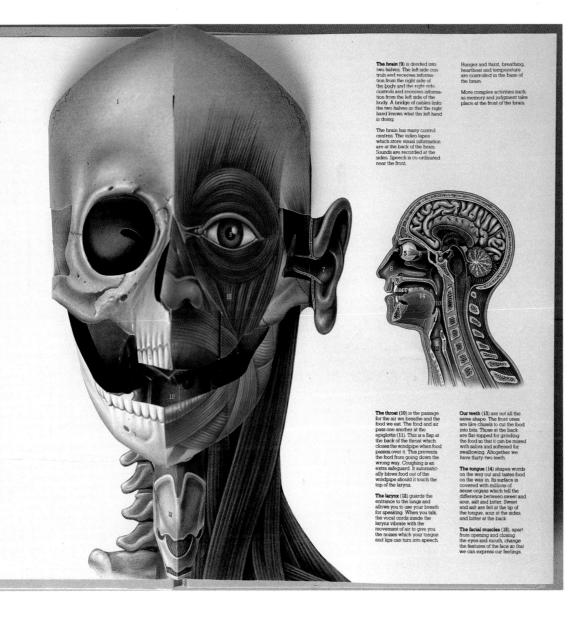

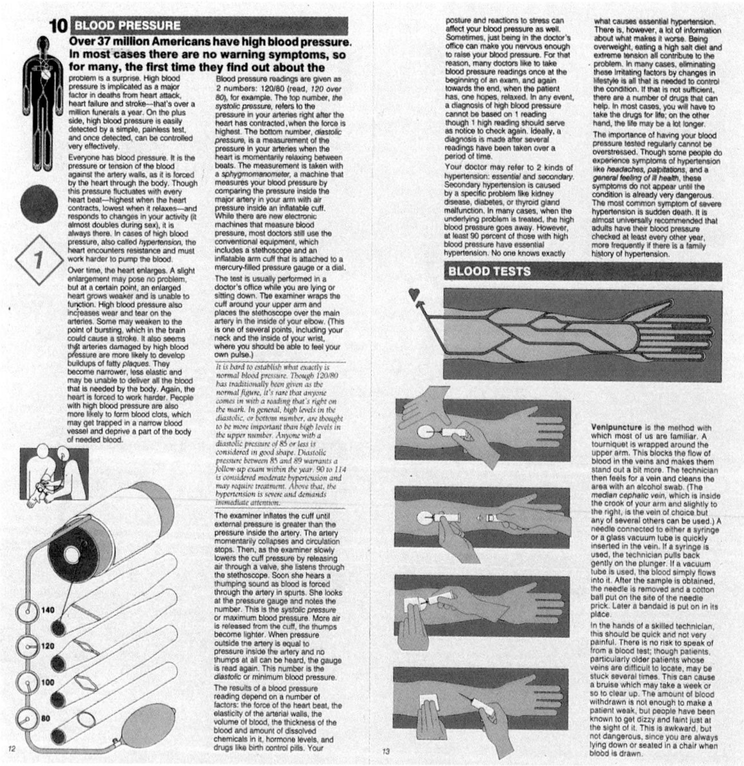

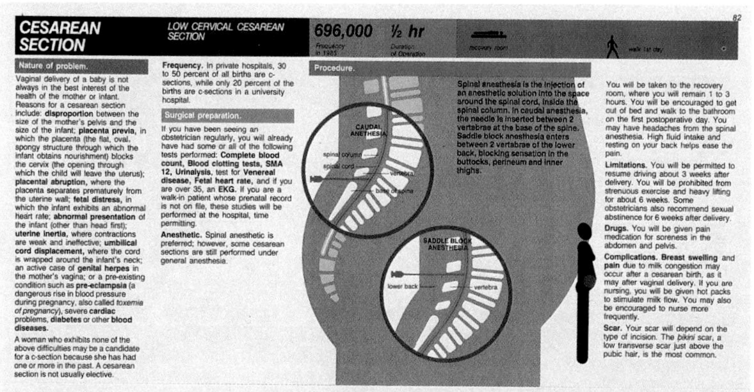

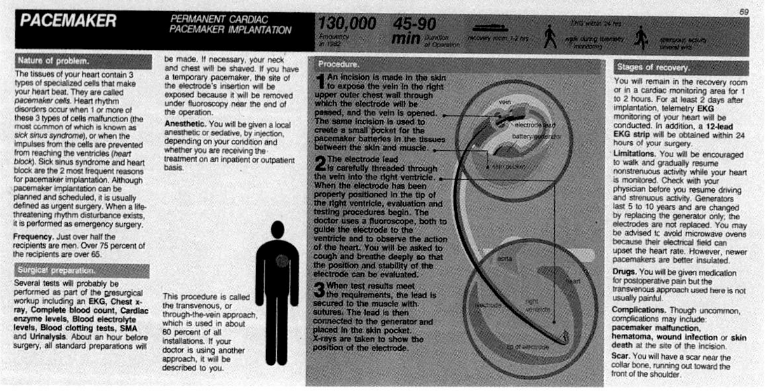

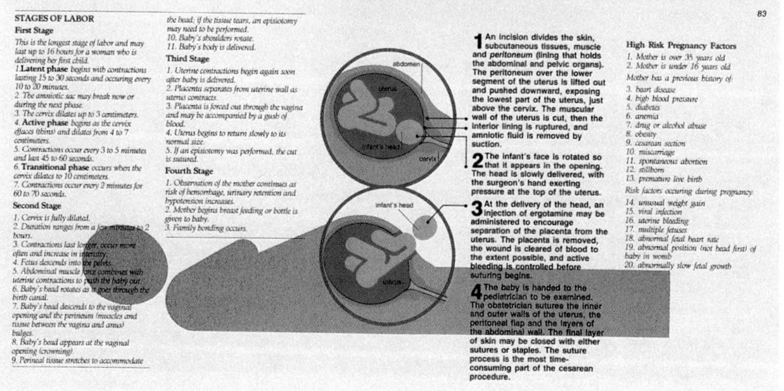

10 BLOOD PRESSURE

Over 37 million Americans have high blood pressure. In most cases there are no warning symptoms, so for many, the first time they find out about the

problem is a surprise. High blood pressure is implicated as a major factor in deaths from heart attack, heart failure and stroke—that's over a million funerals a year. On the plus side, high blood pressure is easily detected by a simple, painless test, and once detected, can be controlled very effectively.

Everyone has blood pressure. It is the pressure or tension of the blood against the artery walls, as it is forced by the heart through the body. Though this pressure fluctuates with every heart beat—highest when the heart contracts, lowest when it relaxes—and responds to changes in your activity (it almost doubles during sex), it is always there. In cases of high blood pressure, also called hypertension, the heart encounters resistance and must work harder to pump the blood.

Over time, the heart enlarges. A slight enlargement may pose no problem, but at a certain point, an enlarged heart grows weaker and is unable to function. High blood pressure also increases wear and tear on the arteries. Some may weaken to the point of bursting, which in the brain could cause a stroke. It also seems that arteries damaged by high blood pressure are more likely to develop buildups of fatty plaque. They become narrower, less elastic and may be unable to deliver all the blood that is needed by the body. Again, the heart is forced to work harder. People with high blood pressure are also more likely to form blood clots, which may get trapped in a narrow blood vessel and deprive a part of the body of needed blood.

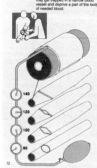

Blood pressure readings are given as 2 numbers: 120/80 (read, 120 over 80), for example. The top number, the systolic pressure, refers to the pressure in your arteries right after the heart has contracted, when the force is highest. The bottom number, diastolic pressure, is a measurement of the pressure in your arteries when the heart is momentarily relaxing between beats. The measurement is taken with a sphygmomanometer, a machine that measures your blood pressure by comparing the pressure inside the major artery in your arm with air pressure inside an inflatable cuff. While there are new electronic machines that measure blood pressure, most doctors still use the conventional equipment, which includes a stethoscope and an inflatable arm cuff that is attached to a mercury-filled pressure gauge or a dial.

The test is usually performed in a doctor's office while you are lying or sitting down. The examiner wraps the cuff around your upper arm and places the stethoscope over the main artery in the inside of your elbow. (This is one of several points, including your neck and the inside of your wrist, where you should be able to feel your own pulse.)

The examiner inflates the cuff until external pressure is greater than the pressure inside the artery. The artery momentarily collapses and circulation stops. Then, as the examiner slowly lowers the cuff pressure by releasing air through a valve, she listens through the stethoscope. Soon she hears a thumping sound as blood is forced through the artery in spurts. She looks at the pressure gauge and notes the number. This is the systolic pressure or maximum blood pressure. More air is released from the cuff, the thumps become lighter. When pressure outside the artery is equal to pressure inside the artery and no thumps at all can be heard, the gauge is read again. This number is the diastolic or minimum blood pressure.

The results of a blood pressure reading depend on a number of factors: the force of the heart beat, the elasticity of the arterial walls, the volume of blood, the thickness of the blood and amount of dissolved chemicals in it, hormone levels, and drugs like birth control pills. Your

posture and reactions to stress can affect your blood pressure as well. Sometimes, just being in the doctor's office can make you nervous enough to raise your blood pressure. For that reason, many doctors like to take blood pressure readings once at the beginning of an exam, and again towards the end, when the patient has, one hopes, relaxed. In any event, a diagnosis of high blood pressure cannot be based on 1 reading though 1 high reading should serve as notice to check again. Ideally, a diagnosis is made after several readings have been taken over a period of time.

Your doctor may refer to 2 kinds of hypertension: essential and secondary. Secondary hypertension is caused by a specific problem like kidney disease, diabetes, or thyroid gland malfunction. In many cases, when the underlying problem is treated, the high blood pressure goes away. However, at least 90 percent of those with high blood pressure have essential hypertension. No one knows exactly

what causes essential hypertension. There is, however, a lot of information about what makes it worse. Being overweight, eating a high salt diet and extreme tension all contribute to the problem. In many cases, eliminating these irritating factors by changes in lifestyle is all that is needed to control the condition. If that is not sufficient, there are a number of drugs that can help. In most cases, you will have to take the drugs for life; on the other hand, the they may be a lot longer.

The importance of having your blood pressure tested regularly cannot be overstressed. Though some people do experience symptoms of hypertension like headaches, palpitations, and a general feeling of ill health, these symptoms do not appear until the condition is already very dangerous. The most common symptom of severe hypertension is sudden death. It is almost universally recommended that adults have their blood pressure checked at least every other year, more frequently if there is a family history of hypertension.

BLOOD TESTS

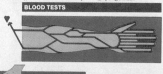

Venipuncture is the method with which most of us are familiar. A tourniquet is wrapped around the upper arm. This blocks the flow of blood in the veins and makes them stand out a bit more. The technician then feels for a vein and cleans the area with an alcohol swab. (The median cephalic vein, which is inside the crook of your arm and slightly to the right, is the vein of choice but any of several others can be used.) A needle connected to either a syringe or a glass vacuum tube is quickly inserted in the vein. If a syringe is used, the technician pulls back gently on the plunger. If a vacuum tube is used, the blood simply flows into it. After the sample is obtained, the needle is removed and a cotton ball put on the site of the needle prick. Later a bandaid is put on in its place.

In the hands of a skilled technician, this should be quick and not very painful. There is no risk to speak of from a blood test; though patients, particularly older patients whose veins are difficult to locate, may be stuck several times. This can cause a bruise which may take a week or so to clear up. The amount of blood withdrawn is not enough to make a patient weak, but people have been known to get dizzy and faint just at the sight of it. This is awkward, but not dangerous, since you are always lying down or seated in a chair when blood is drawn.

It is hard to establish what exactly is normal blood pressure. Though 120/80 has traditionally been given as the normal figure, it's rare that anyone comes in with a reading that's right on the mark. In general, high levels in the diastolic, or bottom number, are thought to be more important than high levels in the upper number. Anyone with a diastolic pressure of 85 or less is considered in good shape. Diastolic pressure between 85 and 89 warrants a follow-up exam within the year; 90 to 114 is considered moderate hypertension and may require treatment. Above that, the hypertension is severe and demands immediate attention.

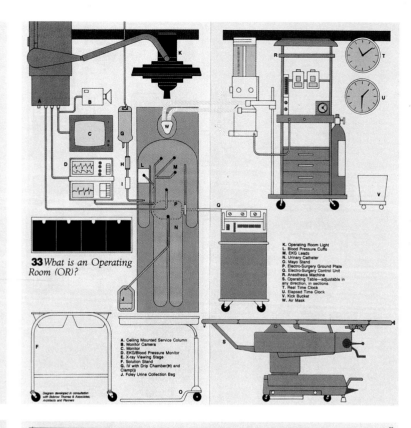

33 What is an Operating Room (OR)?

K. Operating Room Light
L. Blood Pressure Cuffs
M. EKG Leads
N. Urinary Catheter
O. Mayo Stand
P. Electro-Surgery Ground Plate
Q. Electro-Surgery Control Unit
R. X-ray Viewing Stage
S. Anesthesia Machine
T. Real Time Clock
U. Elapsed Time Clock
V. Kick Bucket
W. Air Mask

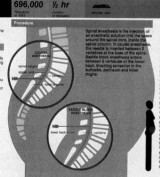

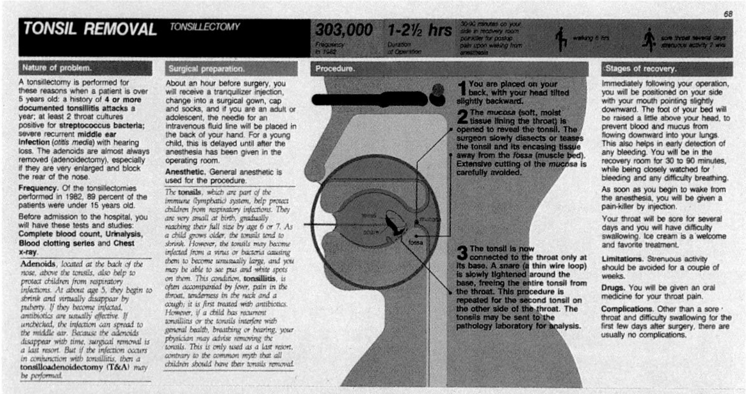

A. Ceiling Mounted Service Column
B. Monitor Camera
C. Monitor
D. EKG/Blood Pressure Monitor
E. X-ray Viewing Stage
F. Solution Stand
G. IV with Drip Chamber(H) and Clamp(I)
J. Foley Urine Collection Bag

Diagram developed in consultation with Bobrow Thomas & Associates, Architects and Planners

---

TONSIL REMOVAL — TONSILLECTOMY

303,000   1–2½ hrs

Nature of problem.

A tonsillectomy is performed for these reasons when a patient is over 5 years old: a history of 4 or more documented tonsillitis attacks a year; at least 2 throat cultures positive for streptococcus bacteria; severe recurrent **middle ear infection** (otitis media) with hearing loss. The adenoids are almost always removed (adenoidectomy), especially if they are very enlarged and block the rear of the nose.

Frequency. Of the tonsillectomies performed in 1982, 86 percent of the patients were under 15 years old.

Before admission to the hospital, you will have these tests and studies: Complete blood count, Urinalysis, Blood clotting series and Chest x-ray.

Adenoids, located at the back of the nose, above the tonsils, also help to protect children from respiratory infections. At about age 5, they begin to shrink and virtually disappear by puberty. If they become infected, antibiotics are usually effective. If unchecked, the infection can spread to the middle ear. Because the adenoids disappear with time, surgical removal is a last resort. But if the infection occurs in conjunction with tonsillitis, then a tonsilloadenoidectomy (T&A) may be performed.

Surgical preparation.

About an hour before surgery, you will receive a tranquilizer injection. You will not be allowed to eat or drink. Heart rhythm disorders occur when 1 or more of these 3 types of cells malfunction and the most common of which is known as sick sinus syndrome, or when the impulses from the cells are prevented from reaching the ventricles (heart block). Sick sinus syndrome and heart block are the 2 most frequent reasons for pacemaker implantation.

Anesthetic. General anesthetic is used for the procedure.

The tonsils, which are part of the immune (lymphatic) system, help protect children from respiratory infections. They are very small at birth, gradually reaching their full size by age 6 or 7. As a child grows older, the tonsils tend to shrink. However, the tonsils may become infected from a virus or bacteria causing them to become unusually large, in which case they are able to see pus and white spots on them. This condition, tonsillitis, is often accompanied by fever, pain in the throat, tenderness in the neck with general health, breathing or hearing, your physician may advise removing the tonsils. This is only used as a last resort, contrary to the common myth that all children should have their tonsils removed.

Procedure.

1 You are placed on your back, with your head tilted slightly backward.

2 The mucous (soft, moist tissue lining the throat) is opened to reveal the tonsil. The surgeon slowly dissects or teases it away from the fossa (muscle bed). Extensive cutting of the mucosa is carefully avoided.

3 The tonsil is now connected to the throat only at its base. A snare (a thin wire loop) is slowly tightened around the base, freeing the entire tonsil from the throat. This procedure is repeated for the second tonsil on the other side of the throat. The tonsils may then be sent to the pathology laboratory for analysis.

Stages of recovery.

Immediately following your operation, you will be positioned on your side with your mouth pointing slightly downward. The foot of your bed will be raised a little above your head, to prevent blood and mucus from flowing downward into your lungs. This also helps in early detection of any bleeding. You will be in the recovery room for 30 to 90 minutes, while being closely watched for bleeding and any difficulty breathing.

As soon as you begin to wake from the anesthesia, you will be given a pain-killer by injection.

Your throat will be sore for several days and you will have difficulty swallowing. Ice cream is a welcome and favorite treatment.

Limitations. Strenuous activity should be avoided for a couple of weeks.

Drugs. You will be given an oral medicine for your throat pain.

Complications. Other than a sore throat and difficulty swallowing for the first few days after surgery, there are usually no complications.

CESAREAN SECTION — LOW CERVICAL CESAREAN SECTION

696,000   ½ hr

Nature of problem.

Vaginal delivery of a baby is not always in the best interest of the health of the mother or infant. Reasons for a cesarean section include: **disproportion** between the size of the mother's pelvis and the size of the infant; **placenta previa**, in which the placenta (the flat, oval, spongy structure through which the infant obtains nourishment) blocks the cervix (the opening through which the child will leave the uterus); **placental abruption**, where the placenta separates prematurely from the uterine wall; **fetal distress**, in which the infant exhibits an abnormal heart rate; **abnormal presentation** of the infant (other than head first); **uterine inertia**, where contractions are weak and ineffective; **umbilical cord displacement**, where the cord is wrapped around the infant's neck; an active case of **genital herpes** in the mother's vagina; or a pre-existing condition such as **pre-eclampsia** (a dangerous rise in blood pressure during pregnancy), also called toxemia of pregnancy), severe **cardiac** problems, **diabetes** or other blood diseases.

A woman who exhibits none of the above difficulties may be a candidate for a c-section because she has had one or more in the past. A cesarean section is not usually elective.

Surgical preparation.

If you have been seeing an obstetrician regularly, you will already have had some or all of the following tests performed: **Complete blood count**, **Blood clotting tests**, **SMA 12**, **Urinalysis**, test for **Venereal disease**, **Fetal heart rate**, and if you are over 35, an **EKG**. If you are a walk-in patient whose prenatal record is not on file, these studies will be performed at the hospital, time permitting.

Anesthetic. Spinal anesthetic is preferred; however, some cesarean sections are still performed under general anesthesia.

Frequency. In private hospitals, 30 to 50 percent of all births are c-sections, while only 20 percent of the births are c-sections in a university hospital.

Procedure.

Spinal anesthesia is the injection of anesthetic solution into the space around the spinal cord. Unlike the spinal column, in caudal anesthesia, the needle is inserted between 2 vertebrae at the base of the spine. Saddle block anesthesia enters between 2 vertebrae of the lower back, blocking sensation in the buttocks, perineum and inner thighs.

You will be taken to the recovery room, where you will remain 1 to 3 hours. You will be encouraged to get out of bed and walk to the bathroom on the first postoperative day. You may have headaches from the spinal anesthesia. High fluid intake and resting on your back helps ease the pain.

Limitations. You will be permitted to resume driving about 3 weeks after delivery. You will be prohibited from strenuous exercise and heavy lifting for about 6 weeks. Some obstetricians also recommend sexual abstinence for 6 weeks after delivery.

Drugs. You will be given pain medication for soreness in the abdomen and pelvis.

Complications. Breast swelling and pain due to milk congestion may occur after a cesarean birth, as it may after vaginal delivery. If you are nursing, you will be given hot packs to stimulate milk flow. You may also be encouraged to nurse more frequently.

Scar. Your scar will depend on the type of incision. The bikini scar, a low transverse scar just above the pubic hair, is the most common.

PACEMAKER — PERMANENT CARDIAC PACEMAKER IMPLANTATION

130,000   45–90 min

Nature of problem.

The tissues of your heart contain 3 types of specialized cells that make your heart beat. They are called pacemaker cells. Heart rhythm disorders occur when 1 or more of these 3 types of cells malfunction and the most common of which is known as sick sinus syndrome, or when the impulses from the cells are prevented from reaching the ventricles (heart block). Sick sinus syndrome and heart block are the 2 most frequent reasons for pacemaker implantation. Although pacemaker implantation can be planned and scheduled, it is usually defined as urgent surgery. When a life-threatening rhythm disturbance exists, it is performed as emergency surgery.

Frequency. Just over half the recipients are men. Over 75 percent of the recipients are over 65.

Surgical preparation.

Several tests will probably be performed as part of the presurgical workup including an EKG, Chest x-ray, Complete blood count, Cardiac enzyme levels, Blood electrolyte levels, Blood clotting tests, SMA and Urinalysis. About an hour before surgery, all standard preparations will

be made. If necessary, your neck and chest will be shaved. If you have a temporary pacemaker, the site of the electrode's insertion will be exposed because it will be removed under fluoroscopy near the end of the operation.

Anesthetic. You will be given a local anesthetic or sedative, by injection, depending on your condition and whether you are receiving the treatment on an inpatient or outpatient basis.

This procedure is called the transvenous, or through-the-vein approach, which is used in about 80 percent of all installations. If your doctor is using another approach, it will be described to you.

Procedure.

1 An incision is made in the skin to expose the vein in the right upper outer chest wall through which the electrode will be passed, and the vein is opened. The same incision is used to create a small pocket for the pacemaker batteries in the tissues between the skin and muscle.

2 The electrode lead is carefully threaded through the vein into the right ventricle. When the electrode has been properly positioned in the tip of the right ventricle, evaluation and testing procedures begin. The doctor uses a fluoroscope, both to guide the electrode to the action of the heart. You will be asked to cough and breathe deeply so that the position and stability of the electrode can be evaluated.

3 When test results meet the requirements, the lead is secured to the muscle with sutures. The lead is then connected to the generator and placed in the skin pocket. X-rays are taken to show the position of the electrode.

Stages of recovery.

You will remain in the recovery room or in a cardiac monitoring area for 1 to 2 hours. For at least 2 days after implantation, telemetry EKG monitoring of your heart will be conducted. In addition, a 12-lead EKG strip will be obtained within 24 hours of your surgery.

Limitations. You will be encouraged to walk and gradually resume nonstrenuous activity while your heart is monitored. Check with your physician before you resume driving and strenuous activity. Generators last 5 to 10 years and are changed by replacing the generator only; the electrodes are not replaced. You may be advised to avoid microwave ovens because their electrical field can upset the heart rate. However, newer pacemakers are better insulated.

Drugs. You will be given medication for postoperative pain but the transvenous approach used here is not usually painful.

Complications. Though uncommon, complications may include: pacemaker malfunction, hematoma, wound infection or skin death at the site of the incision.

Scar. You will have a scar near the collar bone, running out toward the front of the shoulder.

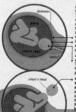

STAGES OF LABOR

First Stage

This is the longest stage of labor and may last up to 16 hours for a woman who is delivering her first child.

1 **Latent phase** begins with contractions lasting 15 to 30 seconds and occurring every 10 to 30 minutes.
2. The amniotic sac may break now or during the next phase.
3. The cervix dilates up to 3 centimeters.

4 **Active phase** begins as the cervix dilates (thins) and dilates from 4 to 7 centimeters.
5. Contractions occur every 3 to 5 minutes and last 45 to 60 seconds.
6. **Transitional phase** occurs when the cervix dilates to 10 centimeters.
7. Contractions occur every 2 minutes for 60 to 70 seconds.

Second Stage

1. Cervix is fully dilated.
2. Duration ranges from a few minutes to 2 hours.
3. Contractions last longer, occur more often and increase in intensity.
4. Fetus descends into the pelvis.
5. Abdominal muscles feel contracted with uterine contractions to push the baby out.
6. Baby's head rotates as it goes through the birth canal.
7. Baby's head descends to the vaginal opening and the perineum (muscles and tissue between the vagina and anus) bulges.
8. Baby's head appears at the vaginal opening (crowning).
9. Perineal tissue stretches to accommodate

the head, if the tissue tears, an episiotomy may need to be performed.
10. Baby's shoulders rotate.
11. Baby's body is delivered.

Third Stage
1. Uterine contractions begin again soon after baby is delivered.
2. Placenta separates from uterine wall as uterus contracts.
3. Placenta is forced out through the vagina and may be accompanied by a gush of blood.
4. Uterus begins to return slowly to its normal size.
5. If an episiotomy was performed, the cut is sutured.

Fourth Stage
1. Observation of the mother continues as risk of hemorrhage, urinary retention and hypotension increases.
2. Mother begins breast feeding or bottle is given to baby.
3. Family bonding occurs.

1 An incision divides the skin, subcutaneous tissues, muscle and peritoneum (lining that holds the abdominal and pelvic organs). The peritoneum over the lower segment of the uterus is lifted out and pushed downward, exposing the lowest part of the uterus, just above the cervix. The muscular wall of the uterus is cut, then the interior lining is ruptured, and amniotic fluid is removed by suction.

2 The infant's face is rotated so that it appears in the opening. The head is slowly delivered, with the surgeon's hand exerting pressure at the top of the uterus.

3 At the delivery of the head, an injection of ergotamine may be administered to encourage separation of the placenta from the uterus. The placenta is removed, the wound is cleared of blood to the extent possible, and active bleeding is controlled before suturing begins.

4 The baby is handed to the pediatrician to be examined. The obstetrician sutures the inner and outer walls of the uterus, the peritoneal flap and the layers of the abdominal wall. The final layer of skin may be closed with either sutures or staples. The suture process is the most time-consuming part of the cesarean procedure.

High Risk Pregnancy Factors

1. Mother is over 35 years old
2. Mother is under 16 years old
3. Mother has a previous history of:
4. heart disease
5. high blood pressure
6. diabetes
7. anemia
8. drug or alcohol abuse
9. obesity
10. cesarean section
11. miscarriage
12. spontaneous abortion
13. stillborns
14. premature live birth

Risk factors occurring during pregnancy
15. unusual weight gain
16. viral infection
17. uterine bleeding
18. multiple fetuses
19. abnormal fetal heart rate
20. abnormal position (not head first) of baby in womb
21. abnormally slow fetal growth

DESIGNER:
RICHARD SAUL WURMAN
ART DIRECTOR:
MICHAEL EVERITT
PUBLISHER:
ACCESS PRESS
■ 341–345

88

SLIPPED DISC

EXCISION OF INTERVERTEBRAL DISC

287,000
Frequency in 1982

3-4 hrs
Duration of Operation

recovery room 1-2 hrs   walk 1st postop day

Nature of problem.

An intervertebral disc (the cushion between 2 bones in your spinal column) is built like a sandwich. It has a tough outer covering called the *annulus fibrosis*, and an inner filling called the *nucleus pulposus*. If the outer layer becomes thinned or injured, the nucleus pulposus may slip out of its covering and bulge into the spinal canal. This is known as a slipped or *herniated* disc, and most commonly occurs between 2 of the *lumbar* (lower back) vertebrae. When this occurs, there is pressure on the roots of the sciatic nerve resulting in sciatica, debilitating pain which runs down the backs of the thighs. When the pain cannot be controlled by other means, elective surgery is undertaken to remove some or all of the herniated disc. Surgery is also considered when pressure on the nerve permanently causes inability of muscles to perform their normal function, i.e., foot drop.

Frequency. Sixty-five percent of all patients were men; 64 percent of all patients were between the ages of 15 and 44.

Surgical preparation.

Before deciding to operate, your doctor has probably ordered regular **x-rays**, and perhaps a **CAT scan** of the spine or **Myelography**, a special x-ray study, where contrast material is injected into the spinal canal. Routine studies before surgery usually include: **Complete blood count, SMA 16, Urinalysis, Blood clotting tests, Chest x-ray** and an **EKG**. Blood will be typed and cross matched in case a transfusion is necessary.

Anesthetic. You will receive a general (gas) anesthetic.

Disc injection or chemonucleolysis is a controversial means of treatment for a herniated disc that may eliminate the need for surgery. A solution containing the same enzyme found in meat tenderizer is injected into the soft central portion of a disc. This part of the disc dissolves and by reducing pressure may greatly ease the pain of **sciatica**. *The procedure, which requires only brief hospitalization, is popular in Europe and Canada where it appears to have a 70 percent success rate. The FDA disallowed the procedure in 1975; however, it has since been reapproved with the use of a drug called chymopapain.*

Procedure.

herniation — vertebrae — disc — neural foramen — spinal cord — sciatic nerve

1 With the patient's x-rays on hand, a lengthwise incision is made over the affected vertebrae. After retracting the nerve root at the appropriate level, several of which merge to form the sciatic nerve (the large nerve that transmits information to and from the muscles and skin of the legs), the prolapsed fragment of the disc is removed. Suction is used to remove any additional fragments from inside the disc.

2 When the disc fragments have been removed, the *neural foramen* (bone channel through which the nerves pass) is examined to ensure free passage of the nerve root that connects the sciatic nerve to the spinal cord.

3 The surgical opening is sutured closed in layers.

Stages of recovery.

You will spend from 1 to 3 hours in the recovery room. You will be encouraged to begin walking on the first postoperative day.

Limitations. Strenuous exercise, lifting and running will be forbidden for the first several weeks. Since driving usually increases any lower back pain, you may be unable to drive during this period. After a couple of weeks, your doctor may instruct you to begin a series of rehabilitation exercises to strengthen your abdominal and back muscles.

Drugs. You will receive medication for pain, which may be severe.

Complications. Urinary retention is a possible complication which would be treated by catheter insertion until normal urinary function returns. Any **infection** is treated with antibiotics.

Scar. You will have a back scar where your surgical incision was made.

89

HIP FRACTURE

OPEN REDUCTION OF FRACTURE OF THE HIP

75,000
Frequency in 1982

3-4 hrs
Duration of Operation

recovery room 1-2 hrs   range of motion exercises after a few days   walk with walker after several days   physical therapy continues

Nature of problem.

When a fracture of the hip occurs in a person who is mobile (not bedridden or wheelchair bound), the broken bone is usually reinforced with a nail and metal plate. This procedure ensures that the break heals with enough sturdiness to permit the individual to resume walking. If the bones have moved out of their proper alignment in the fracture, the break will first be *reduced*. This means that the bones are manipulated until they are brought back into proper position.

Hip reduction is elective only in that the procedure may be postponed for a day or so after the break. However, it is an urgent condition that demands treatment. Because most hip breaks are the result of a sudden fall or traumatic accident, patients are usually admitted to the hospital on an emergency basis.

Frequency. Two-thirds of all patients were women. More than 80 percent of all patients were over 65.

Surgical preparation.

If you are admitted to the hospital as an emergency patient, the preoperative workup, including **Complete blood count, Urinalysis,**

Chest x-ray, EKG, Blood clotting tests and **Blood type** and **Cross match**, in case a transfusion is needed, is carried out either in the emergency room or after your admission to a room. In addition to the usual tests, your pelvis and legs will also be x-rayed to verify the position of your hip. On the day of your surgery, you will receive a sedative and dress in a surgical cap and gown. An IV will be started in the back of your hand or your forearm.

Anesthetic. General (gas) anesthesia is most commonly used. However, sometimes spinal anesthesia is administered as an alternative.

There are 2 different kinds of hip fractures, requiring different procedures. If necessary, the broken hip is realigned or *reduced* before the fracture is repaired. For realignment, the surgeon flexes the injured hip 90 degrees, then pulls up on the femur while rotating the thigh inward. X-rays are taken to verify the position of the hip before proceeding. Then an incision (4 to 6 inches long) is made in the thigh and the underlying muscle is spread apart.

Procedure.

1 The neck, or top segment, of the *femur* (thigh bone) may be broken just below the rounded, ball-like top of the femur that fits into a socket to create the hip joint. In this operation a nail and a screw are placed through the top of the femur, pinning the neck firmly to the rounded top portion of the bone.

neck of femur — nail and screw — femur

2 In the other case, the break is across the *trochanter*, the uppermost segment of the femur that unites the shaft of the bone with the neck. This kind of fracture is repaired by driving a nail through a supporting plate, and the trochanter into the neck of the femur. The plate extends along the shaft of the femur and is held in place with screws.

neck of femur — nail — screw — shaft of the bone — plate

Stages of recovery.

You will spend 1 or 2 hours in the recovery room before returning to your own room. Convalescence is slow and gradual; you will be confined to bed for several days after your surgery. When you are permitted to get out of bed, you will use a walker but will be instructed not to put any weight on the injured leg.

Limitations. Your physician will order a detailed physical therapy plan for you. However, your mobility will be limited for several weeks after surgery.

Drugs. Pain during recovery is considerable. Many patients experience gnawing pain, especially at night. You may be given injections for the first couple of days and then oral medication such as codeine, Demerol or Percodan for several weeks thereafter.

Complications. Possible complications are **infection** and **pulmonary embolism** (blood clot in lungs) which is possible after any long operation followed by enforced bedrest.

Scar. You will have a long scar on your thigh.

■ 341-345 Double spreads from *Medical Access,* one of the tall pocketbook *Access* series. It is a comprehensive layman's guide to diagnostic tests and surgical procedures, and includes information on patient's rights, insurance, choosing a doctor and hospital, emergencies, and many other medical matters. The graphics are basic and clear, and the information is easily understandable. (USA)

■ 341-345 Aus dem Buch *Medical Access,* das allgemeinverständliche Informationen über diagnostische Tests und chirurgische Verfahren vermitteln will. Ausserdem setzt es sich mit Fragen der Arzt- und Spitalwahl, Notfällen, Versicherungen, den Rechten des Patienten usw. auseinander. Zugunsten der Klarheit und leichten Verständlichkeit beschränken sich alle Graphiken auf das Wesentliche. (USA)

■ 341-345 Doubles pages de *Medical Access,* un ouvrage d'information et de vulgarisation sur les tests diagnostiques et les techniques chirurgicales usuels. Sont aussi traités le libre choix du médecin et de l'hôpital, les urgences, les assurances, les droits des malades, etc. Pour augmenter la clarté et la compréhension de l'exposé, tous les graphiques se bornent à représenter des données essentielles. (USA)

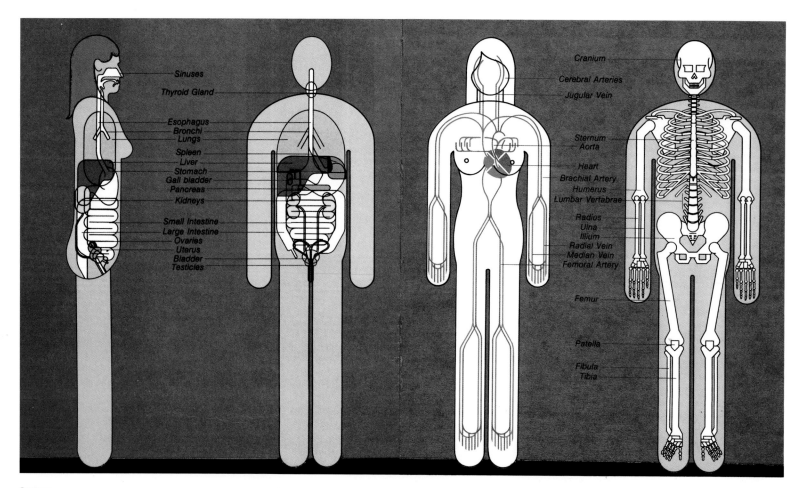

Sinuses
Thyroid Gland
Esophagus
Bronchi
Lungs
Spleen
Liver
Stomach
Gall bladder
Pancreas
Kidneys
Small Intestine
Large Intestine
Ovaries
Uterus
Bladder
Testicles

Cranium
Cerebral Arteries
Jugular Vein
Sternum
Aorta
Heart
Brachial Artery
Humerus
Lumbar Vertabrae
Radius
Ulna
Illium
Radial Vein
Median Vein
Femoral Artery
Femur
Patella
Fibula
Tibia

DESIGNER:
RICHARD SAUL WURMAN
ART DIRECTOR:
MICHAEL EVERITT
PUBLISHER:
ACCESS PRESS
■ 346–348

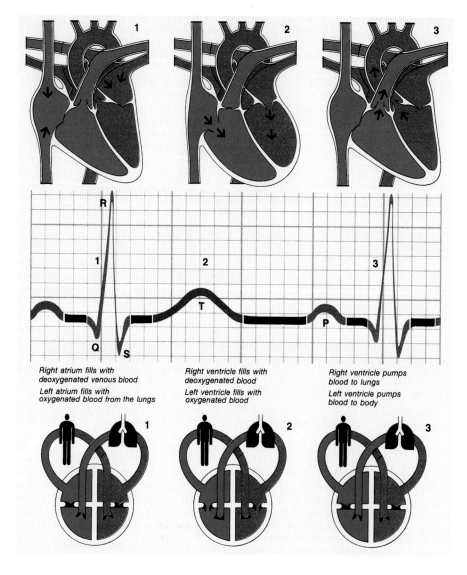

Right atrium fills with deoxygenated venous blood
Left atrium fills with oxygenated blood from the lungs

Right ventricle fills with deoxygenated blood
Left ventricle fills with oxygenated blood

Right ventricle pumps blood to lungs
Left ventricle pumps blood to body

■ 346-348 From the book *Medical Access,* intended for the general public, with clearly presented graphics to explain the field of medicine and hospital care (see also *341-345*). *346:* inner organs of man and woman, blood vessels and skeletal structure, illustration of the introductory double spread. *347:* explanation of an electrocardiogram, the heart beat and the heart function. *348:* diagrams showing the various equipment and function of an intensive care unit. (USA)

■ 346-348 Für den allgemeinen Gebrauch bestimmte, leichtverständliche Darstellungen aus dem Bereich der Medizin und Spitalpflege, aus dem Buch *Medical Access* (s. auch *341-345*). *346:* Innere Organe bei Mann und Frau, Blutgefässe und Knochenbau, Darstellung der einleitenden Doppelseite. *347:* Erläuterung eines EKG bzw. des Herzrhythmus und der Herzfunktion. *348:* Einrichtung und Funktion einer Intensivstation. (USA)

■ 346-348 Représentations simplifiées pour le grand public de données médicales et hospitalières, tirées de l'ouvrage *Medical Access* (cf. *341-345*). *346:* organes internes de l'homme et de la femme, circulation et squelette; ces représentations figurent sur la double page initiale. *347:* explication d'un électrocardiogramme respectivement du rythme et de la fonction cardiaques. *348:* équipement et fonctionnement d'une station de soins intensifs. (USA)

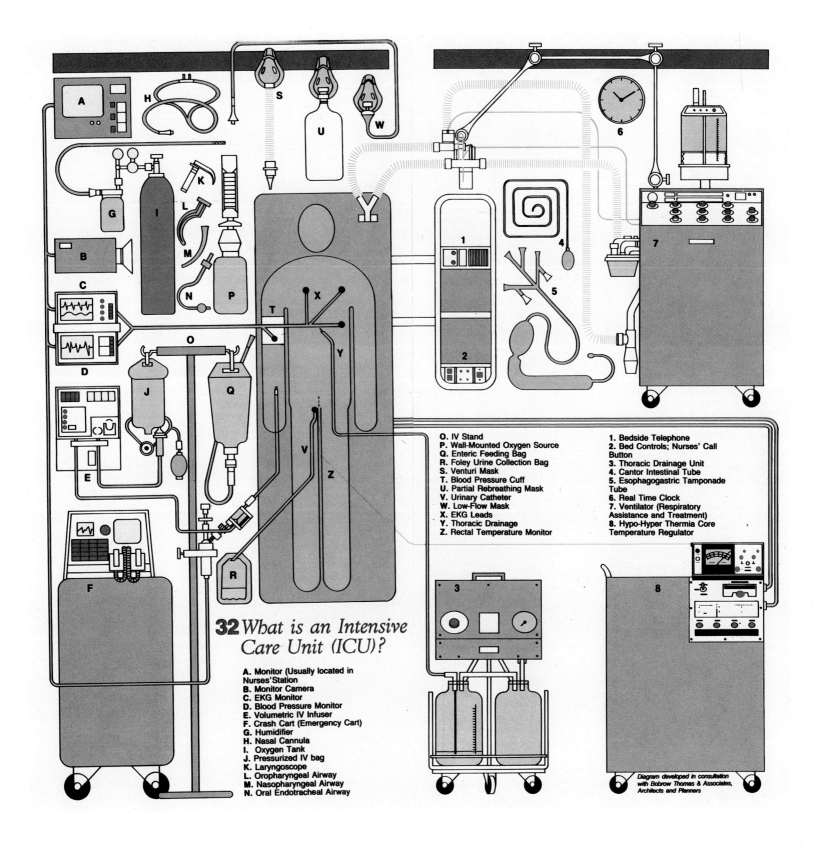

32 *What is an Intensive Care Unit (ICU)?*

A. Monitor (Usually located in Nurses'Station
B. Monitor Camera
C. EKG Monitor
D. Blood Pressure Monitor
E. Volumetric IV Infuser
F. Crash Cart (Emergency Cart)
G. Humidifier
H. Nasal Cannula
I. Oxygen Tank
J. Pressurized IV bag
K. Laryngoscope
L. Oropharyngeal Airway
M. Nasopharyngeal Airway
N. Oral Endotracheal Airway

O. IV Stand
P. Wall-Mounted Oxygen Source
Q. Enteric Feeding Bag
R. Foley Urine Collection Bag
S. Venturi Mask
T. Blood Pressure Cuff
U. Partial Rebreathing Mask
V. Urinary Catheter
W. Low-Flow Mask
X. EKG Leads
Y. Thoracic Drainage
Z. Rectal Temperature Monitor

1. Bedside Telephone
2. Bed Controls; Nurses' Call Button
3. Thoracic Drainage Unit
4. Cantor Intestinal Tube
5. Esophagogastric Tamponade Tube
6. Real Time Clock
7. Ventilator (Respiratory Assistance and Treatment)
8. Hypo-Hyper Thermia Core Temperature Regulator

Diagram developed in consultation with Bobrow Thomas & Associates, Architects and Planners

ARTIST:
PETER ROTH
ART DIRECTOR:
M. G. YASARGIL
AGENCY:
NEUROSURGICAL DEPARTMENT
UNIVERSITY HOSPITAL ZURICH
PUBLISHER:
GEORG THIEME VERLAG
■ 350–352

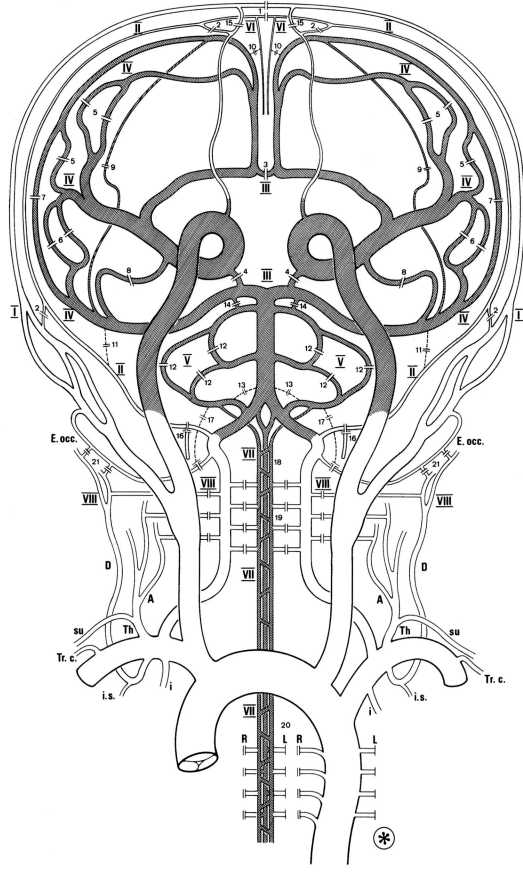

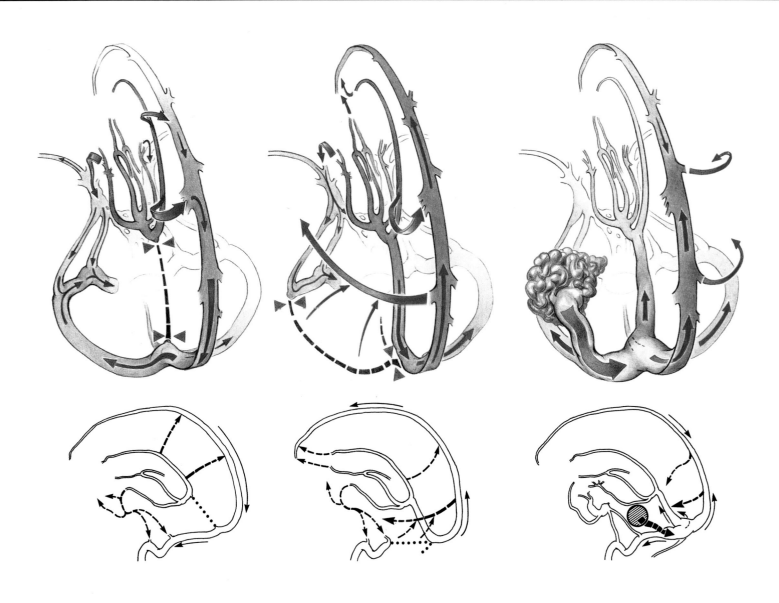

■ 353-357 Medical illustrations from the book *Gesundheit durch Aufklärung* (Health through Knowledge). The subject of these illustrations is the five senses and the corresponding organs: skin, eye, ear, nose, and tongue. (GER)

■ 353-357 Blockdiagramme aus der Partwork-Serie *Gesundheit durch Aufklärung* (Verlag Wort & Bild Rolf Becker). Das Thema sind die fünf Sinne und die entsprechenden Organe: Haut, Auge, Ohr, Nase und Zunge. (GER)

■ 353-357 Illustrations médicales de l'ouvrage *Gesundheit durch Aufklärung* (La Santé par l'information). Les sujets sont les cinq sens et les organes qui leur correspondent: la peau, l'œil, l'oreille, le nez et la langue. (GER)

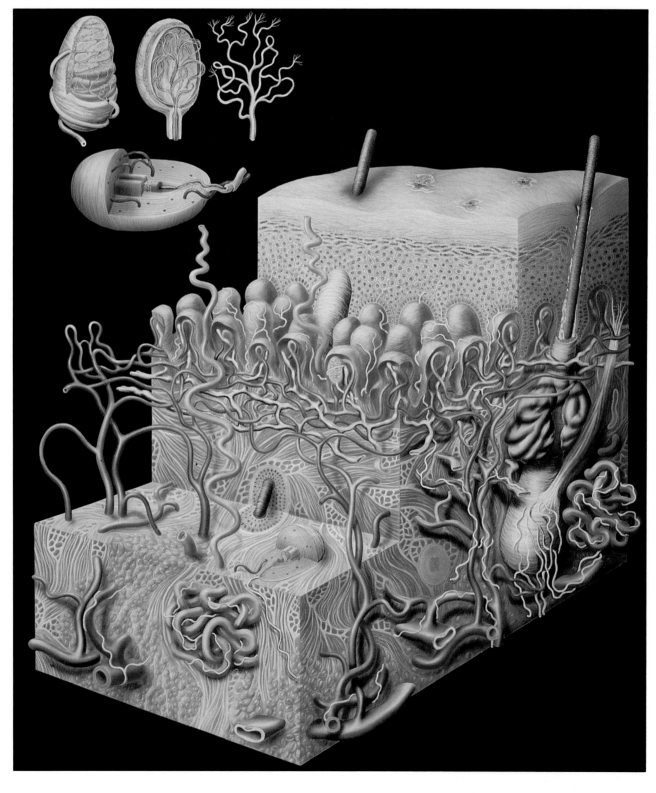

DESIGNER:
VERLAG WORT & BILD ROLF BECKER/ MEDICAL SERVICE MÜNCHEN
ARTIST:
DR. HANS BRÄUER
ART DIRECTOR:
VERLAG WORT & BILD ROLF BECKER
AGENCY:
ATELIER FÜR PLASTISCHE HISTOLOGIE MSM
PUBLISHER:
VERLAG WORT & BILD ROLF BECKER

■ 353-357

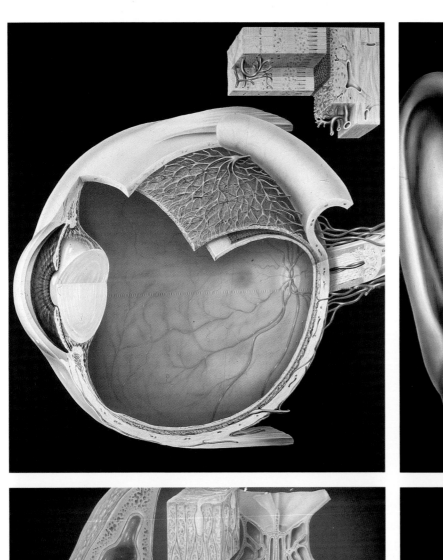

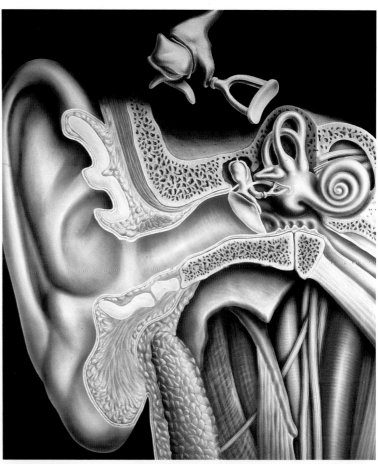

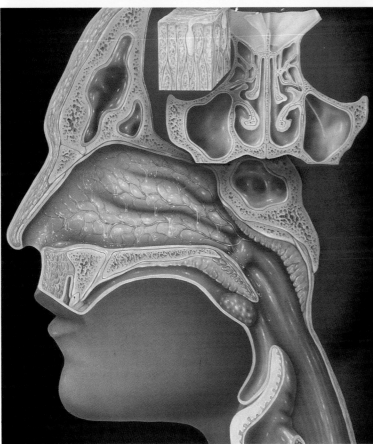

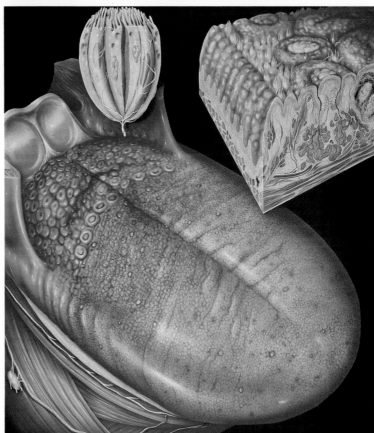

■ 358–364 Medical diagrams from the book intended for the layman *Gesundheit durch Aufklärung. 358* shows skin and hair; *359* the tibia with well developed veins (left) and more strongly developed varicose veins (right); *360* the heart and stimulation and conduction system; *361* tendon and ligament system and the arch construction of the foot; *362* cut-away drawing of a blood vessel; *363* the pericardium and the removal of a coronary construction; *364* blood and lymphatic vessels. (GER)

■ 358–364 Medizinische Diagramme aus der für Laien bestimmten Partwork-Serie *Gesundheit durch Aufklärung* (Verlag Wort & Bild Rolf Becker). *358* zeigt Haut und Haar; *359* Unterschenkel normal (links) und mit starker Ausbildung von Krampfadern (rechts); *360* das Herz und das Erregungs- und Reizleitungssystem. *361* Band- und Sehnensystem und Brückenkonstruktion des Fusses; *362* Aufschnitt eines Blutgefässes; *363* Herzbeutel und Beseitigung einer Koronarverengung; *364* Blut- und Lymphgefässe. (GER)

■ 358–364 Diagrammes médicaux illustrant l'ouvrage de vulgarisation *Gesundheit durch Aufklärung. 358* représente la peau et les cheveux; *359* la jambe avec le réseau veineux bien visible à g., devenu variqueux à dr.; *360* le cœur avec son système de production et de conduction de l'excitation cardiaque; *361* le système de ligaments et d'articulations et la structure en voûte du pied; *362* l'éclaté d'une artère; *363* le péricarde et l'élargissement d'une artère coronaire; *364* le sang et les vaisseaux lymphatiques. (GER)

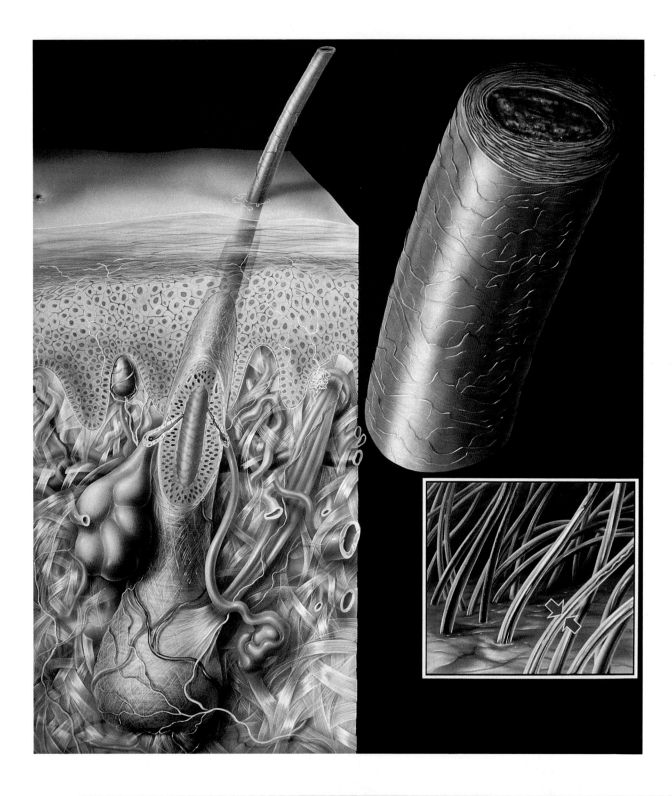

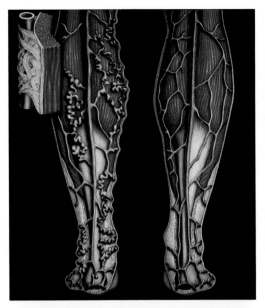
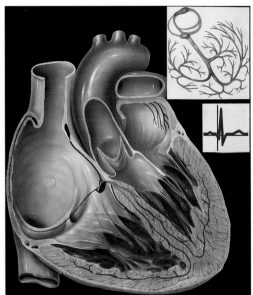
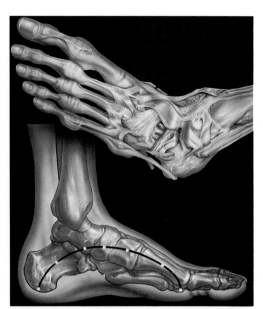
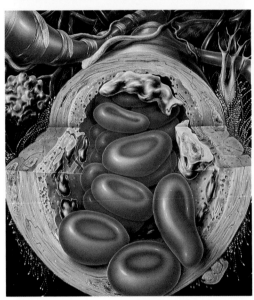
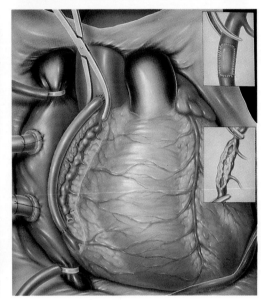
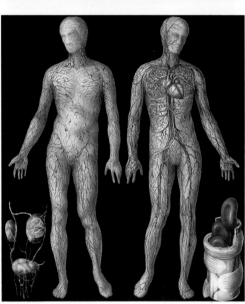

DESIGNER:
Verlag Wort & Bild
Rolf Becker/
Medical Service München

ARTIST:
Dr. Hans Bräuer

ART DIRECTOR:
Verlag Wort & Bild
Rolf Becker

AGENCY:
Atelier für plastische
Histologie MSM

PUBLISHER:
Verlag Wort & Bild
Rolf Becker

■ 358–364

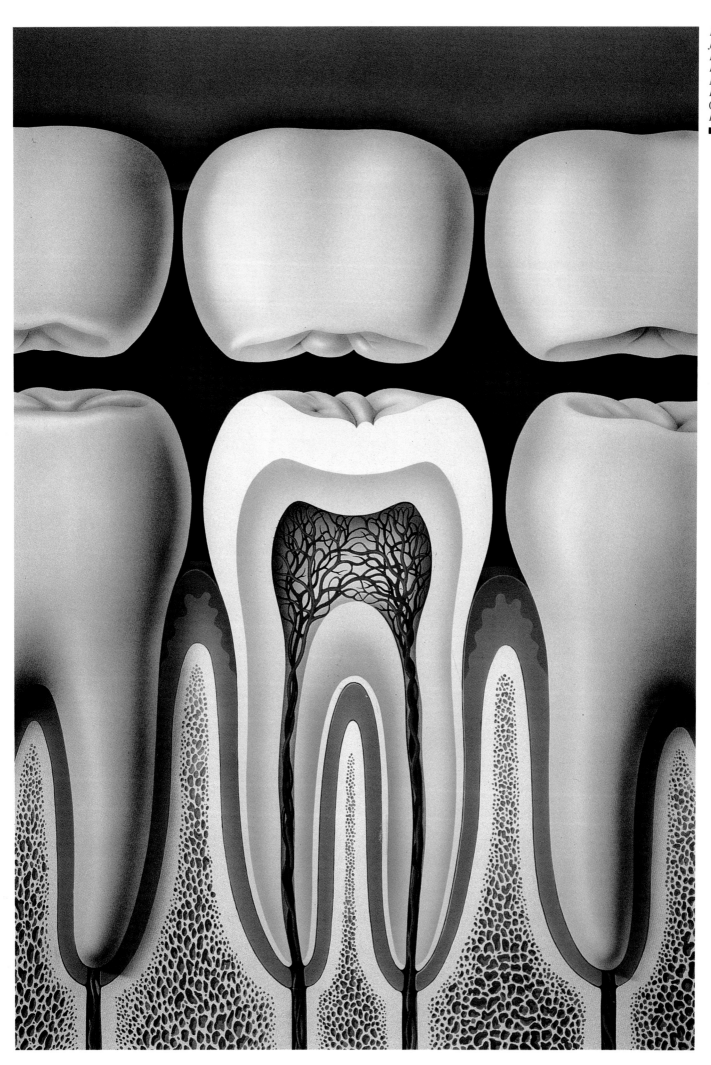

ARTIST:
JOACHIM WIDMANN
ART DIRECTOR:
DIETMAR MEYER
AGENCY:
DIETMAR MEYER
CLIENT:
HENKEL AG
■ 365

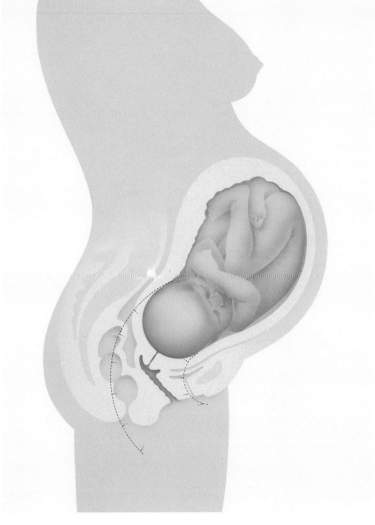

Designer:
*Osterwalder/Widmann
(Graphico)*
Artist:
*Osterwalder/Widmann
(Graphico)*
Art Director:
Dieter Munz
Agency:
Imparc Werbeagentur
Client:
Optiker Verband
■ 366

Artist:
Joachim Widmann
Art Director:
Barbara Saniter
Client:
*Red. Mutter & Kind,
Jahreszeiten Verlag*
■ 367

■ 365 Diagram showing tooth structure, from a brochure issued by Henkel AG. (GER)

■ 366 Illustration of the eyeball from a publication issued by the German Opticians Organization. (GER)

■ 367 Illustration of a fetus in the uterus, from the magazine *Mutter und Kind* (Mother and Child). (GER)

■ 365 Diagramm zur Erläuterung des Zahnaufbaus, aus einer Broschüre der Henkel AG. (GER)

■ 366 Darstellung des Augapfels für eine Publikation des deutschen Optikerverbandes. (GER)

■ 367 In der Zeitschrift *Mutter und Kind* erschienene Darstellung eines Fötus im Mutterleib. (GER)

■ 365 Diagramme explicitant la structure d'une dent. Brochure de Henkel AG. (GER)

■ 366 Représentation du globe oculaire pour une publication de l'Association allemande des opticiens. (GER)

■ 367 Représentation d'un fœtus dans le ventre de sa mère, parue dans le magazine *Mutter und Kind*. (GER)

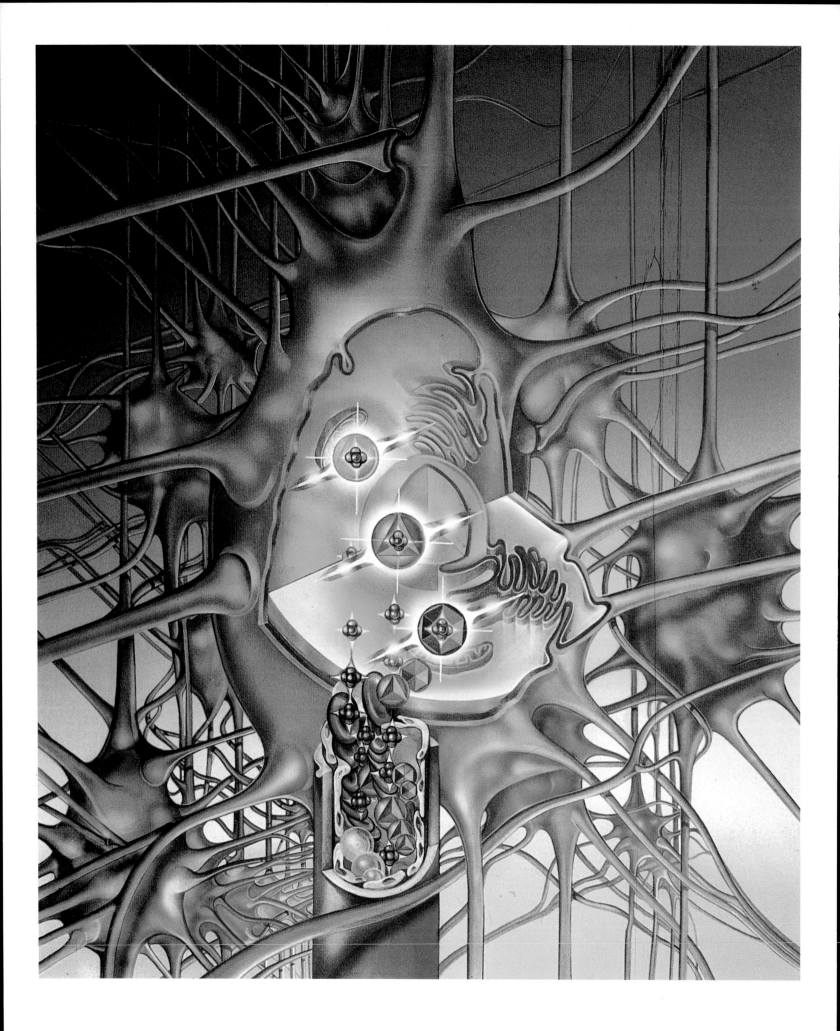

ARTIST:
H. U. OSTERWALDER
ART DIRECTOR:
H. U. OSTERWALDER
AGENCY:
LÜRZER & KONRAD
◄■ 369

ARTIST:
*ROLF CIGLER, SCHULE FÜR
GESTALTUNG ZÜRICH, KLASSE FÜR
WISSENSCHAFTLICHES ZEICHNEN*
ART DIRECTOR:
CHRISTOPH GÖLDLIN
■ 370

■ 369 Diagram of the supply of oxygenated blood to the brain cells. (GER)

■ 370 Reflector elements in the skin of the *Octopus vulgaris*. (SWI)

■ 369 Diagramm der Blut- bzw. der Sauerstoffversorgung der Gehirnzellen. (GER)

■ 370 Spiegelelemente in der Haut der Krake *Octopus vulgaris*. (SWI)

■ 369 Diagramme de la circulation de sang (l'oxygène) dans les cellules du cerveau. (GER)

■ 370 Eléments miroitants insérés dans la peau de l'octopode *Octopus vulgaris*. (SWI)

ARTIST:
JOACHIM WIDMANN
ART DIRECTOR:
WOLFGANG BEHNKEN
CLIENT:
GRUNER + JAHR, STERN
■ 371, 372

■ 371 Diagram of a human cell, to accompany an article in the magazine *Stern*. (GER)

■ 372 Diagram to illustrate a cardiac infarction. It is clearly shown how cholesterol deposits build up in the blood vessels. Even in a baby future danger can be seen through an analysis of the cells. From an article in *Stern*. (GER)

■ 373 Diagram of the AIDS virus according to present scientific knowledge. (Scientific consultant Dr. Michael Koch, Sweden.) (GER)

■ 371 Darstellung einer menschlichen Zelle, verwendet für einen Artikel im Magazin *Stern*. (GER)

■ 372 Diagramm zum Thema Herzinfarkt. Es wird deutlich gemacht, wie es zur Cholesterinablagerung in den Blutgefässen kommt. Schon beim Baby ist durch Zellanalysen eine spätere Gefährdung erkennbar. Aus dem *Stern*. (GER)

■ 373 Darstellung des AIDS-Virus nach dem gegenwärtigen Stand der Wissenschaft. (Wissenschaftliche Beratung Dr. Michael Koch, Schweden.) (GER)

■ 371 Représentation d'une cellule humaine, utilisée dans un article du magazine *Stern*. (GER)

■ 372 Diagramme explicitant l'infarctus du myocarde. On voit le dépôt de cholestérol dans les artères. Les analyses précoces permettent de révéler ce risque chez le nourisson. Article du magazine *Stern*. (GER)

■ 373 Représentation du virus du sida d'après les dernières données de la science. (Conseiller scientifique: le Dr Michael Koch, Suède.) (GER)

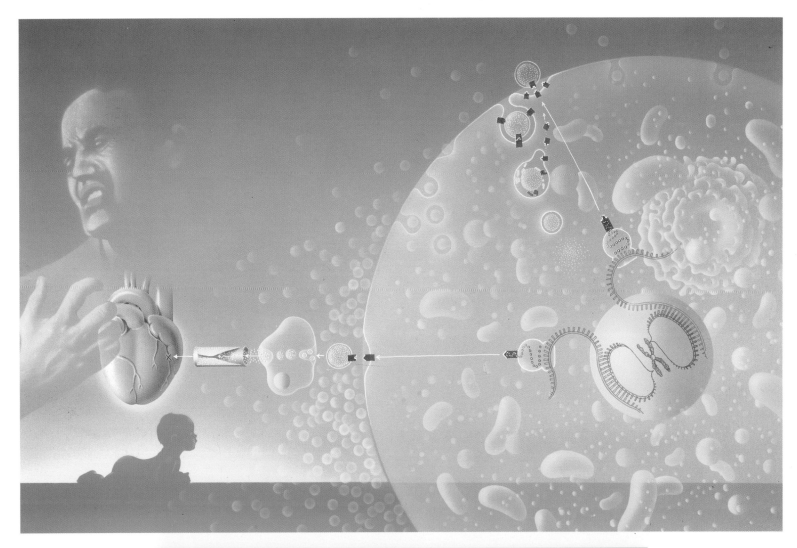

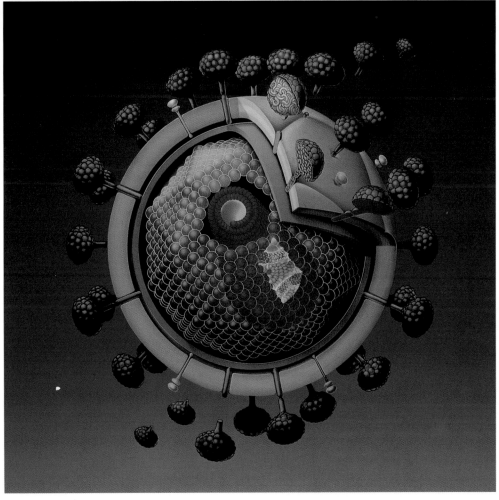

ARTIST:
H. U. Osterwalder

ART DIRECTOR:
H. U. Osterwalder

CLIENT:
Dr. Michael Koch

■ 373

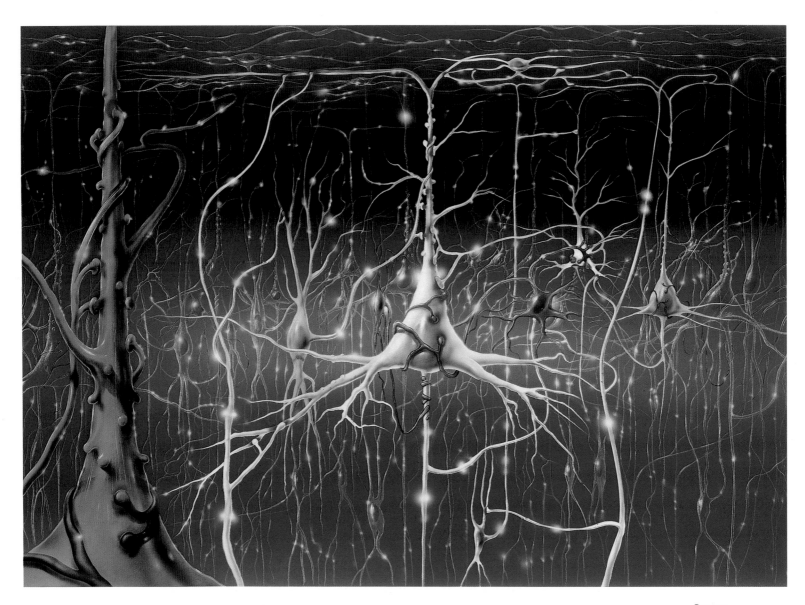

DESIGNER:
CARL-W. RÖHRIG
ARTIST:
CARL-W. RÖHRIG
ART DIRECTOR:
CARL-W. RÖHRIG
AGENCY:
ATELIER CARL-W. RÖHRIG
PUBLISHER:
NATIONAL GEOGRAPHIC
■ 374-375a

■ 374 Diagram of peripheral nerves. From *The Incredible Machine,* published by National Geographic. (USA)

■ 375 Illustration of the defense system of the body, here within a lymph node. Left in the illustration, bacteria and viruses are flowing in and are immediately attacked by the defense cells of the body and rendered harmless. *National Geographic.* (USA)

■ 375a A splinter piercing the skin and the defense reaction of the body is the subject of this illustration. *National Geographic.* (USA)

■ 374 Künstlerische Darstellung des Nervensystems, aus *The Incredible Machine* (National Geographic). (USA)

■ 375 Darstellung des Abwehrsystems des Körpers, hier innerhalb des Lymphknotens. Links im Bild strömen Bakterien und Viren ein, die sofort von den Abwehrzellen des Körpers angegriffen und unschädlich gemacht werden. *National Geographic.* (USA)

■ 375a Darstellung eines in die Haut eingedrungenen Holzsplitters und die Abwehrreaktion des Körpers. Aus *National Geographic.* (USA)

■ 374 Représentation artistique du système nerveux, du livre *The Incredible Machine,* Ed. National Geographic. (USA)

■ 375 Le système immonulogique de l'organisme, ici à l'intérieur d'un ganglion lymphatique. Venant de la gauce, des virus et bactéries pénétrant dans le corps sont attaqués, puis détruits par les cellules immunologiques. *National Geographic.* (USA)

■ 375a La réaction de défense de l'organisme contre une écharde entrée sous la peau. Tiré du magazine *National Geographic.* (USA)

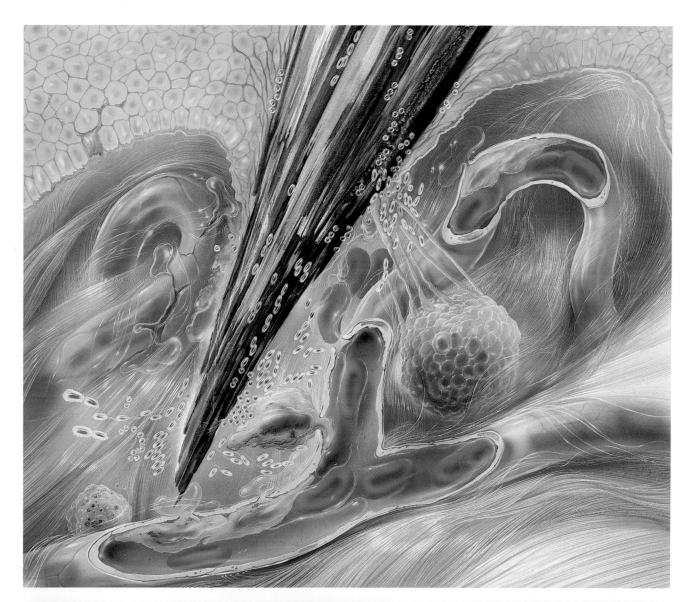

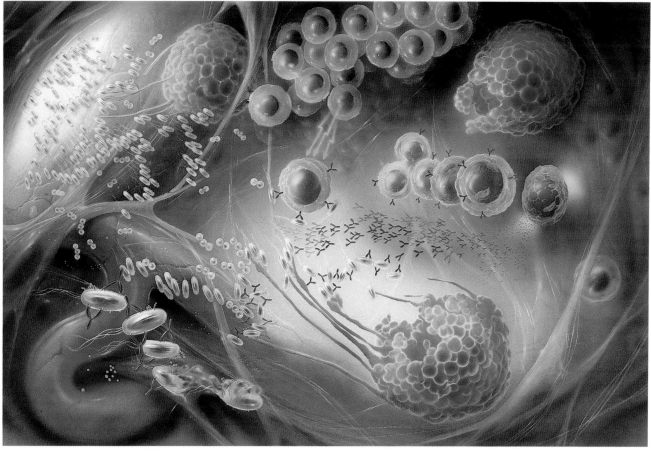

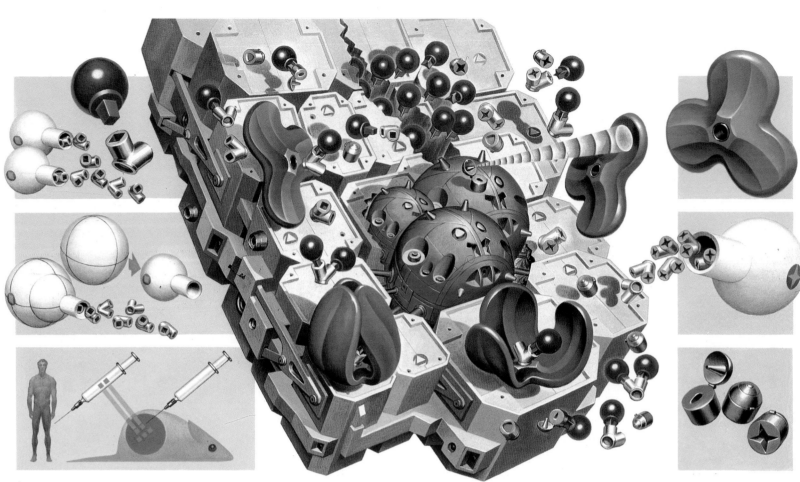

ARTIST:
DAVID MELTZER
ART DIRECTOR:
JAN ADKINS
PUBLISHER:
NATIONAL GEOGRAPHIC
■ 376

■ 376 The "battlefield" shows the daily fight between attackers and the human body's defense system. From the *National Geographic* magazine. (USA)

■ 377, 378 Diagrams from the fields of bacterial genetics, molecular biology and dairy cultures. *377:* conjugation, *378:* specialized transduction. *Nestlé Research News.* (SWI)

■ 376 Dieses «Schlachtfeld» verdeutlicht den täglichen Kampf zwischen Angreifern und Abwehrsystemen im menschlichen Körper. Aus *National Geographic.* (USA)

■ 377, 378 Diagramme aus dem Bereich der bakteriellen Genetik, Molekularbiologie und Milchkulturen aus einem Beitrag in *Nestlé Research News.* (SWI)

■ 376 Ce «champ de bataille» fait saisir l'enjeu de la lutte des systèmes de défense immunitaire de l'organisme contre les agents pathogènes. *National Geographic.* (USA)

■ 377, 378 Diagrammes des *Nestlé Research News* relatifs aux domaines de recherche suivants: génétique bactérienne, biologie moléculaire, cultures laitières. (SWI)

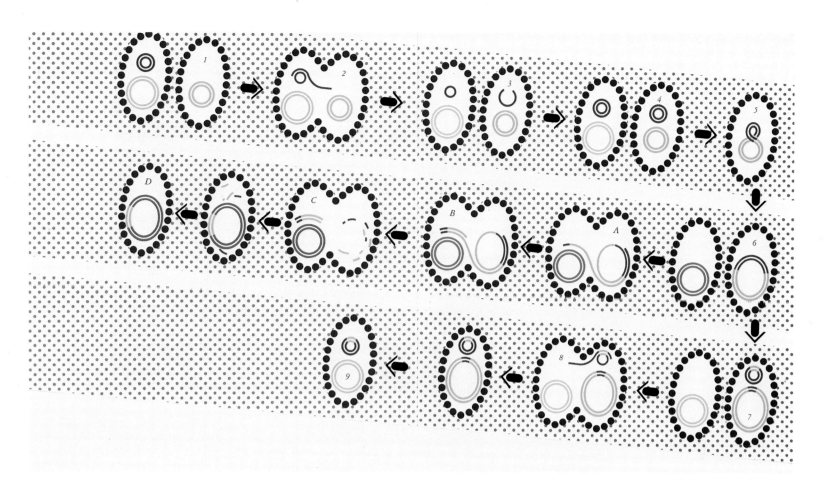

DESIGNER:
YVES RACHETER
ARTIST:
YVES RACHETER
ART DIRECTOR:
AGENCY:
*NESTEC, ETUDES ET
RÉALISATIONS GRAPHIQUES*
CLIENT:
NESTEC
■ 377–378

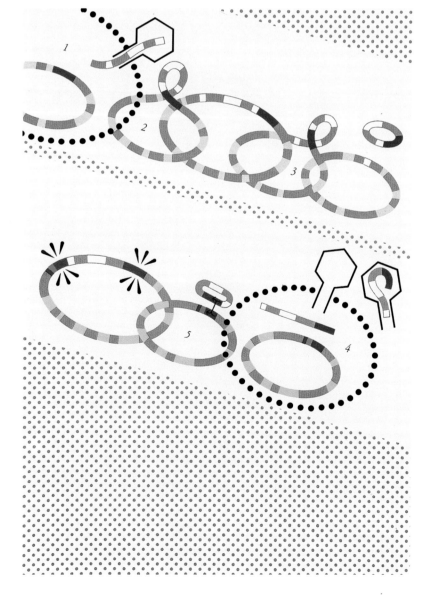

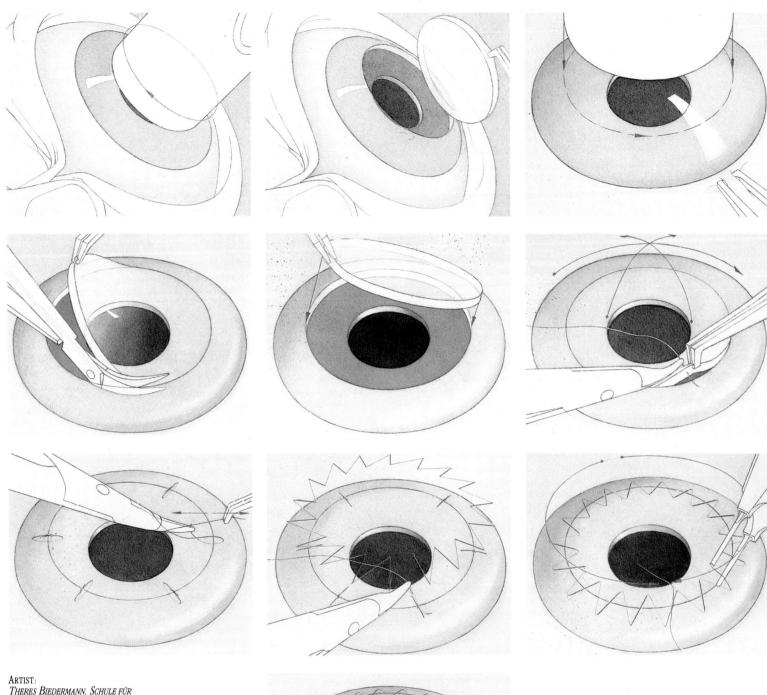

ARTIST:
THERES BIEDERMANN, SCHULE FÜR
GESTALTUNG ZÜRICH, KLASSE FÜR
WISSENSCHAFTLICHES ZEICHNEN
ART DIRECTOR:
CHRISTOPH GÖLDLIN
■ 379-388

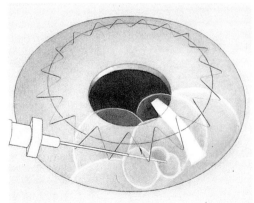

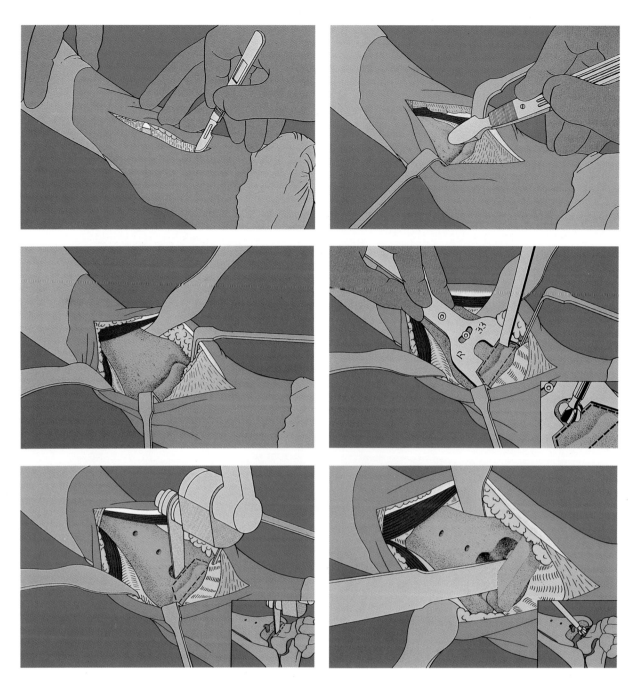

ARTIST:
CAROL DE SIMIO-HILTON,
SCHULE FÜR GESTALTUNG
ZÜRICH, KLASSE FÜR
WISSENSCHAFTLICHES ZEICHNEN
ART DIRECTOR:
CHRISTOPH GÖLDLIN
■ 389-394

■ 379-388 Sequences (watercolor) during a cornea transplant in the eye. The donor eye is shown in green, the recipient eye is shown in blue. (SWI)

■ 389-394 Sequence diagram for an ankle joint operation. The choice of colors contributes not only to the elucidation of the procedures but also to the aesthetics. (SWI)

■ 379-388 Ablauf (Aquarell) einer Hornhaut-(Cornea-) Transplantation am Auge. Das Spenderauge ist grün, das Empfängerauge blau dargestellt. (SWI)

■ 389-394 Ablaufdiagramm für eine Sprunggelenk-Operation. Die Farben tragen nicht nur zur Veranschaulichung des Prozesses, sondern auch zur Ästhetik bei. (SWI)

■ 379-388 Représentation séquentielle (aquarelle) d'une transplantation de cornée. L'œil du donneur est figuré en vert, celui du receveur en bleu. (SWI)

■ 389-394 Diagramme séquentiel d'une intervention sur l'articulation tibio-péronière avec l'astragale. Les couleurs contribuent à la compréhension et à l'esthétique. (SWI)

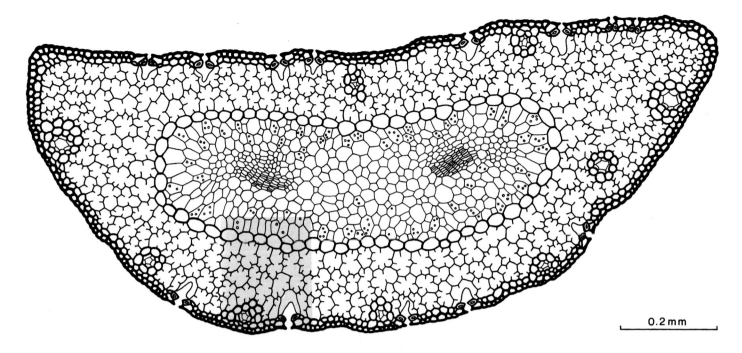

0.2 mm

ARTIST:
GUSTAVE A. FORSTER, SCHULE
FÜR GESTALTUNG ZÜRICH, KLASSE
FÜR WISSENSCHAFTLICHES
ZEICHNEN
ART DIRECTOR:
CHRISTOPH GÖLDLIN
■ 395

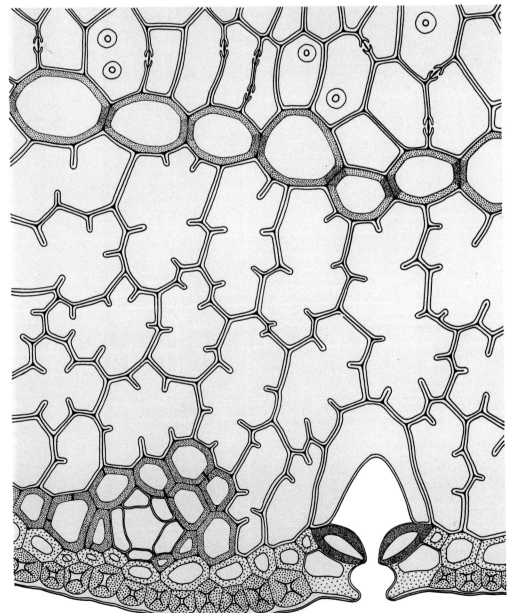

0.1 mm

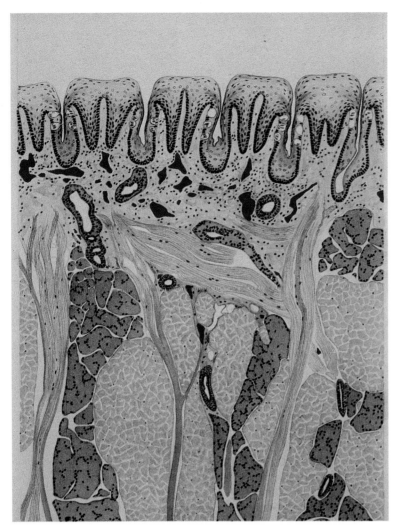

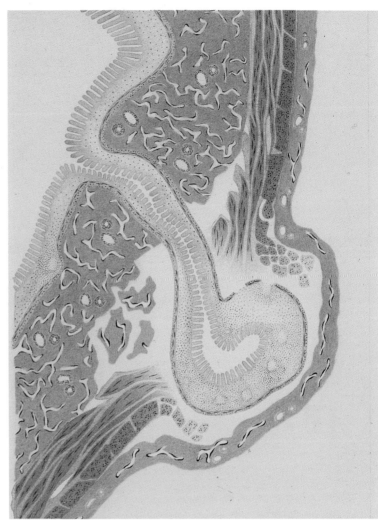

ARTIST:
CHRISTINE PETERHANS-REITER,
SCHULE FÜR GESTALTUNG
ZÜRICH, KLASSE FÜR WISSEN-
SCHAFTLICHES ZEICHNEN
ART DIRECTOR:
CHRISTOPH GÖLDLIN
■ 396

ARTIST:
ROLF CIGLER, SCHULE FÜR
GESTALTUNG ZÜRICH, KLASSE
FÜR WISSENSCHAFTLICHES
ZEICHNEN
ART DIRECTOR:
CHRISTOPH GÖLDLIN
■ 397

■ 395 Cross-section of a needle and enlargement of a section of this diagram. (SWI)

■ 396 Diagram (colored ink, pen and wash) of the surface of the tongue showing the tastebuds. (SWI)

■ 397 Cross-section through the wall of the colon. In this diagram the choice of colors enhances the overall aesthetic impression. (SWI)

■ 395 Nadelquerschnitt und Vergrösserung eines Teils dieser Darstellung. (SWI)

■ 396 Darstellung (farbige Tusche laviert, Feder) der Zungenoberfläche mit Geschmacksknospen. (SWI)

■ 397 Querschnitt durch die Dickdarmhaut. Durch die Wahl der Farben wird auch bei diesem Thema ein ästhetischer Gesamteindruck erreicht. (SWI)

■ 395 Coupe transversale d'une aiguille et agrandissement d'une partie de cette figure. (SWI)

■ 396 Représentation (lavis d'encre de couleur, plume) de la surface de la langue avec les bourgeons gustatifs. (SWI)

■ 397 Partie malade de la paroi de l'intestin. Le choix des couleurs vise à un effet esthétique tout en augmentant la lisibilité du dessin. (Lavis d'encre de couleur.) (SWI)

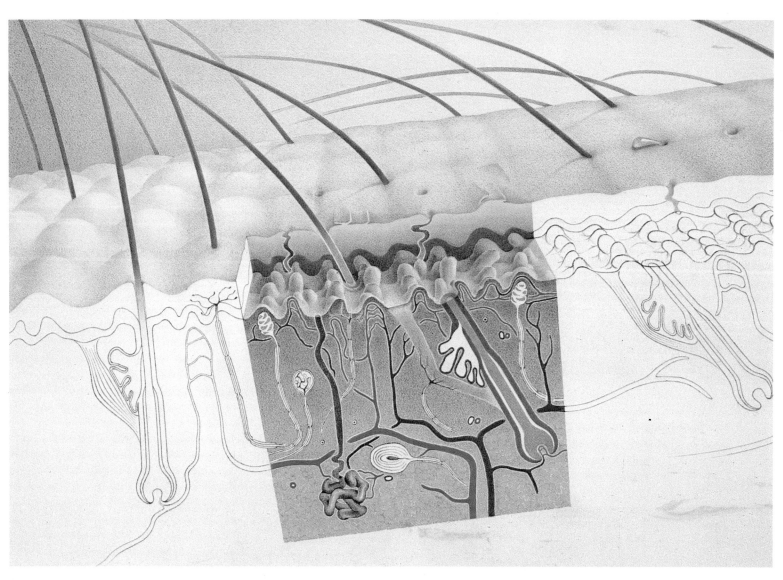

ARTIST:
*PETER ROTH, SCHULE FÜR
GESTALTUNG ZÜRICH, KLASSE
FÜR WISSENSCHAFTLICHES
ZEICHNEN*
ART DIRECTOR:
CHRISTOPH GÖLDLIN
■ 398

■ 398 Diagram (color pencil) on the structure of the human skin. From *Bau und Funktionen unseres Körpers,* Lehrmittelverlag, Zürich. (SWI)

■ 399, 400 *Volvox aureus,* diagram and section (ink drawing) of a green alga with subsidiary colonies. (SWI)

■ 401 Cross-section through the tail of a salamander. Colored ink, pen and wash. (SWI)

■ 398 Blockdiagramm (Farbstift), das über den Aufbau der menschlichen Haut Aufschluss gibt. Aus *Bau und Funktionen unseres Körpers,* Lehrmittelverlag, Zürich. (SWI)

■ 399, 400 *Volvox aureus,* Darstellung und Schnitt (Federzeichnung) einer Grünalge mit Tochterkolonien. (SWI)

■ 401 Querschnitt durch den Schwanz eines Salamanders. Farbige Tusche, laviert, Feder. (SWI)

■ 398 Représentation tridimensionnelle montrant la structure de la peau humaine. Crayon couleur. Tiré de *Bau und Funktionen unseres Körpers,* Lehrmittelverlag Zurich. (SWI)

■ 399, 400 *Volvox aureus:* vue et coupe de cette algue verte d'eau douce et de ses colonies. Dessin à la plume. (SWI)

■ 401 Coupe transversale de la queue d'une salamandre. Encre de Chine de couleur, lavis, plume. (SWI)

ARTIST:
RICCARDO BELLETTATI, SCHULE
FÜR GESTALTUNG ZÜRICH,
KLASSE FÜR WISSEN-
SCHAFTLICHES ZEICHNEN
ART DIRECTOR:
CHRISTOPH GÖLDLIN
■ 399–400

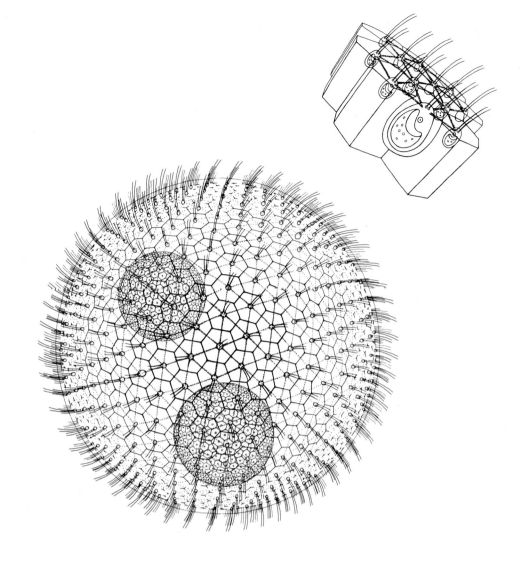

ARTIST:
RUTH BAUR, SCHULE FÜR
GESTALTUNG ZÜRICH, KLASSE
FÜR WISSENSCHAFTLICHES
ZEICHNEN
ART DIRECTOR:
CHRISTOPH GÖLDLIN
■ 401

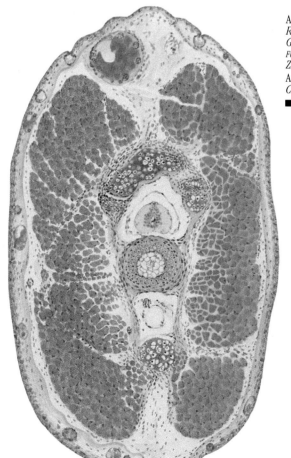

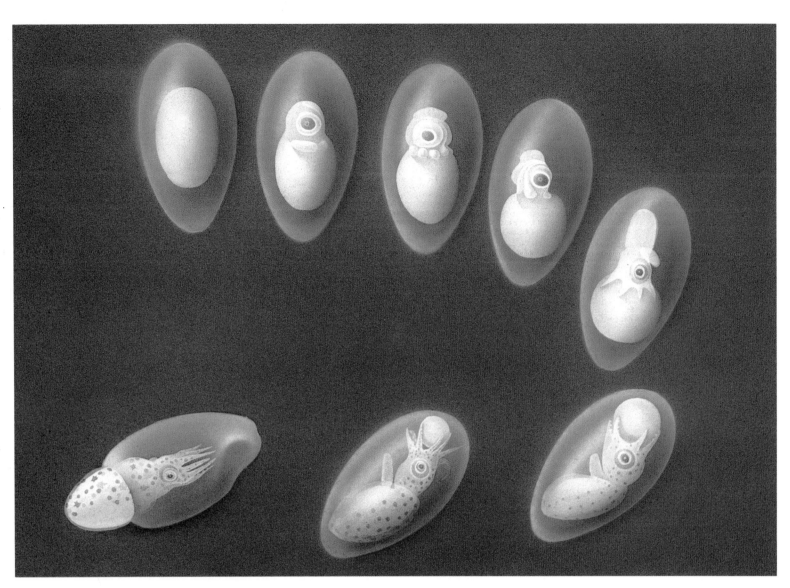

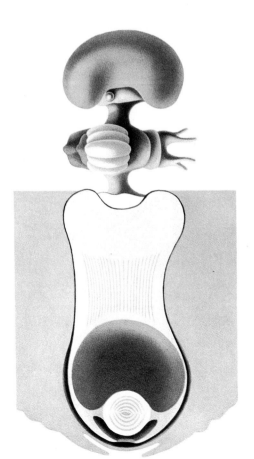

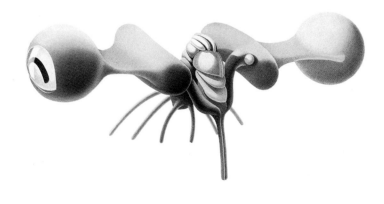

ARTIST:
ROLF CIGLER, SCHULE FÜR
GESTALTUNG ZÜRICH, KLASSE
FÜR WISSENSCHAFTLICHES
ZEICHNEN
ART DIRECTOR:
CHRISTOPH GÖLDLIN
■ 402–404

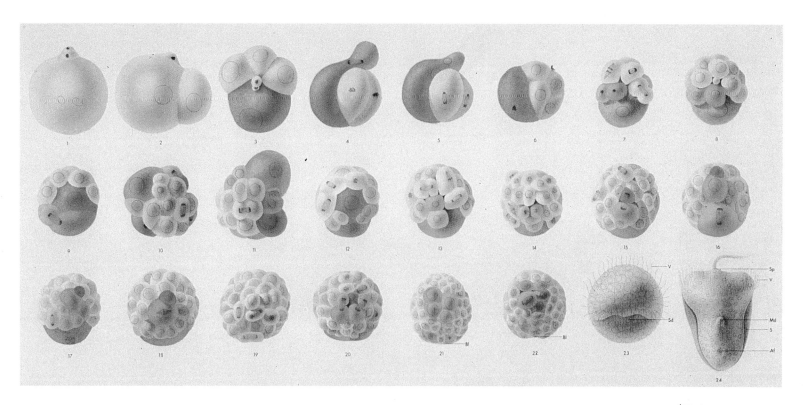

ARTIST:
RUTH BAUR, SCHULE FÜR GESTALTUNG ZÜRICH, KLASSE FÜR WISSENSCHAFTLICHES ZEICHNEN
ART DIRECTOR:
CHRISTOPH GÖLDLIN
■ 405

■ 402 Developmental stages of an octopus embryo up to the hatching out of this cephalopod. (SWI)

■ 403, 404 The optical center in the brain, and the main center of sensory integration (with peripheral nerve cords) of the *Octopus vulgaris*. (SWI)

■ 405 Diagram of the various stages of the development of a microorganism. (SWI)

■ 402 Entwicklungsstadien einer Krake bis zum Ausschlüpfen dieses Kopffüsslers. (SWI)

■ 403, 404 Optische Zentren im Hirn und das Gehirnzentrum mit abgehenden Nervensträngen des *Octopus vulgaris*. (Tusche, laviert.) (SWI)

■ 405 Darstellung der verschiedenen Stadien der Entwicklung eines Mikroorganismus. (SWI)

■ 402 Etapes de développement d'une pieuvre jusqu'à l'éclosion de ce céphalopode. (SWI)

■ 403, 404 Centres visuels cérébrals et le centre cérébral avec cordons nerveux de l'*Octopus vulgaris*. Encre de Chine, lavis. (SWI)

■ 405 Représentation des divers stades de développement d'un micro-organisme. (SWI)

■ 407 Diagram showing development of a tree frog (green-back frog), from spawning through the tadpole stage and finally to the fully-developed frog. The natural enemies during the early development stages are shown below the biotope. (SWI)

■ 407 Darstellung der Entwicklung eines Laubfrosches, von der Ablage des Laiches über die Kaulquappe bis hin zum fertigentwickelten Frosch. Unterhalb des Biotops sind die natürlichen Feinde im frühen Entwicklungsstadium darge-stellt. (SWI)

■ 407 Représentation du développement d'une rainette, depuis le dépôt du frai jusqu'au stade de la grenouille adulte en passant par le têtard. Au-dessous du biotope, on voit quelques-uns des ennemis naturels de la larve et du jeune amphibien. (SWI)

DESIGNER:
ARTIST:
*HARALD CIGLER (SCHULE FÜR
GESTALTUNG ZÜRICH, KLASSE FÜR
WISSENSCHAFTLICHES ZEICHEN)*
ART DIRECTOR:
CHRISTOPH GÖLDLIN
■ 407

■ 408, 409 Diagrammatic illustrations from a book on fruit showing the life cycle of the strawberry and the 5-year growth from the planting/grafting of an orange tree. (JPN)

■ 410 Hypothetical reconstruction of the development of Homo sapiens, whereby the emphasis is placed on the alteration of the skull. From the *National Geographic* magazine. (USA)

■ 408, 409 Aus einem Buch über Früchte: der Lebenszyklus der Erdbeere und eine Wachstumsperiode von 5 Jahren nach der Pflanzung/Veredlung eines Orangenbaumes. (JPN)

■ 410 Hypothetische Rekonstruktion der Entwicklung des Homo sapiens, wobei sich der Zeichner vor allem auf die Veränderung des Schädels konzentrierte. Aus *National Geographic*. (USA)

■ 408, 409 Représentations graphiques dans un ouvrage sur les fruits: cycle de vie de la fraise; phase de croissance quinquennale d'un oranger, écussonnage compris. (JPN)

■ 410 Reconstruction hypothétique de l'homo sapiens. Le dessinateur a porté son attention sur les modifications qui ont affecté le développement crânien. *National Geographic magazine*. (USA)

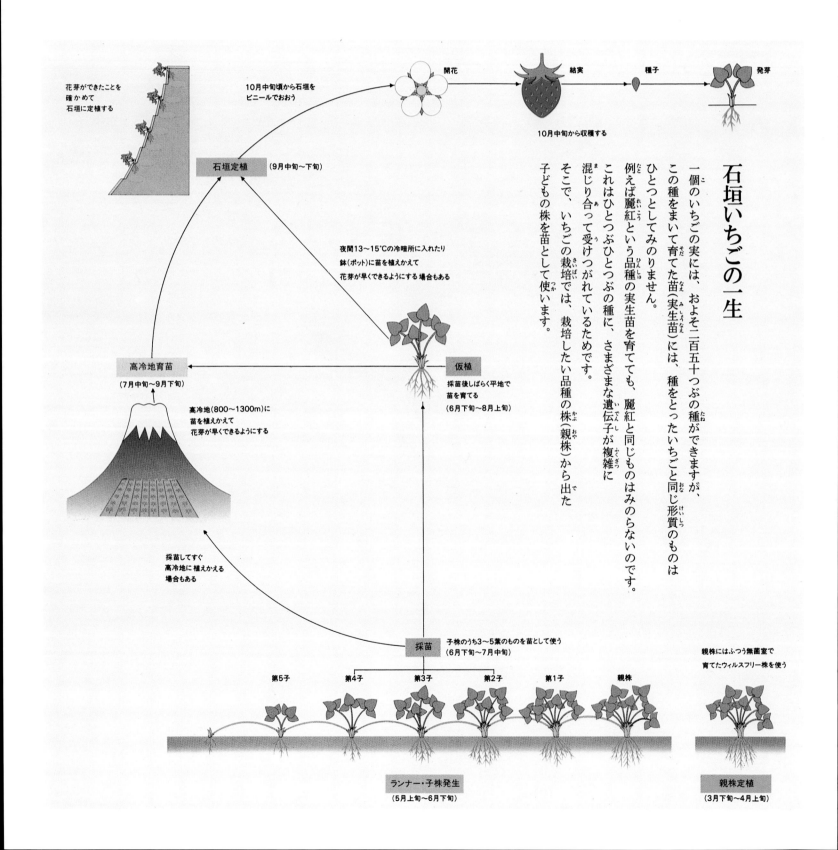

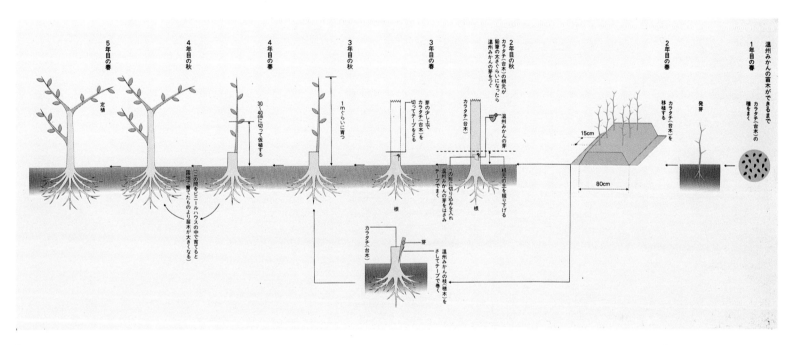

DESIGNER:
MINORU NIIJIMA/CHIAKI AIBA
ART DIRECTOR:
MINORU NIIJIMA
AGENCY:
MINORU NIIJIMA DESIGN STUDIO
PUBLISHER:
KINNO HOSHI SHA
■ 408, 409

ARTIST:
JAY H. MATTERNES
ART DIRECTOR:
J. ROBERT TERINGO
PUBLISHER:
NATIONAL GEOGRAPHIC
▼■ 410

ARTIST:
SHOICHIRO MASUDA
PUBLISHER:
KYOIKUSHA NEWTON
■ 411

■ 411 Diagram to show the origin of geological plates in the mid-ocean ridges. New material issues from the earth's mantle into the crust. Both basalt plates (middle illustration left and right) will be pushed away from each other, possibly through conventional currents (lower arrows). The space existing is filled with fresh basalt (laval). From the Japanese magazine *Newton*. (JPN)

■ 412 Vertical section through the upper layers of soil showing its plants and inhabitants, from microbes to small mammals. The smallest organisms appear again in the enlargements shown in the square and the lens. (USA)

■ 411 Schematische Darstellung eines mittelozeanischen Rückens. Neues Material tritt aus dem Erdmantel in die Erdkruste. Die beiden Basaltplatten (mittlere Illustration links und rechts) werden, möglicherweise durch Konvektionsströmung (die unteren Pfeile) bedingt, voneinander wegbewegt. Der dabei entstehende Raum wird mit frischem Basalt (Lava) ausgefüllt. Aus der Zeitschrift *Newton*. (JPN)

■ 412 Schnitt durch einen kleinen Bereich der Erdschicht mit ihren Pflanzen und Bewohnern, von Mikroben bis zu kleinen Säugetieren. Die kleinsten Lebewesen werden in den Vergrösserungen, dem Kubus und der Linse gezeigt. (USA)

■ 411 Représentation schématique d'une dorsale centrocéanique. Le nouveau matériau remonte du manteau dans la croûte. Les deux plaques basaltiques (à gauche et à droite sur l'illustration du centre) s'écartent, probablement entraînées par des courants de convection (flèches du bas), et du basalte frais (de la lave) occupe le vide entre les plaques. Tiré du magazine japonais *Newton*. (JPN)

■ 412 Coupe d'une petite portion de sol montrant ses habitants végétaux et animaux, des microbes jusqu'aux petits mammifères. Les micro-organismes sont agrandis dans les deux encadrés, le carré et l'ovale. (USA)

ARTIST:
NED M. SEIDLER
ART DIRECTOR:
JAN ADKINS
PUBLISHER:
NATIONAL GEOGRAPHIC
■ 412

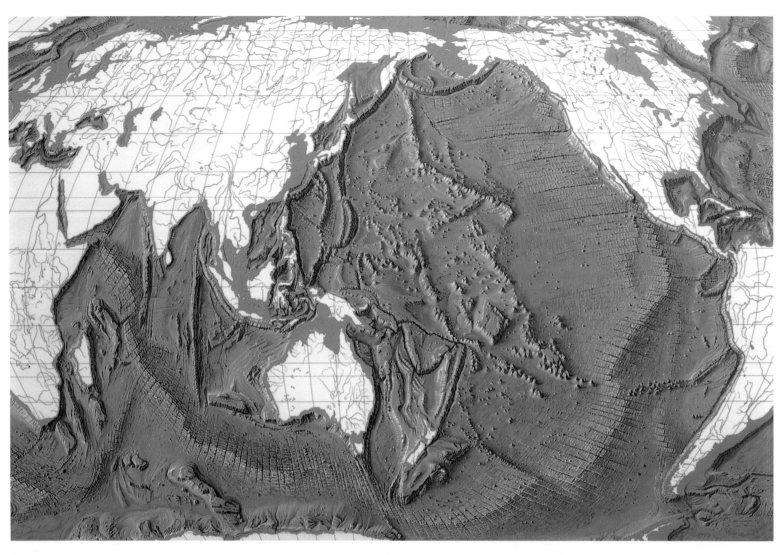

ARTIST:
UKEI TOMORI

ART DIRECTOR:
UKEI TOMORI

CLIENT:
SHIOBUN-SHA. CORP.
■ 413

■ 413 Topographic diagram of the seabed of the Pacific and the Indian ocean. (JPN)

■ 414 Through landslides that are loosened from continental slopes - such as here on the Californian coast near San Francisco - the canyons have crenated at the shale edge and have travelled downslope to the foot. From *Geo.* (GER)

■ 413 Topographische Darstellung des Meeresgrundes des Pazifik und des Indischen Ozeans. (JPN)

■ 414 Durch Schlammlawinen, die sich vom Kontinentalabhang lösen, werden - wie hier an der kalifornischen Küste bei San Francisco - Canyons in den Schelfrand gekerbt. Darstellung aus einem Beitrag in der Zeitschrift *Geo.* (GER)

■ 413 Représentation topographique des grands fonds du Pacifique et de l'océan Indien. (JPN)

■ 414 Des avalanches de boue qui se détachent de la pente continentale constituent des canyons au sein de la plateforme continentale, comme ici au large de San Francisco en Californie. Article du magazine *Geo.* (GER)

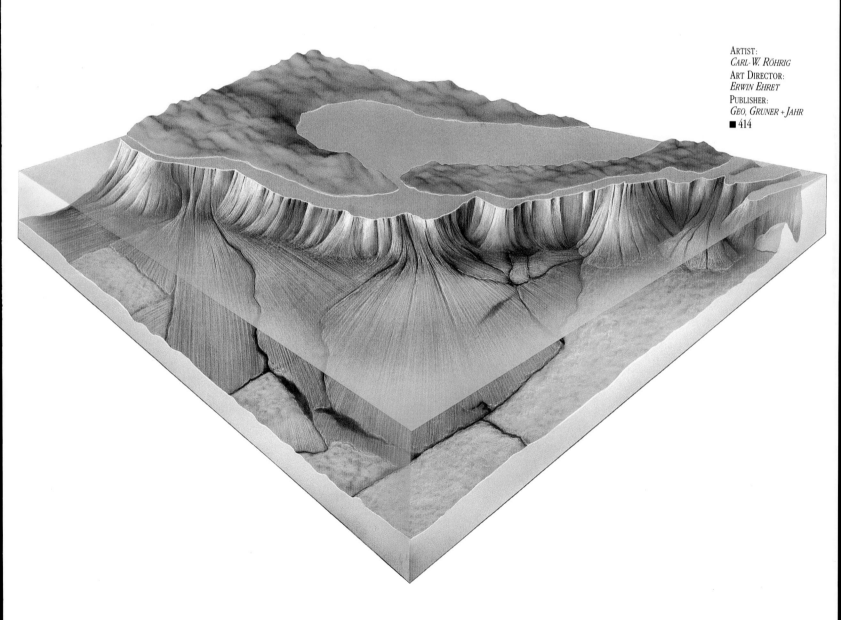

ARTIST:
CARL-W. RÖHRIG
ART DIRECTOR:
ERWIN EHRET
PUBLISHER:
GEO, GRUNER + JAHR
■ 414

ARTIST:
DAVIS MELTZER
ART DIRECTOR:
JAN ADKINS
PUBLISHER:
NATIONAL GEOGRAPHIC
■ 415

■ 415 "Worlds within the Atom", article in *National Geographic* to which this schematic diagram belongs. It concerns the Fermilab's collider now being built and shows how protons will be boosted (red arrows) and then routed to collide with manufactured antiprotons (blue arrows). On collision the particles destroy each other and the resulting energy "congeals" into particles that leave characteristic tracks. The hardware is presented in an exploded view. (USA)

■ 415 «Welten innerhalb des Atoms» ist der Übertitel des Beitrags in *National Geographic,* zu dem dieses Diagramm gehört. Dargestellt sind die charakteristischen Spuren im Magnetfeld, erzeugt von Kleinstteilchen, die durch die beim Aufprall von Protonen und Antiprotonen freigesetzte Energie entstehen. Die roten Pfeile zeigen die Protonenbeschleunigung und den Aufprall mit den Antiprotonen (blaue Pfeile). (USA)

■ 415 «Des mondes à l'intérieur de l'atome», article du *National Geographic* dont est extrait ce diagramme. On y voit les traces caractéristiques laissées par les particules résultant du choc énergétique entre protons et antiprotons à l'intérieur d'un tévatron. Les flèches rouges du circuit montrent le sens de l'accélération des protons, les flèches bleues le sens de circulation des antiprotons sur un cours de collision à l'intérieur du champ magnétique. (USA)

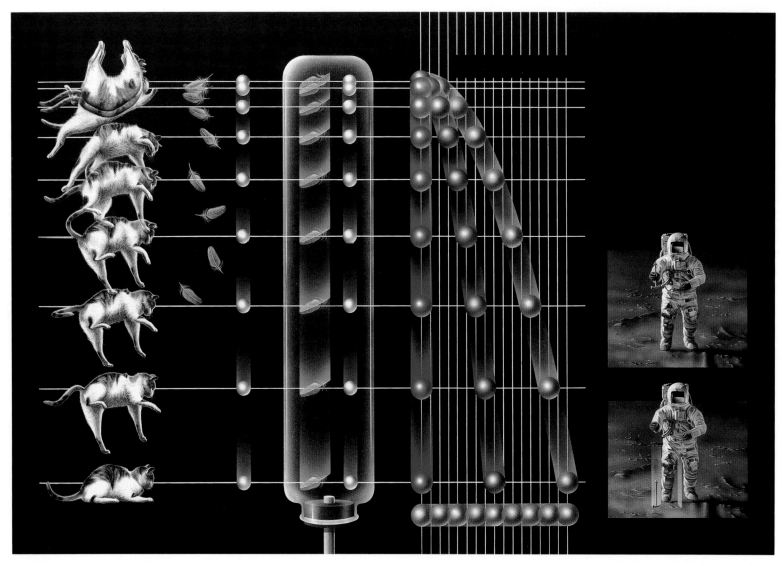

Designer:
Kazuo Itoh
Publisher:
Kyoikusha Newton
■ 416

■ 416 Movement in falling – indicated with various falling matter – is the subject of this diagram, taken from the Japanese *Newton* magazine. (JPN)

■ 417 From an article devoted to nuclear research appearing in the *National Geographic*. Shown is the acceleration of protons and also the collision of protons with graphite, and the smallest particles which are produced as a consequence. Shown in the separate diagram is a carbon atom containing protons and neutrons, and again the splitting up into sub-atomic particles is clearly demonstrated. (USA)

■ 418 Diagram showing the laser beam. The stored energy and its release is compared here with the principle of the arc. From the *National Geographic*. (USA)

■ 416 Bewegung im Fall, dargestellt am Beispiel verschiedener Körper, ist Gegenstand dieser Darstellung aus dem japanischen *Newton*-Magazin. (JPN)

■ 417 Aus einem Artikel über Nuklearforschung im *National Geographic*. In der Darstellung geht es um Protonenbeschleunigung, wobei hier auch der Aufprall der Protonen auf Graphit und die dadurch entstehenden Kleinstteilchen gezeigt werden. In den abgesonderten Darstellungen ist ein Kohlenstoffatom, dessen Aufbau aus Protonen und Neutronen und die Aufsplittung in Kleinstteilchen gezeigt. (USA)

■ 418 Diagramm zur Erläuterung des Laserstrahls. Die gespeicherte Energie und ihre Freisetzung nach dem Prinzip des Bogens. Aus *National Geographic*. (USA)

■ 416 La chute des corps sur la Lune, illustrée de divers exemples dans un article que le magazine japonais *Newton* consacre à la gravitation. (JPN)

■ 417 Pour un article du *National Geographic* consacré à la recherche nucléaire. Il s'agit ici des processus à l'œuvre dans un synchrotron à protons: bombardement d'une cible de graphite avec des protons, création de particules élémentaires. Les encadrés montrent un atome de carbone et ses constituants, protons et neutrons à g., les orbites électroniques à droite. (USA)

■ 418 Diagramme expliquant la génération d'un rayon laser. Le stockage et la libération d'énergie sont comparés au tir à l'arc. Extrait du *National Geographic*. (USA)

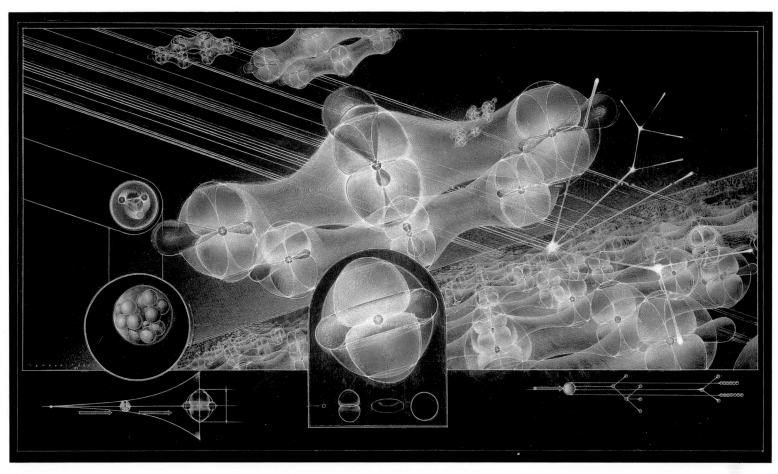

ARTIST:
BARRON STOREY
ART DIRECTOR:
JAN ADKINS
PUBLISHER:
NATIONAL GEOGRAPHIC
■ 417

ARTIST:
DALE GUSTAFSON
ART DIRECTOR:
JAN ADKINS
PUBLISHER:
NATIONAL GEOGRAPHIC
▼■ 418

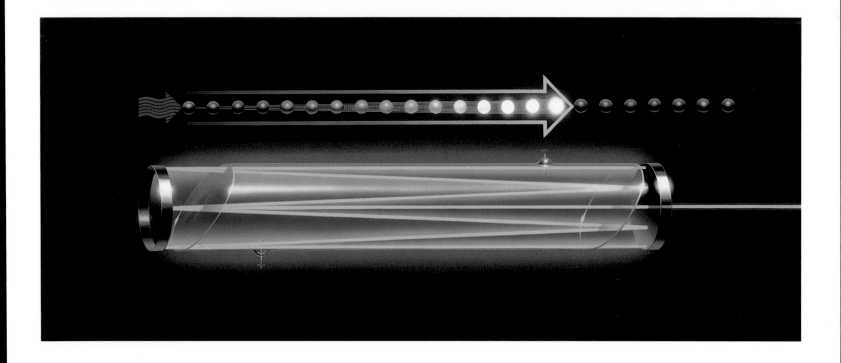

■ 419 Diagram of the energy resources of the earth in global yearly average. The yellow arrows show sun irradiation, whereby part is caught and absorbed or radiated back by the atmosphere. The red arrows show the energy radiated from the earth. As the atmosphere for these longwave rays is largely impermeable, it is radiated back to the earth's surface. From *Klima - unsere Zukunft?* (Climat - our Future?), published by Kümmerly + Frey. (SWI)

■ 420 The same topic as in *419* in another presentation (from *Geo*). The "greenhouse" effect is predominant here. This has influence on the lower region of the atmosphere (troposphere) and is largley due to the imperviousness caused by carbon dioxide. (SWI)

■ 419 Energiehaushalt der Erde im globalen Jahresdurchschnitt. Die gelben Pfeile zeigen die Sonneneinstrahlung, wobei ein Teil von der Atmosphäre abgefangen und absorbiert oder zurückgestrahlt wird. Die roten Pfeile verdeutlichen die von der Erde abgestrahlte Energie. Da die Atmosphäre für diese langwellige Abstrahlung weitgehend undurchlässig ist, wird sie auf die Erdoberfläche zurückgestrahlt. Aus *Klima - unsere Zukunft?*, Kümmerly + Frey. (SWI)

■ 420 Das gleiche Thema wie in 419 aus *Geo*. Hier geht es vor allem um den Treibhauseffekt, der sich im untersten Bereich der Atmosphäre (Troposphäre) auswirkt und auf die grösstenteils von Kohlendioxyd verursachte Undurchlässigkeit zurückzuführen ist. (GER)

■ 419 Le bilan énergétique de la Terre en moyenne annuelle globale. Les flèches jaunes indiquent le rayonnement solaire dont une partie est captée, absorbée ou réfléchie par l'atmosphère. Les flèches rouges se rapportent à l'énergie émise par la Terre. Ce rayonnement de grande longueur d'onde est en grande partie réfléchi par l'atmosphère vers la Terre. Tiré de *Klima - unsere Zukunft?* (Le climat - notre avenir?), Ed. Kümmerly + Frey. (SWI)

■ 420 Le même sujet qu'en 419 est traité dans *Geo*. Il s'agit de l'effet de serre qui naît dans la troposphère, la couche atmosphérique la plus voisine de la Terre, principalement du fait de l'accumulation de gaz carbonique qui empêche le rayonnement terrestre de quitter l'atmosphère. (GER)

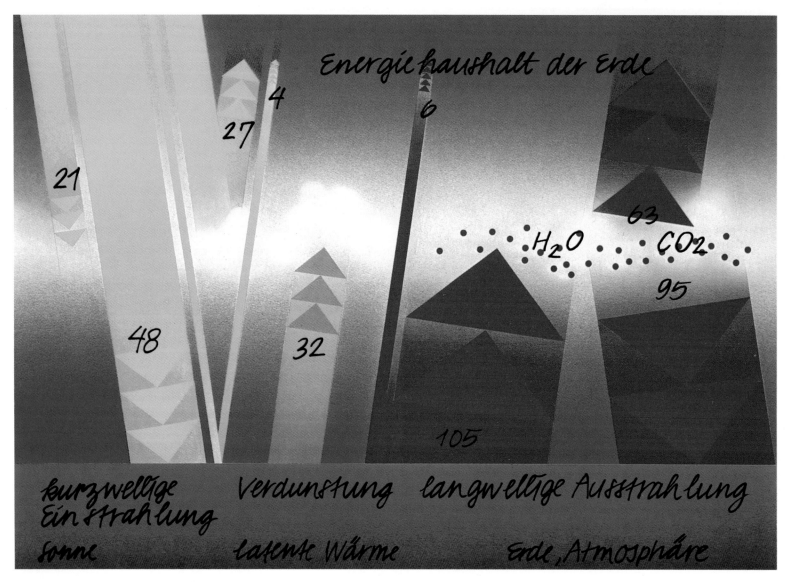

DESIGNER:
ROBERTO RENFER, SCHULE FÜR GESTALTUNG, BERN
ART DIRECTOR:
PETER ANDERMATT/ CLAUDE KUHN-KLEIN
AGENCY:
CCA - SCHWEIZ. KOMMISSION FÜR KLIMA UND ATMOSPHÄREN-FORSCHUNG
PUBLISHER:
KÜMMERLY + FREY
■419

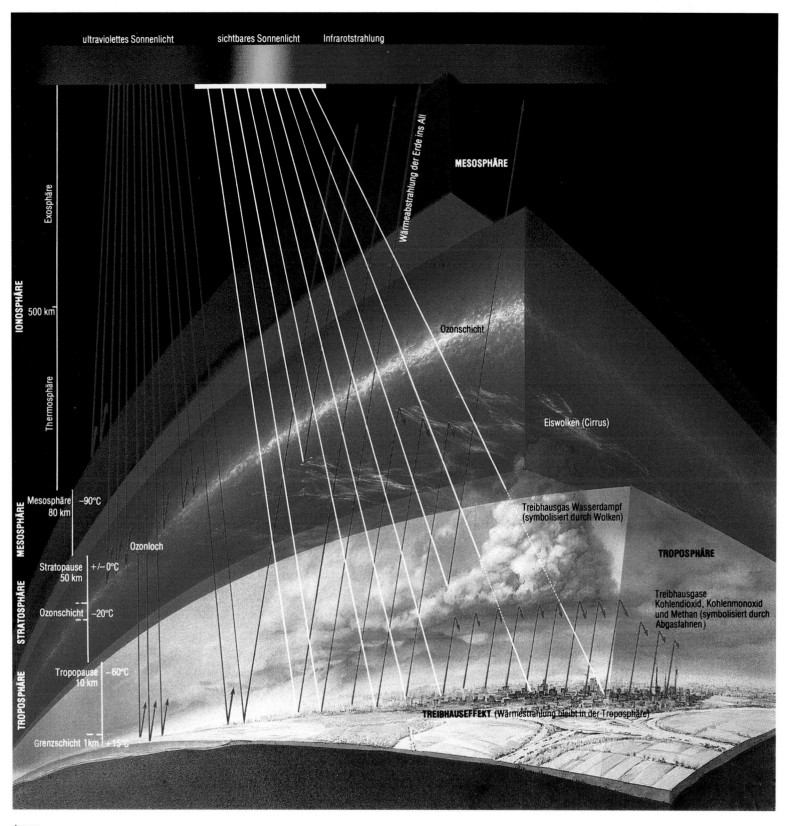

ultraviolettes Sonnenlicht   sichtbares Sonnenlicht   Infrarotstrahlung

Wärmeabstrahlung der Erde ins All

MESOSPHÄRE

IONOSPHÄRE

Exosphäre

500 km

Thermosphäre

Ozonschicht

Eiswolken (Cirrus)

MESOSPHÄRE

Mesosphäre   −90°C
80 km

Treibhausgas Wasserdampf
(symbolisiert durch Wolken)

Ozonloch

TROPOSPHÄRE

STRATOSPHÄRE

Stratopause   +/−0°C
50 km

Treibhausgase
Kohlendioxid, Kohlenmonoxid
und Methan (symbolisiert durch
Abgasfahnen)

Ozonschicht   −20°C

TROPOSPHÄRE

Tropopause   −60°C
10 km

Grenzschicht 1 km   +15°C

TREIBHAUSEFFEKT (Wärmestrahlung bleibt in der Troposphäre)

ARTIST:
JÖRG KÜHN
ART DIRECTOR:
ERWIN EHRET
PUBLISHER:
GEO, GRUNER + JAHR
■ 420

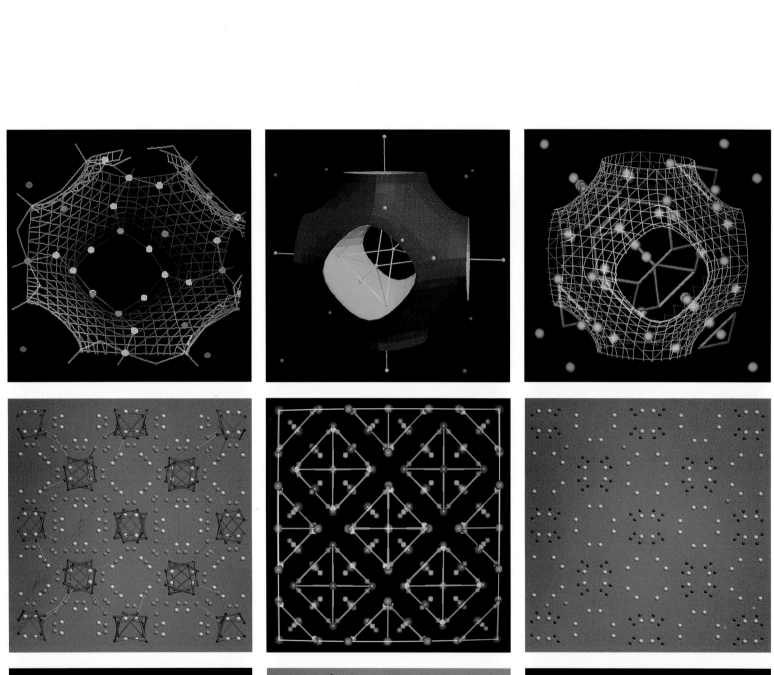

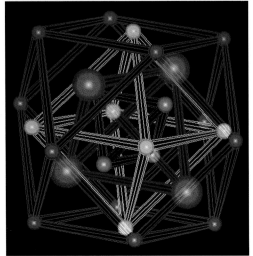

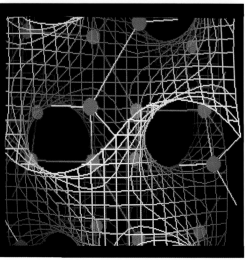

DESIGNER:
H. G. VON SCHNERING,
N. NESPER
CLIENT:
MAX-PLANCK-INSTITUT FÜR
FESTKÖRPERFORSCHUNG
■ 421–429

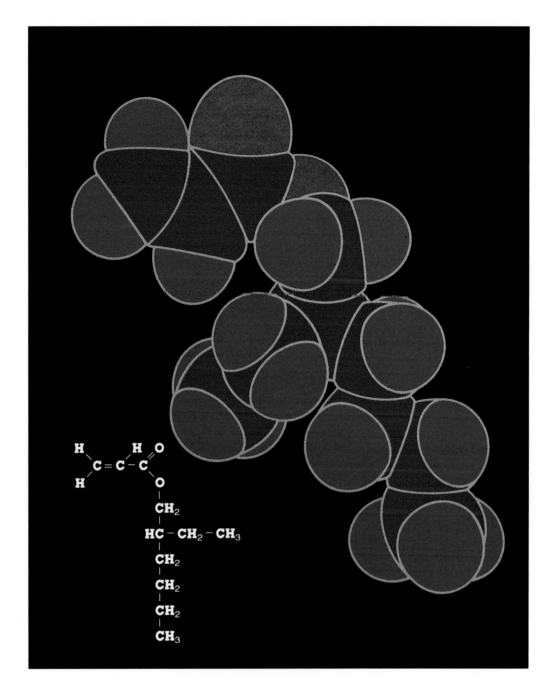

DESIGNER:
M. ALYCE BARKER
ART DIRECTOR:
RON JEFFERIES
AGENCY:
THE JEFFERIES ASSOCIATION
CLIENT:
AVERY INTERNATIONAL
■ 430

■ 421–429 Atom distribution in the structure of crystal and periodic potential surfaces, which through their symmetry alone display certain non-Euclidean spatial divisions. By representing atoms as different colored points, the interatomic bonds as graphic lines, and the composition of the various sub-structures as "organizations" along the spatial dividers, one gains insights into the hierarchical order of complex three-dimensional interconnections. From the article, "The Natural Adaptation of Chemical Structures to Curved Surfaces", first published in *Angewandte Chemie 99* (1987). (GER)

■ 430 Computer-aided design techniques, like this example of a synthetic polymer, greatly increase the understanding of certain chemical and physical properties at the molecular level. Here a diagram from the 1983 Annual Report of Avery International, illustrating advances in adhesive performance, not to mention overall productivity of research and development. The atoms are color-coded: oxygen (orange-red), carbon (dark red), and hydrogen (blue). (USA)

■ 421–429 Darstellungen von Atomverteilungen in Kristallstrukturen und von periodischen Potentialflächen, die allein durch die Symmetrie bestimmte, nicht-euklidische Raumteiler bilden. Mit der Wiedergabe von Atomen als verschiedenfarbigen Kugeln, der Bindungen als Graphen und der Komposition der Ensembles als Organisationen entlang der Raumteiler gewinnt man Einblicke in die hierarchische Ordnung komplexer 3-D-Zusammenhänge. Aus dem Beitrag «Die natürliche Anpassung von chemischen Strukturen an gekrümmte Flächen», zuerst veröffentlicht in *Angewandte Chemie 99* (1987). (GER)

■ 430 Computer-unterstützte Design-Techniken, wie dieses Beispiel von synthetischem Polymer, erhöhen die Verständlichkeit bestimmter chemischer und physikalischer Eigenschaften erheblich. Hier ein Diagramm aus dem Jahresbericht 1983 von Avery International, das Fortschritte der Klebstoffeigenschaften verdeutlicht und damit auch die Bedeutung von Forschung und Entwicklung. Die Atome sind farbkodiert: Sauerstoff (orangerot), Kohlenstoff (dunkelrot), Wasserstoff (blau). (GER)

■ 421–429 Représentation de la répartition des atomes dans diverses structures cristallines et des surfaces périodiques d'énergie potentielle dont la seule symétrie fait fonction de diviseur spatial non euclidien. L'interprétation des atomes sous forme de sphères colorées, des liaisons interatomiques sous forme de traits et la composition des ensembles sous une forme organisée le long des diviseurs font percevoir l'ordre hiérarchisé des interconnexions tridimensionnelles complexes. Illustrations pour un article de *Angewandte Chemie 99* (1987) intitulé «L'adaptation naturelle des structures chimiques aux surfaces incurvées.». (GER)

■ 430 Les techniques de CAO augmentent, comme le montre ici la représentation d'un polymère de synthèse, la compréhension de propriétés chimiques et physiques déterminées au plan moléculaire. Ce diagramme est tiré du rapport annuel d'Avery International pour 1983. Il explicite les propriétés adhésives du matériau et témoigne de l'importance de la recherche et du développement. Les atomes sont codés couleur: l'orange pour l'oxygène, le rouge foncé pour le carbone, le bleu pour l'hydrogène. (GER)

ARTIST:
NED SEIDLER
PUBLISHER:
NATIONAL GEOGRAPHIC
■ 431

■ 431 Pictorial diagram on the subject "Origin of Earth and Life". Four and a half billion years of geological and biological history are depicted along the twining strands of a double helix, the structure of the DNA molecule, the chemical code for life. From *National Geographic.* (USA)

■ 431 Bilddiagramm zum Thema «Ursprung der Erde und des Lebens». 4½ Milliarden Jahre geologischer und biologischer Geschichte sind hier dargestellt, entlang den verdrillten Strängen des Doppel-Helix, der Struktur von DNS, dem chemischen Zeichen für Leben. *National Geographic.* (USA)

■ 431 Diagramme illustrant «l'origine de la Terre et de la vie». On y représente 4,5 milliards d'années d'évolution géologique et biologique sur fond de double hélice porteuse d'ADN, le constituant chimique de base de la vie. Tiré du magazine *National Geographic.* (USA)

VERZEICHNIS

CALL FOR ENTRIES

EINLADUNG

APPEL D'ENVOIS

CALL FOR ENTRIES

FOR GRAPHIS' INTERNATIONAL YEARBOOKS

GRAPHIS DESIGN

ALL ENTRIES MUST ARRIVE ON OR BEFORE JANUARY 31

Advertising: Newspaper and magazine
Design: Promotion brochures, catalogs, invitations, record covers, announcements, logotypes and/or entire corporate image campaigns, calendars, books, book covers, packages (single or series, labels and/or complete packages)
Editorial Design: company magazines, newspapers, consumer magazines, house organs
Illustration: All categories may be black and white or color

GRAPHIS ANNUAL REPORTS

ALL ENTRIES MUST ARRIVE ON OR BEFORE JANUARY 31

All material printed and published in connection with the annual report of a company or other organization.
Design, illustration, photography, typography, as well as the overall conception of the annual report are the criteria to be judged.
In order to do justice to this complex medium, we will present double-page spreads from the annual reports selected which are exemplary in their design and/or illustration.

GRAPHIS PHOTO

ALL ENTRIES MUST ARRIVE ON OR BEFORE JUNE 30

Advertising Photography: Advertisements, promotional brochures, catalogs, invitations, announcements, record covers, calendars.
Editorial Photography for press media – journalism and features – for books, corporate publications, etc. on the following subjects: fashion, cosmetics, architecture, arts, nature, science, technology, daily life, sports, current affairs, portraits, still life, etc.
Fine Art Photography: Personal studies
Unpublished Photography: Experimental and student work

GRAPHIS POSTER

ALL ENTRIES MUST ARRIVE ON OR BEFORE JUNE 30

Culture: Posters announcing exhibitions and events of all kind, film, theater, and ballet performances, concerts etc.
Advertising: Posters for fashion, cosmetics, foods, beverages, industrial goods; image and self-promotional campaigns of companies and individuals
Society: Posters which serve primarily a social and/or political purpose; from the field of education; for conferences and meetings; as well as for political and charitable appeals.

GENERAL RULES

THESE ARE APPLICABLE TO ALL BOOKS MENTIONED.

By submitting work to GRAPHIS, the sender expressly grants permission for his publication in any GRAPHIS book, as well as in any article in GRAPHIS magazine, or any advertising brochure, etc. whose purpose is specifically to promote the sales of these publications.

Eligibility: All work produced in the 12 month period previous to the submission deadlines, as well as rejected or unpublished work from this period, by professionals and students.

A confirmation of receipt will be sent to each entrant, and all entrants will be notified at a later date whether or not their work has been accepted for publication. All the winning entries will be reproduced in a generous format and in four colors throughout.
By submitting work you qualify for a 25% discount on the purchase of the respective book.

What to send:
Please send the actual printed piece (unmounted but well protected). Do not send original art. For large, bulky or valuable pieces, please submit color photos or (duplicate) transparencies.
Please note that entries cannot be returned. Only in exceptional cases and by contacting us in advance will material be sent back.

Entry Fees:
For each single entry: North America: US$ 10.00 West Germany: DM 10,00 All other countries: SFr. 10.00
For each campaign entry of 3 or more pieces: North America: US$ 25.00 West Germany: DM 25,00 All other countries: SFr. 25.00
Please make checks payable to GRAPHIS PRESS CORP. Zurich, and include in parcel. These fees do not apply to students, if copy of student identification is included. (For entries from countries with exchange controls, please contact us.)

How and where to send:
Please tape (do not glue) the entry label provided (or photocopy) – with full information – on the back of each piece. Entries can be sent by airmail, air parcel post or surface mail. Please do not send anything by air freight. Declare "No Commercial Value" on packages, and label "Art for Contest". The number of transparencies and photos should be indicated on the parcel. (If sent by air courier, please mark "Documents, Commercial Value 00.00").

Thank you for your contribution. Please send all entries to the following address:
GRAPHIS PRESS CORP., DUFOURSTRASSE 107, CH-8008 ZURICH, SWITZERLAND

EINLADUNG

FÜR DIE GRAPHIS JAHRBÜCHER

GRAPHIS DESIGN

EINSENDESCHLUSS: 31. JANUAR

Werbung: In Zeitungen und Zeitschriften
Design: Werbeprospekte, Kataloge, Einladungen, Schallplattenhüllen, Anzeigen,
Signete und/oder Imagekampagnen, Kalender, Bücher, Buchumschläge, Packungen (einzelne oder Serien, Etiketten und/oder vollständige Packungen)
Redaktionelles Design: Firmenpublikationen, Zeitungen, Zeitschriften, Jahresberichte
Illustration: Alle Kategorien, schwarzweiss oder farbig

GRAPHIS ANNUAL REPORTS

EINSENDESCHLUSS: 31. JANUAR

Alle gedruckten und veröffentlichten Arbeiten, die im Zusammenhang mit dem
Jahresbericht einer Firma oder Organisation stehen.
Design, Illustration, Photographie, Typographie und die Gesamtkonzeption eines
Jahresberichtes sind die beurteilten Kriterien.
Um diesem komplexen Medium gerecht zu werden, werden aus den ausgewählten Jahresberichten verschiedene typische Doppelseiten gezeigt, die beispielhaft
für die Gestaltung und/oder Illustration sind.

GRAPHIS PHOTO

EINSENDESCHLUSS: 30. JUNI

Werbephotographie: Anzeigen, Prospekte, Kataloge, Einladungen, Bekanntmachungen, Schallplattenhüllen, Kalender.
Redaktionelle Photographie für Presse (Reportagen und Artikel), Bücher, Firmenpublikationen usw. in den Bereichen Mode, Kosmetik, Architektur, Kunst, Natur,
Wissenschaft und Technik, Alltag, Sport, Aktuelles, Porträts, Stilleben usw.
Künstlerische Photographie: Persönliche Studien
Unveröffentlichte Aufnahmen: Experimentelle Photographie und Arbeitenvon
Studenten und Schülern.

GRAPHIS POSTER

EINSENDESCHLUSS: 30. JUNI

Kultur: Plakate für die Ankündigung von Ausstellungen und Veranstaltungen aller
Art, Film-, Theater- und Ballettaufführungen, Musikveranstaltungen.
Werbung: Plakate für Mode, Kosmetik, Lebensmittel, Genussmittel, Industriegüter;
Image- und Eigenwerbung von Firmen und Einzelpersonen
Gesellschaft: Plakate, die in erster Linie einem sozialen oder politischen Zweck
dienen, auf dem Gebiet der Ausbildung und Erziehung oder für die Ankündigung
von Konferenzen und Tagungen sowie für politische und soziale Appelle

TEILNAHMEBEDINGUNGEN

DIESE GELTEN FÜR ALLE AUFGEFÜHRTEN BÜCHER.

Durch Ihre Einsendung geben Sie GRAPHIS ausdrücklich die Erlaubnis zur Veröffentlichung der eingesandten Arbeiten sowohl im entsprechenden Jahrbuch als
auch in der Zeitschrift GRAPHIS oder für die Wiedergabe im Zusammenhang mit
Besprechungen und Werbematerial für die GRAPHIS-Publikationen.

In Frage kommen alle Arbeiten von Fachleuten und Studenten – auch nicht publizierte Arbeiten – welche in den zwölf Monaten vor Einsendeschluss entstanden sind.

Jeder Einsender erhält eine Empfangsbestätigung und wird über Erscheinen oder
Nichterscheinen seiner Arbeiten zu einem späteren Zeitpunkt informiert.
Alle im Buch aufgenommenen Arbeiten werden vierfarbig, in grosszügigem Format reproduziert.
Durch Ihre Einsendung erhalten Sie 25% Rabatt auf das jeweilige Jahrbuch.

Was einsenden:
Bitte senden Sie uns das gedruckte Beispiel (unmontiert, aber gut geschützt).
Senden Sie keine Originale. Bei unhandlichen, umfangreichen oder wertvollen
Sendungen bitten wir um Farbphotos oder Duplikat-Dias.
Bitte beachten Sie, dass Einsendungen nicht zurückgeschickt werden können.
Ausnahmen sind nur nach vorheriger Absprache mit GRAPHIS möglich.

Gebühren:
SFr. 10.00/DM 10,00 für einzelne Arbeiten
SFr. 25.00/DM 25,00 für Kampagnen oder Serien von mehr als drei Stück
Bitte senden Sie uns einen Scheck (SFr.-Schecks bitte auf eine Schweizer Bank
ziehen) oder überweisen Sie den Betrag auf PC Zürich 80-23071-9 oder PSchK
Frankfurt 3000 57-602.
Diese Gebühren gelten nicht für Studenten. Bitte schicken Sie uns eine Kopie des
Studentenausweises.
(Für Einsendungen aus Ländern mit Devisenbeschränkungen bitten wir Sie, uns
zu kontaktieren.)

Wie und wohin schicken:
Bitte befestigen Sie das vorgesehene Etikett (oder eine Kopie) – vollständig ausgefüllt – mit Klebstreifen (nicht mit Klebstoff) auf der Rückseite jeder Arbeit. Bitte
per Luftpost oder auf normalem Postweg einsenden. Keine Luftfrachtsendungen.
Deklarieren Sie «Ohne jeden Handelswert» und «Arbeitsproben für Wettbewerb».
Die Anzahl der Dias und Photos sollte auf dem Paket angegeben werden. (Bei Air
Courier Sendungen vermerken Sie «Dokumente, ohne jeden Handelswert»).

Herzlichen Dank für Ihre Mitarbeit. Bitte senden Sie Ihre Arbeiten an folgende Adresse:
GRAPHIS VERLAG AG, DUFOURSTRASSE 107, CH-8008 ZURICH, SCHWEIZ

APPEL D'ENVOIS

POUR LES ANNUELS INTERNATIONAUX GRAPHIS

GRAPHIS DESIGN

DATE LIMITE D'ENVOI: 31 JANVIER

Publicité: journaux et magazines
Design: brochures de promotion, catalogues, invitations, pochettes de disques, annonces, emblèmes, en-têtes, campagnes de prestige, calendriers, livres, jaquettes, emballages (spécimen ou série, étiquettes ou emballages complets)
Editorial Design: magazines de sociétés, journaux, revues, rapports annuels
Illustration: toutes catégories en noir et blanc ou en couleurs

GRAPHIS ANNUAL REPORTS

DATE LIMITE D'ENVOI: 31 JANVIER

Tous travaux imprimés et publiés en relation avec le rapport annuel d'une entreprise ou d'une organisation.
Les critères retenus pour l'appréciation sont le design, l'illustration, la photo, la typo et la conception d'ensemble des rapports annuels.
Afin de rendre justice à ce média complexe, nous présentons diverses doubles pages types des rapports annuels sélectionnés en veillant à ce qu'elles soient représentatives de la conception et/ou de l'illustration.

GRAPHIS PHOTO

DATE LIMITE D'ENVOI: 30 JUIN

Photographie publicitaire: annonces, brochures de promotion, catalogues, invitations, pochettes de disques, calendriers
Photographie rédactionnelle pour la presse (reportages et articles), livres, publications d'entreprises, etc. dans les domaines suivants: Mode, arts, architecture, nature, sciences et techniques, vie quotidienne, sports, l'actualité, portraits, nature morte, etc.
Photographie artistique: études personnelles
Photographie non publiée: travaux exprimentaux et projets d'étudiants

GRAPHIS POSTER

DATE LIMITE D'ENVOI: 30 JUIN

Affiches culturelles: annonçant des expositions et manifestations de tout genre, des projections de films, des représentations de théâtre et de ballet, des concerts et festivals.
Affiches publicitaires: pour la mode, les cosmétiques, l'alimentation, les produits de consommation de luxe, les biens industriels; publicité institutionnelle et auto-promotion d'entreprises.
Affiches sociales: essentiellement au service d'une cause sociale ou politique dans les domaines de l'éducation et de la formation, ainsi que pour l'annonce de conférences et réunions et pour les appels à caractère social et politique.

MODALITÉS D'ENVOI

VALABLES POUR TOUS LES LIVRES CITÉS.

Par votre envoi, vous donnez expressément à GRAPHIS l'autorisation de reproduire les travaux reçus aussi bien dans le livre en question que dans le magazine GRAPHIS ou dans tout imprimé relatif aux comptes rendus et au matériel publicitaire concernant les publications GRAPHIS.

Sont acceptés tous les travaux de professionnels et d'étudiants – même inédits – réalisés pendant les douze mois précédant le délai limite d'envoi.

Pour tout envoi de travaux, nous vous faisons parvenir un accusé de réception. Vous serez informé par la suite de la parution ou non-parution de vos travaux. Tous les travaux figurant dans l'ouvrage en question sont reproduits en quadrichromie dans un format généreux.
Votre envoi vous vaut une réduction de 25% sur l'annuel en question.

Que nous envoyer:
Veuillez nous envoyer un exemplaire imprimé (non monté, mais bien protégé). N'envoyez pas d'originaux. Pour les travaux de grand format, volumineux ou de valeur, veuillez nous envoyer des photos ou des diapositives (duplicata). Veuillez noter que les travaux ne peuvent pas être retournés, sauf dans des cas exceptionnels et si vous nous en avisez à l'avance.

Droits d'admission:
SFr. 10.00 pour les envois concernant un seul travail
SFr. 25.00 pour chaque série de 3 travaux ou davantage
Veuillez joindre à votre envoi un chèque tiré sur une banque suisse ou en verser le montant au compte chèque postal Zürich 80-23071-9.
Les étudiants sont exemptés de cette taxe. Prière de joindre une photocopie de la carte d'étudiant.
(Si vous résidez dans un pays qui connaît le contrôle des changes, veuillez nous contacter préalablement.)

Comment et où envoyer:
Veuillez scotcher (ne pas coller) au dos de chaque spécimen les étiquettes ci-jointes (ou photocopies) – dûment remplies. Envoyez les travaux de préférence par avion, ou par voie de surface. Ne nous envoyez rien en fret aérien. Indiquez «Sans aucune valeur commerciale» et «Echantillons de spécimens pour concours».
Le nombre de diapositives et de photos doit être indiqué sur le paquet. (Pour les envois par courrier, inscrire «Documents, sans aucune valeur commercial».)

Nous vous remercions chaleureusement de votre collaboration. Veuillez faire parvenir vos travaux à l'adresse suivante:

EDITIONS GRAPHIS SA, DUFOURSTRASSE 107, CH-8008 ZURICH, SUISSE

E N T R Y   L A B E L

Please tape (do not glue) this label or a photocopy to the back of each entry.

SENDER:
Firm, Address, Telephone

ART DIRECTOR:
Name, City, State

DESIGNER:
Name, City, State

ILLUSTRATOR, PHOTOGRAPHER:
Name, City, State

COPYWRITER:
Name, City, State

AGENCY, STUDIO:
Name, City, State

CLIENT, PUBLISHER:
Complete address

DESCRIPTION OF ASSIGNMENT/OTHER INFORMATION:

■ I herewith grant GRAPHIS PRESS non-exclusive permission for use of the submitted material, for which I have full reproduction rights (copy, photography,
illustration, and design).

SIGNATURE:

E T I K E T T / F I C H E

Bitte auf der Rückseite jeder Arbeit befestigen/veuillez scotcher au dos de chaque spécimen.

ABSENDER/ENVOYÉ PAR:
Firma(e), Adresse, Telephon(e)

ART DIRECTOR/DIRECTEUR ARTISTIQUE:
Name, Ort/Nom, Lieu

GESTALTER/MAQUETTISTE:
Name, Ort/Nom, Lieu

KÜNSTLER/ARTISTE, PHOTOGRAPH(E):
Name, Ort/Nom, Lieu

TEXTER/RÉDACTEUR:
Name, Ort/Nom, Lieu

AGENTUR/AGENCE:
Name, Ort/Nom, Lieu

KUNDE/CLIENT:
Adresse

ZWECK/UTILISATION:
INFORMATION:

■ Ich erteile hiermit dem GRAPHIS VERLAG die nicht-exklusive Erlaubnis zur
Veröffentlichung der eingereichten Arbeiten, für die ich die Reproduktionsrechte
besitze (Text, Photographie, Illustration und Design).

■ J'accorde par la présente aux EDITIONS GRAPHIS l'autorisation non exclusive
d'utiliser le matériel soumis à leur appréciation, pour lequel je détiens les droits
de reproduction (texte, photographie, illustration et design).

UNTERSCHRIFT/
SIGNATURE:

A D D R E S S   L A B E L

GRAPHIS PRESS CORP.
107 DUFOURSTRASSE
CH-8008 ZURICH
SWITZERLAND

A D D R E S S   L A B E L

GRAPHIS PRESS CORP.
107 DUFOURSTRASSE
CH-8008 ZURICH
SWITZERLAND